D0243349

Relationship Marketing
Management of Customer Relationships

Manfred Bruhn

FT Prentice Hall
FINANCIAL TIMES

An imprint of **Pearson Education**
Harlow, England • London • New York • Boston • San Francisco • Toronto • Sydney • Singapore • Hong Kong
Tokyo • Seoul • Taipei • New Delhi • Cape Town • Madrid • Mexico City • Amsterdam • Munich • Paris • Milan

Pearson Education Limited

Edinburgh Gate
Harlow
Essex CM20 2JE
England

and Associated Companies throughout the world

Visit us on the World Wide Web at:
www.pearsoneduc.com

First published 2003

© Pearson Education Limited 2003

The right of Manfred Bruhn to be identified as author of this work has been asserted by the author in accordance with the Copyright, Designs and Patents Act 1988.

All rights reserved. No part of this publication may be reproduced, stored in a retrieval system, or transmitted in any form or by any means, electronic, mechanical, photocopying, recording, or otherwise without either the prior written permission of the publisher or a licence permitting restricted copying in the United Kingdom issued by the Copyright Licensing Agency Ltd, 90 Tottenham Court Road, London W1T 4LP.

Translated from the German by Anil Mahyera, Munich.

ISBN 0273-67601-6

British Library Cataloguing-in-Publication Data
A catalogue record for this book can be obtained from the British Library.

Library of Congress Cataloging-in-Publication Data

Bruhn, Manfred.
    [Relationship marketing. English]
    Relationship marketing : management of customer relationships / Manfred Bruhn.
        p. cm.
    Includes bibliographical references and index.
    ISBN 0-273-67601-6
        1. Customer relations--Management. I. Title.

    HF5415.5 .B795413 2002
    658.8'12--dc21

                                                            2002029302

10 9 8 7 6 5 4 3 2 1
06 05 04 03

Typeset by 9.5pt Stone serif by 30.
Printed and bound in Great Britain by Ashford Colour Press, Gosport, Hampshire.

The publisher's policy is to use paper manufactured from sustainable forests.

Relationship Marketing

Pearson Education

We work with leading authors to develop the
strongest educational materials in marketing,
bringing cutting-edge thinking and best
learning practice to a global market.

Under a range of well-known imprints, including
Financial Times Prentice Hall, we craft high quality
print and electronic publications which help
readers to understand and apply their content,
whether studying or at work.

To find out more about the complete range of our
publishing please visit us on the World Wide Web at:
www.pearsoneduc.com

Contents

List of figures

List of figures

Preface and acknowledgements

The fundamental idea of marketing dates back to the late 1940s and emerged in the sixties and seventies. At that time, the surfacing of central principles such as market segmentation or the application of marketing instruments enabled marketing to achieve a breakthrough by utilising the base concept of market-driven corporate management. The concept of the marketing mix entered most marketing textbooks around 1960 and has virtually become the universal model for marketing among academicians and practitioners.

In the following decades, however, the markets and hence the competitive environment changed radically. Marketing established itself as market-driven corporate management not only for consumer goods (the 'dawn of marketing') but also increasingly in the industrial goods, services, and non-profit sectors. This generated new types of problems and challenges associated minimally with marketing's conventional school of thought.

It is thus not surprising that demands surfaced around the mid-eighties for a fresh focus for marketing – which led to the link with the term 'relationship marketing'. These beginnings were observed in the United States as well as in the Scandinavian countries from where they were aggressively pushed forward in the early to mid-nineties, and finally adopted and pursued by the German-speaking regions. The principal aim is to transform marketing from the classic 'inside-out' focus on transactions to an 'outside-in' relationship marketing outlook, whereby the emphasis of the product and the marketing mix management paradigm is replaced with a stronger view of customer relationships as the foundation for analysis.

The goal of relationship marketing is accordingly to place customer relationships on the centre stage in order to arrive at a new structure for marketing activities based on the type of customer relationship. This underlying thought has been debated intensively both for the marketing of industrial goods involving interpersonal relationships between sellers and buyers, and for services where customer integration and the service encounter are prominent. As expected, the credit for the scientific impulse to relationship marketing is owed to the industrial goods and services segment.

Ongoing debates on relationship marketing seem to still be targeted at the supposedly important question of whether this involves a paradigm change or not. These partly controversial debates, however, are missing the key aspect addressed below. This book is thus an attempt to provide a real basis for the reflections on the paradigm change in marketing.

In the light of the above, the purpose of this book is to present the discussions at the forefront of relationship marketing. A comprehensive cardinal principle of relationship marketing is still lacking, even though many of the thought processes, such as the customer life cycle, success chain management with the pre-economic parameters like customer retention and satisfaction among others, do point out the building blocks. As a result, this book seeks to treat the current debates on relationship marketing so as to work out its theoretical and conceptual foundations. An effort will also be made to develop relationship marketing as a management methodology (with analysis phase, strategic focus, operational deployment, implementation, and control), in order to provide a means with the same universal and consistent basis for both scientific and practical problems. This book could just as well have appeared under the title 'Relationship Management'. While working on it, though, it became clear that numerous areas had been barely dealt with either in the literature or in practice. The ideas that emerged in this process are to be taken as suggestions for debates of the future.

This book is aimed equally at the academic community, graduate students who have followed a course in the basic principles of marketing and at practitioners who wish to specialise in the area of relationship marketing. Scientifically-interested readers should acquire not only a 'state of the art' analysis of relationship marketing, but also be able to gain ideas for further research among the abundant unsolved problems. In practice this theme is currently being dealt with under the term 'Customer Relationship Management' (CRM), although management consulting firms are providing information technology 'tool box' solutions for many such cases. The catchword CRM has thus been purposely avoided and it is expected that it will die out over time. The intent of this treatise is basically to handle customer relationships in a systematic manner, rather than to simply present software solutions.

Relationship marketing's principal aim is not to replace traditional marketing, but rather to enhance it as a market- and customer-driven corporate management approach. The fact that relationship marketing applies uniquely to each different segment has been addressed explicitly in a separate chapter on the multi-faceted features of relationship marketing.

Further debates in the practical world will show if and to what extent corporations are able to gain a competitive advantage in the market by implementing relationship orientation both conceptually and operationally. Nevertheless, it is anticipated that relation leadership will certainly establish itself in many segments as a new success factor.

Finally, I would like to acknowledge the valuable contributions of some people and organisations in the process of the development of this book. Special thanks are due, in particular, to the Swiss organisation 'Freiwillige Akademische Gesellschaft' (FAG) who have supported this translation project financially. The publishing of the first English edition of Relationship Marketing would not have been possible without their help and funding. I am also pleased to acknowledge the insightful and helpful comments of four anonymous reviewers. Their critique and suggestions encouraged me to include substantial changes in the translation of this book.

As it takes more than an author to create a book and its supplements, special thanks go to three of my research assistants at the Department of Marketing and Business Administration, Basel. Appreciative thanks are due to Dr. Dominik Georgi, a former research assistant with whom I worked to create the German edition of Relationship Marketing, and to Dr. Silke Michalski, a former research assistant who joined the translation process in the beginning. Furthermore, I would like to thank Dipl.-Kfm. Sven Tuzovic, research assistant in my Department, who has put in hard work during the entire translation process. Warm thanks are due, too, to Peter Neumann for technical assistance who helped to design and prepare many of the PowerPoint graphics that are enhancing both visual appeal and student learning. And, of course, I am very appreciative of all the solid work done by the editorial, production, and marketing staff of Pearson Education UK to transform this manuscript into a handsome published text.

Manfred Bruhn
University of Basel
School of Economics and
Business Administration (WWZ)
January 2002

Publisher's acknowledgements

We are grateful to the following for permission to reproduce copyright material:

Example 6.11 from www.customer.com/crmpulse/case_studies/wachovia_ case.html/ Copyright © 2002 Customer Communications Group

Figures 1.1 and 1.9 from Meffert, H. (2000) *Marketing* (9th edn), Wiesbaden: Deutscher Universitäts-Verlag, 5, 27; Figure 1.3 from Liljander, V. and Strandvik, T. (1995) 'The Nature of Customer Relationships in Services' in Swartz, T. A., Bowen, D. E. and Brown, S. W. (eds.) *Advances in Services Marketing and Management*, Greenwich, 141–67; Figure 1.4 from Reichheld, F. F. (1996) *The Loyalty Effect. The Hidden Force Behind Growth, Profits, and Lasting Value*, Boston: Harvard Business School Press, 36; Figures 1.5 and 3.5 from Reichheld, F. F. and Sasser, W. (1990) 'Zero Defections. Quality Comes to Services', *Harvard Business Review*, 68, (5), 105–11; Figure 2.2 from Zeithaml, V. A. and Bitner, M. J. (2000) *Services Marketing. Integrating Customer Focus Across the Firm* (2nd edn), Boston: McGraw-Hill, 31; Figure 2.3 from Weiber, R. (1993) Was ist Marketing?', Working Paper No. 1 Zur MarketingTheorie der Professor für Marketing an der Universität Trier, Trier, 63; Figures 2.7 and 2.9 from Altman, I. and Taylor, D. A. (1973) *Social Penetration. The Development of Interpersonal Relationships*, New York, Holt, Rhinehart and Winston; Figure 3.2 from Benölken, H. and Greipel, P. (1994) *Dienstleistungsmanagement* (2nd edn), Wiesbaden: Deutscher Universitäts-Verlag, 201; Figures 3.6, 3.16, 3.17 and 8.4 from Georgi, D. (2000) *Entwicklung von Kundenbeziehungen*, Wiesbaden: Gabler Verlag; Figure 3.7 from Roos, I. and Strandvik, T. (1997) 'Diagnosing the Termination of Customer Relationship, Proceeding the "New and Evolving Paradigms: The Emerging Future of Marketing"', Dublin, American Marketing Association, 626; Figure 3.9 from Murmann, B. (1999) *Qualität mehrstufiger Dienstleistungsinteraktionen*, Wiesbaden: Gabler Verlag, 202; Figure 3.14 from Weiber, R. and Adler, J. (1995) 'Informationsökonomisch begrundete Typologisierung von Kaufprozessen' in *Zeitschrift für betriebswirtschaftliche Forschung*, 47, (1), 43–65; Figures 4.3 and 4.10 from Kotler, P. (2000) *Marketing Management. The Millennium Edition* (10th edn), reprinted by permission of Pearson Education, Inc., Upper Saddle River, NJ.; Figure 6.5 from www.hamptonhotel. co.cr/guarantee.html/ Copyright © 2002 Hampton Inn; Figures 6.6 and 6.23 Copyright © 2002 Novell Inc. Screenshots used with permission. All Rights Reserved; Figure 6.8 from www.homfcom/online_banking/HFonline_banking_ TXT.html/ Copyright © 2002 Home Federal Bank; Figure 6.9 from www.porschedriving.com/faqs.html/ Copyright © 2002 Dr. Ing. H. C. F. Porsche AG.; Figure 6.10 from www.ewatchfactory.com/retail/en/index.htm/ Copyright © 2002 ewatchfactory Corp.; Figure 6.11 from Scheuing, E. E. and Johnson, E. M.

(1989) 'A Proposed Model for New Service Development', *Journal of Services Marketing*, 3, (2), 25–34; Figure 6.13 from Laakmann, K. (1995) *Value-added Services als Profilierungsinstrument im Wettbewerb Analyse, Generierung und Bewertung*, Frankfurt, 19; Figure 6.15 from www.rockychoc.com/preferredcard.htm/ Copyright © 2002 Rocky Mountain Chocolate Factory; Figure 6.21 from Lovelock, C. (2001) 'Courses of Action Open to a Dissatisfied Customer' in *Services Marketing: People, Technology, Strategy* (4th edn), reprinted by permission of C. Lovelock, 165; Figure 6.22 from Stauss, B. and Seidel, W. (1998) *Complaint Management* (2nd edn), Munich: Hennser Verlag, 66; Figure 6.24 from Clark, M. (2000) 'Customer Service, People and Processes' in Cranfield School of Management (eds.) *Marketing Management. A Relationship Marketing Perspective*, New York, 210–27; Figure 6.25 from Parasuraman, A., Zeithaml, V. A. and Berry, L. L. (1985) 'A Conceptual Model of Service Quality and its Implications for Future Research', *Journal of Marketing*, 49, (4), 41–50; Figure 6.26 from Zeithaml, V. A., Berry, L. L. and Parasuraman, A. (1996) 'The Behavioral Consequences of Service Quality' in *Journal of Marketing*, 52, April, 35–48; Figure 7.2 from Plinke, W. (1996) 'Kundenorientierung als Voraussetzung der Customer Intergration' in Kleinaltenkamp, M., Fleiß, M. and Jacob, F. (eds.) *Customer Integration*, Wiesbaden, Gabler Verlag, 41–56; Figure 7.3 from Lovelock, C. (2001) 'Using IT to Customize Service to Airline Passengers' in *Services Marketing: People, Technology, Strategy* (4th edn), reprinted by permission of C. Lovelock, 550; Figure 7.4 from Deshpandé, R., Farley, J. U. and Webster, F. E. (1993) 'Corporate Culture, Customer Orientation, and Innovativeness in Japanese Firms', *Journal of Marketing*, 57, (1), 23–7; Figure 8.3 from Parasuraman, A., Zeithaml, V. A. and Berry, L. L. (1994) 'Alternative Scales for Measuring Service Quality: A Comparative Assessment Based on Psychometric and Diagnostic Criteria' in *Journal of Retailing*, 70, (3), 201–30; Figure 8.5 from Homburg, C. (1998) *Kundennähe von Industriegüterunternehmen* (2nd edn), Wiesbaden: Deutscher Universitäts-Verlag; Figure 8.6 from Bailom, F., Hinterhuber, H. H., Matzler, K. and Sauerwein, E. (1993) 'Das Kano-Modell der Kundenzufriedenheit', *Marketing ZFP*, 18, (2), 117–26; Figure 8.16 from Berger, P.D. and Nash, N.I. (1998) 'Customer Lifetime Value. Marketing Models and Applications', *Journal of Interactive Marketing*, 12, (1), 17–30; Figure 8.18 from Hoekstra, J. C. and Huizingh, E. K. R. E. (1999) 'The Lifetime Value Concept in Customer-Based Marketing', *Journal of Market-Focused Management*, 3, (3–4), 257–74; Figures 8.19 and 8.20 from Cornelsen, J. (1998) *Kundenbewertung mit Referenzwerten*, Working Paper No. 64, Betriebswirtschaftliches Institut, University of Erlangen-Nürnberg, Nürnberg; Figure 8.24 from Kaplan, R. S. and Norton, D. P. (1992) 'The Balanced Scorecard – Measures That Drive Performance', *Harvard Business Review*, 70, 71–9; Figure 8.25 from Bütikofer, P. (1999) 'Balanced Scorecard als Instrument zur Steuesrung eines IT-Unternehmens im Wandel', *Die Unternehmung*, 53, (6), 321–32; Figure 8.26 developed from *Criteria for Performance Excellence*, Baldrige National Quality Program, National Institute of Standards and Technology, 2002. Not copyrightable in the United States; Figure 9.2 from Fournier, S. (1998) 'Customers and Their Brands: Developing Relationship Theory', *Journal of Consumer Research*, 24, (3),

343–73; Figure 9.4 from Chojnacki, K. (2000) 'Relationship Marketing at Volkswagen' in Hennig-Thurau, T. and Hansen U. (eds.) *Relationship Marketing*, Heidelberg: Springer-Verlag, 54; Figure 9.5 from Levitt, T. (1983) 'After the Sale is Over', *Harvard Business Review*, 61, 87–93; Figure 9.7 from Lovelock, C. (2001) 'How Much Profit a Customer Generates over Time' in *Services Marketing: People, Technology, Strategy* (4th edn.), reprinted by permission of C. Lovelock, 152; Figure 9.8 from www.kdnuggets.com/solutions/crm.html/ Copyright © 2000 KDnuggets; Figure 9.9 from Payne, A. and Frow, P. (1997) 'Relationship Marketing: Key Issues for the Utilities Sector', *Journal of Marketing Management,* 13, (6), 463–77 © Westburn Publishers Ltd. 1997 (www.westburn.co.uk)

In some instances we have been unable to trace the owners of copyright material, and we would appreciate any information that would enable us to do so.

Reviewers' comments

"I've read the book and I would like to use it in my own postgraduate class teaching. I find the book to be very coherent and well managed in terms of breadth and depth of concepts presented and the way they have been blended to produce relevant managerial skills. The chapters are well ordered. The size and contents selection are highly appropriate for a postgraduate book."

Sofia Daskou, Lecturer in Marketing, University of Strathclyde

"The biggest advantages of the book are its detailed grounding in various theoretical approaches, its clear and consistent management approach and its systematic structure. Much better than many other books about relationship marketing which seem to babble about all kinds of related subjects but fail to present a comprehensive framework. Finally, a good sound book about relationship marketing."

Wim G. Biemans, University of Groningen

"The concept of relationship marketing reflects a marked change in current thinking. As today's marketplace is enormously more complex than in the past, companies are seeking new approaches to develop customer-oriented strategies. Here, this authoritative exploration of key issues represents a 'state of the art' contribution to the literature and will benefit not only the academic field, but also practitioners who are involved with planning and executing relationship marketing strategies and activities."

Dr. Thomas Middelhoff, CEO, Bertelsmann AQ

"Due to market changes such as globalization, technological advances and changing needs of consumers, companies are recognizing the necessity of customer relationships. The book is an invaluable reference for graduate students as well as for managers wishing to improve their knowledge and skills in modern relationship marketing."

Dr. Kay Hafner, President and CEO Germany, Wal-Mart, Germany GmbH & Co. KG

1 The foundations of relationship marketing

Overview

In this chapter we address the foundations of relationship marketing. Specifically, we will elaborate on the following questions:

➤ What are the developmental phases of the relationship marketing concept and how did the relationship marketing school of thought emerge?

➤ What is the domain of relationship marketing and how can relationship marketing be defined?

➤ What is the applicability of relationship marketing?

1.1 The emergence of the relationship marketing school of thought

The discipline of marketing has emerged over many decades (for an extensive overview of the evolution of marketing thought (e.g. Sheth, Gardner and Garrett, 1988). As Parvatiyar and Sheth (2000, p. 9) observed, early marketing thinking primarily focused on efficiency of marketing channels (Cherington 1920; Shaw 1912), whereas in later years, exchange became a central tenet of marketing (Kotler 1972; Alderson 1965). Changes in the economic and competitive framework in the last few years have led again to a new focus in marketing. For instance, today's marketers are faced with a marketplace which is enormously more complex, while in earlier stages marketing thinking focused rather on mass marketing principles and 'making the sale'.

The evolutionary changes can be characterised by **distinct stages of marketing**. According to this concept, management's strategy-related assignments vary over time, for example, with respect to corporate success factors and the use of corporate management analysis techniques (the concept that firms move through different levels of marketing orientation was first suggested in the early 1960s by Keith, 1960, who based his observation on his own managerial experiences at Pillsbury). While the concept is not without criticism because of its general simplification, this approach has been widely used in examining operations of many marketing firms (Tesar, Moini and Boter 2000, p. 2). Figure 1.1 illustrates in a simplified manner how various **developmental phases of corporate management** in the last century can be identified:

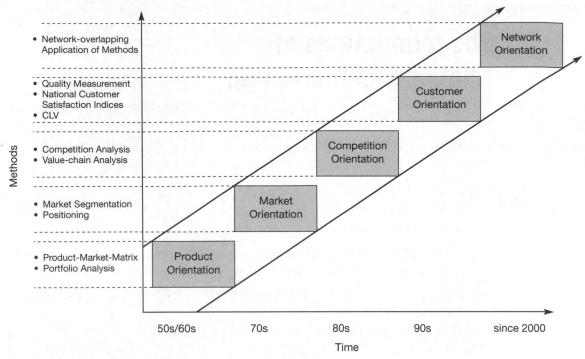

Figure 1.1 Developmental phases of corporate management
(*Source*: adapted from Meffert 2000, p. 5)

1 After World War 2 and during the fifties and sixties, the absence of market bottlenecks resulted in the occurrence of excess demand in the markets. Accordingly, corporate activities could be characterised as **product oriented**, since successful companies were primarily the ones that concentrated on achieving high production efficiency, low costs, and mass production. Assuming that consumers were primarily interested in product availability, corporations essentially aimed at satisfying all of the existing demand. This phase was typically exemplified by corporate management based on existing products, Ansoff's product-market-matrix school of thought, and the application of portfolio analysis among others (Ansoff 1966). Furthermore, as Parvatiyar and Sheth (2000, p. 10) observed, repeat purchase and brand loyalty gained prominence in the marketing literature.

2 In the seventies, the fundamental transformation from a seller's to a buyer's market took place. Excess supply of goods on store shelves and the emergence of saturation in general led to an increasing shortage of end consumers. The outcome of this development was that many corporations recognised the necessity of a **market orientation** approach, defined as the means to address the needs of specific target groups and to turn them into purchasers of the corporate output. The marketing concept evolved and consumers instead of distributors became the focus of marketing attention (Kotler 1972). For instance, one could now observe the application of market research methodologies for the segmentation of markets, and for the positioning of corporate services, etc.

3 In the eighties, the expanding use of similarly directed marketing activities and homogeneous products made it increasingly difficult to achieve market performance by simply focusing on meeting a customer's general needs. Market challenges grew to the extent that the presentation and delineation of one's own offer versus the competitors' took on a central role within the framework of **competition orientation**. New approaches for the identification of strategic competitive advantages and the strategic orientation of corporations became increasingly popular. For instance, organisations now had access to approaches such as competition analysis, value-chain analysis, and so forth. Figure 1.2 illustrates companies which have realised different competitive advantages.

4 In the nineties, it became more and more difficult to differentiate oneself from competitors by catering to customers' general needs. On the contrary, customers increasingly expected individual attention, so that companies had to shift their focus to **customer orientation** by aligning their activities with the specific wishes of a single customer. This development occurred primarily because of changes in consumer behaviour, like the progressively greater heterogeneity of customer expectations or the hybridisation of consumer behaviour. At the forefront of this phase was the application of special methods like SERVQUAL (Parasuraman, Zeithaml and Berry 1988; 1986) for determining quality characteristics, the implementation of the American Customer Satisfaction Index (ACSI) (Fornell 1992), or the calculation of the customer lifetime value (Rust, Zeithaml and Lemon 2000).

5 Corporations are presently in a major globalisation phase and their status is characterised by the growing significance of information and communication technologies that lead to **hyper-competition** (D'Aveni 1994). Consequently, **network orientation** for corporate management will move into the limelight in the future (the development of the interaction and network perspective has actually already started: see Achrol 1997; Cook and Emerson 1984; Håkansson 1982). Small, regional companies must build up strategic networks to strengthen their know-how, while large corporations should enter into strategic alliances to secure their competitive position. Therefore, a growing number of collaborations, with

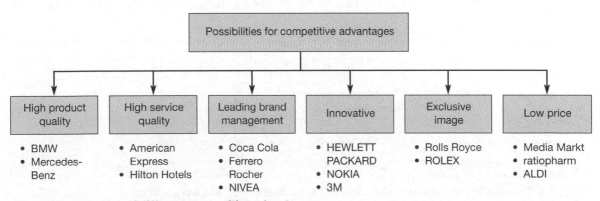

Figure 1.2 Examples of different competitive advantages

company-related and functional overlaps, will occur between firms in the same or in different markets. Entirely new methodologies for these network orientation processes will, however, not be put into practice. Rather, what will follow is the application of existing methods like value-chain analyses or controlling techniques to the entire network.

In the last few years, **customer orientation** has represented the adage of marketing activities in practice. At the same time, the goal of relationship marketing has been the control of customer relationships, each comprised of a combination of various independent transactions (Liljander and Strandvik 1995; Bitner and Hubbert 1994; Rust and Oliver 1994). Additionally, specific relationship episodes can be identified through an explicit evaluation (Figure 1.3).

With the trend of growing concentration on customer relationships, emphasis on **customer retention** fits well within the central goal of marketing activities. This focus is founded on the belief that customer retention promises economic performance in the areas of both turnover and costs (Anderson, Fornell and Rust 1997; Zeithaml, Berry and Parasuraman 1996; Blattberg and Deighton 1996; Rust, Zahorik and Keiningham 1994; Reichheld and Sasser 1990).

From a **turnover perspective**, it is accepted that both turnover and prices are impacted positively by customer retention, which initially contributes towards maintaining the current corporate revenues. Additionally, by retaining customers it is possible to raise the purchasing frequency on the one hand, and to attain the potential of cross selling on the other – which in turn could result in even higher sales. A growth in the readiness of retained customers to pay a premium price in return for reduced risk has also been observed. Hence, it can be assumed that customer retention generates rising sales figures for a corporation.

From a **cost perspective**, additional cost savings are generated by the experience effect. First, the handling of retained customers can result in lower costs than the handling of newly-acquired customers. Second, the customer can apply his experience with the seller in numerous sectors to raise the efficiency of providing the products.

In addition to the direct effects of customer retention on relationships with customers, emphasis is often placed on the indirect impacts of other customer relationships. It has been argued that retained customers possibly refer the company

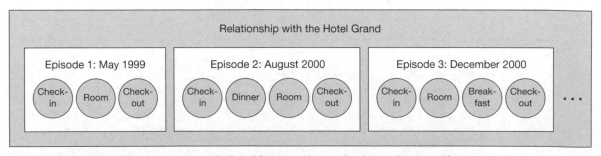

Figure 1.3 Composition of customer relationships based on episodes and transactions
(*Source*: adapted from Liljander and Strandvik 1995, p. 149)

to others while seldom dissuading potential and current customers away from the supplier (Boulding *et al*. 1993). Such **word-of-mouth communication** is believed to have indirect effects on revenues, in that customer losses can be avoided while new customers are being acquired, without any direct action on the part of the supplier.

These arguments, based on plausibility deliberations, have been corroborated through **empirical findings for individual companies or sectors** in a publicly efficacious manner:

- The financial services group MBNA America Bank N.A. analysed and confirmed the **effects of customer retention on turnover**. It was found that a reduction of five per cent in customer losses leads to an increase in profits of 60 per cent over the following five years (Reichheld 1993, p. 107). The results of a sector-overlapping study, as depicted in Figure 1.4, were that a reduction of five per cent in the churn rate generated higher profits of between 25 and 85 per cent (Reichheld and Sasser 1990).

- With respect to the **impact of customer retention on cost savings**, a financial consultancy established that customer-related transaction costs decrease by around 60 per cent between the first and second year of a company-customer relationship (Reichheld and Sasser 1990, p. 106). On the one hand, this occurs because customers encounter fewer problems and difficulties with output provision. On the other hand, awareness of both the customer's financial situation and investment preferences by the financial consultant makes up a measurable share of these cost savings. An investigation in the life insurance sector further demonstrated that a growth in customer retention of five per cent translates into cost reductions of 18 per cent (Reichheld 1993, p. 112).

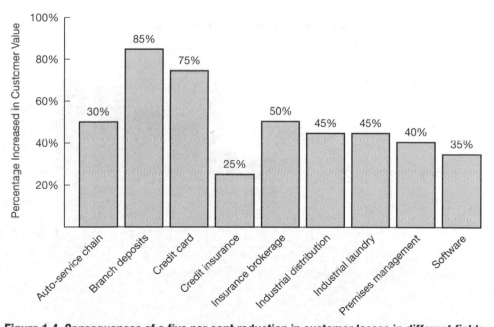

Figure 1.4 Consequences of a five per cent reduction in customer losses in different fields
(*Source*: Reichheld 1996, p. 36)

■ Finally, the development of some of the profit variables described was analysed in connection with the **total impact of customer retention on profits** during the course of an active customer relationship. Figure 1.5 illustrates the relevant results of this impact on profits due to the effects of word-of-mouth communication.

The results of the aforementioned studies have led to the opinion that in different phases of their relationship with a corporation, customers display a different economic sense. This situation is often illustrated in terms of the **relationship ladder** shown in Figure 1.6 (for different depictions of the 'RM ladder of customer loyalty', see Egan 2001, p. 59; Payne 2000b, p. 113). Once a customer has been acquired the relationship with the company can, depending on the customer satisfaction level, develop in two fundamentally different directions. On the one side, if the company is able to keep the customer lastingly satisfied, he or she can ideally turn into an 'enthusiast' of the company. This means that the customer becomes more and more loyal, making significant use of the entire range of company services (cross selling), while not considering competitive offers. Furthermore, this is accompanied by positive word-of-mouth communication, i.e. recommending the company to friends and acquaintances. Contrarily, in the case of a customer developing dissatisfaction, it is possible that he or she could even turn into a 'terrorist' (Jones and Sasser 1995, pp. 96–97) towards the company by not only causing extra costs for the firm, but also by dissuading other current and potential customers away.

It is clear that a corporation needs to **orient** itself towards **total customer relationships**, versus focusing on single transactions with a customer. This implies the linking of separate transactions, because only this approach enables the utilisation, for example, of the cost savings potential of customer retention. If the company does not succeed in continuing and extending the relationship on the basis of earlier transactions, a customer will have to be 'newly-acquired' prior to each transaction, and the corporation will incur additional acquisition costs each

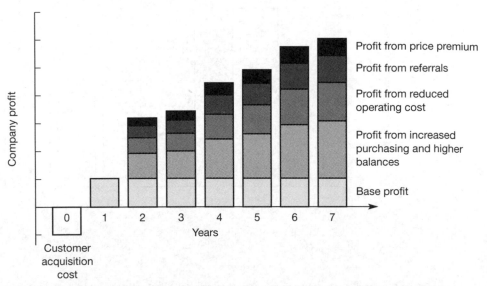

Figure 1.5 Development of value categories in the course of a customer relationship
(*Source*: Reichheld and Sasser 1990, p. 108)

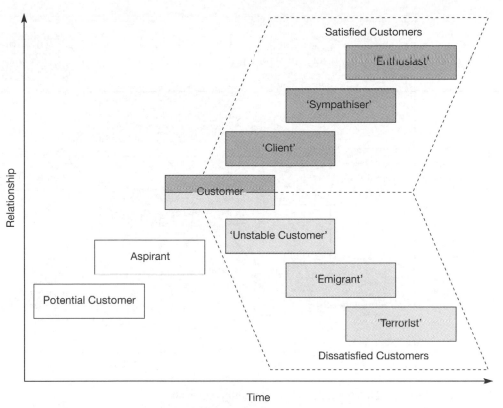

Figure 1.6 The 'ladder' of customer relationships

time (e.g. for customer access within the realm of corporate promotion). Moreover, when a company cannot readily call up data stored on a customer (e.g. on his or her use of the different products), the information must be re-recorded for each transaction.

Apart from the practical perspectives, there is an intense debate in the field of **marketing science** on customer relationships and the new leading approach of relationship building and management which is termed 'relationship marketing'. Examining the existing literature, one can then identify various **origins of relationship marketing**, illustrated in Figure 1.7 (for a discussion of early relationship marketing ideas, see Parvatiyar and Sheth 2000, pp. 10–13, on the difference between 'relationship marketing' and 'marketing relationships', see El-Ansary 1997):

- In the mid-seventies, Bagozzi (1975; 1974) began to gain an understanding of **marketing activities as an exchange process** between the seller and buyer – thereby forming a basis for subsequent conceptualisation of relationship marketing.

- Accepting the view that a customer relationship comprises various exchange processes, the question arises as to how the relationship changes over time. In this regard, one recognises several **relationship phases** that first came under discussion in the early eighties (Dwyer, Schurr and Oh 1987; Ford 1980).

- The possibility of being able to delineate phases within a relationship makes it necessary to **design relationship marketing explicitly**. This conceptualisation was seen for the first time in the early eighties in the research field of services

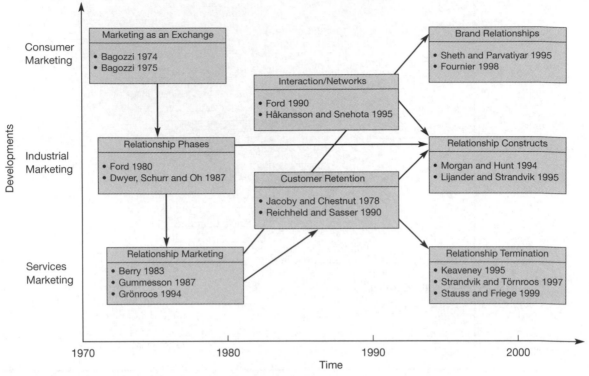

Figure 1.7 Developments in relationship marketing research

marketing (Berry 1983). Building upon Berry's conceptualisation of three levels of relationship marketing (Berry 1995), the published literature on this field can be classified into three broad approaches (Palmer 1996): at a **tactical** level, relationship marketing is used only as a sales promotion tool; at a more **strategic** level, the process by which suppliers seek to 'tie in' customers through legal, economic, technological, and time bonds becomes more relevant; and at the **philosophical** level, relationship marketing refocuses marketing strategy away from products and their life cycle towards customer relationship life cycles.

■ Around 1990, particularly in the industrial sector, it was established that exchange processes occurred not only between two individual exchange parties, but also to a degree between several parties directly or indirectly in contact with each other. The result was that the attributes of **interaction** and **networking** became the subject of further research on relationship marketing (Håkansson and Snehota 1995; Anderson, Håkansson and Johanson 1994; Ford 1990).

■ At the beginning of the nineties, an after-effect of analyses and discussion on customer relationships was that **customer retention** entered the centre stage of marketing research as marketing's target parameter (Reichheld and Sasser 1990).

■ Relationship marketing, originally applied only in the areas of capital assets and services, has since the tail-end of the last millennium been related to consumer goods also in that **brand relationships** are being considered as research elements (Fournier 1998; Sheth and Parvatiyar 1995).

- Additionally, diverse **relationship constructs** like commitment, trust (Morgan and Hunt 1994), and relationship quality (Liljander and Strandvik 1995) have shifted into the midst of marketing science, to help shed light on the emergence of customer retention and long-term customer relationships.

- The research field of **relationship termination** whose essence is the breaking-up and recovery of customer relationships, is being increasingly subsumed under relationship marketing (Roos 1999; Stauss and Friege 1999; Stewart 1998; Roos and Strandvik 1997; Strandvik and Törnroos 1997; Keaveney 1995).

Developments in customer relationship research in the marketing science field have had an impact on both the direction of the research and the concept of relationship marketing.

1.2 The domain and dimensions of relationship marketing

The emergence of relationship marketing (i.e. Hennig-Thurau and Hansen 2000; Gummesson 1999; Peck *et al.* 1999; Payne 1995; Grönroos 1994; McKenna 1991; Berry 1983) is founded on **a criticism of pure transaction-focused marketing**. Critics claim that traditional marketing concepts and methods developed over decades are based exclusively on **transactions** (Brodie *et al.* 1997; Jüttner and Wehrli 1994). Not only strategic marketing approaches, but also operative marketing instruments (e.g. product merchandising, pricing, sales promotion, etc.) are accordingly aimed at the initiation of transactions with customers often not even clearly defined. However, purely transaction marketing is fraught with problems with respect to the underlying marketing philosophy, the structuring of instruments, and the marketing organisation.

All along, customer needs have been, by definition, at the centre of deliberations on the **marketing philosophy**. However, in a corporation's guidelines or other strategic documents on corporate practice, this essential customer related aspect is seldom seen to an adequate degree. On the contrary, structuring of marketing activities exclusively in line with the marketing mix leads to a production and services-based marketing definition (Grönroos 1994, p. 6; for the definition, see Figure 1.8), frequently used in practice as a customer manipulation instrument (Gummesson 1994, p. 9).

In addition, it has been pointed out that the **structuring of instruments** in line with the marketing mix entails deficient selectivity (van Waterschoot and van den Bulte 1992, p. 85). This becomes particularly apparent with the integration of new instruments and concepts for attaining customer orientation, for example, when quality and complaint management are assigned either arbitrarily to the marketing mix or considered in isolation from them.

Another criticism is the isolated focus of a **marketing organisation** around the marketing mix. This is evidenced by the fact that marketing departments in a company are entrusted with catering for customer needs (Grönroos 1994, p. 7). Precisely within this framework of customer-oriented corporate management, marketing should have been assigned a function stretching across departments.

Berry 1983	Relationship marketing is attracting, maintaining and enhancing customer relationships.
Grönroos 1990	The goal of relationship marketing is to establish, maintain and enhance relationships with customers and other parties at a profit so that the objectives of the parties involved are met.
Shani and Chalasani 1992	Relationship marketing is an integrated effort to identify, maintain and build up a network with individual consumers and to continuously strengthen the network for the mutual benefit of both sides, through interactive, individualised and value-added contacts over a long period of time.
Möller 1992	Marketing is about understanding, creating and managing exchange relationships between economic parties; manufacturers, service providers, various channel members and final consumers.
Grönroos 1994	Marketing is to establish, maintain, enhance and commercialise customer relationships so that the objectives of the parties involved are met. This is done by a mutual exchange and fulfilment of promises.
Morgan and Hunt 1994	Relationship marketing refers to all marketing activities directed towards establishing, developing and maintaining successful relational exchanges.
Sheth and Parvatiyar 1995	Relationship marketing is a marketing orientation that seeks to develop close interactions with selected customers, suppliers and competitors for value creation through cooperative and collaborative efforts.
Gummesson 1996	Relationship marketing is marketing seen as relationships, networks and interaction.
Parvatiyar and Sheth 2000	Relationship marketing is the ongoing process of engaging in cooperative and collaborative activities and programs with immediate and end-user customers to create or enhance mutual economic value, at reduced cost.

Figure 1.8 Selected definitions of relationship marketing

Taking the aforementioned criticism into consideration, the domain of relationship marketing seems to be clear: while the goal of transaction marketing is to initiate individual transactions with customers, **relationship marketing** concentrates on managing and controlling customer relationships. However, in marketing literature neither the domain nor the conceptual foundations of relationship marketing are fully developed yet. For instance, Nevin (1995) points out that relationship marketing has been used to reflect various themes and perspectives which differ between a more narrow functional approach on the one side and a broader paradigmatic view on the other side. Figure 1.8 illustrates some of these different perspectives currently in the literature summarising definitions of relationship marketing (for another overview of selected definitions, see Gummesson 1999, p. 243; for further discussion, see Parvatiyar and Sheth 2000, pp. 3–5).

As can be seen from some of the definitions, the understanding of relationship marketing differs somewhat. Berry (1983), for example, has a rather strategic viewpoint, stressing the importance of attracting new customers but also of maintaining loyal customers in the marketing process. Grönroos (1990) and Gummesson (1996) take a broad perspective advocating that customer relationships should be the focus of marketing. Some scholars (e.g. Peck *et al.* 1999; Morgan and Hunt 1994) propose a more inclusive definition of relationship marketing, that is, they include buyer partnerships, supplier partnerships, internal partnerships, and lateral partnerships within their view.

However, following the opinion of Parvatiyar and Sheth, it is important for an emerging discipline to 'develop an acceptable definition that encompasses all facets of the phenomenon and also effectively de limits the domain ... ' (Parvatiyar and Sheth 2000, p. 6). Therefore, it is reasonable to limit the domain of relationship marketing to only those actions that are focused on serving the needs of customers (Sheth 1996; Parvatiyar and Sheth 2000). However, to achieve a mutually beneficial relationship with its customers, corporate management may need to consider other organisational relationships, i.e. with suppliers, competitors, or internal divisions (Parvatiyar and Sheth 2000, p. 7). Considering these aspects, the following underlying definition will be used in this book:

> **Relationship marketing** covers all actions for the analysis, planning, realisation, and control of measures that initiate, stabilise, intensify, and reactivate business relationships with the corporation's stakeholders – mainly customers – and to the creation of mutual value.

The following four **dimensions of relationship marketing** can be derived from the above definition:

- Stakeholder orientation
- Decision orientation
- Time-horizon orientation
- Value orientation

An underlying concept of relationship marketing is **stakeholder orientation** involving the corporation's relations with its stakeholders. Even if marketing activities apply to different groups, customers represent the core stakeholders (Figure 1.9). The following two **forms of relationship marketing** can be differentiated:

- From an **insular perspective**, relationship marketing solely concerns customer relationships.
- From a **broader perspective**, relationship marketing entails the corporation's relationship with all of its stakeholders.

Customer relationships are the decisive factor for corporate success, and their quality in turn is dependent on the company's relationships with the remaining stakeholders. Therefore, this book focuses mainly on customer relationships, and deals with relationships to the remaining stakeholders as required.

Relationship marketing covers a management approach that involves the implementation of measures for analysis, planning, realisation, and control as part of a **decision orientation**. Consequently, relationship marketing represents an integrated approach under whose umbrella all of a company's marketing activities can be dealt with. In this manner, the concept is linked to an action orientation, where measures conducive to the control of relationships are supposed to be established.

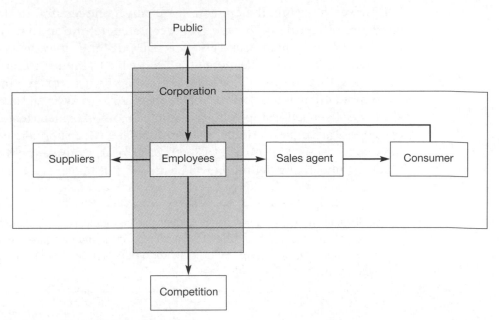

Figure 1.9 Marketing's stakeholders
(*Source*: adapted from Meffert 2000, p. 27)

Relationship marketing involves not only the initiation of relationships, but also its subsequent stabilisation, intensification, and reactivation (in case of a termination of the relationship by the customer). Consequently, through a **time-horizon orientation** appropriate consideration is given to the dynamic character of customer relationships, above all to the concept of a customer relationship cycle.

Relationship marketing also pursues a **value orientation** approach, in that the value for the relationship party comes first. With respect to customer relationships, the value for the customer stems from the satisfaction of his or her needs by the company, while the value to the corporation shows up as profits attained.

The development of relationship marketing has been partly designated as a **paradigm shift** (Brodie *et al.* 1997; Grönroos 1994; Kotler 1991; Kuhn 1962). However, since a relationship is formed of single transactions, relationship marketing must not be understood as a new definition of the marketing school of thought but rather as an extension of traditional marketing (Payne 2000a; Baker, Buttery and Richter-Buttery 1998). This viewpoint becomes clear by comparing the **distinctive features** of transaction marketing versus those of relationship marketing:

■ In terms of the **assessment horizon**, transaction marketing has more of a short-term character, while relationship marketing is primarily long-term oriented. Whereas transaction marketing focuses on the short-term initiation of product sales, relationship marketing's chief focus is on the creation of long-term customer relationships.

- With respect to the **purpose of marketing activities**, the seller's products and services are at the focal point of transaction marketing measures, whereas relationship marketing actions relate to both the outcome and the customer.

- In the case of relationship marketing, **key concepts** are interaction, relationships and networks, while the 4Ps, segmentation, and branding are more important for transaction marketing.

- In reference to **marketing goals**, transaction marketing activities are aimed at solely acquiring new customers, in contrast to relationship marketing that concentrates not only on acquiring customers but also on their retention and recovery.

- For transaction marketing, the **marketing strategy** involves presenting the product. Relationship marketing strives to achieve a dialogue with the customer in order to align the seller's products and services with specific customer needs.

- The **promotion strategy** differs with respect to the personal interaction. While transaction strategy uses non-personal advertising, relationship marketing is characterized through a personal interaction.

- Under relationship marketing itself, customer-specific indicators such as the customer profit contribution or the customer value enhance classic economic **profit and control ratios**.

Figure 1.10 compares the central tenets of the transaction marketing and the relationship marketing approach.

Criteria for differentiation	Transaction Marketing	Relationship Marketing
World view	Managing a company's product portfolio, setting and modifying marketing mix parameters to achieve optimal 4P configuration	Managing a company's customer portfolio, building long-term business relationships
Assessment horizon	Short-duration	Long-duration
Key concepts	4Ps, segmentation, branding, etc.	Interaction, relationships and networks
Marketing focus	Product/service	Product/service and customer
Marketing goal	Customer acquisition	Customer acquisition, customer retention, customer recovery
Marketing strategy	Presentation of outcome	Dialogue
Marketing interaction	One-way communication, formal market studies	Interactive communication, mutual learning and adaptations
Promotion strategy	Non-personal advertising, brand and image management	Through personal interaction, developing identity as a reliable supplier in a network
Economic profit and control parameters	Profit, profit margin contribution, sales, costs	Additionally: customer profit contribution, customer value

Figure 1.10 Differentiation between transaction marketing and relationship marketing

1.3 Relationship marketing and the scope of application

An analysis of the origin of relationship marketing showed that the **applicability of relationship marketing** could depend on the types of sectors and outputs considered (Dwyer, Schurr and Oh 1987). This thesis stems from a differentiation of markets in terms of a spectrum of extremes ranging from 'always-a-share' to 'lost-for-good' markets (Jackson 1985). In **'always-a-share' markets** demand exists for exchangeable goods, whose customers incur lower switching costs and as such have a lower state of dependence. On the one side, buyers can rely on a mix of suppliers without incurring significant variation in performance. On the other hand, multiple suppliers have a share of a customer's business either now or in the future. Examples of 'always-a-share' markets are logistics, basic supplies, catering. For these markets relationship marketing is less relevant (Jackson 1985, p. 122). **'Lost-for-good' markets** are characterised by a distinguishable output, whose customers are confronted with high switching costs (e.g. specific investments, economic penalties, cost of finding a new supplier) and have a high state of dependence. In these markets, relationship marketing is highly significant (Jackson 1985, p. 123). If treated badly and lost, then the chance of winning a 'lost-for-good' customer back is very low. Examples of 'lost-for-good' markets are office automation systems and heavy construction equipment.

Underlying this market-based differentiation, however, is an isolated analysis of relationships and transactions. Often, such a differentiation cannot be upheld for one and the same product. Also, the normative character of an isolated assessment of relationships and transactions leads to **misleading implications for marketing**. It suggests a differentiation for markets where only the 'lost-for-good' model can be applied to strive for control of customer relationships. In contrast, the achievement and maintenance of customer relationships is a marketing challenge even for sellers in 'always-a-share' markets.

| Example 1.1 | In the case of **theatres**, both types of customers, 'always-a-share' and 'lost-for-good', can be differentiated even so the service is identical, for instance, attending a première of a new play. While subscribing theatregoers would be classified more under the 'lost-for-good' model, non-subscribers instead fall into the category 'always-a-share'. As a consequence, an isolated view could lead to misleading implications for the theatre's marketing actions. |

Hence, in order to discuss the applicability of relationship marketing, it appears appropriate, on the one hand, to distinguish between the different types of products. On the other hand, it is necessary to conduct a more refined differentiation between the types of output, as is the case when comparing the 'lost-for-good' and 'always-a-share' markets. As the core of a spectrum of outputs, the following fundamental **output types** can be identified on the basis of features such as contacts, outputs, and customers (Figure 1.11):

- Customised outputs
- Standardised outputs

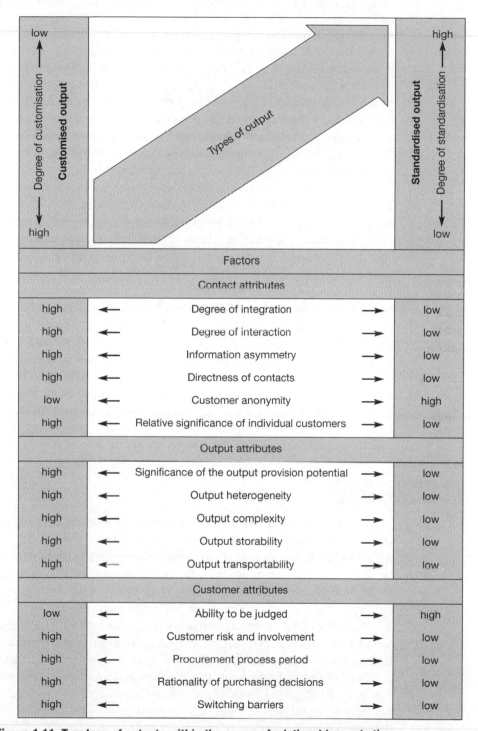

Figure 1.11 Typology of outputs within the scope of relationship marketing

Contact attributes are related to the procedure for contacts between the seller and buyer in the context of the provision of outputs. Customised services demonstrate a high level of integration compared to standardised products. For customised services, it is required that the customer or the instruments at his or her disposal participate in the process of service provision. Consequently, these services have a higher level of interaction: the more a customer is involved in the provision process the greater the importance of interactions between the seller and buyer for the service. Customised services are, however, disadvantageous for a customer as a result of information asymmetries, since the seller often has an information head start vis-à-vis the customer. By the same token, because of the high integration level, customers calling for customised outputs are not as anonymous to the seller. Ultimately, the relative significance of single customers to a seller is often greater for customised services than for standardised products.

As a consequence of contact characteristics, two general types of **output attributes** can be identified. Customised services, more than standardised products, require the seller to always be capable of providing the outcome. Further, customised service types exhibit greater heterogeneity and complexity, and since the customer's presence is required to provide the services they can often be neither stored nor transported.

The characteristics of both contact and output related factors thus originate from **customer attributes**, primarily those associated with the purchasing behaviour of customers. Customised services are initially more difficult for customers to judge than standardised products. This is justified by a predominance of belief and experience qualities in comparison with search qualities (Friedman and Smith 1993; Zeithaml 1991; Darby and Karni 1973). Consequently, the purchase of such services by a customer is linked with higher risks that lead to greater involvement of the customer, a higher level of rationality, and a longer purchase decision period. Because of these aspects, the customer is faced with greater switching barriers when purchasing customised outputs versus standardised ones.

Summary

This chapter has dealt with the foundations of relationship marketing. Looking at the emergence of the relationship marketing school of thought, we see that there is a shift in the perception of the fundamentals of marketing taking place, which can be described as a paradigm shift. However, relationship marketing is not supposed to become just a contrary philosophy to transaction marketing. We understand this concept rather as an extension of the traditional marketing perspective. For the applicability of relationship marketing it makes sense to distinguish between different types of corporate output as well as to differentiate products and services in more detail than just between 'lost-for-good' and 'always-a-share' markets.

The following chapters on the theoretical foundation, conceptualisation, and design of relationship marketing activities are in general valid for sellers of all product and service types. However, the implication can differ in numerous aspects depending on the specific output type. In this case, we will point out these differences explicitly at the appropriate location.

2 The theoretical foundation of relationship marketing

Overview

Looking at the recent discussion, there still seems to be a lack of understanding with regard to the theoretical foundation of relationship marketing. However, we feel that for understanding the concept, developing a management process, and the implementation of specific activities, the reader needs to have a knowledge of fundamental theories that build the framework of relationship marketing as a science. Therefore, we present a comprehensive conceptualisation basis in which single theories stemming from the neoclassical, the neo-institutional, and the neo-behavioural school are analysed from the point of view of their benefits for explaining the concept of relationship marketing. While each theory is examined in respect to six requirements, the reader will also find a summarised illustration at the end of this chapter. Specifically, the following questions form the focus of our interest:

➤ What are the theoretical requirements for relationship marketing?

➤ Which theories are (or can be) differentiated within the neoclassical paradigm, the neo-institutional paradigm, and the neo-behavioural paradigm?

➤ What are the benefits and the disadvantages of these theories for the theoretical explanation of relationship marketing?

2.1 Elements of a theoretical foundation for relationship marketing

Marketing, a part of the science of business administration, is interdisciplinary in nature with a theoretical foundation in various research fields that present a framework for marketing-relevant questions. The interdisciplinary character applies particularly to relationship marketing, where diverse theories of various origins are used for different aspects investigated (e.g. reasons for the emergence of customer retention). These theories can be related to three **marketing paradigms** (Kaas 2000):

1 Neoclassical paradigm

2 Neo-institutional paradigm

3 Neo-behavioural paradigm

The first two paradigms mentioned originate from the school of microeconomics and differ primarily in terms of their postulates. Whereas the **neoclassical paradigm** is founded on an extremely simplified assumption (e.g. complete information, perfect rationality), the premises of the **neo-institutional paradigm** (e.g. information asymmetry, limited rationality) are more realistic. The **neo-behavioural paradigm** is interdisciplinary, empiric-positivistic, and application-based. The interdisciplinary character means that theories from different disciplines such as

	Theory	Authors	Focus
Neoclassic	Value theory	Implicit application based on a series of marketing publications	Significance of quality, customer satisfaction, perceived value, and relationship quality within relationship marketing
	Profit theory	Blattberg and Deighton 1996	Evaluation of customer relationships from a corporate perspective
Neo-institutional paradigm	Information economics	Klee 2000	Explanation of interaction uncertainties and derivation of strategies to reduce uncertainty
		Ahlert, Kenning and Petermann 2001	Trust as success factor for services-based corporations
	Transaction cost theory	Klee 2000	Pre-conditions for an advantageous initiation of customer relationships
		Grönroos 1994	Profitability of long-term business relationships
	Principal-agent theory	Jensen and Meckling 1976; Bergen *et al.* 1992	Elucidation of customer and employee behaviour within customer relationships
Neo-behavioural paradigm	*Psychological theories*		
	Learning theory	Sheth and Parvatiyar 1995	Clarification and influencing factors for the emergence of customer relationships
	Risk theory	Sheth and Parvatiyar 1995	Clarification and influencing factors for the emergence of customer relationships
		Fischer and Tewes 2001	Trust and commitment as intermediary variables for service processes
	Cognitive dissonance theory	Sheth and Parvatiyar 1995	Clarification and influencing factors for the emergence of customer relationships
	Socio-psychological theories		
	Interaction/Network approaches	IMP Group 1982; Grönroos 1994	Structuring of interaction processes
	Social exchange theory	Houston and Gassenheimer 1987	Emergence and maintenance of customer relationships; evaluation, long-duration, and stability of customer relationships
	Social penetration theory	Altman and Taylor 1973	Emergence and development of customer relationships

Figure 2.1 The theoretical foundation of relationship marketing

psychology, sociology, or socio-psychology are applied to explain marketing-relevant circumstances. The qualities of empirical positivism are used to express the hypotheses, while relevant research enables the inference of recommended actions for corporate management in light of the paradigm's application base. Within this framework, numerous existing theories can be applied to clarify questions on relationship marketing (Figure 2.1).

The applicability of theories for expounding on questions related to relationship marketing can be assessed in terms of the following **theoretical requirements for relationship marketing**:

1 The central elements of relationship marketing are the corporation's customer relationships. Hence, the theories must be able to clarify the **forms and types of customer relationships**.

2 It should be feasible to explain the **different customer relationship phases**, from their build-up through to termination.

3 It is required that the **processes for the emergence of customer relationships** are elucidated, i.e. how these phases flow and take place.

4 In the context of customer relationship phases, it is additionally important to illuminate the **dynamic aspects of a customer relationship**.

5 The **conditions for the emergence and maintenance of customer relationships** should be highlighted.

6 It should be possible to express the viewpoints of both relationship parties, i.e. the **point of view of the buyer and the seller**.

The theories applied in the literature to relationship marketing will be evaluated critically on the basis of these requirements.

2.2 Neoclassical paradigm theories

The **neoclassical paradigm**, stemming from the microeconomic theory, analyses decisions of households and corporations under certain initial conditions akin to information security and rationality (Kaas 2000). An examination of both the sellers' and buyers' perspectives can be related to the following central **theories**: the Value Theory and the Profit Theory:

■ The **value theory** explains consumer behaviour related to the corporate products and services. It fundamentally posits that in view of value maximisation, the greater the usage value of a product to a customer, the more likely that he or she will demand it from the company. Subsequently, the incremental value of the product taken decreases: for instance, the greater the units of products available to the customer the smaller the value gained by the customer from incremental units. For customer relationships, this means that the greater the likelihood of a relationship representing value to a customer the sooner it will be initiated with the corporation. With these arguments, dimensions such as quality, customer satisfaction, perceived value, or relationship quality (see Chapter 3), develop implicit significance for relationship marketing.

■ The **profit theory** illustrates corporate behaviour with respect to product and service offers made to consumers. According to the thesis of profit maximisation, corporations orient their activities towards the economic consequences of their alternative actions. A central application of the profit theory to relationship marketing can be found in models of the customer lifetime value (CLV), which is an economic evaluation of customer relationships from a corporate standpoint. The CLV of a customer refers to the customer's net present value to a seller (Berger and Nasr 1998; Dwyer 1989). To arrive at the CLV of a particular customer the net value has to be calculated and discounted at a chosen discount rate (usually a rate that takes into account the company's cost of capital and risk). This requires the projection of the period of relationship and of future revenues and costs which, however, is often difficult to determine in practice.

A **critical evaluation** of the neoclassical paradigm is conducted below in respect of the theoretical requirements for relationship marketing:

■ The neoclassical theory does not explain the form and nature of customer relationships (requirement 1).

■ Similarly, neither the phases nor the processes for the emergence of customer relationships can be clarified. The dynamic character of customer relationships is also not taken into account (requirements 2, 3, and 4).

■ The emergence and maintenance of customer relationships can be elucidated fundamentally (requirement 5). From the customer's outlook, a customer relationship comes into existence because of value maximisation, whereas from the corporations' viewpoint it originates from profit maximisation. Particularly from the customer's perspective, however, details of how value is derived from an output are not provided.

■ In all cases, both the seller and the buyer are considered (requirement 6).

Overall, the neoclassical theory has the **advantage** of being able to withstand stringent theoretical and mathematical scrutiny, but the **disadvantage** of being very abstract and empirically barely provable. Since it does not fulfil the majority of the enumerated requirements, the neoclassical theory is thus of significantly lower relevance for clarifying questions related to relationship marketing, when compared with the neo-behavioural and forthcoming neo-institutional paradigms.

2.3 Neo-institutional paradigm theories

In the realm of the neo-institutional paradigm, specific circumstances involving customer relationships can be clarified with the help of the following theories:

- Information economics
- Principal-agent theory
- Transaction cost theory

2.3.1 Information economics

Information economics covers the functioning of markets under the uncertainty of information. The primary goal of this theory is to explain and reduce interaction uncertainties. Applying information economics, any type of product can be subdivided into search, experience, and credence qualities:

- **Search qualities** can be judged by the relationship party even prior to the contract or purchase
- **Experience qualities** can be judged only on or after purchase
- **Credence qualities** cannot be judged even after consumption

While search qualities apply more to goods, experience and credence qualities are more characteristic of services. Figure 2.2 arrays the possible continuum of evaluation for different types of products and services (Zeithaml and Bitner 2000, p. 31). Another perspective is illustrated in Figure 2.3. Based on the respective degrees of the relevant qualities, products and services can be arranged more specifically in an **economic information pyramid**.

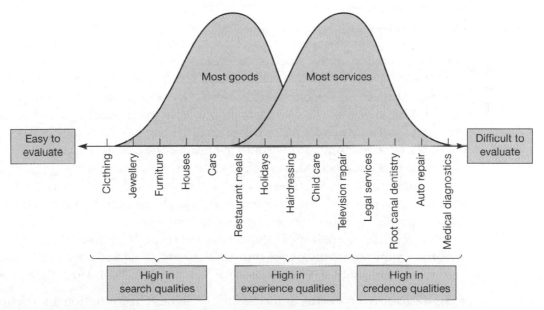

Figure 2.2 Evaluation process for various types of goods and services
(*Source:* Zeithaml and Bitner 2000, p. 31)

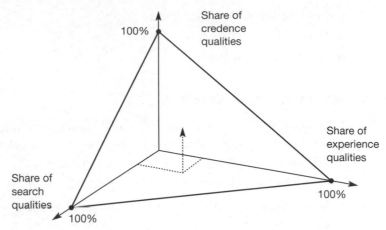

Figure 2.3 Economic information pyramid of products/services
(*Source*: Weiber 1993, p. 63; Adler 1996, p. 72)

These output qualities could represent the **purchase decision criteria** for a potential or current customer. Search qualities, which can be clearly imparted to the customer through impersonal communication, are not the only ones relevant for the customer's decision. Hence, during the initiation and control of customer relationships, corporations must also concentrate on aspects that have more of a relationship character. **Trust as the purchasing decision criteria** is an important construct that plays a particularly valuable role here. Corporate outputs can be better defined under the guidance of these qualities. The classification of them holds consequences for both the corporation and the customer.

From a **corporate perspective**, these qualities can be applied to plan the output offering depending on the phase of a customer relationship. For customer acquisition, it is meaningful to offer products and services with a high share of search qualities. This should be done in such a way that, in the course of a customer relationship and in view of cross selling of products, they can be enhanced with higher proportions of experience and credence qualities. From a **customer perspective**, the qualities of an output change during a relationship. While experience and credence qualities dominate prior to or at the start of a relationship, the proportion of search qualities (i.e. qualities assessable by the customer) increases as the experience of a customer with the seller grows. Hence, the insecurity of the customer is reduced during the course of the corporate relationship.

To address the uncertainty of information, the corporation and the customer can undertake **appropriate measures**, through both signalling and screening actions as follows (Kirmani and Rao 2000; Kaas 1995; Spence 1976; 1974; 1972; Figure 2.4):

■ **Signalling** refers to the transmission of reliable information by the more informed market participant, to the less informed participant in the market

■ **Screening** represents search activities for information on the more informed participant in the market, by the less informed market participant

Perspective \ Action	Signalling Transmission of information	Screening Search of information
Seller	**I** **More informed of own capabilities** • Depiction of own potential • Reference customers	**III** **Less informed of external factors** • Credit rating for loan request
Buyer	**II** **More informed of external factors** • Disclosure of specific data on customisation needs	**IV** **Less informed of seller's potential** • Comparison of several offers

Figure 2.4 Examples of information activities on corporations and customers

A **corporation's signalling activities** (Field I) are used to deliver reliable information on its capabilities to solve problems for the customer. This occurs primarily through promotion policy related measures that, for example, depict the firm's potential or present its highly satisfied reference customers. This is supposed to exemplify that the corporation can fulfil the requirements of potential customers, in order to convince the customer to commence a relationship with the corporation. Customers are normally only in a position to find out the validity of this information after utilisation of a product or service. In the course of a relationship a customer gains ever more experience of the corporation and its output, with the result that corporate signalling activities increasingly lose their effectiveness.

Signalling activities of a customer (Field II) are also relevant for numerous outputs, for example, when the customer informs the company about his or her output-related demands (e.g. data on customisation requirements). This applies chiefly to outputs for which the customer's experience and knowledge are meaningful (e.g. a management consulting project). The customer's signalling enables the highest possible satisfaction level. In this instance, if the corporation gathers and can call up data on the customer, the need for signalling activities also decreases in a relationship over time.

Active collection of customer data is achieved by the setting up of **corporate screening activities** (Field III). Since the gathering of individual customer data is often too costly, representative screening activities are regularly conducted, particularly in the area of market research. For certain outputs (e.g. services) that involve frequent contact between the seller and buyer, it is possible to integrate screening activities into the usual activities for output provision such as the monitoring of customer expectations by customer relations personnel. In this way, the uncertainties over the customer's situation decrease continuously during the term of the relationship.

Similarly, one also finds **screening activities by a customer** (Field IV) in which he or she collects data on the company. Just prior to selecting a seller customers probably conduct an intensive search for information on different providers. During a relationship as well, further screening activities will be performed. On the one hand, the current seller will invariably be scrutinised regarding its fulfilment of customer requirements. On the other hand, the customer gathers additional data on alternative providers that form the basis for the decision to switch sellers.

Based on the theoretical requirements for relationship marketing, information economics can be subjected to the following **critical evaluation**:

■ It is possible to differentiate between the various types of customer relationships by distinguishing among search, experience, and credence qualities (requirement 1).

■ The phases of a customer relationship cannot be explained (requirement 2).

■ However, it is feasible to clarify the general process of a customer relationship (requirement 3), since signalling and screening activities lose their significance in a relationship over time.

■ The dynamic character of customer relationships is, as such, given due consideration (requirement 4). However, the fact is that information economics does not permit an explanation of subsequent relationship stages.

■ Other than that, neither the emergence nor the maintenance of a customer relationship is elucidated (requirement 5).

■ Perspectives of the seller and the buyer are also taken into account (requirement 6).

2.3.2 Principal-agent theory

The **principal-agent theory** (Bergen, Dutta and Walker 1992; Eisenhardt 1989; Jensen and Meckling 1976) deals with uncertainty and information asymmetries in the realm of socio-economic relationships. The relationship party with greater dependence on the opposing party is designated as the principal (i.e. contract issuer), while the opposing party (i.e. contract recipient) represents the agent. In classical agency theory models, the agent is always assumed to be more risk-averse than the principal, who may be risk-neutral (Gibbons 1998). In practice, a definitive allocation of these two roles is not always possible since both the customer and the seller are in a state of inter-dependence and thus exhibit information asymmetries. Customers are seldom experts on the output acquired and the seller normally has an information head start in this respect. The customer, nevertheless, is found to have an advantage over the seller because the seller cannot have all the information about the customer.

A relationship party is distinguishable from its counterpart in terms of three **types of uncertainties** (Spremann 1990; 1987):

1 'Hidden characteristics' – information asymmetry on specific output attributes from a customer's viewpoint or customer attributes from the corporate viewpoint

2 'Hidden actions' – activities of the relationship party, which the other party cannot judge or which could be harmful to it

3 'Hidden intentions' – information asymmetry on the intentions of the other relationship party (e.g. profit orientation versus a corporation's expense)

Hidden characteristics are of relevance in the event of basically complex outputs (i.e. customised services). In such cases, customers are seldom able to judge services before making use of them, because of a high proportion of inherent credence qualities. Consequently, they may enter into a disadvantageous business relationship – a situation referred to as 'adverse selection'.

Hidden actions take effect on execution of a contract or in other words on establishment of a business relationship. It is possible that the behaviour of the relationship party cannot be evaluated as a result of cognitive, time, or cost-related reasons ('moral-hazard situation'). This is especially true in the case of customised products or services, where it is often not feasible even after occurrence of the behaviour.

During the course of a relationship, **hidden intentions** can also become obvious. The situation where an agent acts in compliance with the contract, but nevertheless generates value disadvantages for the principal, is labelled as a 'Hold-up' (Goldberg 1976). These negative consequences of information asymmetries, however, appear to be relevant only for a short period (Kumar, Scheer and Steenkamp 1995). Hidden characteristics, hidden actions, and hidden intentions should thus not occur in long-duration relationships.

A **critical evaluation** shows that the theoretical requirements for relationship marketing are fulfilled to the following degree:

- A differentiation of different types of customer relationships is fundamentally possible in terms of hidden characteristics, hidden actions, and hidden intentions (requirement 1).

- A customer relationship's phases and its development process are not explainable by the theory (requirements 2 and 3).

- The dynamic aspect and especially the long duration of customer relationships is also not taken into account by the theory (requirement 4).

- The reasons for entering into a business relationship are clarified, since the information asymmetries and their negative consequences can be avoided in this way (requirement 5).

- Within the scope of this theory, the points of view of both the seller and the customer are considered since both sides could be affected by the asymmetries in information (requirement 6).

2.3.3 Transaction cost theory

The **transaction cost theory** (Williamson 1975; Coase 1937) explores the costs that are a part of the coordination of a business relationship, i.e. the transaction costs. These are comprised of costs for the initiation, handling, control, modification, and termination of contracts as well as the opportunity costs (Picot 1982). According to the transaction cost theory, these costs increase disproportionately with rising uncertainty, specificity, and frequency of a transaction (Williamson 1991). For transactions under long-term **cooperative business relationships**, it can thus be assumed that these costs should be lower:

- the higher the uncertainty to be overcome (e.g. due to high market dynamics)
- the higher the specificity of the resources to be brought in from both sides (e.g. special tools for the manufacturer of special machines)
- the greater the frequency of exchange transactions (e.g. banking transfers)

All socio-economic output relationships should ideally be designed such that by taking the relevant influencing parameters into account, the appropriate **coordination form to minimise transaction costs** can be chosen (Picot and Dietl 1990, p. 182). According to the transaction cost theory, the hierarchy (vertical integration), the business relationship (cooperation), and market competition (confrontation) are the fundamental coordination forms that exist.

The following arguments are a **critical evaluation** of the transaction cost theory in view of the theoretical requirements for relationship marketing:

- On the one hand, it is possible to apply the transaction cost theory to differentiate between types of relationships by highlighting the various coordination forms. On the other hand, applications of the theory are limited to contractually regulated customer relationships (requirement 1).
- An explanation of the different phases and the development processes for customer relationships is not possible (requirements 2 and 3).
- Customer relationship dynamics are partly considered by the frequency of transactions assessed as a factor influencing the transaction costs (requirement 4).
- Further, the emergence of customer relationships is illuminated by the maxim of transaction cost minimisation (requirement 5).
- The perspectives of both the seller and the buyer are taken into account, since transaction costs can be incurred for both relationship parties (requirement 6).

Apart from these relationship-specific arguments, the neo-institutional theories demonstrate an overall **advantage** of greater transparence and integration capability versus other theories. Additionally, compared to neoclassical theories, they are based on more realistic base-assumptions. Nevertheless, these theories have the **disadvantage** that their argumentation lies on a relatively high abstract plane, thus making the derivation of specific actions difficult.

2.4 Neo-behavioural paradigm theories

In the scope of the neo-behavioural paradigm, there are very many theories that can be applied to explain problems related to relationship marketing. These can be generally grouped as follows: **psychological theories** and **socio-psychological theories**.

2.4.1 Psychological theories

The **psychological theories** that are of primary relevance to customer relationships include the Learning Theory, the Risk Theory, and Cognitive Dissonance Theory.

■ Among the many different **learning theories** (as per an overview by Bower and Hilgard 1984), the one referred to in this context is learning through the principle of reinforcement. This proposes that value-generating behaviours of the past are maintained, while those behaviours that have little benefit lead to behavioural changes (Wilkie 1994; Engel, Blackwell and Miniard 1993). When applied to customer retention, this suggests that customers are more likely to patronise the business relationship in which they perceive clear value or are satisfied.

■ The **risk theory** (Bettman 1973; Cunningham 1967; Bauer 1960; 1967) states that individuals seek to hold their subjectively perceived purchasing-specific risk as low as possible. Subjective risk is comprised of the importance of negative outcomes from a possible misjudgment together with the uncertainty of occurrence of these negative consequences. Perceived risk has been conceptionalised traditionally as a multidimensional phenomenon. In the literature, the overall risk has been subdivided into several kinds (e.g. the five types: performance, physical, financial, psychological, and social, were identified by Kaplan, Szybillo and Tocoby 1974). The risk theory can also contribute towards an elucidation of customer retention, since through repetition of a familiar purchase-decision or seller selection a customer can seek to minimise the risk of potential dissatisfaction as much as possible.

■ The **cognitive dissonance theory** (Festinger 1957) assumes that individuals continuously strive to maintain a balanced cognitive system. The goal of an individual is to reduce existing discordance and thereby reinstate balance. For a business relationship this implies that following a purchase, an attempt will be made to avoid dissonance-escalating information while simultaneously seeking discordance-reducing information. Reevaluation, enhancement, and suppression of data all represent typical behaviours of a customer wishing to reduce the dissonance. If the cognitive dissonance and along with it the switching intentions decrease in the course of a business relationship, then an explanation as to why long-term business relationships develop can be provided by the cognitive dissonance theory. In this respect, a problem area should be pointed out. Assuming that cognitive dissonance is present after an initial product purchase, then this theory could also explain a repetition of the first decision. However, the critical question is whether any clarification is provided beyond this first decision. Studies conducted in the eighties have clearly shown that even after multiple purchases, the likelihood of cognitive dissonances existing is very low.

Psychological theories can be subjected to the following **critical evaluation** with regard to the questions and theoretical requirements related to relationship marketing:

- Psychological theories do not permit a differentiation with respect to the form and type of customer relationships (requirement 1).

- Similarly, the various phases and processes of customer relationships can be explained no more than the dynamic aspects of psychological theories (requirements 2, 3 and 4).

- The value of psychological theories lies in their capability to clarify the emergence and maintenance of customer relationships (requirement 5). With the help of these theories it is feasible to identify specific arguments for the commencement of a relationship by a customer.

- However, that is possible only from the standpoint of a customer, but not from that of a corporation (requirement 6).

2.4.2 Socio-psychological theories

The following theories are of particular relevance for a **socio-psychological clarification** of questions on relationship marketing:

- Interaction and network theories
- Social exchange theory
- Social penetration theory

Interaction and network theories

Interaction theories stemming from the field of capital assets marketing cover the analysis and design of interactions. Fundamentally, one can distinguish the following four types of interactions and related theories in terms of two dimensions: the number of and type of participants (Figure 2.5):

1 Dyadic-person theories for interactions between two individuals
2 Multi-person theories for interactions between several individuals
3 Dyadic-organisational theories for interactions between two organisations
4 Multi-organisational theories for interactions between several organisations

Types of participants \ Number of participants	Two	More than two
Persons	Dyadic-person interaction theories	Multi-person interaction theories
Organisations	Dyadic-organisational interaction theories	Multi-organisational interaction theories

Figure 2.5 Types of interaction theories
(*Source*: adapted from Backhaus 1999)

Among the dyadic-person theories, **investigations** of socio-psychological constructs like perceived similarity, power or social cost-benefit calculations are themes that have found applications in marketing. The significant extension to multi-person theories has been not as much in terms of the additional variables studied, but rather in its application to more individuals. A fundamental extension also occurred in organisational interaction theories that strive to depict all links between corporations.

Organisational approaches form the basis of **network theories**. Since relationships between the seller and buyer are determined not only by interactions between them but also by their dependence on indirect personal and organisational links, the interaction theories help in the analysis of relevant interdependencies. The direct and indirect relationships between the network members that change over time are examined more closely on a meta-plane with respect to their quantity, intensity, links, and substance. The networks are thus characterised by the following **attributes**:

- The central element of a network is the **cooperation** between the network members, where cooperation implies joint execution of activities on the provision of products to achieve higher profitability and economic efficiency for the members. An example of this are strategic cooperations in the airline industry (see 'Insights 2.1: Strategic Networks between Airlines' for more information).

- Networks function only if their members have faith in the reciprocity of network relationships, i.e. each product or service will generate an output in return over the medium to long term (Johanson and Mattson 1987, p. 36).

- Another constituent element of networks is the power of their members, used by them to emphasise their interests, solve problems, or push through individual strategies (Benson 1975, pp. 231–232). The sanctioning capability of respective corporations provides the basis for exercising power (Sydow 1992, p. 92).

- To some extent all network members are more or less **economically dependent** on each other. This dependence implies that corporations cannot reach certain strategic decisions without considering the other members.

Insights 2.1

Strategic Networks between Airlines

As international airline traffic has grown in recent decades, cooperation and strategic alliances among international airline carriers in the provision of service has become widespread. The most visible form of a strategic network is found in the international airline alliances that link U.S. carriers to partners in other countries worldwide (Brueckner 2000, p. 2). Networks in the airline industry may assist in a decrease of costs, improved earnings, and increased profitability. Examples of different existing airline alliances are: Star Alliance (www.star-alliance.com), Oneworld (www.oneworld.com), Skyteam, and KLM/Northwest. Established in May 1997, Star

Alliance nowadays has the most complete global coverage, including 15 member airlines: Air Canada, Air New Zealand, All Nippon Airways (ANA), Ansett Australia, Austrian Airlines, bmi british midland, Lauda Air, Lufthansa German Airlines, Mexicana Airlines, SAS Scandinavian Airlines (SAS), Singapore Airlines, Thai Airways International, Tyrolean Airways, United Airlines and Varig Brazilian Airlines. This partnership was designed to provide customers with the benefits of a global and 'seamless' travel experience, lessening some of the inconveniences of a traditional interline, or multi-carrier, trip (Brueckner 2000, p. 2). Travellers thus have access to almost 900 airports in 129 countries. Furthermore, the elements of this arrangement include cooperation in scheduling and ticketing (e.g. harmonised timetables), frequent flyer programmes (e.g. customers can earn and redeem air miles or points on any member airline), airport clubs (e.g. access to over 500 lounges), baggage handling and customer service across airlines. As a result of this network, the member airlines are able to achieve cost savings and to better utilise capacity through the operation of joint venture services and code sharing. Besides this, they benefit from millions of customer data, one of the most valuable assets, from their individual frequent flyer programs.

(*Sources*: The information on Star Alliance is based, in part, on several articles published on its website on April 7, 2000, December 3, 2001, and April 16, 2002 (www.star-pr.com/web/press_room/index.htm, accessed on May 10, 2002). See also Brueckner, J.K. (2000): The Benefits of Codesharing and Antitrust Immunity for International Passengers, with an Application to the Star Alliance, unpublished study, University of Illinois at Urbana-Champaign, www.brueckner-report.com/bruecknerreport.pdf, accessed on January 17, 2002.)

Direct and indirect relationships between network members form the substance of network theories, which can, hence, be viewed as both the requirements and the action parameters for network management. The goal of network theories is the optimal allocation of scarce resources among network members by means of exchange processes benefiting all parties involved. On the one hand, network theories offer a framework for analysing the totality of corporate relationships. On the other hand, they have a highly descriptive character whose implicit conceptual recommendations more likely represent common sense inferences.

Based on the theoretical requirements for relationship marketing, interaction and network theories can be subjected to the following **critical evaluation**:

- An analysis of various types of interaction and network relationships enables a differentiation among different types of customer relationships (requirement 1).

- The theories, however, can explain neither the phases nor the dynamic character of a customer relationship (requirements 2, 3 and 4).

- In particular, network theories can clarify the emergence and maintenance of customer relationships (requirement 5).

- Perspectives of both the seller and the buyer are also taken into account (requirement 6).

Social exchange theory

The **social exchange theory** (Blau 1964; Homans 1961) elucidates the emergence and continuance of social relationships, specifically customer relationships (Bagozzi 1975). The central element of exchange relationships is the mutual

exchange of values (Houston and Gassenheimer 1987; Bagozzi 1975). From a medium-term perspective the supply of a value by the one party will be compensated sooner or later by the delivery of a value by the other party.

The **goal of equality** is the foundation of exchange processes, i.e., both exchange parties strive for attainment of justice between themselves (Sahlins 1972; Homans 1961). This does not imply that only one exchange party ensures that it is not taken advantage of by the other. Rather, each of the exchange parties is aware that any advantage gained by the other at its expense entails negative consequences for itself. Corporations realise that they cannot retain customers over the long term, especially if the customers feel that the seller has taken advantage of them (e.g. very high price demands by the seller). This has been demonstrated in an analysis of different output types, particularly customised services, in which the customers were able to judge the company comprehensively because of their close contact with the firm.

Three **types of exchange processes** can be distinguished in terms of social exchange processes (Bagozzi 1975; Ekeh 1974; Lévi-Strauss 1969):

1 **Restricted exchange processes** involve two exchange parties, where each party delivers something to its respective counterpart and receives something in return.

2 **Generalised exchange processes** occur between at least three exchange parties. In contrast to restricted exchange processes, however, the parties are not in direct contact with each other. In the minimal case of three exchange parties, the first party delivers a certain value to the second party, which in turn delivers it to the third, which eventually delivers a value back to the first party.

3 **Complex exchange processes** take place foremost in networks, and are characterised by relationships between at least three exchange parties. As opposed to a generalised exchange, it is possible here that an exchange party that has delivered a certain value to another party receives one in return. In the extreme case, relationships exist between all the exchange parties considered. The box 'Insights 2.2: Multi-Exchange Process of Television Ads' illustrates an example of complex exchange processes.

Insights 2.2

Multi-Exchange Process of Television Ads

Television advertisements are a clear example of complex exchange processes. The parties in this exchange are the advertising firm, the television station, and the viewer. The firm delivers its advertisement to the station and pays for its transmission. The station transmits a programme to the viewer, who gives her or his attention and thereby facilitates not only indirect media penetration, but as a recipient of the programme also perceives the firm's advertisement. If the viewer ends up acquiring the firm's product, possibly as a result of the advertisement, the firm then supplies its product and the viewer as a customer pays the due price, thereby completing a three-way exchange process. Figure 2.6 illustrates the exchange processes between the different parties.

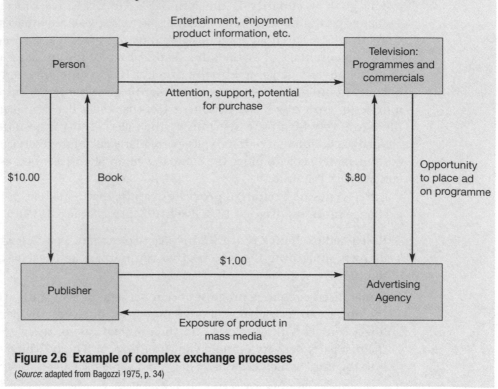

Figure 2.6 Example of complex exchange processes
(*Source*: adapted from Bagozzi 1975, p. 34)

Various types of exchanges can be differentiated, depending on their content. A value exchange and a symbolic exchange can be identified as the base types. The possibility of a combined exchange as a mixture of the two general types also exists (Houston and Gassenheimer 1987; Bagozzi 1975). Under a **value exchange**, goods are exchanged for money or other goods. The motivation for the exchange comes from the subsequent usage of the exchanged goods or money. Hence, the value exchange can be specified as a pure economic exchange. The underlying reason behind a **symbolic exchange** is that the product is not taken purely for its usage, but also for its symbolic perception. In general, a symbol exists in either the absence of direct experience or when an object is not perceived for itself alone, but instead in the form of aspects such as feelings associated with the object. For relationship marketing, the existence of symbolic exchanges implies that consumers become customers of the corporation not solely because of the product offered, but also because of the attendant symbolism.

> **Examples of symbolic exchanges:** The image that customers associate with clothing or cars; security that goes along with life insurance; attention associated with football club merchandise.

On the basis of these fundamental deliberations on social exchange processes, the social exchange theory serves to explain the **occurrence and continuance of cus tomer relationships**. The theory provides a framework that helps to explain customer behaviour in the realm of customer relationships, and thereby demonstrates a close bearing to customer retention – a central target parameter for marketing.

From the customer's perspective, the decisive factor for continuing a relationship is called **relationship judgment**. Economic calculations form the basis for evaluating relationships. The customer maintains a relationship when the net outcome (**OC**) is positive. The OC value is the difference between the exchange value (of service quality, for example) and the exchange costs like the price. The theory further postulates a decreasing incremental value for repeated exchanges.

For modelling of evaluation processes, it is assumed that parties apply the **comparison levels** (**CL**) (Thibaut and Kelley 1959, p. 21) to judge a relationship. On the basis of these levels, the relationship parties determine the relationship costs and values. Satisfaction is derived when the OC value is greater than the CL value. The form of the CLs depends mainly on prior experiences of the customer with similar categories of outputs. The CL is established by customer expectations, representing the basis for considering customer satisfaction and perceived service quality.

In spite of economically sound modelling of the assessment process, the exchange theory emphasises the **relevance of social aspects** within relationship behaviour. This is because the theory's underlying view of the value of a relationship is broad. It is thus postulated that social aspects such as trust, recognition, and affection are a part of the central elements of value.

One of the important organisational aspects of relationship marketing is the **evaluation of available relationship alternatives** (Thibaut and Kelley 1959). A customer judges the relationship to a seller not only on the basis of experiences with this seller, but also on the basis of additional experiences with other sellers in equivalent product or service categories. Alternatives are compared by contrasting the CL versus an alternative comparison level CL_{alt}.

A **critical evaluation** of exchange theories can be done on the basis of the theoretical requirements for relationship marketing:

- The different forms and types of customer relationships can be clarified by the theory for restricted, generalised and complex exchange processes (requirement 1).

- The social exchange theory cannot illustrate the phases and emergence processes for customer relationships (requirements 2 and 3).

- The dynamic character of customer relationships is considered partly (requirement 4), but only in that experiences with a seller and her or his competition are accounted for in the form of CL and CL_{alt}. The long-term nature of relationships is thus explicitly accentuated.

- In addition, the emergence and maintenance of relationships are explained on the basis of these variables (requirement 5). Here too, a wide range of influencing parameters is included, since aspects such as trust are considered as possible value elements for the customer. However, an explicit and detailed analysis of different factors that influence the emergence and maintenance of customer relationships does not follow.

■ The social exchange theory's decision methodology can, hence, be applied to all relationship parties such that both the seller and buyer viewpoints are given due consideration (requirement 6).

Social penetration theory

The **social penetration theory** (Altman and Taylor 1973), like the social exchange theory, explains the emergence and continuation of relationships. In contrast to the latter, the former takes a micro view by explaining the emergence of a relationship through individual interactions between relationship parties. According to this theory, individuals continuously discover additional elements of the **relationship party's personality** in the course of the relationship. In this way, the relationship develops fully through ever more forays into the counterpart's personality. The personality is described as a systematic organisation of an unknown number of elements (Altman and Taylor 1973, p. 15) structured around the following two dimensions (Figure 2.7):

1 Personality breadth
2 Personality depth

The **personality breadth** has two sub-dimensions: categories and frequency. Categories refer to main topics handled by the relationship party during the development of a relationship. Family and hobbies are examples of such categories and each of these is made up of a series of elements. For example, the category 'family'

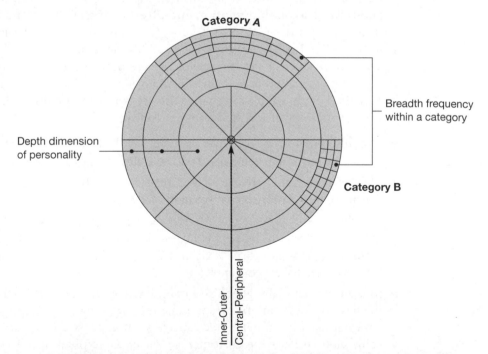

Figure 2.7 Human personality development according to the social penetration theory
(*Source*: Altman and Taylor 1973, p. 16)

is comprised of elements like attitudes towards family life or experiences with one's own family. Frequency then refers to the number of interactions with the relationship party in one such category (Altman and Taylor 1973, pp. 29–30).

Customer needs and the various products offered by the corporation are examples of categories in **customer relationships**. These categories like a clarification on the company's products may be encountered many times, such that the frequency of the dealings could impact the relationship. For example, when the customer has dealt often enough with the company's products and services, he or she becomes an expert who influences positively the provision of products and services.

Example 2.1	In reference to a relationship between a bank and its customer, an example of a personality category is the customer's handling of money. Elements of this category are the customer's risk aversion, the significance assigned to money, and the duration required for money-related decisions. At the beginning of a relationship, banks seek to set up an investment profile of the customer in order to identify general aspects of the customer's personality within this category. However, only after a specific period, if at all, will the bank advisor know these personality elements well.

Personality depth refers to the path from the surface into the core of the personality. Just like an onion, the personality structure is made up of different layers with outer layers having more elements of personality than inner layers. Additionally, the outer layer elements are more superficial than any of the inner ones. Central personality characteristics are found on the inner layers and they influence the appearance of outer layer elements. With increasing personality depth, it becomes more difficult to penetrate into even deeper layers of the counterpart's personality. This is because the disclosure of deep-seated personality characteristics has a higher level of risk-association than the disclosure of outer layer elements (Altman and Taylor 1973, p. 27).

When applied to **customer relationships**, the personality depth from a customer's perspective depicts the corporation's profoundness of knowledge on the customer. In terms of product use, for example, the knowledge as to whether the customer uses the product at all is more general than knowledge of how the customer uses the respective product. Similarly, various layers of the customer's knowledge on the company can be distinguished. For example, in the category 'manufacturing a product' the information 'ingredients' is classified as more 'superficial' than the information 'manufacturing process'.

A relationship is formed of many **interactions between the relationship parties**. In such interactions the relationship parties penetrate the personality of the other by continuously getting to know more confidential aspects (personality depth) in more areas (personality breadth) of the other party (Altman and Taylor 1973, p. 29). During a relationship, corporations and customers will exchange requirements and outputs more and more intensively.

According to the social penetration theory, the **social penetration process** that describes the effect of a relationship on interactions between the parties represents inroads into the relationship party's personality. This process can be characterised in eight **dimensions** (Altman and Taylor 1973, p. 129):

1 In terms of the **interaction diversity** between relationship parties, there is an increase in not only the topics (personality breadth) that are the substance of interactions but also in the types of interactions. On commencement of a relationship individuals know little about the other and a majority of the interactions are verbal. These are subsequently supplemented by non-verbal forms of interaction. In the aforementioned banking example, the bank and its employees at first obtain information on customers through an investment-profile questionnaire. After a certain amount of time and several advisory discussions, the bank representative will be able to increasingly interpret the customer's unconscious remarks as well as gestures and expressions.

2 Along with the use of new forms of interaction, relationships generate rituals that only the parties involved can interpret. This results in the existence of **interaction uniqueness** between the relationship parties. For instance, when a person has repeatedly visited a restaurant, café, or club, he or she gets to know the establishment's employees better. Thus, certain greeting rituals such as waving may be used.

3 **Replaceability and equivalence** of interactions is reached due to their vast breadth and uniqueness. The better the parties in the relationship know each other the sooner the facts can be communicated in different ways. For instance, if a restaurant employee and the guest know each other well, they can also communicate non-verbally with each other. That is, in the situation where the guest wishes to order her or his usual drink, while the waiter is attending another table, the guest just signals with his hand.

4 Furthermore, a relationship leads to increasing **openness** between the relationship parties. The first time a patient visits a new doctor he or she will not mention all health problems. In contrast, a patient that has known this doctor for a long time will be able to speak more openly about the problems.

5 During the development of a relationship, the relationship parties gain an increasingly better **understanding of roles**. For joint activities, both then know the role each has to play for the respective activity. In an ongoing management-consulting project, certain tasks often have to be done by both the consultants and the firm that is receiving consultation. Once the relevant processes have been implemented, the respective tasks (e.g. information preparation done on a regular basis) will be executed without asking the relationship party.

6 The better a relationship the greater the **informality** in interactions between the parties. For example, in the Business-to-Business (B2B) segment, the first time a company places an order with a supplier the process is relatively formal (e.g. written order confirmation). Once many orders have transpired between the two companies and their respective employees, it is likely that subsequent ones will be placed informally by telephone or email.

7 With mounting relationship intensity, an augmented **possibility and acceptance of criticism** develops with the result that the relationship parties become

increasingly willing to give and accept criticism and to take it seriously. This can be illustrated with the following example: once an insured person and the insurance clerk become familiar with each other, both parties will handle problems more easily. The customer will then find it easier to express dissatisfaction to the insurance company over a damage claim.

8 The first seven dimensions result in increasing **exchange efficiency** with regard to interactions between the relationship parties. In comparison with earlier relationship stages, the better the state of knowledge between the relationship parties the more precise and rapid the communication.

With growing relationship intensity, these dimensions become more effective. Under closer examination and respective structuring of the dimensions it becomes apparent that the customer's knowledge and behaviour improve during the course of a relationship (Figure 2.8).

As a result of **customer knowledge**, the high relationship intensity has a positive impact on the form of interactions, since the trust between the relationship partners leads to an improvement in seller-buyer contacts. In this way, trust results in the development of better solutions. This is justified primarily because the strong relationship contributes to the achievement of a constructive 'conflict culture' between the transaction parties (Moorman, Zaltman and Deshpandé 1992, p. 318).

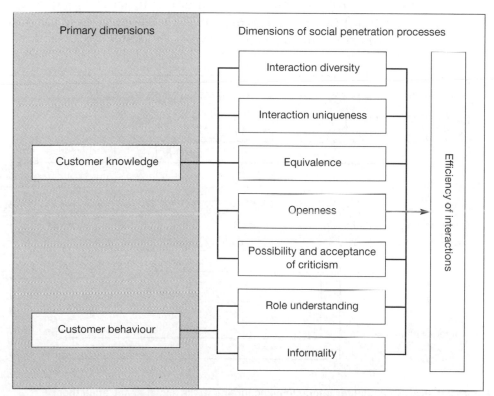

Figure 2.8 Dimensions of the social penetration theory process
(*Source*: Georgi 2000, p. 61)

Accordingly, the relationship parties can openly discuss problem-laden elements of interactions and reach an improved basis jointly.

Customer behaviour, which plays the role of a quality driver among external factors integrated in the provision of products and services, can also lead to improved interactions due to the intense relationship. If a customer trusts a seller, for example, then he or she is more likely to provide the corporation with clear and specific information at the right time (Dwyer, Schurr and Oh 1987; Moorman, Zaltman and Deshpandé 1992, p. 318; Halinen 1996, p. 328). Hence, with the social penetration process it becomes apparent how an improvement in the relationship intensity can have a positive impact on interactions between the seller and buyer.

Only after several transactions between parties have taken place is it designated as a relationship. The social penetration theory focuses on explaining the occurrence of follow-on transactions. To illustrate these subsequent transaction decisions by a relationship party, this theory forms the basis for a **process model of follow-on interactions** according to which, individuals make judgments, predictions, and decisions on interactions with others (Figure 2.9; Altman and Taylor 1973, p. 34).

A relationship starts with the **first interaction** between parties. This is assessed by a judgment standard patterned after the CLs of the social exchange theory (Kelley and Thibaut 1978, p. 8). Additionally, following an interaction, the individual predicts the outcome of future interactions that arise with potential relationship parties. The individual then applies these prognoses to decide on whether to continue or terminate the relationship.

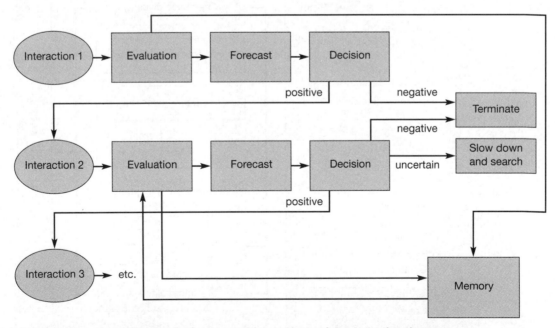

Figure 2.9 Process model for interactions according to the social penetration theory
(*Source*: adapted from Altman and Taylor 1973, p. 35)

Continuing the relationship means initiation of a **second interaction** that will eventually be judged in turn. It will also be verified if the prediction comes true and a new decision will be based on these results. In addition to the alternatives of terminating or continuing the relationship after the second transaction, a third possibility of softening up of the relationship comes into the picture.

The information processed by the individual for the assessments and forecasts will be stored in one's **central memory** and recalled for later judgments and predictions. This information represents the link between the transaction and relationship planes within the framework of thought. The relationship parties store the information gained in the interaction so that it can be called up for later opportunities. Following the second transaction, the decision to continue the relationship is dependent on not just one single interaction but rather on an evaluation of the whole relationship to date.

The following **critical evaluation** of the social penetration theory results from the framework of the theoretical requirements for relationship marketing:

- A differentiation between the different forms and types of customer relationships is possible (requirement 1), in that various characteristics of the personality breadth and depth can be distinguished (Altman and Taylor 1973).

- The different phases of a customer relationship and thereby its emergence process can be explained by the dimensions of the social penetration theory (requirements 2 and 3).

- The process model focuses explicitly on the dynamic character of the development of customer relationships (requirement 4).

- Similarly, the emergence and maintenance of customer relationships is clarified by adapting the process model to the social exchange theory (requirement 5).

- The social penetration theory's statements can also be applied to all relationship parties and as such to the seller and customer perspectives (requirement 6).

It is apparent that the social penetration theory fulfils the theoretical requirements for relationship marketing to a high degree. Consequently, it should be viewed as an important foundation of relationship marketing. The base deliberations of the theory are reflected in the customer relationship life cycle, which forms the basis for the conceptualisation of relationship marketing.

Summary

This chapter presented a methodical and comprehensive conceptualisation basis in which single theories stemming from the neoclassical, the neo-institutional, and the neo-behavioural school were analysed. After developing six requirements, each theory was examined on its contribution and benefits for explaining the concept of relationship marketing. Figure 2.10 gives a brief summary of the aforementioned critical evaluations based on the requirements.

Theories	Requirements					
	1	2	3	4	5	6
Neoclassical Theory	–	–	–	–	o	+
Information Economics	+	–	+	o	–	+
Principal Agent Theory	+	–	–	–	+	+
Transaction Cost Theory	+	–	–	o	+	+
Psychological Theories	–	–	–	–	+	o
Interaction/Network Theories	+	–	–	–	+	+
Social Exchange Theory	o	–	–	o	+	+
Social Penetration Theory	+	+	+	+	+	+

Figure 2.10 Summary of the aforementioned critical evaluations ('+' = positive contribution, 'o' = some contribution, '–' = no contribution)

Resulting from the critical evaluation, we can say that the social penetration contributes the most to explaining the concept of relationship marketing. All other theories fulfil only partly the requirements necessary for the theoretical foundation.

3 The conceptualisation of relationship marketing

Overview

After examining the theoretical background, the next step deals with deriving specific concepts which can be used for a conceptualisation of relationship marketing. So far there has been only a superficial discussion of single aspects but none of the approaches in this chapter have been analysed comprehensively in context with relationship marketing. However, taking a closer look at the relevant concepts is important if relationship marketing is seen and understood as a science. Therefore, we present the most relevant and fundamental theoretical approaches which form the basis for the development of a conceptualisation of relationship marketing. Specifically, we will address the following questions:

➤ Which approaches should be considered for the conceptualisation and design of relationship marketing?

➤ What are the benefits of the customer life cycle concept for the conceptualisation of relationship marketing?

➤ How do the concepts of perspective taking and the success chain influence the conceptualisation of relationship marketing?

➤ What is the relevance of customer relationship perspectives for the conceptualisation of relationship marketing? How can we manage to harmonise our own view with others' viewpoint of expectations and actual outputs?

➤ What does an idealised planning process of relationship marketing, with its phases for analysis, planning, execution of actions, and control, look like?

3.1 The customer life cycle as a reference base

Customer relationships are dynamic in nature, resulting in various phases in the relationship that can be presented and analysed uniquely through the life cycle concept. Hence

■ the customer requirements life cycle, and
■ the customer relationship life cycle

can be the starting point for systematic modelling of relationship marketing.

3.1.1 Fundamentals of the life cycle concept

The **life cycle concept** emerged out of research on adoption and diffusion of innovation that originally dealt with the achievement of innovation within target groups. This concept has already been applied to numerous aspects investigated in the business administration field and in other areas such as the economic analysis of firms (Mueller 1972; for more recent research, Gup and Agrrawal 1996). Fundamental deliberations centre around the concept that, just as for human beings, each and every item examined has a limited life cycle. During this period each item goes through idealised phases similar to the ones of childhood, adolescence etc. for humans. Each respective phase is characterised by specific attributes that permit conclusions to be made about the particular item involved.

In **marketing**, the life cycle concept has been applied primarily in the sense of product, market, and brand life cycles. A major application is in the area of **product life cycles (PLC)** (Palmer 2000; Day 1981; Cox 1967; Levitt 1965) where the development of a product in the market is presented in terms of economic figures like turnover and market share. The PLC concept thus describes the evolution of a product, illustrated by its sales pattern from the time of market entry to its demise (Cox 1967, p. 375). This permits identification of six development phases: introduction, growth, and maturity under rising or stable revenues, and saturation, decline, and collapse under falling revenues. For each respective phase, product specific strategic and operative recommendations can be deduced for marketing actions. Figure 3.1 depicts an example of a typical PLC-curve representing different products.

With the transition from mainly product-oriented to more intensive customer-oriented marketing, it is logical to apply the life cycle concept to the **development of customer relationships** (Stauss 2000). In the course of a customer relationship, both customers and sellers go through different stages independent of the relationship's strength. From a customer orientation perspective, customer requirements during a relationship are decisive for the course of a relationship life cycle. These requirements are in turn dependent on the natural life phase of the customer. An analysis of the development of customer relationships, hence, identifies **two life cycles** – for customer requirements and customer relationships – that are discussed below.

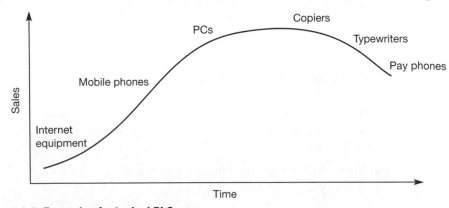

Figure 3.1 Example of a typical PLC-curve

3.1.2 Customer requirements life cycle

The **customer requirements life cycle** structures the **life phases of an individual**. Customers do not only have different needs and wants (Kotler 2000, pp. 21–22), these needs can also differ during different phases in each market considered. Insights 3.1 describes the principle of the customer requirements life cycle regarding the example of financial services in Germany. Within relationship marketing the customer requirements life cycle concept has two central functions. First, it has a **present control function** aimed at assessing the current exploitation of the customer potential. This includes aspects such as the realisation of the cross selling potential for a customer or a product differentiation in line with her/his needs. Second, it has a **future control function** that enables determination of the corporation's medium to long-term profit potential from the customer, based on the latter's needs in various phases in life. For instance, when the customer is in a phase with significant future needs in the respective market, like a student who intends to pursue a management career and raise a family, he or she is more attractive for the corporation over the medium to long-term than an 80-year old formerly unemployed individual without any net worth. This permits the early matching of specific customer requirements through materialisation of customer acquisition ('lock-in' effect) and product differentiation aspects.

The examples above demonstrate that the life cycle phase alone is inadequate for predicting future customer sales. The phase must, instead, be considered in combination with other customer attributes such as socio-economic or demographic factors. Nevertheless, the customer requirements life cycle does express the idealised profit potential of a specific customer. For a real life example, see the box 'Customer requirements life cycle for financial services in Germany'.

Insights 3.1

Customer requirements life cycle for financial services in Germany

The concept of the customer requirements life cycle can be explained very easily. For example, a family will face many financial issues, problems, and challenges during its entire life cycle (Garman and Forgue 1994). Furthermore, families use a variety of financial assets for various goals (Xiao 1996, p. 21). That is, some financial assets, such as checking accounts, are held by most families whereas other assets, such as stocks, are held only by a minority of families (Kennickell and Shack-Marquez 1992). While some research suggests that family savings can be associated with life cycle variables, such as age, number of children (Hefferan 1982), and household size (Hogarth 1991), this idea can be extended to a life cycle of an individual person. Figure 3.2 depicts an application of the customer requirements life cycle to the financial services sector in Germany.

In the early years, various forms of savings make up the majority of financial services offered. In subsequent life cycles the offers may be enhanced by insurance and liquidity-supportive services. With growing emphasis on the future, financial services that focus on insuring the individual or family move to the forefront. As the needs and thus the demands for financial services change from one life phase to another, providers of these services can profit from such information: they can increase the added value by offering life cycle tailored products and services, or by bundling outputs for the potential customers.

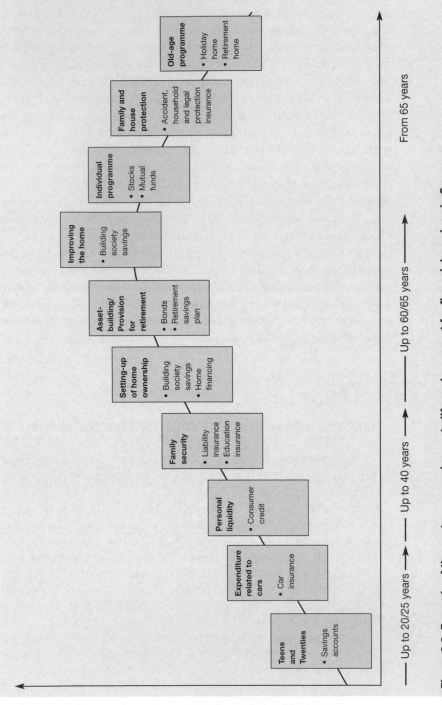

Figure 3.2 Example of the customer requirements life cycle concept for financial services in Germany

(*Source:* Benölken and Greipel 1994, p. 201)

3.1.3   Customer relationship life cycle

The customer requirements life cycle is valid irrespective of the sellers dealt with by the customer. It also represents the framework within which an analysis of the customer relationship development can be conducted in the context of the **customer relationship life cycle** (Stauss 2000; Dwyer, Schurr and Oh 1987, p. 15):

> The customer relationship life cycle describes idealised phases that occur regularly in the relationship over time, and enables conclusions to be drawn for relationship marketing on the basis of the relationship's intensity.

Referring to the customer relationship life cycle axes, the abscissa represents the **business relationship duration** and the ordinate reflects the **relationship intensity**. Consequently, the various phases in the cycle differ fundamentally according to the intensity of the relationship considered.

Since the intensity of a customer relationship can be expressed in terms of diverse constructs, a core formal difficulty surfaces when using the customer relationship life cycle to determine its ordinate. The following **three types of constructs for determining the relationship intensity** are applicable to a customer, either in isolation or preferably in combination (Figure 3.3):

a The relationship intensity's **psychological indicators** that could, for instance, be used are the relationship quality from the customer's perspective, or the customer's trust in or commitment to the seller (detailed in section 3.3).

b Behaviours that could, for instance, be subsumed under **behavioural indicators** are the purchasing behaviour, information behaviour like the extent of a search for competitive products, integration behaviour covering the disclosure of factors relevant for the provision of products, and word-of-mouth communication by the customer on the seller.

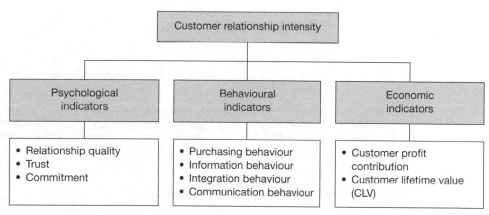

Figure 3.3 Indicators of the customer relationship intensity

c **Economic indicators** of the relationship intensity are the customer profit contribution from a static perspective, and the customer lifetime value from a dynamic viewpoint. Depending on the conceptualisation of customer value (Chapter 8), psychological and behavioural indicators are also included here.

Additional factors are considered for a clear **designation of the phases in a customer relationship life cycle**. These relate to the buyer-seller relationship and can be sub-divided into customer and corporation related attributes. **Customer attributes** help to specify relevant aspects in each phase. Variables such as the relationship quality, which can be applied to put the life cycle diagram ordinate into effect, come into play. Among these attributes are: the customer's goals with regard to the relationship with the seller plus the psychological, behavioural, and economic facets. **Corporation attributes** apply to the derivation and recommendation of strategic and operative actions for marketing. Of relevance are the primary goals, tasks, target groups, marketing focus, customer processing, and taking account of the competition.

The **relationship life cycle phases** are divided and characterised in several different ways (e.g. Stauss 2000; Dwyer, Schurr and Oh 1987; Dubinsky and Ingram 1984). In general, they can be classified in three **core phases** (Stauss 2000; Bruhn 1999a; Figure 3.4):

a Customer acquisition

b Customer retention

c Customer recovery

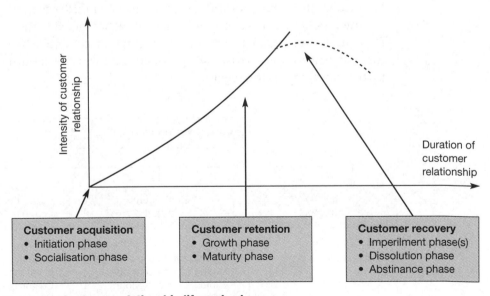

Figure 3.4 Customer relationship life cycle phases

These three customer relationship life cycle phases can be characterised in greater detail in terms of stated customer and corporation associated attributes (Figure 3.4). The **customer acquisition phase**, comprising the initiation and socialisation phases, describes the initiation of a buyer-seller relationship, wherein the initiation and socialisation phases can be differentiated precisely. The **initiation phase** is the precursor to transactions involving an exchange of goods between the seller and buyer. The customer obtains data on the seller, while the latter undertakes measures such as promotion to acquire the customer. This phase ends with the first exchange of goods, thereby initiating the **socialisation phase** in which the seller and buyer become familiar with each other. The customer gains preliminary experience with the seller's product, which enables the seller to collect data on the customer for subsequent preparation of customised outputs. Since both customer acquisition and familiarisation entail start-up costs, this acquisition phase is generally uneconomic for the company.

In the case of positive developments the buyer-seller relationship grows during the **customer retention phase**, which can be separated into the growth and maturity phases (Stauss 2000). The **growth phase** for a corporation is characterised by full utilisation of the customer's potential, in that an effort is made to broaden the relationship through increased output use by the customer as for cross buying. In the **maturity phase**, since the respective customer's potential has been utilised almost fully the goal is now aimed at maintaining the sales level reached. Regarding empirical research analysing the benefits of long-term customer loyalty or relationship quality during a relationship, the box 'Insights 3.2: Empirical findings' provides the reader with more information.

Insights 3.2

Empirical findings

In connection with the initially growing economic relationship strength, one of the studies most often quoted is that by Reichheld and Sasser (1990). Figure 3.5 illustrates examples of the profit made per customer as a function of the relationship length by credit card organisations, laundries, wholesalers, and automobile servicing companies.

With regard to the development of the relationship quality as a psychological indicator of the relationship intensity, this variable was measured from a student's perspective at eight stages in an empirical study conducted during a tutorial at the university. The results showed significant growth in the relationship quality occurring in the middle of the relationship, i.e. between the third and sixth period. Beyond that, the value balanced out at a relatively high level (Figure 3.6).

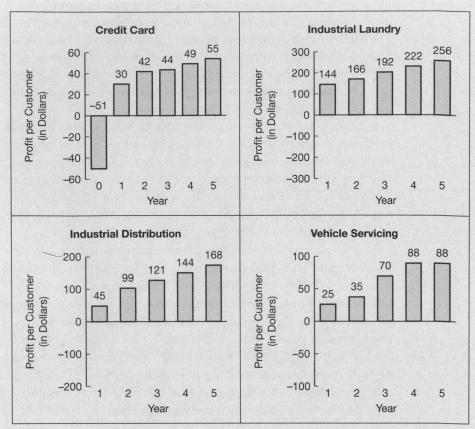

Figure 3.5 Empirical findings on profit generated per customer in different sectors
(*Source*: Reichheld and Sasser 1990)

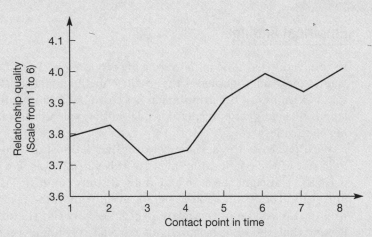

Figure 3.6 Empirical example of the development of relationship quality during a relationship
(*Source*: Georgi 2000, p. 137)

The **customer recovery phase** is concerned with termination of the relationships by the customers and covers the imperilment, dissolution, and abstinence phases. In the **imperilment phase**, as a result of certain events the customer begins to mull over the idea of not using the seller's products and services any more. A decision is then reached in the **dissolution phase** to stop using the seller and the customer openly cancels the relationship especially in case of a membership, or just gives it up quietly. This leads to the **abstinence phase** where the customer refrains from using any of the relevant sellers' products or services. The relationship could commence again, because of either customer-originated reasoning or due to recovery measures undertaken by the provider.

In the recovery phase, customer losses can take place in different ways. Depending on the length of the process and the intensity of the reaction, four **types of defection processes** can be identified (Figure 3.7). An example of one type is a radical loss, meaning a rapid defection with a strong reaction and possibly additional negative word-of-mouth communication.

The customer relationship life cycle is idealised and can vary in terms of the following attributes **depending on the output type** applicable to the respective sector:

- Occurrence of phases
- Duration of phases

The **occurrence of phases** implies that a customer does not have to go through all phases. An initiation phase occurs mainly for customised services (e.g. tax advice), where the customer's risk and involvement lead to longer decision-making processes. The growth phase could be bypassed if the customer requires only one of the seller's products or the latter offers few outputs, as is usually the case with standardised services such as visits to the cinema. Otherwise, both the growth and maturity phase could be skipped if service provision errors crop up early during the socialisation phase and lead to commencement of the imperilment phase.

The **duration of phases** cannot be defined precisely. For standardised products like daily-use consumer goods, the socialisation and growth phases could be very

Strength of reaction \ Length of termination process	Short	Long
Strong	**Type 1** The relationship is terminated quickly and completely	**Type 2** The relationship termination process is long but leads to a complete termination. No return intentions.
Weak	**Type 3** The relationship is terminated quickly but not completely (shift of patronage pattern)	**Type 4** The relationship is terminated gradually and not completely or with return possibilities.

Figure 3.7 Types of defection processes
(*Source*: adapted from Roos and Strandvik 1997)

short. With customised services such as capital assets the phases are longer due to their heterogeneity and complexity. The imperilment phase for a standardised output also tends to be shorter, because the lower barriers allow the customer to switch sellers quickly. For example, if a customer is very unhappy with a restaurant meal, he or she will not visit again. At the other end of the scale, one does not switch doctors as swiftly.

The **customer relationship life cycle** is a clarification model that embraces a customer relationship in an idealised and explanatory form. As is apparent from a description of the individual phases the customer relationship life cycle can be considered from both the seller and buyer perspectives. This **duality in examining a customer relationship** is a fundamental principle that a corporation needs to take into account for all its activities on analyses, planning, implementation, and control.

3.2 Principles of relationship marketing

The above-referenced duality perspective of customer relationships is reflected by two essential principles of relationship marketing: **perspective taking as a behavioural principle** and the school of thought on the **success chain as a management principle**. Both concepts reflect important insights for the conceptualisation of relationship marketing.

3.2.1 Perspective taking as a behavioural principle

Perspective taking reflects an individual's ability to adopt the perspective, or the psychological point of view, of another (see Davis 1983). It involves shifting from a self-oriented reaction to others' distress to an other-oriented reaction (e.g. 'Before making a decision I try to look at all sides of a disagreement'). Based on the underlying assumption that, as a cognitive dimension of empathy, perspective taking is a core condition for social interactions (Davis 1983, p. 115) the **perspective taking concept** is very important for substantiating and shaping relationship marketing. In **customer relationships** the customer must take the corporate perspective into account, but more importantly the corporation and its employees have to consider customer perspectives for successful interactions. Perspective taking thereby represents a behavioural principle with guidelines that can be derived especially for the behaviour of corporate members towards customers. The following aspects are examples that highlight the **relevance of perspective taking within relationship marketing**:

- Corporations must recognise customer problems reactively and expectations proactively to ensure long-term relationships with their customers.
- The perspective taking concept provides a means to fully trace the purchase decision process from the customer's viewpoint (e.g. with the blueprinting methodology described in Chapter 8).

- Customer retention measures can be successfully implemented only if their effect on the customer can be predicted or regularly verified.

- Relationship marketing is only successful if companies know and give due consideration in their planning to customer-specific influencing factors such as satisfaction, commitment, trust, and relationship quality.

Perspective taking is designed to perceive a person's background and is characterised as a **multi-dimensional construct** (Long and Andrews 1990; for recent research on a model of perspective taking, see Steins 2000). The following three **dimensions of perspective taking** can be identified under a multi-dimensional assessment:

1 **Visual-spatial** (or perceptual) **perspective taking** is aimed at the perception of spatial and visually ascertainable elements from an extrinsic perspective such as the customer's facial expression displaying dissatisfaction over a transaction.

2 **Conceptual** (also: informational, cognitive, social-cognitive, or role-related) **perspective taking** involves an understanding of the customer's complete situation (e.g. consideration of the customer's assets and family situation for financial advice).

3 In the case of **emotive perspective taking**, recognition of the interaction party's feelings is at the forefront (e.g. customer's time-pressure).

Various **pre-conditions** have to be met in order to be able to implement the perspectives taken. These include the detachment from the interaction problem and oneself, closeness to the interaction party, and the underlying relationship quality between the interacting parties.

So far, the **meaning of perspective taking** has been demonstrated empirically for human relations. For instance, Bromme and Nückles (1998) have done research on perspective taking between medical doctors and nurses. The capability, execution, and perception of perspective changes are the significant factors that govern satisfaction in partnerships (Long and Andrews 1990; Franzoi, Davis and Young 1985). In contrast, perspective changes could have a negative impact if applied repeatedly in an interaction and if the reflection processes are arbitrarily continued and strengthened. The danger lies in the fact that these processes could become predominant within the interaction.

The concept of perspective taking is the logical consequence of a demand for **customer orientation**, which can be implemented only when the corporation and its employees are able to fulfil customer expectations. Seeing the vantage point of the customer through perspective taking is imperative. Conceptually, as clarified in the discussion on the customer relationship life cycle (section 3.1), this results in the necessity to analyse customer relationships from the customer's perspective. The analysis and design of perspective taking permits three main **perceived constructs** to be identified:

1 Extrinsic image

2 Self-image

3 Triadic-image

Extrinsic images represent an assessment of the direct relationship party (e.g. judgment of a customer representative by the customer). During the development of a **self-image**, the relationship parties evaluate their own behaviour by comparing expectations of their own output against the way it is perceived.

 Example 3.1

Figure 3.8 elucidates the relevance of perspective taking by the seller. The findings of an empirical study clearly show the differences in perception between a seller and customer, i.e. between the seller's self-image and its extrinsic image held by the customers. For various service attributes the seller rates its performance markedly better than the customer.

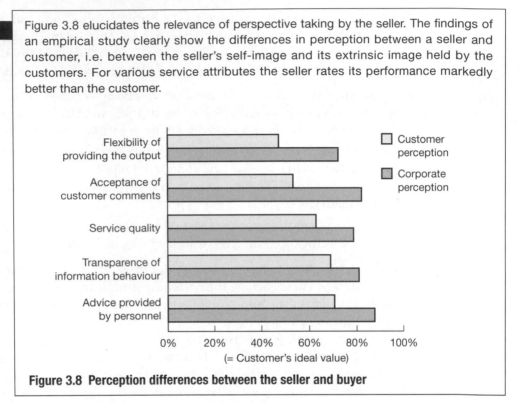

Figure 3.8 Perception differences between the seller and buyer

Triadic-images occur in relationship structures involving more than two parties. As an example, in the insurance sector, a triadic relationship structure comprises a seller, a buyer, and an agent. Here, the service provider judges the agent's quality of service to the customer, while the agent assesses the service provider's quality of service to the customer.

If companies discover problems in perspective taking by their employees or sales agents when in contact with customers, it is necessary to improve the social and psychological competencies of the employees and agents. One of the main instruments for attaining higher levels of customer orientation is to offer classes and seminars on perspective taking. The objectives of **perspective training** are the development, promotion, and application of perspective taking as well as a perspective change for agents and sellers.

Various methods have been developed for the teaching of perspective taking (Goldstein and Michaels 1985; Chandler 1982). The main **training theories** can be divided into two factions based on their content. One set considers imparting fun-

Example 3.2

Figure 3.9 shows empirical findings of a study conducted in the insurance sector on the extrinsic image (quality judgment), self-image, and triadic-image. Here, an arithmetic average between one and two means that the expectations have been fulfilled or are judged as being fulfilled; values above two imply a deficiency in expectation-fulfillment. By analysing the single judgments depicted, one recognises similar structures for quality judgment, the self-image, and the triadic-image among various interactions. For instance, the customer's extrinsic image of the corporation is better than the corporation's (or management's) self-image, whereas the customer's extrinsic image of the agent is worse than the agent's self-image. Also, the seller and agent classify their respective triadic-images as very weak. These results should be viewed as indicators of flawed trust between the seller and agent.

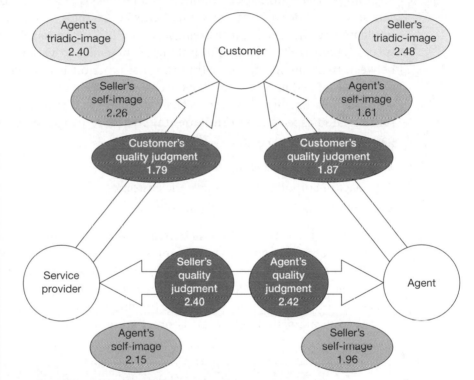

Figure 3.9 Study of extrinsic, self, and triadic-images in the insurance sector
(*Source*: Murmann 1999, p. 202)

damental knowledge on perspective taking combined with behavioural tests and feedback discussions as adequate training for achieving a perspective change. The other rejects the conveying of knowledge on perspective taking, focusing instead exclusively on capability training. On the basis of research and training results of these different approaches, **component training** has been specially developed for this purpose. This comprises of six components ranging from manual skills training, cognitive analyses, and consciousness attainment, through to actual applications in customer contacts (Goldstein and Michaels 1985).

Perspective taking represents a general principle that should be kept in mind by the parties involved. In customer relationships, this applies to both companies and customers. Hence, management must utilise both the customer and corporate viewpoints as the basis for relationship marketing.

3.2.2 Success chain as a management principle

With respect to customer relationships, relevant buyer and seller perspectives can be structured in the form of **success chains** (e.g. service profit chain) that function as the intellectual foundation for planning, directing, and controlling relationship marketing (Anderson and Mittal 2000; Bruhn 1999a; Heskett, Sasser and Schlesinger 1997; Storbacka, Strandvik and Grönroos 1994). The box 'Insights 3.3: The service profit chain at Sears' highlights an example of a company which has implemented the service profit chain successfully. The **underlying idea** behind the success chain is the meaningful linking of inter-related variables. The influences between them are illustrated within the chain, permitting structured analysis and derivation of actions. Based on buyer-seller based deliberations in the context of a customer relationship, this success chain can help to intellectually link buyer- and seller-related aspects. The **fundamental structure of the success chain** encompasses three elements (Figure 3.10):

1 Corporate activities (corporate input)

2 Impact of corporate activities on the customer

3 Economic performance (corporate output)

It is important to consider the **link between corporate and customer related variables** in the success chain. On the one hand, the effects of corporate measures (input) on a customer should be investigated, including the extent of each effect. On the other hand, the economic performance (output) that is related to these effects should be analysed. The extent to which economic performance (output) comes from a given effect on a customer should also be established. The links

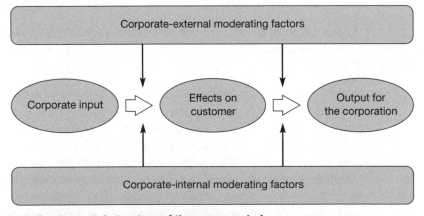

Figure 3.10 Fundamental structure of the success chain

within a success chain are, however, not definitive. They can vary depending on the sector, customer, etc. In other words, a dependent variable is not 100 per cent contingent on the independent variable. For instance, while assertions of a positive association between customer satisfaction and financial performance are commonplace, the results are not conclusive, and there is still no shortage of skepticism about both the conceptualisation of customer satisfaction and the satisfaction-loyalty relationship (i.e. Jones and Suh 2000; Babin and Griffin 1998; Woodruff and Gardial 1996; Yi 1991). Thus, customer satisfaction does not always lead to customer retention, nor does retention automatically increase profitability. This can be seen as a consequence of **moderating factors**, described later, influencing both chain elements and their inter-relationships.

Insights 3.3

The service profit chain at Sears

Sears, Roebuck & Company, which is the leading US department store chain, provides a good example of the success of the service profit chain model. The company has undergone a radical transformation in recent years to reverse its business decline. Much of the company's success is due to its measurement systems which track employee attitudes as well as their effect on customer satisfaction and profitability. Critically, management alignment has been organised around these metrics and there is a clear understanding throughout the company of how the service profit chain model works.

In 1992, the company reported massive losses of $3.9 billion on sales of $52.3 billion. Arthur Martinez was appointed to lead the merchandise group with the goal of streamlining the business. First, he set up task forces to identify world-class status in key areas of the business. Gradually, it became apparent that what was needed was a model to show direct causation from employee attitudes, through customer satisfaction, to company profits. The company needed to know how management action, such as investment in sales training, would directly translate into improved customer satisfaction and retention, and finally, higher revenues.

Links between employee measures, customer measures, revenues and profitability were identified using sophisticated modelling techniques. The results showed that the attitudes of employees towards their jobs and the company were critical to employee loyalty and customer service quality, while customer satisfaction directly affected customer retention and the likelihood of customer referrals. After further refinement, the model was used as a predictor of revenue growth: a 5-unit increase in employee attitude would drive a 1.3-unit increase in customer satisfaction and a 0.5 unit increase in revenue growth.

It can be stated that the results at Sears Roebuck have been impressive. By 1993, the company reported a net income of $752 million: a dramatic improvement for a business in such a mature industry. While employee satisfaction at Sears had risen by four per cent, customer satisfaction had likewise increased by almost four per cent. These improvements created more than $200 million additional revenue, which was achieved through the value creation activities of both managers and employees. Even though not every company will be able to be as sophisticated as Sears in implementing the service profit chain model, customer retention should always be a key business priority.

(*Source*: adapted from Payne, A. (2000b): 'Customer Retention' in Cranfield School of Management (ed.), *Marketing Management. A Relationship Marketing Perspective*, New York, p. 121 (Case Study 1: The connection between customer retention and profitability). This case study is based on: A.J. Rucci, S.P. Kim and R.T. Quinn (1998), *The Employee-Company-Profit Chain*, Harvard Business Review, January-February, pp. 83–97.)

An examination of relationship marketing's success chain 'customer satisfaction – customer retention – economic performance' (Figure 3.11) shows that the heterogeneity among customer expectations, for example, is a moderating factor for the link between relationship marketing and customer satisfaction. The more heterogeneous the expectations the greater the difficulty in raising the general level of customer satisfaction through certain marketing measures. A customer's variety-seeking behaviour influences the connection between her or his satisfaction and retention. The more a customer seeks a change in a particular output category the less likely that her or his retention can be impacted by satisfaction. A customer's output has a moderating effect regarding the link between retention and economic

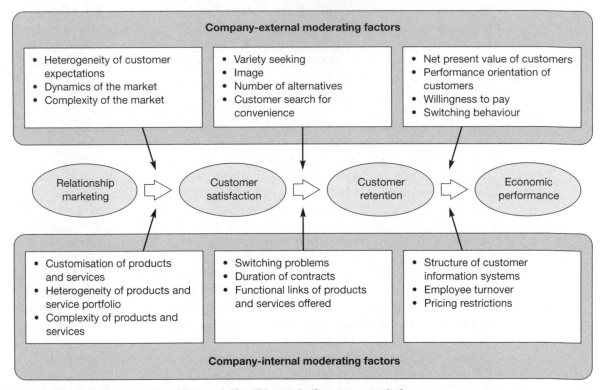

Figure 3.11 Detailed structure of the relationship marketing success chain

success. If a customer already uses all the outputs desired from a corporation even an increase in customer retention will not, for instance, generate any cross selling potential, thereby resulting in no additional revenues.

Although a corporation's input and output factors are each set in principle at the same level, the links between the **effects on customers** are often more complex. Figure 3.12 shows a model that adapts diverse theories and empirical knowledge from marketing research to structure various customer-related pre-economic variables. According to this, customer expectations influence both the output quality and customer satisfaction. The product and service quality in turn impacts perceived value, customer satisfaction, and relationship quality, etc.

Precise management of customer relationships is enabled by an analysis of the effects within a success chain by considering relevant moderating factors. In this case, as for the perspective taking principle, both the buyer and seller standpoints must be taken into account.

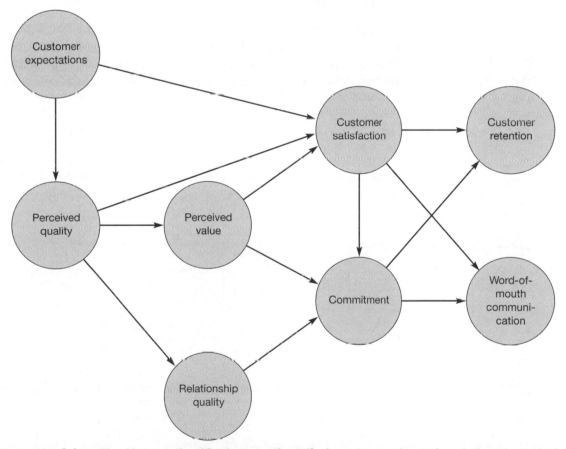

Figure 3.12 Schematic of interrelationships between theoretical constructs relevant for relationship marketing

3.3 Customer relationship perspectives

3.3.1 Buyer's viewpoint of customer relationships

In the fundamental structure of a success chain, the chain link 'effects on the buyer' needs to be examined more closely for a detailed evaluation of a **buyer's viewpoint of customer relationships**. This link can be precisely sub-divided into the elements 'relationship judgment by the customer', 'psychological consequences' of this judgment, and 'behavioural consequences' of the psychological consequences (Figure 3.13). Within the context of these chain links, a few behavioural science constructs have been peer-reviewed among relationship marketing researchers. The following is a presentation of these constructs along with an investigation of their relevance to relationship marketing (for controlling relationship marketing, the measurement of the constructs is treated in detail in Chapter 8).

Customer assessment of relationships

A relationship judged positively by the customer represents, on the one side, the desired outcome of relationship marketing measures and, on the other, the basis for successful effects of relationship marketing. In this respect, the **output quality**, **perceived value**, and **relationship quality** have corresponding impacts on corporate success.

(1) Output quality

The construct **output quality** is defined as the capability of the corporation to meet customer expectations with its products and services. This definition includes two main **views of quality** (Garvin 1988; 1984):

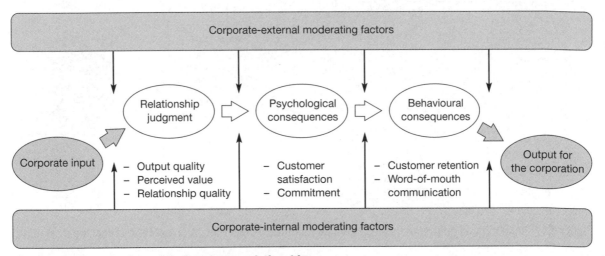

Figure 3.13 Buyer's viewpoint of customer relationships

- **Product-based quality perception**: Quality is the sum or the level of existing product or service qualities. The aim is to measure the quality in terms of objective criteria.

- **Customer-based quality perception**: Quality is defined by the customer's discernment of product features or outputs. The quality is accordingly measured in terms of subjective criteria.

The coexistence of different abstract opinions on quality calls for specification of the relevant **output quality dimensions**. In this respect, the perception of various quality characteristics by the corporation's internal and external target groups is taken as the quality dimension. Here, the focus of discourse in the marketing literature has been on a differentiation into the three dimensions – potential, process, and outcome (Donabedian 1980). The **potential dimension** includes the seller's technical, organisational, and personal output requirements. The **process dimension** is based on all processes during the provision of products and services, and the **outcome dimension** judges the final result.

A differentiation of the quality dimension is also possible within the scope and type of output provided (Grönroos 1990). In this sense, the **technical dimension** covers the scope of the output programme, and questions the 'what' of a product or service. In contrast, the **functional dimension** questions the 'how', i.e. the form in which the product or service is offered.

A further sub-division of the quality dimension relates to the customer's expectation attitude on the output programme (Berry 1986): The **customary components** include all qualities that are normally a part of a product and service. Any negative variances could result in 'penalty points' being assigned by the customer. In contrast, **occasional components** include supplementary services provided by the seller but unanticipated by the customer and honoured with 'bonus points' by the latter.

By sub-dividing an output into search, experience, and credence components (Chapter 2), the following three quality dimensions answer the question of how well the customer knows the product or service when making a judgment (Zeithaml 1981, p. 186). At the **search quality** stage the customer has no experience with the seller and is on the lookout for prior indicators to assess the output. Opposed to this, for **experience qualities**, the customer is in a position to pass judgments because of experiences that occurred during or at the end of the service delivery process. **Credence quality** components encompass all output attributes that either elude a precise evaluation or permit estimation only at a later point in time.

Finally, **five quality dimensions** will be presented. These include all the subdivisions enumerated, and are the outcome of not only conceptual deliberations but also empirical tests (Zeithaml, Parasuraman and Berry 1992; Parasuraman, Zeithaml and Berry 1988; 1985):

- 'Tangibles' comprise the seller's outward appearance, in particular the room furnishings and appearance of personnel.

- 'Reliability' designates the seller's capability to supply the promised outputs at the stated level.

- ■ 'Responsiveness' asks the question as to whether the corporation is in a position to respond to and satisfy the customer's wishes. A willingness to react and the reaction speed play a role here.

- ■ 'Assurance' relates to the seller's capability to deliver the output, specifically in terms of the knowledge, politeness, and trustworthiness of the employees.

- ■ 'Empathy' characterises both the seller's willingness and capability to respond to individual customer desires.

The number of purchasing relevant quality dimensions varies markedly with the **output type**. For customised services, because of the greater difficulty in judging them, the number of attributes taken into account by the customer for output evaluation will be higher than for standardised services (e.g. experience, speed, and reputation of a consulting firm, versus price as the main decision criteria for raw material procurement). Figure 3.14 depicts output-related differences based on their search, experience, and credence qualities.

In assessing the quality the customer orients her or his expectations to the requested output. This means that **customer expectations** can also be analysed and directed systematically. An individual's expectations represent a psychological state that relates to future behavioural consequences for that person (van Raaij 1991, pp. 401–2).

The marketing literature has numerous interpretations on the concept of **customer expectations** (Figure 3.15), which can be classified into predictive and normative expectations (Ngobo 1997, pp. 63–4; Liljander 1994). **Predictive expectations** have an anticipatory nature in that the customer states in advance the level of output foreseen as being taken or considered likely to be utilised (Tse and Wilton 1988, p. 205; Cadotte, Woodruff and Jenkins 1987, p. 305; Oliver 1980, p. 460). In

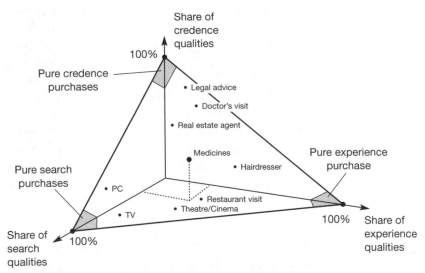

Figure 3.14 Classification of different types of products and services based on their share of search, experience, and credence qualities

(*Source*: Weiber and Adler 1995, p. 61)

contrast, **normative expectations** represent a demand for provider services and characterise the output level required by the customer from the firm (Teas 1993, p. 19; Parasuraman, Zeithaml and Berry 1988).

These two types of expectations differ with respect to their classification on a scale of output levels and the reference item (Figure 3.15). The criterion for the type of **classification on an output scale** represents a specific, objectively comprehensible output level in terms of the expectation type. This classification is given for normative expectations. Hence, an ideal expectation is always at a high output level whereas the minimally acceptable level is relatively low. Predictive expecta-

Types of Expectations			Affiliation to basic types	Classification on a scale	Reference object	
Authors[1]	Definition	Description			broad, not company-focused	narrow, company-focused
Miller 1977; Tse and Wilton 1988	Perception of an ideal level which cannot be exceeded	Ideal level	Normative	Given (High)	x	
Parasuraman, Zeithaml and Berry 1988; Boulding et al. 1993	Level which is desired by customers or which should be provided through the organisation	Desired level	Normative	Given		x
Cadotte, Woodruff and Jenkins 1987	Customer perception of the product and service quality of the best provider in a single category	Best-brand-level	Normative	Given	x	
Cadotte, Woodruff and Jenkins 1987	Perception of a typical and average quality of all product or services known to the customer in one category	Product-type-level	Normative	Given	x	
Zeithaml, Berry and Parasuraman 1993	Minimum level which is accepted by customers	Moderate level	Normative	Given	x	
Miller 1977	Level which is just tolerated by customers	Minimum tolerable level	Normative	Given (Low)	x	
Miller 1977; Boulding et al. 1993	Perception of the level that the customer feels he or she deserves to get	Deserved level	Predictive	Not given		x
Olson and Dover 1979; Oliver 1980; Cadotte, Woodruff and Jenkins 1987; Boulding et al. 1993	Perception of the product and service quality of a specific provider	Predicted level	Predictive	Not given		x
Miller 1977	Likelihood of the occurrence of an event	Most likely level	Predictive	Not given		x

[1] These authors provide an introduction into each type of expectation in the literature. An overview of more types can be found in Liljander and Strandvik 1993; Oliver 1996; Ngobo 1997.

Figure 3.15 Overview of expectation types

tions, on the contrary, are not bound to any specific level (Oliver 1996, pp. 71–2). In relation to a firm's offer, customers can foresee or probably envision either a relatively high or low output level. This state of affairs becomes clear on examination of different types of **reference items** anticipated. Normative expectations do not relate to any specific seller, whereas predictive expectations always do.

(2) Perceived value

In **relationship marketing** the perceived value construct for evaluating the customer perspective of a relationship with the seller influences customer satisfaction above all, and is a lever for instituting switching barriers for the latter (Ravald and Grönroos 1996). From the customer perspective, the perceived value has four different **aspects** (Zeithaml 1988, p. 13):

1 Customers can disregard the benefits and interpret **price** as the perceived value.

2 By overemphasising the benefit components the perceived value can also be defined as a **benefit** derived from the output.

3 Alternatively, the perceived value is often viewed as the **benefit at a given price**.

4 Additionally, the perceived value could be inferred as a **cost-benefit relationship**.

The third and fourth interpretations above represent the most frequently encountered **definition of perceived value**. The perceived value is generally defined as the relationship between the customer's **perceived benefit** and effort (Monroe 1991; Zeithaml 1988). Often, the customer's perceived benefit is seen primarily as the service quality perceived by her or him. Nevertheless, the relationship-related benefit elements of relationship marketing should definitely be taken into account (Ravald and Grönroos 1996).

The **perceived effort** comprises all costs involved in the purchase of a product or service. In addition to search, acquisition, transport, installation, maintenance, error risk, and defective quality-related costs, the primary cost is for the price of the output used (Ravald and Grönroos 1996).

In contrast to output quality, the perceived value within customer perception lies on a higher abstract plane. The output quality and value differ in two ways. First, the value is more of an individual and personal construct than the perceived quality. Second, in an extended sense, perceived value includes benefit components and also price elements.

Ensuring an analysis of perceived value within the framework of relationship marketing avoids analysis and control based purely on the outputs. Even if it represents the main aspect of customer benefit, due **consideration of relationship aspects** is guaranteed by an extended definition of customer benefit within a perceived value construct. Particularly from a **dynamic standpoint** the perceived value variable can take on an important function, in that it enables the customer to model and weigh the benefit and price components against each other. It happens, for instance, that customers first choose the seller with the lower price, although customer benefit is subsequently of primary relevance for customer retention. Conclusions of this type can be reached through a differentiated analysis of the perceived value.

(3) Relationship quality

With the aim of meaningfully linking transactions attributable to relationships, the **relationship qualit**y can be fundamentally characterised as the capability of one of the relationship parties to reduce the complexity of transactions, lower the uncertainty, and raise the interaction efficiency between the relationship parties (Smith 1998; Hennig-Thurau and Klee 1997, p. 751; Bitner 1995, p. 251; Crosby, Evans and Cowles 1990, p. 70). A high relationship quality thereby simplifies transactions between the parties. The relationship quality has the following five **attributes** (Georgi 2000; Figure 3.16):

1 Perspective
2 Reference object
3 Temporal orientation
4 Transaction reference
5 Type of construct

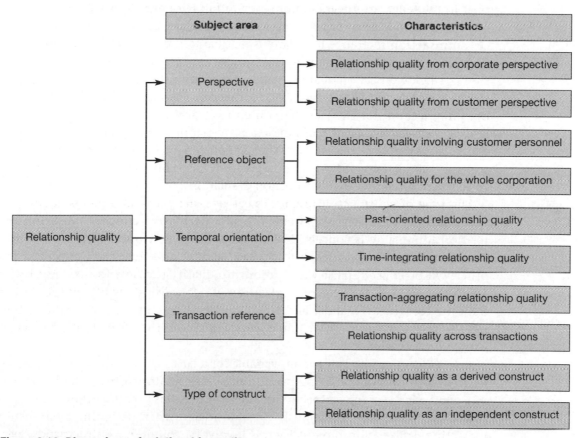

Figure 3.16 Dimensions of relationship quality
(*Source*: Georgi 2000, p. 42)

From a relationship judgment perspective the corporate and customer standpoints can be differentiated. From a corporate viewpoint, the corporate-customer relationships can be assessed according to both economic criteria such as customer lifetime value and pre-economic ones such as customer commitment. The customer assesses the sellers' capability to reduce complexity and uncertainty in the relationship in the form of trust in the seller. From a customer viewpoint the relationship quality is defined by an evaluation of the relationships from her or his perspective.

A customer can perceive the customer representative (Bejou, Wray and Ingram 1996; Crosby, Evans and Cowles 1990) and the whole corporation (Hennig-Thurau and Klee 1997; Liljander and Strandvik 1995) as differentiated relationship quality reference objects. In assessing the relationship quality over time, one can distinguish between its past and time-integrated orientation. The **past orientation** relates to the relationship quality of all prior contacts with the seller as judged by the customer (Liljander and Strandvik 1993; Crosby, Evans and Cowles 1990, p. 70). Additionally, a future orientation is found in the **time-integrating orientation** approach. The future orientation deals with estimating the upcoming course of the relationship from the customers' viewpoint expressed as a result, for example, of trust in the seller. An integration of past and future orientations is necessary, since relationships should be construed as lasting beyond the current point in time.

A **transaction reference** for relationship quality is closely related to time orientation. A **transaction-integrating interpretation** sees relationship quality as the sum of single transaction qualities within the relationship as perceived by the customer (Liljander and Strandvik 1995; Bitner and Hubbert 1994). This, however, does not account for the fact that a high relationship quality guarantees a link among transactions. Hence, a transaction-overlapping interpretation of relationship quality should be undertaken. The relationship quality will be perceived in the realm of transactions, although its judgment is based on attributes such as trust in the corporation rather than transaction evaluations.

The **type of construct** distinguishes between derivative and independent conceptualisation of relationship quality. Under **derivative conceptualisation** the relationship quality is conceived as a 'higher-order' construct, within which different constructs (e.g. trust, customer satisfaction) and their correlation to each other will be conceptualised as relationship quality (Crosby, Evans and Cowles 1990). An **independent conceptualisation** of relationship quality interprets it as the total construct (Liljander and Strandvik 1995). In this way, marketing activities can be focused on relationship quality, which can then function as the target and control variable.

Relationship quality is the main variable for a customer to assess a relationship, whereas relationship marketing permits **customer relationships to be managed**. As a consequence of the perspective taking principle, it is very important that a customer's perception of a relationship be considered when designing relationship marketing. For relationship quality this involves a complex construct whose perception takes place in different dimensions. In general, two **relationship quality dimensions** can be identified (Georgi 2000):

1 Customer's trust in the corporation

2 Familiarity between customer and corporation

The **trust** construct, whose function is the reduction in complexity of human relationships (Loose and Sydow 1994; Rotter 1967; Deutsch 1958; for an overview of definitions, see O'Malley and Tynan 1997, p. 494), represents a component of relationship quality focused on the future. Trust is defined as the customer's willingness to forego any additional investigation and just rely on the corporation's behaviour in the future (adapted from Morgan and Hunt 1994, p. 23).

As a **trust-building requirement** one must be vulnerable, i.e. consequences of decisions must be uncertain and of importance to the trusting person (Doney and Cannon 1997; Moorman, Zaltman and Deshpandé 1992). Trust occurs particularly when 'modified re-buys' are involved instead of 'straight buys', as in the case of customised purchases of modified re-buys of complex machines versus straight buys of refreshments. Modified buys raise the degree of uncertainty in the purchasing decision (Johnston and Lewin 1996).

Various processes for the emergence of trust can be identified in the context of the **trust-building process** (Doney and Canon 1997, p. 37):

- In a **calculated process**, one relationship party assumes trustworthy behaviour of the other if the benefit of non-trustworthy behaviour is lower than the costs incurred when caught (Rao and Bergen 1992; Lindskold 1978).

- For **predictive processes**, trust is dependent on one's capability to anticipate the other party's behaviour.

- The **capability process** relates to an estimation of the relationship party's ability to accomplish its job.

- According to the **intent process**, trust is based on the goals and intentions of the other party (Lindskold 1978).

- With regard to the **transferring process**, trust building is subject to an estimation of the relationship party by an outsider.

The customer's **familiarity** with the corporation is another dimension of relationship quality. Familiarity is closely related to trust and is based on the past. It encompasses the degree of familiarity with an object (e.g. situation) or subject. In the context of a corporate-customer relationship, familiarity characterises the **degree of conversance** with the respective relationship party in terms of its attitudes and modes of behaviour.

On the basis of **reciprocal dependence** of the parties in a relationship (Håkansson and Snehota 1993, p. 2), customer familiarity comprises not only her or his familiarity with a corporation but also the familiarity of the corporation with the customer as perceived by the customer. On the one hand, it is important for the customer to be aware of the corporate processes as long as he or she is involved in the provision of products or services. On the other hand, the customer is possibly very conscious as to whether the company is familiar with her or him. Knowing the party's name is a sample indicator of a corporation's familiarity with a customer, but awareness of specific requirements such as a non-smoking room in a hotel is more meaningful.

A central task of relationship marketing lies in the **building-up of familiarity**. In cases where familiarity appears partly and to a certain degree without action on the part of the company, the latter can support the emergence of familiarity through appropriate familiarity-building measures. The higher the relationship quality perceived by the customer the less critical he or she is of individual interactions and the sooner can positive psychological consequences be reached with the customer.

Psychological consequences

While the evaluation of a relationship is chiefly cognitive in nature, it is necessary for a successful customer relationship to ensure that the psychological consequences of the assessment are positive. The customer wittingly or unwittingly signals her or his judgment of the relationship in terms of the service quality, perceived value, or relationship quality. Such signalling articulates the customer's feelings about the relationship. The customer's satisfaction and commitment are the relevant **psychological consequences** of an assessment process.

Customer satisfaction involves a construct whose conceptualisation is closely associated with output quality. Customer satisfaction is defined as the balancing of customer demands (customer desires/expectations) against the perception of services delivered by the company (Kotler 2000, pp. 36–40; Oliver 1996, pp. 11–12). In this way, customer satisfaction also relates to customer expectations. Within product quality, customer expectations play a role when judging individual output attributes. Customer satisfaction, on the other hand, relates to the degree of fulfilment of the customer's expectations. Additionally, since customer satisfaction is notably influenced by judgment parameters, particularly the product and service quality, it represents a central determinant of behavioural consequences (primarily customer retention) within the relationship marketing success chain. It thus represents a construct often emphasised in connection with customer relationships. Furthermore, customer satisfaction is both a goal and a marketing tool.

Example 3.3	According to Kotler (2000, p. 37), companies achieving high customer satisfaction ratings make sure that their target market knows it. For instance, Dell Computer's growth in the PC industry is attributed in particular to achieving and advertising its number one rank in customer satisfaction. Another example is the Honda Accord which has received from J.D. Powers the number one rating in customer satisfaction for several years. The company's advertising of this fact has helped to sell even more Accords (Kotler 2000, p. 37).

Consequently, an enormous effort has been made in recent years to **model customer satisfaction**. In this regard, the **confirmation/disconfirmation paradigm** has often been used to explain the emergence of customer satisfaction (Oliver 1996, p. 98). According to this paradigm, customer satisfaction occurs precisely when customer expectations are met by the product and service delivered. In the event of over-fulfilment of expectations some theories speak not of satisfaction but instead of enthusiasm or delight (Oliver 1996). The confirmation/disconfirmation paradigm has the advantage that the measurement of customer satisfaction is both easy to follow and practical. Its disadvantage, however, is that it is a statistical approach that simplifies the construct by distinguishing between just satisfaction and dissatisfaction of a customer.

This aspect is taken into account by the qualitative satisfaction model (Stauss and Neuhaus 1995) that identifies different qualities of customer satisfaction and dissatisfaction. Five different types of **customer satisfaction/dissatisfaction** are accordingly identified:

1 A high level of contentment characterises the 'satisfied but insistent'. However, constantly growing customer demands call for fulfilment over and over again.

2 As opposed to the first type, the 'satisfied and stable' exhibit passive behaviour.

3 The 'satisfied but resigned' show certain indifference to the relationship with the seller.

4 Similar to the 'satisfied and stable', the 'dissatisfied but stable' display a weak activity level, but are definitely unhappy with the output.

5 The 'dissatisfied and insistent', in contrast, articulate their displeasure with the corporation and would not patronise the same seller again.

Unlike the confirmation/disconfirmation paradigm, the qualitative satisfaction model permits a unique assessment of the **effects of customer satisfaction/dissatisfaction** that are of relevance for analysing cause-effect correlations in customer satisfaction. In addition to satisfaction, the customer commitment to the seller has a major impact on the person's attitude towards the relationship. Commitment refers to the strong belief by a relationship party in the importance of a relationship to the extent that every possible measure is taken to maintain it (Morgan and Hunt 1994, p. 23). Customer commitment relates invariably to the seller or a relationship with the seller but not to any of the seller's specific outputs. Commitment thereby represents a core relationship construct. The better the relationship in the eyes of the customer the more pronounced the commitment to the company. In turn, the higher the commitment, the sooner a customer becomes tied to the corporation. A high commitment level can thus represent a significant emotional switching barrier. In general, **commitment dimensions** can be classified into the following three types (Kumar, Scheer and Steenkamp 1995; Morgan and Hunt 1994; Allen and Meyer 1990):

- **Emotive commitment** denotes the degree of the customer's emotional ties to the seller

- **Continuation commitment** denotes the customer's willingness to continue the relationship with the seller

- **Obligation commitment** denotes a type of forced commitment

Continuation commitment, in particular, is a **control variable for relationship marketing** that provides the means for relationship maintenance by the customer. Thus, commitment is very closely associated with behavioural consequences for customers.

Behavioural consequences

Customer behaviour in the form of customer retention and word-of-mouth communication is the outcome of the assessment and psychological consequences. Customer retention encompasses all psychological awareness processes and observed modes of her or his behaviour, in which certain bonding reasons manifest the intentional or actual maintenance and intensification of the relationship with the firm (Keaveney 1995; Auld 1993). According to this definition, the following four **customer retention aspects** become apparent (Figure 3.17):

1 Degree of behavioural reference

2 Degree of behavioural explicitness

3 Causes of customer retention

4 Degree of relationship modification

The degree of behavioural reference comprises three customer retention dimensions (Oliver 1996, p. 392):

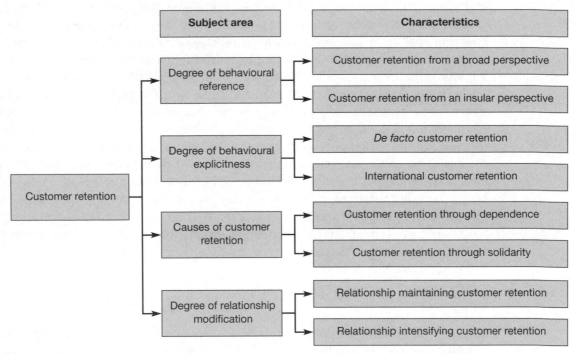

Figure 3.17 Customer retention facets
(*Source*: Georgi 2000, p. 48)

a **Cognitive dimension** (e.g. specialised know-how of a financial advisor)

b **Emotive dimension** (e.g. sympathy for the customer representative)

c **Conative dimension** (e.g. repetition intention)

The conative aspect alone relates to customer retention in an **insular perspective**. Combined with the cognitive and emotive aspects one can speak of customer retention on a **broader perspective**. Based on the **degree of behavioural explicitness**, one can distinguish between intentional and real customer retention. **Intentional customer retention** relates to the customer's intentions, for example, to repeat a selection. Conversely, **real customer retention** is manifested in specific customer behaviour such as the actual repetition of a selection.

The **causes of customer retention** can be further classified into **dependence** and **solidarity**, both of which result in risk minimisation from the customer's standpoint. Dependence characterises a bonding state over a specific time-period. Even if the customer can manoeuvre more or less freely in this state, within this period he or she has limited freedom to make decisions on using the seller's products or services because of conditions such as a contract. The **forms of dependence** can be of three types: contractual, technical/functional, and economic.

The customer's dependence directly affects her or his selection repeating behaviour. Solidarity can emerge either within the framework of dependence or can be separate from it, depending on the bonding state originating from psychological causes and parameters such as trust. Solidarity evokes voluntary customer retention that can be traced to the customer's perceived advantages of the existing relationship with the firm in comparison to a situation without a relationship and/or relationships with other companies.

Solidarity has a **stronger influence on customer retention** than dependence. Without solidarity, dependence can affect customer retention only as long as contractual, technical/functional, or economic reasons exist. In contrast, solidarity leads to customer retention without the existence of dependence.

The **degree of relationship modification** specifies whether customer relationship is concerned with maintenance or intensification of the relationship. In a **relationship maintaining customer retention** situation, repeated selection of previously used outputs holds the same significance for the customer. In a **relationship intensifying customer retention** situation, however, the customer extends the relationship (Danaher and Rust 1996; Dick and Basu 1994). These aspects are interdependent, in that maintaining customer retention is a necessary requirement for its intensification.

The idealised customer relationship life cycle (in Chapter 3, section 3.1) clarifies the significance of customer relationship in relationship marketing. The goal of relationship marketing thereafter is to not only build up the relationships, but above all to intensify them over time. Through relationship maintaining activities, a type of 'relationship base' is created that reflects the maintenance of the customer relationship. As such, it is possible to intensify customer retention as seen in the form of cross selling activities. Only in this way can an ascending relationship life cycle curve be attained.

In this respect, it must be kept in mind that only **retention of profitable customers** gives hope for success. Customer retention measures can become inefficient if applied blindly to the whole body of customers. Consequently, it is the task of relationship marketing to identify each relationship that should be upheld through such measures.

In addition customer retention that involves purchasing behaviour, the customer's **communication behaviour** in the form of word-of-mouth communication is relevant. **Word-of-mouth communication** is a phenomenon that can have just the same behavioural effect on the recipient as active direct marketing. It is a promotion process promulgated not by the company itself, but rather by its customers (Richins 1983, p. 69). The communication can be classified into positive (recommendations) and negative (purchase warning) forms. In particular, consistent relationship marketing promotes **recommendations** by satisfied customers.

While the corporation pursues marketing activities like corporate communication that seek to control specific recipient target variables, word-of-mouth communication does not necessarily have any underlying objective (Zeithaml, Berry and Parasuraman 1993, p. 9). A firm that is in touch with current and potential customers anticipates a rise in the recipients' cognitive, emotive, and conative target variables, whereby positive impacts on economic variables such as sales and profits are finally supposed to be achieved. When a customer uses word-of-mouth communication with someone else regarding a company or its products, in most cases he or she has unknowingly influenced the other party in its behaviour with the company.

Accepting the **significance of word-of-mouth communication in relationship marketing** is an argument for bestowing significance on customer retention. Customers are considered particularly loyal when they not only maintain and intensify their relationship with the firm, but also recommend the firm to friends, acquaintances, and colleagues. Assuming appropriate customer profitability, a primary target of relationship marketing is to develop the relationships so as to attain such customer loyalty.

3.3.2 Sellers' viewpoint of customer relationships

On the basis of findings related to a customer relationship from the buyers' perspective, there are also consequences from its consideration from a sellers' perspective. Customer relationships are considered from the sellers' perspective through implementation of relationship marketing – the subject of this book. The following chapters **focus on the corporate perspective**, which encompasses the customer-end of the relationship marketing success chain (Figure 3.18).

Effects on the customer that lead mainly to customer retention behaviour, impact the company's economic performance. This represents the last link – **output of the relationship marketing success chain**. Here, one can differentiate between output at the corporate level (e.g. profit) and that at the customer level (e.g. customer profit contribution) – the latter because of the particular relevance to relationship marketing of individual customers. The box 'Insights 3.4: How

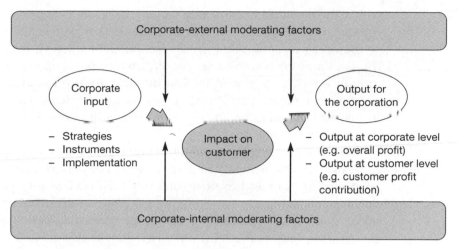

Figure 3.18 The providers' viewpoint of customer relationships

Measurement Begins' illustrates in a simple manner which parameters should be calculated (refer to Chapter 4 for a discussion on the relationship marketing target parameters and to Chapter 8 for its control variables).

Insights 3.4

How Measurement Begins

- **Customer reactivation**: Number of inactive customers who have been enticed to purchase again

- **Customer repurchase rate**: Percentage of existing customers who have made a repeat purchase within a specific period of time

- **New customer acquisition rate**: Rate at which new customers are being acquired: first time buyers to repeat buyers

- **Channel penetration**: Tracks the number and types of channels used: indicator of loyalty

- **Customer profitability**: Value of the total customer relationship over time across all product lines and channels, after the cost of servicing the customer

- **Customer lifetime value**: Uses current per-customer profitability to forecast the customer's value over the predicted life of the relationship

- **Customer satisfaction**: Percentage of existing satisfied customers derived from surveys

Relationship marketing's task is to put the success chain into motion. This occurs through the appropriate **relationship marketing success chain input** activities, which cover related strategies (Chapter 5), instruments (Chapter 6), and its implementation (Chapter 7). These activities are supposed to drive the effects on customers within the relationship marketing success chain. For example, a customisation strategy can strive to mould corporate activities as best as possible to customer needs to attain a high level of customer satisfaction. Subsequently, relevant product policy measures must be executed (e.g. customisable output elements) accompanied by promotion activities (e.g. information on customisation possibilities and enabling customers to impart specific wishes). For strategy implementation in the firm, it will be necessary to train the employees dealing with customers in line with their customisation requirements.

In this way, the corporate input sets into practice the effects on relationship judgment by the customer and the psychological and behavioural consequences. These effects in turn can lead to increasing profitability. This interpretation of the relationship marketing success chain, however, has an **idealised character** in that the profit chain is not absolutely valid (as mentioned earlier). This can be traced to **moderating factors** that bear on correlations between various links in the chain (section 3.2.2). As a result of these factors, correlations within the success chain need not be to 100 per cent, for instance, between relationship marketing and customer satisfaction, customer satisfaction and retention, or between customer retention and economic success. The role of relationship marketing is thus to take these moderating factors into account in the realm of **relationship activities** as follows:

■ For **customer segmentation** (Chapter 4), it is necessary to identify those customer relationships for which the respective correlations are valid. Only for these can the success chain be continuous, thereby enabling relationship marketing to be set up profitably.

■ Equally, it is only for these relationships that appropriate marketing **strategies** (Chapter 5) can be developed and **relationship actions** (Chapter 6) confirmed.

■ In the **control phase** (Chapter 8), it is also necessary to monitor if the measures taken for the customer relationships referred to actually generate economic benefits along the success chain. If not, within the scope of the segmentation, a new relationship marketing direction must be planned.

An outcome of these deliberations is that it is worthwhile to design relationship marketing with the help of a planning process.

3.4 Relationship marketing as a planning process

A specific market focused decision-making system has proven itself for solving various tasks under the umbrella of market-driven corporate management. Hence, it makes sense to use this approach as a basis also for relationship marketing. In this context, the literature offers the **decision theory**, which helps marketing personnel to develop the capability to structure and analyse decision-related problems. In presenting the decision-making structure marketing variables such as the situation, targets, and instruments are differentiated. These groups of variables may not be considered in isolation. Rather, in developing marketing concepts, it is more important to take the correlations and relationship structures between the groups of variables into consideration and to integrate them into a management process.

Relationship marketing thus calls for systematic decision-making behaviour that can be achieved through a **management process** (e.g. Ryals 2000a, pp. 235–244). Figure 3.19 depicts an idealised relationship marketing process with classic phases for analysis, planning, execution, and control. This management process highlights how marketing as a corporate function can justify its role as the initiator of systematic corporate management. Continuous marketing planning, the core of this management system, includes the analysis and planning phases of the process. It thereby generates a **marketing plan** that helps the marketing managers in implementing the management process stepwise. Specifically, relationship marketing is made up of the following **phases**:

- Analysis
- Strategic direction
- Operational focus
- Implementation
- Control and monitoring

The **analysis phase** (Chapter 4) involves an investigation of all aspects relevant for controlling customer relationships. In addition to a SWOT-analysis, emphasis is laid on customer analysis aimed at relationship marketing effects within the success chain. From the findings, relationship marketing goals are derived at both the corporation and customer levels. To guarantee the setting-up of customer-specific activities, systematic customer segmentation is necessary. It is particularly important to give due consideration to the customer relationship life cycle comprising the acquisition, retention, and recovery of customers.

The **strategic direction phase** (Chapter 5) covers the determination of relationship marketing's strategic focus. In this phase, decisions that could fundamentally impact the strategy for customer acquisition, retention, or recovery related to the customer relationship life cycle have to be taken. For a given business area, besides its segmentation and market area strategy determination, it is critical to define the company's competitive advantage. Relationship orientation plays a central role in the realm of relationship marketing. Above all, customer-directed strategies need to be developed while keeping the market participants in mind. Also, supplementary to a decision on the degree of differentiation between market and relationship processing, it is relevant to specify the focus on customer acquisition, retention, and recovery.

The **operational focus phase** (Chapter 6) encompasses the strategic aim of relationship marketing, wherein the marketing instruments for customer acquisition, retention, and recovery phases are determined. For each phase, the respective instruments that result in the most appropriate fulfilment of the tasks within the phase are instituted for policies related to the 4Ps. Furthermore, for the management of quality and complaints and for internal marketing, supportive activity across all phases is used.

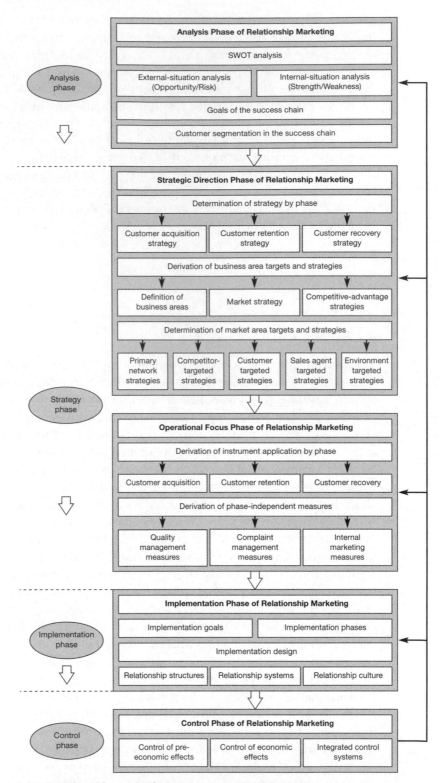

Figure 3.19 Relationship marketing as a management process

Transformation and implementation of established measures for all corporate members follows in the **implementation phase** (Chapter 7). The spotlight here is on a modification of corporate structures, systems, and culture. The **control phase** (Chapter 8) involves comprehensive controlling of relationship marketing activities. Initially, an evaluation is conducted of non-economic target variables such as customer satisfaction. This is followed by measurement of economic target variables such as the customer lifetime value and an integrated control assessment aimed at the effects within the relationship marketing success chain. Looking at the whole planning process, this control ideally represents the last phase, although it is interdependent with the other four planning process phases.

Summary

This chapter has presented the most relevant and fundamental theoretical approaches which form the basis for the development of a conceptualisation of relationship marketing. The deeper examination of concepts such as customer life cycle, perspective taking, the success chain, or customer relationship perspectives is essential for understanding the sense of relationship marketing as well as for developing the planning process later on. The customer relationship life cycle helps to understand the duality of relationships, that is, each phase can be regarded from both the buyer's and the seller's viewpoint. Perspective taking which refers to the ability to adopt others' perspective is also a fundamental principle of relationship marketing. The concept applies to both the company and the customer, and management must acknowledge both viewpoints when planning its activities. In this sense also, examining customer relationship perspectives, together with the principle of structuring relationships in the form of a success chain, gives a clear insight into the psychological and behavioural consequences of relationships. Consequently, considering these principles will be useful for developing a management process of relationship marketing.

4 The analysis phase of relationship marketing

Overview

In this chapter we take a close look at the analysis phase of relationship marketing which comprises two main tasks: (1) the analysis of the internal and external environment (SWOT-analysis) with the aim of target planning and (2) customer segmentation that is based on various levels of the success chain. Specifically, we will address the following questions:

➤ How can the SWOT-analysis be applied in relationship marketing?

➤ What does target planning in relationship marketing mean, for instance: what types of target relationships can be identified and which targets should be formulated for each customer segment?

➤ How can the concept of the success chain be applied to the task of segmentation?

The initial task of the analysis phase is to analyse the general situation for solving relationship marketing's special problems. One proceeds on the assumption that the conceptualisation of relationship marketing is based on both the success chain as the management principle and the planning process as a structuring approach. The priority of customer orientation within relationship marketing puts particular significance on a **SWOT-analysis** (Strengths, Weaknesses, Opportunities, and Threats with emphasis on customer analysis). These analysis findings are then applied at various levels of **target planning**. **Customer segmentation** based on the success chain thus serves to identify activity areas for differentiated market processing.

In considering relationship marketing's analysis phase, specifically in the upcoming planning process phases, it will be necessary to conduct the analysis by relating it to different output types. In this way, the multi-faceted nature of relationship marketing for the marketing of consumer and industrial goods and services will be taken into account.

4.1 SWOT-analysis and target planning

4.1.1 SWOT-analysis

A SWOT-analysis (Kotler 2000, pp. 76–9; Ryals 2000a, pp. 238–41) provides an understanding of the situation in which relationship marketing is to be implemented. Customer-relevant problems should be addressed from the buyers' perspective. From the market standpoint it is necessary to establish the possibilities of maintaining customer relationships through strategic competitive advantages. Further, one needs to identify approaches to building up, holding, and intensifying customer relationships from the sellers' perspective. Accordingly, the fundamental SWOT-analysis can be divided into two categories:

1 External analysis of opportunities and threats

2 Internal analysis of strengths and weaknesses

External analysis

An **external opportunity-threat analysis** investigates aspects of relevance to the corporation but not controllable by the corporation. These aspects represent a framework that the company uses to direct its relationships with the marketing stakeholders for whom the external analysis covers the following areas: markets, customers, sales agents, suppliers, competitors, and the business environment (Figure 4.1).

Under relationship marketing, an opportunity-threat analysis is primarily concerned with identifying significant circumstances for shaping the corporation's **relationships with its stakeholders**. The major focus here is on an assessment of the **networking capability** of these stakeholders (Cravens and Piercy 1994). The investigation must establish the possible extent of any cooperation that could exist with customers, suppliers, sales agents, competitors, and also the business environment.

Analysis of Opportunities and Threats					
Market	Customers	Sales Agents	Suppliers	Competitors	Environment
• Market breakdown • Polarisation • Technological change • Market volume • Degree of saturation • Heterogeneity • Output attributes	• Customer demography/ structure • Attitudes • Quality/service requirements • Purchasing power • Experience with the seller • Experience with the output category	• Purchasing-decision behaviour • Needs • Technical equipment • Power application through trade • Trade concentration • Readiness to cooperate	• Number of suppliers • Dependence on suppliers • Delivery reliability • Readiness to cooperate • Technical equipment	• Number and size of competitors • Competition intensity • Competitors' market position • Power relationships • Cooperation possibilities	• Political framework (requirements) • Competition law • Environmental legislation • Social norms • Overall national economic growth

Figure 4.1 Areas for analysis of opportunities and threats

Looking at **different output types**, any cooperation with suppliers and customers is especially important for customised products and services. For instance, a high level of customer integration and a high relative importance of specific customers (e.g. for capital goods or management consulting) are more likely to necessitate cooperation with the customers. For customers, output utilisation in this area also means higher risk when compared to standard products or services, as he or she will also have a greater interest in cooperating.

According to the customer orientation maxim of relationship marketing, the analysis of the 'customer' is of particular importance for lending depth to an investigation of opportunities and threats to the company's customer relationships. As per the relationship marketing success chain, the **analysis content** relates to the effect of relationship marketing measures on corporate customers and can be divided into the following three areas:

1 All relationship marketing measures are initially aimed at the customers' **economic effects** such as sales, contribution margin, and CLV.

2 These economic effects are influenced to a great degree by **behavioural effects** such as the buying/communication behaviour and customer retention.

3 The customers' various **psychological effects** such as familiarity, image, quality perception, customer satisfaction, and relationship quality in turn determine the behavioural effects.

In general, the **analysis** can be conducted on two **planes**:

1 On an **accumulated plane** information covering the whole customer group is gathered (e.g. customer satisfaction rate). An analysis of these data specifies customer-related key variables and identifies general opportunities and threats for the regular customers.

2 On a **distributed plane** the focus is on individual customer relationships. In contrast to the accumulated plane, where information is assembled and identified for all customers, this analysis deals with corporate opportunities and threats for each individual relationship. An **analysis of individual customers** is, however, often impossible without a massive data collection effort. In such cases an effort should be made to conduct at least a **customer group analysis** by adapting existing corporate segments. This permits identification of more specific marketing problems than on an accumulated plane (Peck *et al.* 1999, p. 37).

On the basis of the three key customer relationship life cycle phases, three customer **analysis groups** can be identified. These are the **potential** customers (acquisition phase), **current** customers (retention phase), and **lost** customers (recovery phase). A differentiated analysis of these groups is required because of closely related but probably differing marketing problems for each group. This applies to both the contents of the analysis and to the implications of the findings, which can vary greatly depending on the customer group. For example, customer satisfaction is a valid analysis criterion for current and lost customers only. When dealing with potential customers, however, emphasis could be placed on making them familiar with the products and services offered. Most of the current and retained customers, on the contrary, should already be familiar with the existing outputs.

The main task of an opportunity-threat analysis is an **evaluation** of the observed facts. Depending on the characteristics of the criteria studied these could be interpreted as either an opportunity or a threat. Hence, a high customer satisfaction level is seen as an opportunity, while a low satisfaction level is judged as a threat.

Internal analysis

While an external analysis highlights the possibilities in relationship marketing, an internal **strength-weakness analysis** helps to weigh which activities make sense for the corporation to undertake in this respect. A strength-weakness analysis is thus an **analysis of resources** in the following possible areas (Figure 4.2): finance, research and development, procurement, marketing, and so on.

Performing a resource analysis requires a company to undertake the following three steps:

1 Initially, a **resource profile** is developed to identify and assess the relevance of the resources.

2 The next step recognises **the strengths and weaknesses** of the corporation, while the resources available are balanced against market requirements.

3 Finally, a strength-weakness comparison against competitors is done to **identify specific competencies**.

Each business should evaluate its internal strengths and weaknesses periodically. Figure 4.3 illustrates a checklist which can be used to review the aforementioned areas. Each factor is rated as a major strength, minor strength, neutral factor, minor weakness, or major weakness.

Analysis of Strengths and Weaknesses				
Finance	Research and Development	Procurement	Organisation	Marketing
• Capitalisation • Cost status • Cost flow • Productivity • Stock price development	• Number of patents • Number of new developments per year • Innovativeness of new developments • Quality of research personnel	• Procurement systems (e.g. Just in time) • Quality of materials • Warehousing costs • Error rate	• Visionary, capable leadership • Dedicated employees • Employee retention • Sickness rate • State-of-the-art of production equipment • Production flexibility	• Product and service quality • Company reputation • Market share • Customer retention • Pricing effectiveness • Complaint management

Figure 4.2 Areas for analysis of strengths and weaknesses

Checklist for performing Strength/Weakness Analysis								
	Performance					Importance		
	Major strength	Minor strength	Neutral	Minor weakness	Major weakness	High	Medium	Low
Marketing								
● Product and service quality	——	——	——	——	——	——	——	——
● Company reputation	——	——	——	——	——	——	——	——
● Market share	——	——	——	——	——	——	——	——
● Customer satisfaction	——	——	——	——	——	——	——	——
● Commitment	——	——	——	——	——	——	——	——
● Customer retention	——	——	——	——	——	——	——	——
● Pricing effectiveness	——	——	——	——	——	——	——	——
● Complaint management	——	——	——	——	——	——	——	——
Finance								
● Capitalisation	——	——	——	——	——	——	——	——
● Cost status	——	——	——	——	——	——	——	——
● Cash flow	——	——	——	——	——	——	——	——
● Productivity	——	——	——	——	——	——	——	——
● Stock price								
Organisation								
● ...								

Figure 4.3 Checklist for performing a strength and weakness analysis

(*Source*: adapted from Kotler 2000, p. 78)

Contrasting internal and external analyses in a SWOT-matrix

In order to systematically present the findings of opportunity-threat and strength-weakness analyses, use is made of the **SWOT-matrix**. This identifies the strengths that can be applied to avoid certain threats and/or gain specific opportunities (Figure 4.4).

Internal Environment \ External Environment	Opportunity	Threat
Strength	Suppliers' readiness to cooperate Good position in suppliers' portfolio	Rapidly changing customer needs Close cooperation with customers
Weakness	Few sellers Low customer retention	High share of unprofitable customers Low customer satisfaction

Figure 4.4 Illustrative SWOT-matrix in relationship marketing

Based on the customer life cycle concept, the following scenarios are typical examples of a SWOT-matrix applied to **relationship marketing problems**:

- **Customer acquisition phase**: an automobile corporation has been losing its market share for years. It has been established that consumers that have never tried out any of the company's vehicles have a weak perception of the company. The main competitor, in contrast, brings new models on the market much more frequently, thus attracting more new customers. One possibility of improving the situation is to enhance innovativeness or the speed of the company's product development versus its competitors.

- **Customer retention phase**: an insurance firm has continuously declining sales and profits from its current customers, even though the number of customers has remained at least constant over the last few years. In the insurance business new firms are constantly entering the market (e.g. banks, automobile manufacturers). The insurance company should contemplate the wisdom of increasing the attractiveness of its services in order to utilise the cross selling potential more effectively.

- **Customer recovery phase**: a telecommunication company has a very high customer churn rate. The market is characterised by handing out gifts to win new customers with the result that it is impossible to generate profits within the first half year of a customer relationship. In this situation there are two possibilities: one, it could make sense to cooperate with the competition; two, it may also make sense to look at ways of improving product offers to supplement the gifts.

The findings of the SWOT-analysis form the basis for target planning within relationship marketing, as discussed below.

4.1.2 Target planning

Target categories

In the composition of relationship marketing different goals have to be pursued at different levels. It makes sense to structure the feasible goals to permit their systematic application and follow-up of those targets. Applying the success chain idea (Chapter 3) results in the five **categories of goals** below, each with different relevant variables depending on the output type (Figure 4.5):

1 Economic corporate goals

2 Psychological corporate goals

3 Economic customer goals

4 Customer behavioural goals

5 Psychological customer goals

Psychological, economic, as well as behavioural customer goals form a link in the **customer success chain**. These can be extended to the corporation's economic goals, which are direct results of the economic customer targets. In addition, psychological corporate goals correlate directly with the corporation's economic goals and also indirectly through the customer success chain.

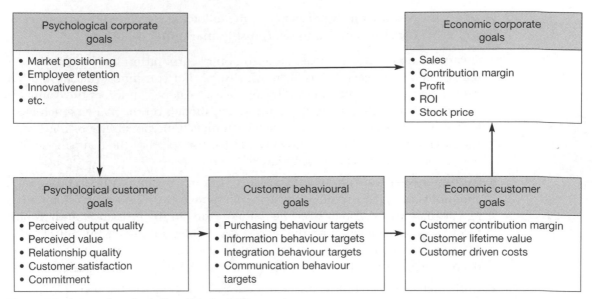

Figure 4.5 Categories of relationship marketing goals

The prime targets of relationship marketing mirror the prime objectives of a company and could be characterised as **economic corporate objectives**. These variables are indicators of the corporation's overall performance and include the sales, cost recovery, contribution margin, profit, return on investment, or the stock price. The main variables of interest from a profit perspective are sales, profit, and possibly the return on investment. In contrast, cost recovery represents a significant economic target variable from a non-profit viewpoint.

Furthermore, it is necessary to follow up on the **psychological corporate goals** including aspects such as market positioning, employee retention, and innovation. Achieving these objectives may have a direct impact on the attainment of economic corporate targets. Cost savings can ensue, for example, by retaining experienced employees, or motivated ones operating at high productivity levels (Heskett, Sasser and Schlesinger 1997; Reichheld and Sasser 1990). Additionally, psychological corporate goals are closely related to those of customers. For instance, satisfaction of employees and customers as well as employee and customer retention are closely connected (Payne 2000b, p. 118). These correlations are relevant primarily for customised products and services. At a high degree of integration and interaction, employee–customer contacts are a central element of output provision. In numerous sectors (e.g. banking), customer retention is strongly dependent on keeping the same customer representatives – i.e. employee retention.

On the one hand, psychological targets pursued at the corporate level directly affect the economic targets at that level. On the other hand, the psychological corporate goals can help to initiate the relationship marketing success chain through realisation of customer-related psychological, behavioural, and economic targets.

The consequences of the success chain's impacts in turn influence economic corporate objectives.

Goals such as familiarity, image, customer satisfaction, or trust are a part of **psychological customer goals**. Image and familiarity are particularly relevant for standardised products like beverages. Since potential and current customers are anonymous, it is very critical for companies in this field that the customers view corporate products as part of their evoked set. The image can be the deciding factor for customised products and services, since customers find these more difficult to judge and they are more risk-bound than standardised ones. Reasons lie in the fact that credence and experience qualities are over-weighted for customised outputs while standardised outputs are characterised mainly by search qualities (Friedman and Smith 1993; Zeithaml 1991; Darby and Karni 1973). Variables such as customer satisfaction and trust are also core target variables of customised products and services.

Attaining psychological customer goals can lead to the achievement of **behavioural customer goals** (Oliver 1996). This includes purchasing behaviour targets (e.g. buying, re-buying, increase in the buying frequency, cross buying), information behaviour targets (e.g. limiting customer desires to look for competitive information), integration behaviour targets (e.g. strong customer involvement in the provision of products and services), and communication behaviour targets (e.g. positive word-of-mouth communication).

For purchasing behaviour targets, the major **differences in importance** need to be determined **depending on the output type**. Customer retention targets such as re-buying, buying frequency increase, and cross buying are much more important for customised products or services than for standardised ones. This is basically because individual customers are relatively significant for a seller of customised services (e.g. an auditing firm, portfolio management broker), when large amounts are invested on commencement of the relationship with the seller. Subsequently, customer retention enables cost savings to be attained for customised outputs. For one thing, this occurs because of the high degree of integration and interaction and the attendant effect of the sellers' experience with the customer. Additionally, in these areas, information asymmetries are often to the disadvantage of the customer. Retained customers that have already had experiences with the firm can contribute much more at a qualitatively high level towards the provision of products and services than inexperienced customers. Cross buying effects are also more relevant here. In particular, companies in the capital goods and services sectors frequently offer a wide range of outputs, which become economic only if many customers use most of the outputs. Additionally, as an important purchase-decision making criterion, word-of-mouth communication for customised products is related to the customers' risk.

In order to set customer-specific targets, the prime economic objectives need to be formulated at both the individual customer and group level. Among the **customer economic targets** that could be affected by their behavioural targets, are aspects such as the customer contribution margin, the CLV, or the customer impacted itemised costs (Egan 2001, p. 63; Ryals 2000b, p. 256; Berger and Nasr 1998; Dwyer 1997). Comparable with the economic corporate goals, the most important facets from a profit perspective are the customer contribution margin and the CLV that result from customer sales. On the other end, the targets to be pursued from a non-profit perspective are the customer-cost variables.

Each target has a different meaning depending on the **customer relationship life cycle** phase. The purchasing behaviour targets should thus be formulated depending on the relationship phase involved: e.g. the first purchase in the customer acquisition phase versus a re-purchase in the customer retention phase.

The various **target formulation and application requirements** must always be taken into consideration when planning relationship marketing. This includes **considering the compatibility of goals**, where it is necessary to ensure that the customer targets determined are in accord with fundamental corporate positions such as its vision, model, and philosophy. The **operating aspects** of selected goals must also be kept in mind. Setting firm targets makes sense only if the achievements and any resulting variances can be reviewed and appropriate adjustment measures implemented. Hence, it is critical that any target parameters set be measurable or assessable (Chapter 8). The focus during goal setting should thus be on **relationships and goal hierarchies**.

Target relationships

Generally the following two types of **target relationships** can be identified (Becker 1998):

1 **Complementary goals** are ones closely connected with each other, i.e. realisation of one target leads to achievement of the other. Examples of such goals are correlations between sales and profits, customer retention and sales, customer satisfaction and customer retention, and quality perception and customer satisfaction.

2 **Polar goals** are precisely the opposite of the types above, i.e. attaining one target precludes attainment of the other. The connection between a reduction in cost of sales and an increase in sales is one such example.

These goal relationships are extremely important because of the **effectiveness and efficiency of goal achievement**. On the one hand, if two targets are complementary, synergy effects can be utilised to implement measures efficiently. On the other, being aware of polar relationships enables one to consider the dangers of measures with conflicting impacts.

Target hierarchies

It is necessary to consider **target hierarchies** since they are closely related to target relationships. The success chain school of thought makes it clear that all relationship marketing goals are correlated with each other at one level or another. Relationship marketing's targets reinforce each other, such that when pursuing the objective of a primary category a secondary objective can always be achieved indirectly.

As is apparent from Figure 4.6, relationship marketing's various strategic and operational goals should be considered in a detailed **system for relationship marketing targets**. The **Analytic Hierarchy Process (AHP)** developed by Saaty (1980) is part of the decision and planning theories offering a means for the structuring and analytically consistent application of the targeting system. The AHP theory helps the quality control personnel in a firm to set up their own target type preferences in a hierarchically organised system. This can then be applied to calculate preference values for each goal. These calculated values clearly show if goals located at the hierarchy's lower levels adequately reflect the aspired for prime objectives.

In this way, the sub-targets for corporations and customers contribute to realising the prime objective. It should be taken into account that goals on the same plane can be interdependent. In the target hierarchy depicted, the innovativeness aspect as a corporate sub-target impacts the perceived output quality that is a customer sub-target.

Target formulation in the success chain

An effort should be made to formulate targets for each customer segment (Kotler 2000). Apart from economic goals most of the other relationship marketing goals are not as relevant for all of the corporation's target groups. Irrespective of a specific

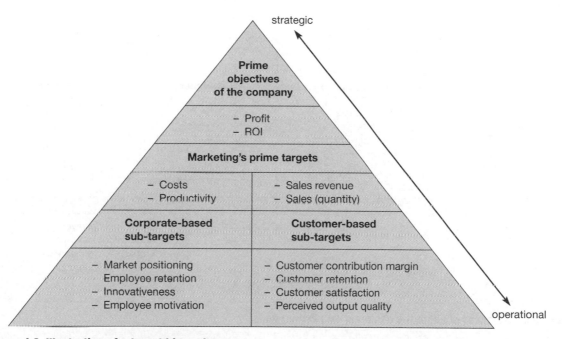

Figure 4.6 Illustration of a target hierarchy

customer segment (section 4.2), the relationship marketing goals vary greatly with potential, current, and lost customers. This becomes clear from an assessment of the success chains in the customer acquisition, retention, and recovery phases.

During the **customer acquisition phase** (Figure 4.7), marketing measures are put into action to kindle the customers' interest in the corporation and its products to generate attention for and familiarity with the outputs, and to create preferences and a positive image. Accordingly, the behaviour related to the first purchase and information should be controlled to improve the resultant economic targets, while initiating a dialogue and interaction with the customer.

During the **customer retention phase** (Figure 4.8), the relationship marketing measures serve to secure a positive perception of quality plus a high level of customer satisfaction, relationship quality, and commitment by the customer to the corporation. These psychological goals are supposed to help raise the customer retention level and generate positive word-of-mouth communication, both of which represent the basis for turnover and profits.

During the **customer recovery phase** (Figure 4.9), the focus is on determining the causes for customer defections. One outcome can be the goal of improved qual-

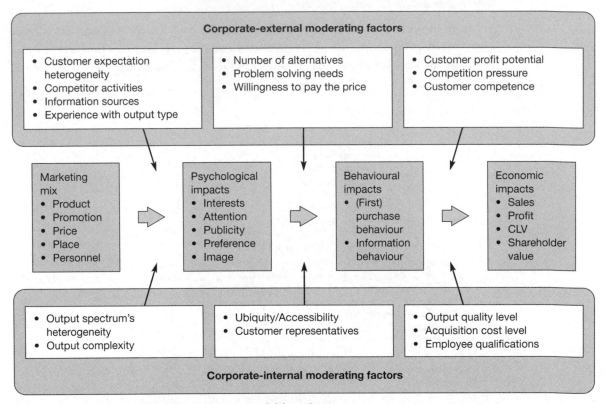

Figure 4.7 Success chain in the customer acquisition phase

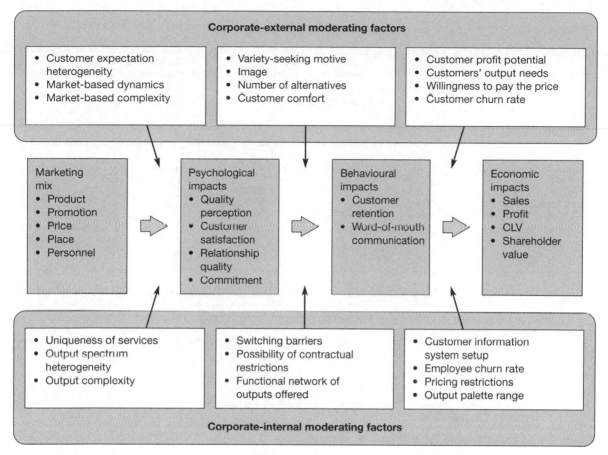

Figure 4.8 Success chain in the customer retention phase

ity perception and image enabling repeated stimulation of interests and preferences among lost customers. In this way, a first buy is achieved and can be repeated through the re-establishment of the relationship and avoidance of negative word-of-mouth communication, all of which results in higher revenues and profits.

It is apparent, that the prime objectives in different phases are similar. These targets should be improved through achievement of the psychological and behavioural customer goals that, however, are not the same for each phase.

Relationship marketing's relationship orientation also requires that the target formulation be made dependent on the customers' type of relationship with the corporation. The **type of relationship** represents an extremely broad based **macro-segmentation**. In order to guarantee focused market processing it makes sense to conduct a more detailed **micro-segmentation** that takes relationship marketing's success chain into account.

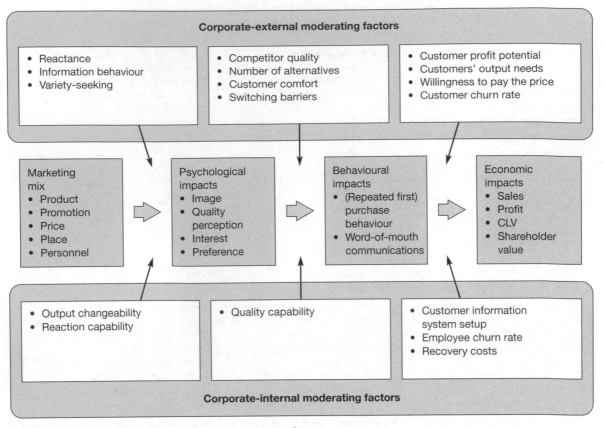

Figure 4.9 Success chain in the customer recovery phase

4.2 Customer segmentation in relationship marketing

4.2.1 Foundations of customer segmentation

Customer segmentation refers to a classification of all potential and current customers, based on their market reaction, into inherently homogeneous but externally heterogeneous sub-groups (i.e. customer segments) (Freter 1983). In view of relationship marketing's background the **classical segmentation criteria** must be expanded (Oldano 1987). When selecting segmentation criteria, certain requirements must be given due consideration.

Segmentation criteria requirements

To be able to fulfil the task of building inherently homogeneous but externally heterogeneous segments for all customers the segmentation criteria, as for classical marketing, must satisfy the following **requirements** (Dickson and Ginter 1987; Plummer 1974):

- **Measurability**: It must be feasible to measure and record segmentation criteria with current market research methods. This is a critical condition for the statistical procedures to be able to identify customer segments. Application of theoretical constructs of buyer behaviour such as customer satisfaction or trust demand a high degree of expertise.

- **Buying frequency relevance**: Suitable indicators of expected buying behaviours of consumers need to be selected. Qualities and behaviours that represent the requirements for a particular purchase are to be recorded and delineated on the basis of their inherently homogeneous and externally heterogeneous market segments. A focused segment-specific application of marketing instruments and the possibility of a behaviour-prognosis of segments ascertained is dependent on the degree of fulfilment of these requirements. In the services sector, in particular, the danger exists that a demographic and/or psychological criterion-driven segmentation leads to clustering with inadequate behavioural differences.

- **Accessibility**: The segmentation criteria must be chosen such that targeted access is assured for the demarcated segments. Fulfilment of these requirements impacts the extent to which the corporation can directly access consumers within a target segment by applying segment-specific marketing activities.

- **Capacity to act**: Only if the segmentation criteria permit the design and targeted application of marketing instruments, are they suitable for customer segmentation. If so, a link is achieved between an understanding and manipulation of the market.

- **Economic efficiency**: The criteria should be investigated such that the benefit resulting from the segmentation is greater than the costs incurred. As long as the requirement cannot be verified *ex ante*, the criteria should at least enable recognition of the extent of the segment-specific demand.

- **Stability over time**: The information collected *per* the criteria must be highly stable across the planning horizon. Customer segmentation makes sense only if the customer and market results are valid for the time period covering the execution and outcomes of the market processing activities.

These requirements need to be applied to judge the segmentation criteria to be analysed. It must be ensured that each and every criterion is measurable and stable over time. In any case, the range of criteria for customer segmentation must fulfil the remaining requirements.

Segmentation criteria types

In the literature, some authors have complained that there is no generally accepted and validated way to segment markets (Schauermann 1990; Beane and Ennis 1987). Regarding consumer market segmentation, four forms have emerged as the most popular (Elliott and Glynn 2000; Kotler 2000, pp. 263–270): geographic segmentation, demographic segmentation, psychographic segmentation, and behaviouristic segmentation (for specific segmentation criteria in the business-to-business market, see Bonoma and Shapiro 1983).

Example 4.1	Blockbuster Entertainment has invested in complex databases to track the video-borrowing behaviour of its 85 million members by buying additional demographic data from outside companies (Kotler 2000, p. 263). Through demographic segmentation the company is able to offer videos that reflect the population of individual cities. Oldsmobile, however, rather relies on psychographic segmentation. The company goes after golfers because research has shown that people who play golf are 143 per cent more likely to buy a new car than the average person. With this in mind, Oldsmobile started to hold a Oldsmobile Scramble golf tournament for Olds dealers and prospective buyers at country clubs across the United States (Kotler 2000, p. 266).

For customer segmentation, a range of criteria can also be applied. These **segmentation criteria** can be differentiated in terms of both their usefulness for conducting the segmentation and their ability to be controlled by the firm. Structuring criteria can be separated from descriptive ones depending on the **criterion usefulness** within the scope of customer segmentation. **Structuring criteria** are used to classify the customer segments, which are then designated with **descriptive criteria** to make the segments understandable. The segmentation criteria contents differ in their **ability to be controlled by the seller**, resulting in two types – endogenous and exogenous criteria. Endogenous criteria can be controlled by the seller and relate to relationship marketing goals. By adapting the success chain, the following endogenous groups of segmentation criteria can be applied for customer segmentation:

- Economic endogenous criteria (e.g. customer contribution margin, CLV)
- Behavioural endogenous criteria (e.g. customer retention, word-of-mouth communication)
- Psychological endogenous criteria (e.g. customer satisfaction, relationship quality)

Based on these endogenous criteria, for example, profitable and unprofitable customers (customer contribution margin as criterion) or satisfied and dissatisfied customers (customer satisfaction as criterion) can be separated from each other.

In contrast to endogenous criteria, **exogenous criteria** represent aspects that the company either cannot control at all or only to a limited degree. Nevertheless, they are relevant for the customers' buying behaviour and, hence, for the corporation's success. The following criteria can be differentiated (Peltier, Schibrowsky and Davis 1998):

- Demographic exogenous criteria (e.g. age, gender)
- Socio-economic exogenous criteria (e.g. income, social level)
- Psychological exogenous criteria (e.g. general quality demands, attitude towards a product)
- Behavioural exogenous criteria (e.g. variety seeking behaviour, general information behaviour)

Among exogenous segmentation criteria, there are major differences between consumptive and investment areas. Thus, in the **B2B field**, the demographic attributes apply primarily to organisational attributes with the foremost being company size. Among psychological and behavioural criteria, those such as the buying centre must definitely be considered since investment decisions are often reached by purchasing committees or buying centres. Figure 4.10 depicts some major segmentation criteria which apply for business markets.

Customer segmentation procedure

In general, customer segmentation within relationship marketing should be conducted in three steps:

1 **Segment building**: Initially, the customer segments are formed with guidance from selected aspects of the structuring criteria.

2 **Segment description**: These customer segments are then described on the basis of the description criteria to derive a basis for dealing with customers.

3 **Segment processing**: The last step involves the processing of selected segments, including the attendant planning and implementation activities.

Demographic Factors

- **Industry**: Which industries should we serve?
- **Company size**: What size companies should we serve?
- **Location**: What geographical areas should we serve?

Operating Variables

- **Technology**: What customer technologies should we focus on?
- **User or non-user status**: Should we serve heavy users, medium users, or non-users?
- **Customer capabilities**: Should we serve customers needing many or few services?

Purchasing Approaches

- **Purchasing-function organisation**: Should we serve companies with highly centralised or decentralised purchasing organisations?
- **Power structure**: Should we serve companies that are engineering-dominated, financially-dominated, and so on?
- **Nature of existing relationships**: Should we serve companies with which we have strong relationships or simply go after the most desirable companies?
- **General purchase policies**: Should we serve companies that prefer leasing? Service contracts? Systems purchases? Sealed bidding?
- **Purchasing criteria**: Should we serve companies that are seeking quality, service, or price?

Situational Factors

- **Urgency**: Should we serve companies that need quick and sudden delivery or service?
- **Specific application**: Should we focus on certain applications of our product rather than all applications?
- **Size of order**: Should we focus on large or small orders?

Personal Characteristics

- **Buyer-sellers similarity**: Should we serve companies whose people and values are similar to ours?
- **Attitudes towards risk**: Should we serve risk-taking or risk-avoiding customers?
- **Loyalty**: Should we serve companies that show high loyalty to their suppliers?

Figure 4.10 Major segmentation criteria for business markets
(*Source*: Kotler 2000, p. 272)

As a consequence of distinguishing between exogenous and endogenous segmentation criteria, two basic **customer segmentation procedures** are available:

1 The endogenous criteria for building segments can be applied in the context of an **endogenous segmentation**. The resulting segments are then described on the basis of the endogenous criteria.

2 The alternate approach in the form of an **exogenous segmentation** is also feasible, whereby one applies exogenous criteria for building the segments and endogenous criteria for describing them.

Example 4.2

Depending on their satisfaction with the company, customers can be segmented under the first approach. The segments are simply 'satisfied customers' and 'unsatisfied customers', both of which can be described by exogenous criteria (e.g. age). One possible outcome could be that satisfied customers are normally older than the dissatisfied. A resulting implication could be that measures should be taken to raise the level of satisfaction among younger customers. The second approach takes the contrasting procedure. Customers are divided between 'old' and 'young' and described in terms of their level of satisfaction. One possible outcome could be that older customers are more satisfied than younger customers.

It is clear that the customer segmentation findings for both approaches do not differ significantly. Nevertheless, the endogenous approach has the advantage that it enables **targeted customer segmentation**. The relationship marketing goal is hence fulfilled by considering the effects within the success chain when forming, describing, and processing the segments.

Insights 4.1

Customer segmentation procedure of Deutsche Bahn

The German railroad corporation Deutsche Bahn (a company with more than 220,000 employees and revenues of €15 billion in 2000) uses a combination of the aforementioned segmentation procedures. While perceived customer value is used as an endogenous criterion, the purpose of travelling by train is the exogenous criterion. With conjoint analysis perceived customer value was differentiated in three different segments of values: Travellers who try to minimise travel time, travellers who are price sensitive, and travellers who are comfort-oriented. Regarding the purpose for taking the train, three more segments were found: business travellers, private reasons, and office travellers who are persons who take the train as a means of travelling between home and office. After combining both dimensions in a portfolio Deutsche Bahn was able to differ nine customer segments. The results showed that the biggest group of customers are those who are price-sensitive private travellers (33 per cent). As more than half of all customers regard price as the most important perceived value, the relationship marketing strategy thus focuses on price policy for private travellers. Figure 4.11 illustrates the segmentation of this example.

Values Purpose of travelling	Minimising travel time 31%	Price-sensitive 51%	Comfort-oriented 18%
Business travel 30%	12%	12%	6%
Private travel 58%	15%	33%	10%
Travel to office 12%	4%	6%	2%

Figure 4.11 Example of a combined segmentation procedure on the basis of exogenous and endogenous segmentation criteria at Deutsche Bahn, Germany

(*Source*: adapted, in part, from Perrey, J. (1998). *Nutzenorientierte Marktsegmentierung im Verkehrsdienstleistungsbereich, Dargestellt am Beispiel der Deutschen Bahn AG*. Working Paper No. 124, Organisation for Marketing and Business Administration e.V. at the University of Münster, Münster.)

4.2.2 Customer segmentation based on the success chain

Relationship marketing's targets can be structured as success chains for the customer relationship life cycle phases. Using the appropriate success chain, a **multi-level targeted segmentation** can be based on the individual chain links. The purpose is to highlight mainly those customers with whom the relationship marketing targets have been either well or poorly achieved. Additionally, the appropriate moderating factors allow the relevant chain to be used to identify grounds for any deficiencies in the success chain's functioning (e.g. low customer retention despite a high satisfaction level). The segmentation can be based on either individual success chain elements (**intra-efficacy segmentation**) or several success chain elements (**inter-efficacy segmentation**).

Intra-efficacy segmentation

For **intra-efficacy segmentation** based on single chain elements like customer satisfaction, a two-dimensional segmentation is conducted by considering the variables applicable to the formation of the chain links. A **portfolio analysis** is one possible form for displaying the resulting segments. This analysis enables derivation of various portfolios for relevant chain elements like the three success chains applicable to the customer acquisition, retention, and recovery phases. Since the **customer retention phase** is the most important one for relationship marketing, the intra-efficacy segmentation approach will be illustrated for this phase by identifying three **segmentation forms** that lead to the portfolios portrayed in Figure 4.12:

1 Satisfaction based segmentation

2 Customer retention based segmentation

3 Relationship success based segmentation

Under **satisfaction based segmentation** (portfolio 1), the emergence of customer satisfaction is analysed in greater detail to identify the satisfaction drivers, i.e. the particular product attributes with which the firm can satisfy its customers (Anderson and Mittal 2000). In a strict sense, satisfaction based segmentation does not represent any customer segmentation theory but instead serves mainly to prioritise customer-oriented output attributes. Since customer satisfaction occurs on fulfilment of the customers' expectations, an **attributes portfolio** with the following four **types of output attributes** can be developed on the basis of the significance and assessment of these attributes:

▪ **Routine attributes** are evaluated positively, although they are of little significance to the customer.

▪ **Success attributes** demonstrate a high level of significance and are also assessed positively.

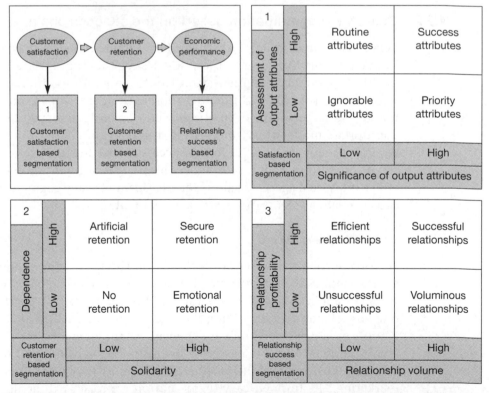

Figure 4.12 Segmentation based on individual success chain elements in the customer retention phase (portfolios)

- **Ignorable attributes** are judged neither positively nor are they important for customers.

- **Priority attributes** are important for customers but nevertheless assessed negatively.

Under customer-retention-based segmentation (portfolio 2), an analysis of the reasons for customer retention is done. Fundamentally, customer retention can be related to customer solidarity or dependence (Chapter 3). Based on these two dimensions, the following four customer types or customer retention types can be classified:

- **Artificial retention** occurs at a low solidarity level and higher dependence level.

- **Secure retention** results if a high level of dependence and solidarity occur simultaneously.

- **No retention** occurs if the customer feels neither dependence nor solidarity.

- **Emotional retention** is observed when the customer has a high level of solidarity to the corporation but is not dependent on it.

In terms of the economic performance of a customer relationship, both the relationship volume (i.e. sales volume from a customer) and the relationship profitability with that customer could be possible segmentation criteria (Storbacka 1997, p. 488). Using these two dimensions for relationship-success-based segmentation (portfolio 3) permits the following four customer or **relationship types** to be identified:

- **Efficient relationships** are profitable even at a low relationship volume.

- **Successful relationships** show both a high relationship volume and profitability level.

- **Unsuccessful relationships** lack both volume and profits.

- **Voluminous relationships** are characterised by a high relationship volume simultaneously associated with a low profitability level.

Intra-efficacy segmentation enables precise analysis of the occurrence of specific effects within the chain. Hence, it is highly relevant for relationship marketing, since it provides a means to differentiate and show the impact on customers. It also permits customer-specific control of relationship marketing targets.

This segmentation is, however, isolated in that the extent of the success chain's impact on each customer cannot be verified. For that, an **inter-efficacy segmentation** needs to be conducted.

Inter-efficacy segmentation

The **inter-efficacy segmentation** is based on not just one but on two of the success chain's links. This type of segmentation can also be depicted in the form of a portfolio recognisable by its two dimensions or four customer types (Storbacka, Strandvik and Grönroos 1994). In addition, it can be differentiated according to the customer relationship life cycle phases.

(1) Segmentation in the customer acquisition phase

During the customer acquisition phase it is necessary to identify those customers that the corporation should seek to acquire (Hansotia and Wang 1997). Within this phase, the success chain 'actions–image–first purchase–economic performance' could be applied to allocate potential customers (Figure 4.13) into the resulting three groups depending on the **segmentation criteria**:

1 Segmentation based on the action potential
2 Segmentation based on the image potential
3 Segmentation based on the first purchase potential

Segmentation based on the action potential (portfolio 1) highlights the following **customer types** within the first chain link:

■ For **involved customers** a positive image is achieved despite the low level of activities undertaken. Without any major effort on the part of the firm, these customers deal intensively with the corporation and its products and have a high image.

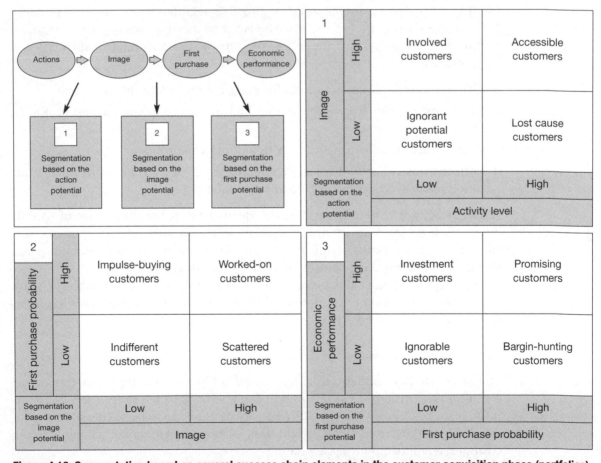

Figure 4.13 Segmentation based on several success chain elements in the customer acquisition phase (portfolios)

- For **accessible customers** the success chain is valid for the correlation considered. For such customers intensive measures are undertaken and the firm has a positive image. The firm should work on these customers further as long as the image improves continuously.

- Lost cause customers are not reached in spite of significant activities undertaken. Since the measures are ineffective, the activity level should be turned down.

- For ignorant customers both the customers and the firm are poorly informed. The customers do not monitor the company and the firm does not attend to them. Should these customers not represent an attractive group and if it is not possible to deal with them, the firm ought to reconsider any further associations with this group.

The second chain link involves a correlation between the image and the first purchase and permits a **segmentation based on the image potential** (portfolio 2), enabling recognition of the following **customer types**:

- **Impulse-buying customers** want to at least select the firm in spite of its poor image. If these customers are profitable, the company should weigh the application of image-enhancing actions to stabilise the probability of a first-buy.

- The chain applies to **worked-on customers**. Since the firm has managed to build a positive image here with a high purchasing probability, additional image-enhancing actions could make sense.

- **Scattered customers** do not want to deal with the firm, despite its high image. The high image thus does not generate a positive outcome for the firm. In case these customers are attractive it needs to be verified if there are other factors affecting their buying decisions.

- **Indifferent customers** hold neither a positive image nor exhibit a high buying likelihood. Hence, the firm should check if image enhancement makes sense with these customers.

The following **customer types** can be highlighted by comparing the first purchase probability to the economic success under **segmentation based on the first purchase potential** (portfolio 3):

- **Investment customers** are those with a low probability of a first purchase and a high probability of future economic success. Due to the potential for success, investment in this relationship could be worthwhile.

- The chain applies to **promising customers** since they have a high probability of making a purchase and a high level of economic success. The corporation should ensure that the buying probability is retained at the existing level.

- **Bargain-hunting customers** are not profitable for the firm in spite of a high likelihood of making a first purchase. In the event that the first-buy probability can be traced to the firm's efforts, investments in this customer group should be reviewed again.

- **Ignorable customers** barely exist in either dimension. They most likely do not belong to the corporate target groups and should thus not be dealt with.

(2) Segmentation in the customer retention phase

The success chain 'actions – customer satisfaction – customer retention – economic performance' can be applied in the **customer retention phase** as the basis for the **segmentation of existing customers**. This segmentation results in these **three customer portfolios** (Figure 4.14):

1 Segmentation based on the satisfaction potential

2 Segmentation based on the customer retention potential

3 Segmentation based on the success potential

The first portfolio applies to **segmentation based on the satisfaction potential** of current customers, in that the dimensions 'action activity level' and 'customer satisfaction' are compared. The activity level refers to the extent of the firm's efforts aimed at raising or securing customer satisfaction among the customers considered (e.g. quality management or complaint management actions). An identification of the following **customer types** results from this:

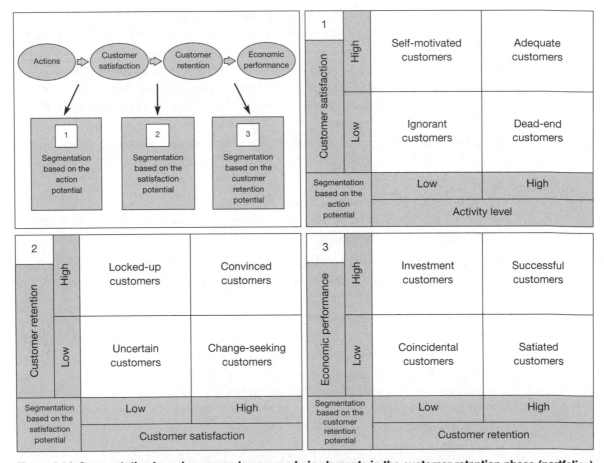

Figure 4.14 Segmentation based on several success chain elements in the customer retention phase (portfolios)

- **Self-motivated customers** have a high level of satisfaction at a low activity level. Even though the firm invests little in satisfying these customers they are nonetheless satisfied. One possible reason for the lack of a correlation between the actions and the satisfaction level could be the complexity of the offered products and services, leading to a low level of critical judgment by the relevant customers. Another reason could be the stability in the requirements made by the respective customers, whose fulfilment needs no additional investments.

- **Adequate customers** are highly satisfied and have a high level of activity. For them the measures executed are adequate, i.e. they lead to the desired outcome – customer satisfaction.

- **Ignorant customers** have a low level of satisfaction at a low level of activity. For these customers the correlation between actions and satisfaction is also linear but inverse compared with the one for investment customers. If they display general attraction for the firm, measures should be undertaken to expand this group of customers.

- **Dead-end customers** have a high level of activity but a low level of satisfaction. Although the firm makes an effort to raise the satisfaction level, the respective customers are not satisfied. One reason for this could be the uniqueness of the products. In that case, it is possible that the actions were too general for the customers involved and, since the targets have not been achieved, they are uneconomic. Hence, the actions should be modified to help elevate the satisfaction level of the respective group.

Comparing the dimensions 'customer satisfaction' and 'customer retention' results in derivation of the second portfolio for **segmentation based on the retention potential** (Storbacka, Strandvik and Grönroos 1994). Customers are segmented according to whether their satisfaction leads to their retention and permits the following **customer types** to be identified:

- **Locked-up customers** display a high level of retention at a low satisfaction level. For them there is no correlation between satisfaction and retention. Even though they are dissatisfied with the firm's products or services they have no intentions to switch. One reason here could be the lack of alternatives (e.g. monopolies) that provide no options for a switch. In most sectors, even after abolition of a monopoly, long-term retention is more likely at a higher as opposed to a lower level of satisfaction. The firm should, hence, undertake measures to either raise the satisfaction level or seek to preserve the motives for the retention despite the dissatisfaction.

- **Convinced customers** have a high level of both satisfaction and retention. Such customers are characterised by a linear correlation between satisfaction and retention. The corporation should pay attention to fulfilling customer expectations in the future also and to keeping them satisfied accordingly.

- **Uncertain customers** depict a low level of satisfaction and also retention. With them, as well, there is a linear correlation between satisfaction and retention. If the particular customers are attractive for the company, it should be confirmed if the facts also apply for the positive case, i.e. the possibility of attaining retention through high satisfaction. An effort should then be made to implement measures to raise the satisfaction level among them.

■ **Change-seeking customers** have a low level of retention at a high level of satisfaction. This applies to those that cannot be made dependent on the firm although they are highly satisfied. A correlation either does not exist between the two variables or at most to a small degree. One possible reason for this may be the variety-seeking behaviour of these customers who are on the lookout for a change. The implications are that it may make sense for the firm to avoid any further investments to elevate the satisfaction level. Additionally, an analysis should be conducted to establish the extent to which other customer retention drivers (e.g. contractual obligations) could lead to at least a medium-term enhancement in retention of these customers.

By comparing the dimension 'customer retention' against 'economic performance', a third portfolio is derived in the context of the customer retention phase for **segmentation based on the success potential** (Mulhern 1999). From this, the following **customer relationship types** can be classified:

■ **Investment customers** have low retention but high economic performance. For them, the supposed correlation between customer retention and economic performance does not exist. The respective customers have low solidarity with the firm but nevertheless high profitability. It is possible that the economic performance stems from past practices, but the customers still intend to switch to another seller. In this situation the firm should institute retention measures since the customers are profitable.

■ For **successful customers** both retention and economic performance are at significant levels. In this 'normal' case, due to the presumption of a positive correlation, the firm is able to secure its profitability through retention of the particular customers. Hence, customer retention should be maintained for certain at the high level.

■ For **coincidental customers** both retention and economic performance are low. For them also customer retention and profitability are linearly related. It should be verified here if the low economic performance can be traced to low retention. This could occur if the customers display a high success potential (e.g. need for the corporate products until now taken from others). If so, the corporation should undertake actions to improve the retention of the respective group.

■ For **satiated customers** retention is high but the economic performance is low. For such customers high retention does not, as generally suspected, lead to economic performance. A possible reason for these circumstances could be the customers' low success potential, for example because the firm has not been able to achieve much cross selling or because the handling of these customers is costly. As such, investments to retain these customers are not justified. If the problem appears to be ongoing, thought should be given to separating oneself from them.

Conducting a **retrograde application** helps to link these three portfolios and to determine the focus of relationship marketing. Since economic performance of customer relationships is the final decisive element, segmentation helps to identify approaches to take advantage of the economic success potential. The segments could thus be examined at first to highlight customers with the potential for economic performance. This could then be followed by recommendations for actions based on a classification in terms of the retention and satisfaction potential.

Example 4.3	If a firm determines that the investment-customer group with a high success potential but low customer retention makes up a large share of all its customers, the segment should be analysed in greater detail. Accordingly, an assessment should be made of the segments to which the respective customers are to be allocated on the basis of their retention potential. If the outcome is that a large share of the investment customers are uncertain customers, a check should be made to see why they are not satisfied. If these are ignorant customers, for whom the firm has expended little effort, thought should be given to investing in customer retention here, because of the potential for high economic performance.

(3) Segmentation in the customer recovery phase

The **customer recovery phase** should be segmented to enable recovery management to be designed precisely (see section 6.2.3). The classification can be done on the basis of the success chain 'actions – regained interest – reactivation intention – economic success'. This results in the following **segmentation types** (Figure 4.15):

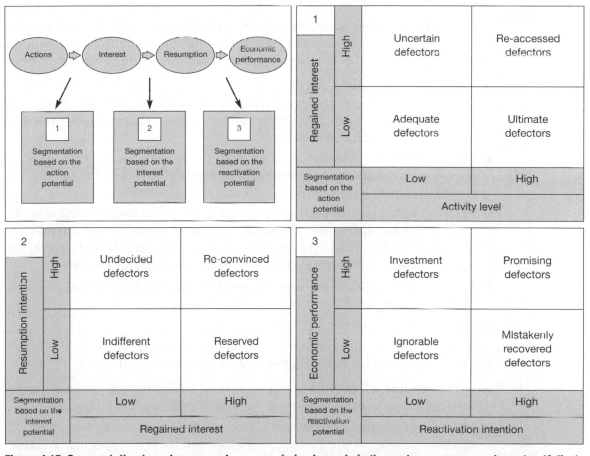

Figure 4.15 Segmentation based on several success chain elements in the customer recovery phase (portfolios)

101

1 Segmentation based on the action potential

2 Segmentation based on the interest potential

3 Segmentation based on the reactivation potential

By comparing the activity level with the regained interest in the context of the **segmentation based on the action potential** (portfolio 1), an analysis is conducted to determine the customers among whom the corporate measures generate interest in the firm. The following **customer types** can thus be pinpointed:

- **Uncertain defectors** are interested in resuming the relationship with the firm without any of its influence. It should be assessed if the firm also has the same interests and if recovery measures should be instituted.

- **Re-accessed defectors** come into play if the corporation implements intensive actions and the former customers dealt with exhibit interest in resuming the relationship. The firm should finally undertake actions to reactivate the relationship.

- **Ultimate defectors** are customers that show no interest in the corporation in spite of a high activity level.

- In the case of **adequate defectors** neither the firm nor former customers are interested in reactivating the relationship.

The **segmentation based on the interest potential** (portfolio 2) is achieved by considering the second chain link, i.e. the connection between interest and the intention to resume. This results in recognition of the following **customer types**:

- **Undecided defectors** display strong intentions to resume the relationship despite little interest. This has occurred, for example, with customers that switched to private firms in the liberalised telecommunications market and were disappointed in their expectations.

- **Re-convinced defectors** exist when both the interest and the intention to resume occur simultaneously. The firm thus manages to apply appropriate measures to convince lost customers to reactivate their relationship.

- **Reserved customers** have a high level of interest in the company and exhibit a certain amount of recovery potential, in spite of a lack of any intention to resume. This interest just needs to be stimulated by the firm through appropriate recovery actions such as taking care of transfer formalities by a bank.

- The success chain does not apply to **indifferent defectors** in that corporate measures are not expected to be worth undertaking.

Working on the last chain link, which reflects the correlation between reactivation intention and economic success, the following **customer types** can be ascertained from the **segmentation based on the recovery potential** (portfolio 3):

- With **investment defectors** the firm could try to achieve the potential success with these customers by enhancing the level of the intention to resume.

- Recovery of **promising defectors** is both feasible and the success potential is apparently high, but the question of if and when the recovery could be accomplished needs to be addressed.

- **Mistakenly re-acquired defectors** are not profitable for the corporation and therefore it should not pay much attention to them.

- In the case of **ignorable defectors** neither side has any interest in recovery activities.

Evaluation of segmentation approaches

In relationship marketing it is necessary to identify each customer relationship that can be shaped profitably. This can be achieved through the aforementioned classification approaches based on relationship marketing's success chain concept. The customer portfolios therein are a possible form of illustration that is easy to follow, although each of them permits only two dimensions at a time to be taken into consideration.

This limitation can be overcome through a **multi-dimensional segmentation**. For instance, in the customer retention phase all links of the success chain 'relationship marketing – customer satisfaction – customer retention – economic performance' can be segmented. Here, each customer to whom the chain applies can be identified. A disadvantage of such a multi-dimensional segmentation lies naturally in its complexity.

Customer segmentation represents a basis for individualised customer processing, which must be a part of relationship marketing. Looking at the relevant state of research it becomes clear that many questions still remain unanswered. Discourses on segmentation problems in the literature on relationship marketing are quite limited. In practice, on the other hand, there is definitely a certain degree of mistrust of segmentation based on psychological attributes. This is explainable by the fact that a classical segmentation on the basis of aspects such as socio-demography is much easier to understand and the respective segmentation criteria are easy to measure. Nevertheless, since the classical attributes have little impact on the success of a customer relationship as compared to the success chain variables, customer-oriented firms must look into how they could implement more effective customer segmentation instead.

Summary

This chapter dealt with the analysis phase of relationship marketing. Taking a close look at the two main tasks within the analysis phase, we first learnt that organisations have to consider their internal and external environment before implementing relationship marketing. While the SWOT-analysis provides a tool for companies to examine their current situation, target planning structures feasible goals on the basis of the success chain. Before formulating specific targets the organisation should consider target relationships and target hierarchies as well. However, the analysis phase also includes the task of customer segmentation. After discussing general segmentation criteria we demonstrated a new way of segmenting customers. That is, the segmentation can be based on various levels of the success chain. We developed segmentation portfolios for individual success chain elements, thus helping companies to differentiate their customers and manage their activities accordingly.

5 The strategic focus of relationship marketing

Overview

This chapter deals with the strategic focus of relationship marketing. A corporation's relationship-oriented appearance is a combination of numerous activities. The success of these activities is sustainable only if the enterprising actions are founded on a strategically focused control mechanism. The fundamental role of relationship marketing is to identify the primary thrust for the initiation, build-up, and intensification of customer relationships. In doing this, it is necessary to establish the corporation's general strategic direction and to assess the options for any special focus for relationship marketing. Specifically, we will cover the strategic options of three main areas, addressing the following questions:

➤ What are the requirements for developing strategies in relationship marketing?

➤ When differentiating strategies on the basis of the customer relationship life cycle phases, which different strategies can be pursued for customer acquisition, customer retention, and customer recovery?

➤ What tasks have to be done when pursuing business area strategies? Which single strategic options can be differentiated?

➤ Finally, regarding the field of market participant strategies, which specific strategies can be pursued when addressing, for example, customers, competitors, or the business environment?

5.1 The foundations of strategic relationship marketing

5.1.1 Relationship marketing – its strategic attributes and tasks

Relationship marketing's strategies establish a framework of actions that show the path to realising its goals. These strategies result from diverse decisions on controlling corporate relationships and are fixed in the form of conditional, medium to long-term, global behavioural plans for the corporate strategic business units.

This conditionality of relationship marketing's strategies illustrates that these will be set under due consideration of the corporation's existing internal and external situations. The medium to long-term time horizon means that commitment to the strategies covers several planning periods/years. These strategies should encompass an easily graspable time horizon, in view of the anticipated business environment and strategic aspects. A further attribute of the marketing strategy is its **global nature**. No single measures are prescribed as a connecting link between relationship marketing's targets and operational measures, but instead the focus of relationship marketing is ascertained.

The following general requirements must be put into effect when developing the relationship marketing strategies, such that they fulfil their function as a global action plan:

- Ability to depict the directions for achieving the scheduled relationship marketing targets (e.g. enhancement of satisfaction among current customers; increasing new customer acquisition through cooperation with sellers in other sectors)
- Ability to simultaneously identify the market and customers' segments to be processed and those not to be processed based on the success chain
- Setting up a channelled application of the methods as well as targeted control of the application of instruments in various phases of the customer relationship life cycle
- Highlighting the consequences resulting from the strategies laid down in terms of the methods used, the organisation, and the personnel
- Ability to verify target achievement over time on the basis of appropriate indicators within relationship marketing's success chain

Strategy development for relationship marketing is both a planning and a creative marketing management task. The **planning task** involves setting up and controlling a market- and customer-focused action plan with the help of strategic analysis instruments such as SWOT, life cycle, or portfolio analysis. The **creative task** involves the achievement of alternative or innovative solutions within the given activity framework. Relationship marketing strategies are the result of structured thinking, a creative awareness process, and intuitive marketing management capabilities.

5.1.2 Strategic options for relationship marketing

Relationship marketing is not a replacement for but rather an enhancement of classical marketing. Its possible strategies cannot be totally isolated from classical marketing strategies, but instead the aims of a strategic marketing concept are partly shifted. In general, two types of relationship marketing strategies can be classified:

1 First, **modified classical marketing strategies** can be pursued. In other words, traditional strategic marketing approaches become heavily relationship-oriented through a stronger focus on business relationships.

2 Second, **original relationship strategies** whose design is founded on the fundamentals of relationship marketing can also exist.

In addition to these formal delineations for possible relationship marketing strategies, three fundamental types can be identified (Figure 5.1):

1 **Phase-driven strategies** are based on the customer relationship life cycle and indicate whether a corporation strives for customer acquisition, retention, or recovery. From the operational aspects of relationship marketing, phase-driven strategies are specified in terms of classical marketing instruments (e.g. 4Ps) such that, in contrast to classical marketing, no special instrumental strategies are fixed.

2 **Business area strategies** highlight the markets in which the corporation intends to be active. For these strategies the implications that arise depend on the phase-driven strategies selected.

3 **Market participant strategies** show how the corporation plans to handle its relationships with various market members like customers, competitors, sales agents, and the business environment. The overall networking strategy plays a special role here as a result of various interlaced value chain steps.

Phase-driven Strategies		
Customer acquisition strategy	Customer retention strategy	Customer recovery strategy
• Stimulation • Persuasion	• Solidarity • Dependence	• Restitution • Improvement
Business Area Strategies		
Definition of business areas	Market segment stragey	Competitive advantage strategy
• Functions • Technologies • Customer groups • Regions	• Market penetration • Market development • Output development • Diversification	• Relationship advantage • Quality advantage • Innovation advantage • Brand advantage • Programme breadth advantage • Cost advantage • Value advantage

Market Participant Strategies				
Customer targeted		Competitor targeted	Sales agent targeted	Business environment targeted
Market handling	Relationship handling	• Avoidance • Cooperation • Conflict • Adjustment	• Avoidance • Cooperation • Conflict • Adjustment	• Innovation • Adjustment • Resistance • Avoidance • Retreat • Passiveness
• Undifferentiated • Differentiated • Segment-of-one	• Active relationship handling • Passive relationship handling			
Overall networking strategies				

Figure 5.1 Strategic options for relationship marketing

5.2 Phase-driven strategic decisions as the basis

Phase-driven strategies specify the general relationship marketing direction (customer orientation) that can be derived from the SWOT-analysis. For example, if they show that a company has a high churn rate, more emphasis must then be placed on customer retention and recovery. Three **strategic options** can be differentiated on the basis of the customer relationship life cycle phases:

1 Customer acquisition strategy
2 Customer retention strategy
3 Customer recovery strategy

5.2.1 Customer acquisition strategy

The primary aim of a **customer acquisition strategy** is to acquire new customers by having the firm direct its marketing activities accordingly. A customer acquisition strategy is always appropriate, as winning new customers is important for the economic performance of an organisation. However, there are some aspects which clearly show that the focus should be mainly on customer acquisition, for instance, if the corporation:

■ gains relatively fewer customers than its competitors
■ still has a small group of regular customers
■ has less profitable customers than could be acquired
■ has current customers that are less profitable than new ones entering the market

The **customer acquisition strategy** can be made concrete by differentiating between a stimulation and a persuasion strategy. A **stimulation strategy** offers customers incentives to enter into a relationship with the firm. A **persuasion strategy** depicts the firm's capabilities to fulfil customer needs and expectations. These fundamental strategy types can differ thereafter depending on whether they are to be implemented effectively or symbolically. Under effective as opposed to symbolic implementation customers are stimulated or convinced with specific corporate attributes. In all, this results in four **strategy types** for dealing with customers in the acquisition phase (Figure 5.2):

1 An **effective stimulation strategy** could be implemented by means of special offers.
2 Image building is one measure that is part of a **symbolic stimulation strategy**.
3 Product samples could be used to implement an **effective persuasion strategy**.
4 Measures to direct word-of-mouth communication are instruments of a **symbolic persuasion strategy** for winning advocates of the corporation that speak positively of the firm and its products with potential customers.

Task \ Means	Effective	Symbolic
Stimulation	Effective stimulation strategy Examples: ● Special offers ● Competition	Symbolic stimulation strategy Examples: ● Image building ● Classic advertising testimonials
Persuasion	Effective persuasion strategy Example: ● Product samples ● Before & after advertisements	Symbolic persuasion strategy Example: ● Controlling recommendations ● Quality guarantees

Figure 5.2 Types of customer acquisition strategies

A customer acquisition strategy could be aimed at various customer groups. If the company has a low penetration rate in **current market segments**, the strategy is directed at these segments. If these segments have already been exhausted, customers acquisition could be focused on **new segments**. If all the market segments have been sapped, the customer acquisition strategy could instead be applied to **new markets**.

5.2.2 Customer retention strategy

A **customer retention strategy** is aimed at raising the retention level of current corporate customers. Such a strategy should be pursued for several reasons. For instance, research has shown that keeping loyal customers is five to seven times cheaper than winning new customers (Keaveney 1995, p. 71; Hart, Heskett and Sasser 1990, p. 149). However, there are some other aspects which show a need of a strategic focus on customer retention, for example, if the corporation:

■ has a generally high churn rate

■ immediately loses numerous new customers

■ achieves cross selling only to a low degree

■ cannot utilise any of the cost savings potential for current relationships

■ has many customers that also use products or services from competitors

However, one has to keep in mind that customer retention *per se* should not be a goal. Every company has customers with different levels of profitability based upon, for instance, their purchase frequency and value. The key objective is thus to retain the maximum number of customers who are profitable, or who demonstrate characteristics which will render them of above average profitability in the future.

Solidarity and dependence strategies can be identified among the **types of customer retention strategies**. A **solidarity strategy** strives for customer retention by means of psychological determinants like relationship quality and customer satisfaction, whereas a **dependence strategy** sets up barriers to switching to achieve customer retention.

When developing the customer retention strategy, it is initially necessary to bear in mind the time horizon for eventual implementation of the strategy. Both the solidarity and dependence strategies could be applied over the short or long term, as depicted by the following examples for each strategy type (Figure 5.3):

- **Short-term dependence strategy**: short-term agreements with customers (e.g. 1-month contract from mobile phone companies)

- **Long-term dependence strategy**: long-term agreements with customers (e.g. 2-year contracts from mobile phone companies)

- **Short-term solidarity strategy**: low-price offers over a short period to build up trust by demonstrating fairness towards the customer

- **Long-term solidarity strategy**: securing a high level of employee retention by having the same customer representatives for familiarity development

A customer retention strategy has the advantage over a new customer acquisition strategy that the corporation and customers already know each other. Due to the experiences already gained in the context of customer retention, past transactions can be used as a basis for handling markets. Additionally, the company can identify current customers more easily than potential ones.

Example 5.1

While there can be a specific need for customer retention, some companies have always cared passionately about customer loyalty. According to Kotler (2000, pp. 47–8), Lexus took a long-term strategy from the beginning as it chose dealers that had demonstrated a high commitment to customer service and satisfaction. The company even communicates to their dealers how much improved customer retention is worth to them in dollars. Constructing a specific model, Lexus can calculate how much each dealership could earn by achieving higher levels of repurchase and service loyalty.

Type of customer retention \ Time horizon	Short-term	Long-term
Dependence	**Short-term dependence strategy** Examples: • Short-term agreements • Volume rebates	**Long-term dependence strategy** Examples: • Long-term agreements • Subscriptions
Solidarity	**Short-term solidarity strategy** Example: • Low price offers • Surprise through gifts	**Long-term solidarity strategy** Example: • Employee retention • Product customisation

Figure 5.3 Types of customer retention strategies

5.2.3 Customer recovery strategy

A **customer recovery strategy** includes the emotional recovery of likely defectors and the actual recovery of lost customers. Such a strategy should be pursued for several reasons. Regaining lost customers can be profitable (Stauss 1997), e.g. these customers show a higher loyalty than before. Furthermore, research by Bain & Company shows that when retaining just five per cent more of the best customers, corporate profits can be boosted 25 to 85 per cent, depending on the industry (Griffin 1999). Primarily, this strategy of customer recovery should be pursued if:

- the firm has a high churn rate
- the firm's mistakes are the cause of this churn rate
- recovery appears to be more profitable than acquiring new customers

Studies show that high customer turnover is a problem that many organisations have to deal with. For instance, the average company in America today loses, at minimum, 20 per cent of its customers every year, while for many companies, customer losses are even higher (Griffin 1999). Among car dealers and internet service providers, customer turnover can be as high as 50 per cent. Among mobile phone companies, customer turnover averages 30 per cent, while newspaper subscriber turnover averages 30 to 50 per cent. Yet, many managers do not even know exactly their own churn rate. As a recent study demonstrates, 1,000 senior managers from America's largest corporations were asked if they knew how many customers they lost per year. While 60 per cent of the respondents said 'no', those who said they knew their defection rates estimated them at 12 per cent or less. In fact, the average company loses about 20 per cent of its customers annually (Griffin 1999).

It is important to decide in general how a **customer recovery strategy** should be pursued. It is necessary to differentiate between the recovery of defecting customers from an emotional perspective and that of already lost customers from a factual perspective. The recovery can either make amends or improvements to address the main problems leading to the defections. Accordingly there are four **types of recovery strategies** (Figure 5.4):

- If by making amends it is possible to avoid termination of a relationship with defecting customers, then a **compensation strategy** is implemented (e.g. replacing damaged products, reimbursements).

- An **improvement strategy** covers subsequent improvements of problems for defecting customers (e.g. repairing damaged products).

- Just as in the case of customer acquisition, if the firm offers to make amends for lost customers it is pursuing a **stimulation strategy** (e.g. discounts on reinstatement of the relationship).

- Just as in the acquisition phase a **persuasion strategy** is likewise undertaken by improving service for lost customers (e.g. the provider promises to meet customer needs)

Type of recovery \ Customer situation	Defecting customers	Lost customers
Restitution	**Compensation strategy** Examples: • Replacement of damaged products • Reimbursements	**Stimulation strategy** Examples: • Rebates • Gifts
Improvement	**Improvement strategy** Example: • Repairing damaged products • Service recovery	**Persuasion strategy** Example: • Adjustment of the product offer • Innovation to meet customer wishes

Figure 5.4 Types of customer recovery strategies

In addition to the customers' status, i.e. defecting versus lost customers, there are other criteria that play a role in the selection of the relevant strategy. A key aspect here is the ability to repair or alter the product or service. In case the product cannot be repaired or altered neither the improvement nor the persuasion strategy can be applied.

A recovery strategy also has an advantage over a new customer acquisition strategy, since the corporation usually knows the customers. This can be clearly shown when looking at sales statistics (Griffin 1999): e.g. the average company has a 60 to 70 per cent probability of selling again to active customers and a 20 to 40 per cent probability of successfully selling to lapsed customers. Contrasting these two statistics with the fact that a company has, on average, only a five to 20 per cent probability of making a successful sale to a new prospect. In addition, marketing costs are generally higher since the number of contacts typically required to turn a prospect into a first-time buyer is much higher than the contacts required to reactivate a lapsed customer. The bottom line is that lost customer recovery represents a substantial investment for any company.

Although it is often particularly easy to identify lost customers, their attractiveness for the firm should be evaluated, e.g. by estimating what a lapsed customer is worth in future purchase potential (Griffin 1999). In many instances customers defect probably because they have inappropriate expectations of the firm and as such are not part of the firm's target group. For such situations the company should focus instead on strategies for new customer acquisition or retention.

Besides the firm's current market situation the sector and hence the **output type** can influence the relevance of individual phase-driven strategies. For customised products and services the significance of individual customers is thus much greater, for example, in the capital investment area than in the consumer goods field. Consequently, customer defections entail higher financial burdens with the result that strategies for customer retention and recovery take on greater significance.

5.3 Business area strategic decisions

5.3.1 Definition of business areas and market coverage

The business areas are defined in order to **develop strategic business units**. Strategic business units are thought constructs that represent a firm's separate, heterogeneous fields of activity that have to fulfil their independent market tasks. The various approaches for business area delineation differ mainly in terms of the number of variables taken into account. Approaches based on a single-dimension (e.g. product) or dual-dimension (e.g. product and region) seldom suffice. Rather, the three-dimensional approach by Abell (1980) provides the basis for differentiating business areas. The corporate activity fields examined are accordingly depicted in a 3-D view. Analysing and combining the features of the following **dimensions**, which need to be adjusted in line with relationship orientation, enables the development of the strategic business units (Figure 5.5):

■ For the **customer groups** dimension a classification is done according to the target groups whose needs could or should be satisfied.

■ For **functional fulfilment** the solutions to be earmarked for these customer groups are specified, i.e. which target group needs are to be fulfilled.

■ Moreover, the business areas can be separated according to the **technologies** with which customer needs should be satisfied. For certain output types like services the term technology within a dimension is to be interpreted very broadly. Here, technology is not a part of the supplier's output but instead an element of the services provision process.

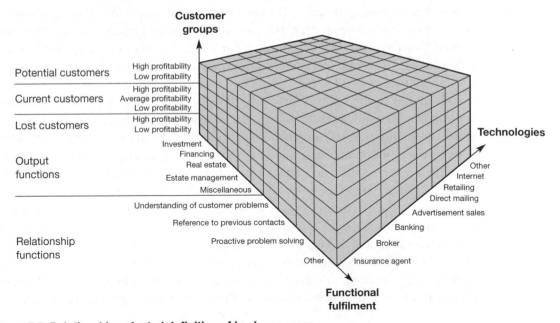

Figure 5.5 Relationship-oriented definition of business areas

The above approach must give greater consideration to relationship orientation. For this purpose, particularly the customer groups and functional fulfilment dimensions offer the means for a stronger relationship focused selection of the business area.

For the **customer groups** dimension it is necessary to employ relationship criteria to identify the customer groups. At first, the customer relationship life cycle can be taken to examine potential customers (acquisition), current customers (retention), and lost customers (recovery). These can be supplemented by utilising additional economic and pre-economic relationship criteria. Owing to relationship marketing's profitability focus the relationship or **customer profitability** plays an important role (Storbacka 1997). The selected criteria can also be applied together such that for each customer group developed on the basis of the customer relationship life cycle, a further breakdown can be made into highly profitable, less profitable, and low or even unprofitable potential, current, and lost customers (Figure 5.5).

Particularly for **output types** that call for high investments by the seller at the start of a relationship, profitability should be a central criterion for separating the business areas. This applies primarily to certain customised products and services. For example, a machinery manufacturer must frequently make special tools to produce customised machines for its customers. In contrast, since a chewing gum producer invests little in specific customer relationships, the profitability based business segment demarcation is of less relevance.

Furthermore, the functional fulfilment dimension can be extended with a relationship component by differentiating at a primary level between transaction and output functions on the one hand and relationship functions on the other. Besides output needs like investments, financing, and real estate in the financial services area, relationship needs such as a reference to earlier customers or the knowledge of customer problems are also taken into consideration. These can be conceptualised in terms of the relationship quality by construing trust and familiarity as the relationship function.

In the light of the relevance of relationship functions, customer risk is pertinent for different **output types**. The higher the risk that a customer incurs in using a particular product the more important it is that he or she be able to trust the seller: i.e. relationship functions will be fulfilled by the seller. Contrasting the commensurate dimensions that have been modified allows the feasible strategic business areas to be identified. Figure 5.6 depicts **examples of strategic business segments** for relationship marketing:

- **Low profitability customers** for whom output functions (product or service-related) are fulfilled by a concentrated application of technologies (e.g. only automated provision of products through dispensing machines and the Internet; strategies of banks to reduce direct contact with less profitable customers through greater use of online banking)
- **Potential customers** offered fulfilment of product functions through differentiated application of technologies (e.g. local offices, telephone banking, internet)

Function \ Application of technologies	Concentrated	Differentiated
Ouput functions	Unprofitable current customers	Potential customers
Output and relationship functions	Lost customers	Profitable current customers

Figure 5.6 Examples of relationship marketing's business segments

■ **Profitable current customers** for whom the application of technologies is enhanced with the personal contact of the seller to satisfy the output and relationship functions (e.g. customer reps to secure familiarity with customers)

■ **Lost customers** for whom output and relationship functions are made available by the concentrated application of technologies such as direct mailing

5.3.2 Market segment strategies

The strategic focus of **market segment strategies** needs to be defined for the selected strategic business segments. On the basis of an output-market matrix one can identify market penetration, market and output development, and diversification strategies (adapted from Ansoff 1966). These general foci have different weightings **depending on the phase-driven strategic decisions** (Figure 5.7).

Market penetration strategy means full utilisation of the potential of existing markets with existing products. All phase-driven strategy types can be applied to market penetration. Through market penetration during acquisition an organisation acquires new customers that have so far used competitors' products. This occurs because the firm can apply its experiences already gained in existing relationships. For customer retention, market penetration involves cross selling of

Outputs \ Markets	Existing	New
Existing	Market penetration • Acquiring new customers from competitors • Cross selling • Recovery	Market development • Gaining new segments • Regional expansion
New	Output development • Cross selling • Switching barriers • Recovery	Diversification • New customer acquisition • Partial cross selling

Figure 5.7 Relationship-focused market segment strategies

products to existing customers that have so far not made use of them. Customers that have already used competitors' products but are not doing so at the moment are re-acquired with the support of a recovery strategy.

Existing products and services are offered and sold in existing and new markets through a **market development strategy**. This involves the winning of new market segments (e.g. upgrading the corporate services for a higher price segment) or the regional extension of business activities. In this way market development exclusively serves to acquire new customers.

An **output development strategy** covers the offering of new products and services in the form of innovations or product palette expansions in existing markets. Within relationship marketing this strategy best suits a customer retention or recovery strategy. To retain customers, output developments can be undertaken for cross selling and for the setting up of switching barriers. These developments also contribute towards recovery, if customers are planning to defect or have defected because the corporate products could not meet their needs comprehensively.

A **diversification strategy** refers to the offering of new products/services in new markets, that is, corporate management reviews opportunities to develop new products to extend the present business (Yip 1982). According to Kotler (2000, p. 75), three types of diversification can be differentiated. The horizontal diversification describes a strategy where new products or services are supposed to appeal to current customers. In case of the concentric diversification-related products are aimed at a different group of customers. The third option is the conglomerate diversification. That is, a company diversifies into completely unrelated product or service areas that have no relationship to the company's current technology or business (e.g. an airline expands by purchasing a car dealership). Diversification primarily supports a new customer acquisition strategy. Beyond that, diversification permits the partial pursuit of a retention strategy if a corporate customer is active in various markets (e.g. a customer purchases a small transporter for her or his small business, the transporter is part of a diversification by a former manufacturer of automobiles only, and this customer currently owns a private car from this very firm).

5.3.3 Competitive advantage strategies

Various strategies exist for gaining competitive advantages over the competition (Figure 5.1). Among these are the classic quality, cost, brand, programme breadth, and innovation strategies. For marketing it is necessary that the appropriate competitive advantages be examined from a **relationship perspective**. This involves three approaches:

1 Pursuit of relationship orientation as the primary competitive advantage

2 Modification of the definitions of competitive advantages by accounting for relationship aspects

3 Matching the application of competitive advantages with the relationship life cycle phase

Relationship orientation as the primary competitive advantage

By aligning the corporate activities with the fundamental ideas of relationship marketing, the key marketing activities should be aimed at achieving a **competitive advantage in relationships**. This implies that besides aligning marketing activities to the relationship life cycle, the firm should establish its relation **leadership market** position – i.e. become the seller with the best customer relationships. Many facets can be applied to specify this position: for example, trust and familiarity as the core relationship quality dimensions complemented by the customer relationship life cycle phases (Figure 5.8). Even if relationship quality is a primary goal in the retention phase, strategies that possess the necessary character for building relationship quality can be implemented during both the customer acquisition and recovery phases.

Accordingly, materialisation of relationship orientation involves **trust building** during the three key relationship life cycle phases in the three dimensions – trustworthiness, reliability, and acceptance of criticism.

In the customer acquisition phase the desired orientation is an outcome of the seller's **trustworthiness** for the customer. Prior to using the seller's products, the customer has no related experience on which to base trust in the firm. Hence, in this phase the firm must seek to undertake suitable activities to attain quality indicators (such as cost versus reputation for a hairdresser's), such that the firm can be trusted even without the necessary experience. Here, one can differentiate between

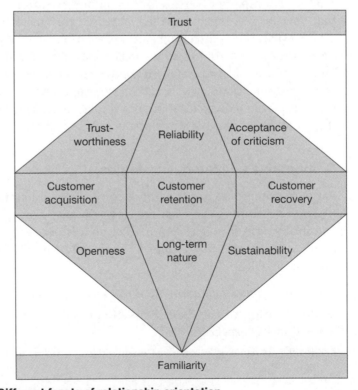

Figure 5.8 Different facets of relationship orientation

personal and impersonal trustworthiness. The impersonal aspect has to do with the customers' trust in the firm as an institution such as a bank, whereas the personal aspect involves trust in the bank's advisor, for example, during the first contact.

Reliability in this context comes into play when the customer already has experience with the firm. This is not associated with purely output reliability, as in the case of product quality dimensions, but rather with the seller's reliability in general. For instance, this could include the customers' trust in the firm's ability to anticipate her or his future needs. It may also involve aspects such as expert tax-advice or medical services that the customer is not knowledgeable about, but ones that would be handled in her or his interests.

In the event that serious problems occur in the buyer-seller relationship, the company's **acceptance of criticism** becomes important for the recovery phase within relationship orientation. The customer must have the feeling that the organisation accepts probable mistakes without seeking to resolve existing conflicts to her or his disadvantage (Czepiel 1990). This can be done, for example, through an active complaint management policy, showing consumers that the company is open to complaints. A critical element here is the ability of the firm to learn how to accept and apply mistakes and the attendant criticism towards future activities. An outstanding example is the Ritz-Carlton, granting its employees considerable latitude in handling problems with its hotel policy.

Similarly, relationship orientation can be materialised through the primary dimension of **familiarity**, which is comprised of a sub-dimension in each of the three relationship life cycle phases. For customer acquisition, familiarity can be supported by broad-based **openness**. The customer thus has the chance to quickly become familiar with the firm, for example, through the availability of numerous communication channels from which to select the most appropriate one. In addition the openness towards the customer indicates the firm's readiness to build up on familiarity in the course of the relationship.

If the customer has already had experiences with the firm in the retention phase, familiarity is consolidated through the **long-term nature** of customer-related corporate activities. All relationship aspects in which a change would lead to deterioration in the relationship are maintained here over the long term. In this way, the firm's customer familiarity is secured through constancy among base aspects such as the same customer representative.

In the recovery phase, **sustainability** is necessary for implementing relationship orientation on the familiarity side. Although this phase often involves compensation for negative aspects that have led to defections, positive aspects of the relationship must nevertheless be maintained. On the one hand, it is easier for the customer to re-establish the relationship. On the other, the firm can achieve cost savings by viewing the break-up as just an interruption and maintaining continuity in the relationship.

The usefulness of relationship orientation as a central competitive advantage can vary depending on the **output type**. Thus, relationship based aspects are decisive for the customer mainly for purchasing of complex outputs that are high-risk bound – as in the case of many customised services such as those of dentists and management consultants.

Relationship orientation of classic competitive advantages

Besides relationship orientation as a general competitive advantage of relationship marketing, other classic competitive advantages can sometimes be strongly relationship focused. This applies to the following competitive advantages:

■ Value orientation

■ Innovation orientation

■ Variety orientation

Quality and cost orientation are the main competitive advantages discussed within traditional marketing. Both these strategies are considered as opposing approaches and applied as outpacing strategies either together or alternately (Gilbert and Strebel 1987). A consistent combination of both competitive advantages can be reached by implementing **value orientation**. The perceived value is relationship marketing's primary target parameter and the first step in achieving relationship quality. A value strategy includes both quality and costs or price from the customer perspective as competitive advantages. As such, the perceived value can be used as a control parameter for the various customer groups ('value-for-money' strategy). Under **innovation orientation** the corporation's purpose is to gain a competitive advantage through its innovation capabilities (Alpert and Kamins 1995). These advantages within a relationship focus can come about in two ways:

■ Relationship-driven output innovation

■ Relationship innovation

Relationship-driven output innovation involves the implementation of relationship aspects for the innovation of core and supplementary outputs. This refers to the provision of innovative services that supplement existing key products depending on customer assertions. For key products, innovation involves the achievement of new types of core outputs to satisfy specific customer needs such as the use of one set for both mobile and conventional phone calls. The outcome of relationship-driven output innovation **impacts performance** on two fronts. One is that the cross selling potential and the customer's greater readiness to pay can be utilised to increase sales. The product offer becomes incomparable with that of competitors through innovative customisation, thereby creating a market of its own for the respective customers. The other is that the innovative process enables reductions in costs, since the customer can contribute to the development process.

Relationship innovation covers innovation that is not directly related to corporate products. This has to do primarily with offers for the customer involving the whole relationship. Examples of relevant measures of such a strategy are cards, magazines, or bonus programmes for certain customers. The early frequent-flyer programmes in the airline industry are examples of such relationship innovation.

A **variety orientation** can also become a competitive advantage that leads to a stronger relationship orientation, in that the corporation's output programme is enhanced by the offers mentioned above. Particularly among airlines, respective components of programme offers represent decisive initial and repeated purchase grounds, since a frequent-flyer membership can play a central role in the reasons for a purchase.

Application of classic competitive advantages in the customer relationship life cycle

In addition to a strengthened relationship orientation as per the definition of classic competitive advantages, these advantages can be differentiated further in terms of their **significance and form in the relationship life cycle phases**. The following orientation types apply to all classic competitive advantages: quality, cost, brand, variety, and innovation (Figure 5.9).

Under **quality orientation** the product and service quality is the most important competitive advantage. This orientation is the aim during the **customer retention phase**. High product quality represents the minimum level from which a relationship can be built up and the retention of customers secured (Boulding *et al.* 1993). Cross selling a follow-on project with a management consulting firm could, for example, strengthen relationships on this basis. Quality orientation has more of an indirect significance for customer acquisition and recovery. In the **customer acquisition phase** the product and service quality has a successful impact as a competitive advantage for potential customers, only if they experience it in ways other than through the firm's output quality. One alternative would be personal communication through friends and acquaintances and impersonal word-of-mouth communication, for instance, through professional articles on automobile tests in magazines (Richins 1983). This promotion enhances the corporation's quality image that could then be the decision criterion for first-time customers. In the **customer recovery phase** product and service problems are the reasons for customer defection processes (Keaveney 1995). Hence, a generally high service quality

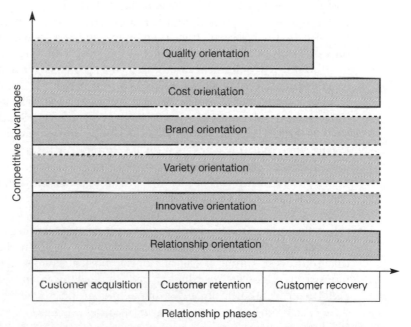

Figure 5.9 Competitive advantages in the customer relationship life cycle phases

is the basis for recovery. Conversely, recovery works only if the customer has trust in the firm's future quality. Accordingly, a relationship orientation is the foremost decisive competitive advantage for recovery.

Cost orientation comes into play as a competitive advantage mainly during customer acquisition and recovery. From the customer perspective, cost orientation in the **customer acquisition phase** forms the basis for a competitive price that is the main first-buy decision criterion in many sectors like raw materials procurement. From a corporate perspective customer relationships are often unprofitable to start with (Reichheld and Sasser 1990). Cost orientation can help to make these relationships profitable as soon as possible through rapid amortisation of the customer acquisition costs. The box 'Insights 5.1: The Low Fare Airline' describes how Southwest Airlines has attracted new customers with its low fares and managed to stay profitable.

Insights 5.1

The Low Fare Airline

Southwest Airlines which is known as a maverick and an innovator in the U.S. airline industry, bills itself as 'the Low Fare Airline'. The company's pricing strategy is to keep all fares consistently low regardless of what the market will bear. Furthermore, the company always offers lower fares than its competitors. For example, when Southwest entered Sacramento in 1991, its everyday fare between Sacramento and Ontario was $118 return compared with $440 for the competition.

One of Southwest Airlines' secret recipes for keeping fares low is cost orientation and a clear focus on serving a specific market niche. That is, the company does not buy jumbo jets or fly international routes. Instead the company serves only point-to-point flights between cities, thereby maximising its use of aircraft. In utilising only one type of aircraft – the Boeing 737 – Southwest is able to keep costs low. First of all, training requirements are simplified as pilots, flight attendants and mechanics concentrate on knowing the 737. Also the whole crew is qualified to the same standard. Thus, the company can substitute aircraft, reschedule flight crews, or transfer mechanics quickly and efficiently. Furthermore, Southwest has reduced its parts inventory and simplified record-keeping, which has also resulted in savings. Finally, the company keeps its business simple. For instance, Southwest has never joined the computer reservations system which is owned by competitors and still does not serve any meals on the flights. Through not subscribing to this system, the company has saved $2 for each segment booked, resulting in millions of dollars a year. And, through only serving peanuts and other snacks, the empty space that would be required for food galleys to permit meal service can be used for extra seats.

While questioning the focus on cost orientation and simplicity, one has to admit that Southwest Airlines is still one of the most profitable companies in the airline industry. Its customers are willing to trade some of the amenities for low fares, on-time performance, and the company's unique ability for positively exceptional service.

(*Source*: based on Freiberg, K. and Freiberg, J. (1996): *NUTS! Southwest Airlines' Crazy Recipe for Business and Personal Strategies.* Austin: Bard Press.)

In the **customer recovery phase**, the effects of prices have two sides. On the one hand, they can be the reason for defections. On the other hand, prices can account for customer returns in form of a compensation for service mistakes. Hence, cost orientation represents a significant competitive advantage. In the **customer retention phase** cost orientation is not very meaningful, since customer relationships are typically self-driven, for example, due to the customer's greater willingness to pay (Reichheld and Sasser 1990). The emphasis in this phase is more on raising revenues.

A **brand orientation** (Aaker 1996) offers a competitive advantage mainly in the customer acquisition phase. In many sectors a customer who has not had any contact with an output does not knowingly look for that brand. A brand thus fulfils various functions like orientation, trust, recognition, or interest awakening at the point of sale (Mintzberg 1988). During the **customer retention and recovery phase** brands take on more functions related to the customers' cognitive dissonance. In the retention phase brands can both confirm and help develop cognitive dissonance. In the recovery phase the brand can remind the customer of the firm and could possibly lead to the emergence of cognitive dissonance resulting in the customer terminating the relationship.

In each of the three customer relationship life cycle phases **variety orientation** also has a competitive advantage, even though it is subordinate to the other leading competitive advantages in each of the phases. In the acquisition phase a broad range of products could be the deciding criterion to buy. In the retention phase raising the range of products or services enables more cross selling. In the recovery phase a lack of the firm's product palette could be a reason for defections. The same applies to **innovation orientation** as a competitive advantage – a less innovative company will encounter long-term problems in acquiring new customers. Besides, deficiencies in a firm's innovative character not only do not help to retain customers but could also be the grounds for defections. A relationship orientation relates to all three of the customer life cycle phases (Chapter 3; Figure 5.9), since it represents an essential basis for customer acquisition, retention, and recovery.

5.4 Market participant strategies in relationship marketing

5.4.1 Overall networking strategy

Among strategies for market participants a networking strategy is the overlapping one (Figure 5.1) within which all market participants such as suppliers, customers, competitors etc. are to be taken into account (Grönroos 2000, p. 300; Gummesson 1994). **Networks** are more or less fixed linkages between these participants pursuing common goals. Examples of the links are **collaborations**, **capital investments**, or **typical business relationships**. The main purpose of setting up a network is to raise efficiency levels. The network members can be located at all stages of a value chain with each taking on a specific task aimed at reaching the mutual targets. The following aspects apply to **network targets**:

- Refraining from activities that neutralise each other
- Avoidance of duplicate activities
- Overcoming of inadequacies in the factor configuration

The main role of networking within relationship marketing is **customer collaboration**. This means striving for more extensive cooperative work with customers than required for simple integration. The collaboration between TV production firms and TV stations is an example of very close cooperation, whereby the TV stations often have a major influence on the production.

Implementation of a network strategy leads to **changed competitive dimensions** of competition between the members of a network as well as among the networks. Between the network members, competition in certain areas like functional or product groups will be replaced through collaborations. In other areas competition between the members can continue as before. Additionally, in the respective markets complete networks as opposed to corporations compete with each other. In this way, individual members have a stronger competitive position compared to their presence alone in the market. A good example of this is the 'Star Alliance' network of 15 airlines (www.star-alliance.com) that competes against the 'Oneworld' network (www.oneworld.com).

The significant **benefit of networks** within relationship marketing's customer focus is in its **acquisition potential** due to cooperation between network members. For example, the following approaches could help utilise members' competencies:

- Acquisition of sales competence through cooperation with the firm best qualified in this area
- Building up of 'lead users', for instance, by developing opinion leaders within the network
- Acquisition of new customers by bringing currently satisfied customers together with potential customers

The pursuit of a network strategy, however, is to a certain extent also associated with **risks**:

- Collective network strategies or the funds assigned for them lead to restrictions in the freedom of choice and strategy flexibility for network members.
- Networks often have a trusting atmosphere promoting a flexible and open exchange of information. This enables potential competitors that are network members of sub-markets not related to the network to receive strategic information on the company involved.
- Furthermore, restructuring the value adding processes within networks can cause disturbances among related processes and also instigate duping due to a shortage of data.
- The close cooperative links within a network and the resulting inflexibility of single firms raises the susceptibility of the whole network to external disruptions.

Example 5.2

Collaborative work between producers, traders, and service providers in the material goods industry is an example of a network. Typical trading tasks in relevant networks are: electronic recording of sales, generation of electronic orders and their transmission, inventory management across networks for inventory optimisation, and transfer of direct deliveries over to central warehouse deliveries. The producer has the following tasks: sales-driven production planning and control, distribution-based packaging arrangements, transmission of electronic shipping tickets, and automatic re-stocking due to the electronically transmitted inventory status. The service provider takes on the following tasks: maintenance of warehouse capacities, acceptance of administrative and organisational tasks for managing the producer and trader warehouses, and the placing and taking of orders on commission.

The firm can improve the quality of its relationships with individuals by focusing on networks for its relationships with various market participants. Customers are particularly dependent on their relationships with other participants. As such, a comprehensive network strategy can contribute markedly towards making relationship marketing successful.

5.4.2 Customer-targeted strategies

Market-handling strategies

Among the **market-handling strategies** that corporations could follow are the **undifferentiated** and **differentiated handling of the market** and the **segment-of-one strategy**. Although these are traditionally established for the whole market, it is realistic and appears reasonable to implement them to match the customer relationship life cycle phase involved (Figure 5.10). Contrary to traditional approaches, this implies that the organisation should meet the requirements for all the three strategies, rather than committing itself totally to just one of them.

Market handling strategy \ Life cycle phase	Customer acquisition	Customer retention	Customer recovery
Undifferentiated market treatment	Mass communication with potential customers	Retention instruments at the whole customer level	Form letters with special offers for relationship resumption
Differentiated market treatment	Target group communication with potential customers	Specific offers for faithful and profitable customers	Online recovery of online customers
Segment-of-one approach	Focused offers for high-potential customers	Product customisation for each single customer	Personal discussions to make a recovery offer

Figure 5.10 Examples of market-handling strategies in the customer relationship life cycle

Under **undifferentiated market handling**, standard products offered are geared to the target group's common needs to meet the typical expectations. Such handling of markets allows the same quality to be maintained under declining costs. In the customer acquisition phase, for example, undifferentiated market handling is possible through mass communication with potential customers via, for example, TV advertisements. In the retention phase, instruments can be applied at the whole customer level (e.g. customer cards). In the recovery phase, for instance, form letters can be sent with special offers for resumption of the relationship.

A **differentiated market handling** gives due consideration to the differences in needs between the firm's various target groups. This differentiation could involve all marketing instruments. In the customer acquisition phase, a differentiated market handling can be implemented through target group communication such as advertisements in magazines directed at the particular groups. In the retention phase specific offers like free coupons can be used for faithful and profitable customers. In the recovery phase a new acquisition of former lost customers is possible, for instance in recovery of online customers.

The **segment-of-one strategy** represents a special form of differentiated market handling, whereby the marketing activities are aimed at individual customer needs. For each customer a differentiated relationship marketing approach is undertaken (personalisation). In the customer acquisition phase, focused offers can be designed for high-potential customers. In the retention phase product customisation for each individual customer becomes feasible. In the recovery phase personal discussions facilitate the drawing-up of recovery offers.

While the concept of mass customisation has already been discussed in the literature for more than a decade (e.g. Pine 1993; Mueller-Heumann 1992; Kotler 1989), increased practical implementation of this strategy can been found only in the last few years (Piller 2000). While the lack of sufficient technologies to handle the information flows connected with mass customisation have been the primary reason for this time lag, new **internet technologies** will be the main enabler for mass customisation in the future. The development of the Internet has given manufactures a platform for taking orders from a mass audience at almost no expense. For instance, more and more consumer markets offer customised products via the world wide web (www), such as cycles, clothes, cosmetics, or shoes (Agrawal, Kumaresh and Mercer 2001).

Relationship handling strategies

In addition to handling markets, companies can generally also pursue various relationship handling strategies at the individual customer level, whereby a separate decision is made on the strategy that should be followed for each particular relationship. Therefore, this concerns the strategic focus of relationship marketing for individual customer relationships. Two **fundamental types of relationship treatment** can be differentiated (Figure 5.11).

1 Active relationship handling
2 Reactive relationship handling

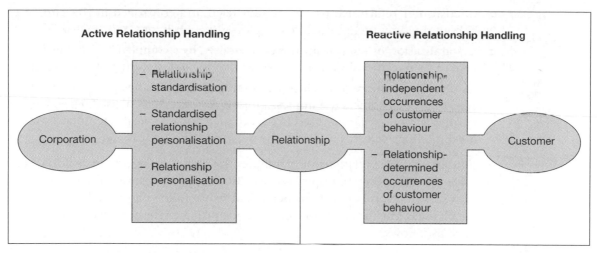

Figure 5.11 Fundamental types of relationship handling

Active relationship handling means that firms are permanently involved in controlling their customer relationships. One indicator of such active involvement could be the planning of customer relationships covering the setting of definitive targets such as customer sales that must be reached for each relationship within a given time period. If these goals are not achieved, the customer is allocated to a less actively handled customer/relationship segment. Three fundamental **strategies** can be identified depending on the **degree of personalisation of the customer relationship** (Figure 5.12 lists a number of sample companies that provide personalised products and services over the Internet):

Customised Products	Companies
Clothing	Land's End, Incredible Clothing, Levi
Automobiles	Smart Car
Computers	Dell, HP, Compaq, Apple
eBooks	Gemstar eBook, Glassbook
Golf Clubs	Golf-to-Fit, Chip Shots
Greeting Cards	Hallmark, Blue Mountain
News	MyCNN, MyYahoo
Shoes and Orthotics	Active Feet Orthotics, Doctor Foot, Nike, customatix
Watches	ewatchfactory
Weather	Weather Channel
Wine	Wine.com

Figure 5.12 Companies providing personalised products and services

- All **customer relationships are standardised** and controlled in the same way, without dividing them into different groups (e.g. A, B, or C customers).

- **Personalisation of relationships** is characterised by a completely individual alignment of each relationship. The company acts fully in line with customer needs.

- **Standardising the relationship personalisation** means designing the relationships to give customers the impression that they are personalised. However, the personalisation is standardised in accordance with a specific template such as direct mailings adjusted to match the needs of various customer groups.

In contrast to active relationship handling, the company resorts to **reactive relationship** handling only to respond to specific occurrences during the relationship. The base assumption here is that each relationship follows a normal course. If the course changes, the firm controls the relationship. The relevant occurrences can be grouped as follows:

- **Relationship-independent occurrences**: The course of the relationship can be affected by events that are not related to the customer relationship. These could mainly be in customer attributes that have changed in the course of a relationship. These attribute changes could be either positive or negative, as in the case of a bank customer's salary rise or job loss. The firm then alters its activities towards the customer (e.g. cross selling actions after a salary increase versus a reduced credit limit in the case of joblessness).

- **Relationship-determined occurrences**: Aspects directly connected to the relationship can influence its course. Here too, the occurrences can be positive and negative, as for successful completion of a management consulting project versus losses resulting from the recommendations of the consulting project. In such cases, depending on the occurrence the firm undertakes appropriate measures such as cross selling following a successful project versus compensation payments for losses incurred due to the advice given.

Generally, the type of relationship handling must not be specified. Thus, the two strategy types can either be switched over time or depending on the specific customer attributes such as profitability, different strategies can be applied to different customer groups.

5.4.3 Competitor, sales agent, and business environment targeted strategies

Even though customer relationships are the main focus of relationship marketing, corporations should also direct their strategic concept based behaviour towards the other **stakeholders** represented by the competitors, sales agents, and the business environment.

Competitor-targeted strategies

The seller's specific behaviour towards its main competitors is defined within a **competitor targeted behavioural strategy**. Competitor targeted strategies are systematised on the basis of two dimensions:

- The first dimension distinguishes between the firm's **innovative** (active) and **imitative** (mainly passive) **behaviour** (Murray 1984; Miller and Friesen 1982).

- The second dimension distinguishes between competitor evasive and competitor confronting behaviour. For this purpose every criterion discussed in the literature on offensive and defensive or proactive and reactive aspects could be applied (Easton 1987).

The following four **competitor targeted behavioural strategies** can be derived by combining the above two dimensions:

- Management contracts, joint ventures, and licenses are examples of a **cooperation strategy** (passive/competitor confronting). The instrument of functionally specific joint ventures is very significant in the airline and telecommunications industries (Porter and Fuller 1989).

- A **conflict strategy** (active/competitor confronting) is linked primarily to the goal of winning market share and possibly attaining market leadership as in the telecommunications industry through adoption of aggressive behaviour distinctly different from that of the competitor.

- An **evasion strategy** (active/competitor evasive) is characterised by an attempt to overcome competitive pressure through enhanced innovative activities compared with the competition (e.g. innovative online offer).

- **Adjustment strategies** (passive/competitor evasive) are aimed at holding on to the product-market position achieved. One's own behaviour follows the competitor's reaction (e.g. price reductions in the petrol filling station market to match each move by a neighbouring competitor).

Sales-agent-targeted strategies

In certain segments, besides strategies aimed at the competition, **sales-agent targeted-strategies** must be formulated to cover the firm's global behavioural plans towards its sales agents.

By combining the seller's behavioural activity/passivity dimensions in designing the sales channels with the sales agents' activity/passivity in reaction to the seller's activities, one can identify the following **sales-agent-targeted strategies**:

- A corporation can remain passive in organising its sales channels. If it also agrees to possible trade demands without opposition, then one speaks of an **adjustment strategy**.

- A **circumvention strategy** involving the development of one's own sales network to bypass existing sales agents is the most costly and risk-bound. Furthermore, some firms have opted for output sales exclusively over **direct sales** channels such as the Internet. These are also a part of a circumvention strategy, since it is clear that in certain segments the line between competitor and sales-agent-targeted strategies is not very distinct.

- In contrast, a **cooperation strategy** provides for contractually specified performance like the presentation of a particular tour operator's offer by travel offices.

■ A **conflict strategy**, on the other hand, arises if the seller takes on an active role in organising existing sales channels and attempts to push its notions through against the interests of the sales agent.

Business-environment-targeted strategies

Relationship marketing is also directed at additional stakeholders of the corporation such as politics, the society, or the financial markets. These groups are subsumed under the company's business environment. The following **strategy types** are a part of this environment:

■ An **innovation strategy** is designated by the firm's proactive behaviour. Social claims are addressed through initiation at an early stage, and innovative solutions are developed (e.g. movie advertisements by Smirnoff that use solely blurred images – symbols – that have been altered to meet future advertising bans for alcohol).

■ If a company uses an **adjustment strategy** it means a wait-and-see attitude. The company reacts only if it has no other option open as in the case of a dismissal of the football coach by the association due to strong demands by the fans.

■ Under a **resistance strategy** the corporation continues with its current behaviour by not making any effort to solve a problem, as done by the tobacco industry's opposition to the knowledge that smoking is dangerous to one's health.

■ Through the **circumvention strategy** the firm seeks to withdraw from social demands by somehow displacing the problem and attempting deception (e.g. moving genetic research to another country because of restricting laws in the home country).

■ A **retreat strategy** goes even further by giving up a business area completely due to social pressure (e.g. abandoning trips into ecologically sensitive regions as part of a tour operator's programme).

■ Under a **passive strategy** the company does not react at all to accusations made by social groups.

5.5 Assessment of strategic relationship marketing

Relationship marketing can be implemented systematically only if it is based on an appropriate strategic concept – otherwise it will get lost in a myriad of single actions. In practice then, one can identify three groups of firms. Some corporations can be called **natural relationship managers** since they set up their marketing activities aimed at customer relationships very early in the game. Such firms are usually in the B2B-market where networking ideas and associated relationship orientation, for instance, matured very early. Consequently, systematic relationship management is seldom implemented in these segments.

Another group of firms can be described as **selectors**. These companies establish single relationship marketing concepts such as CLV measures, complaint management, and quality management, but without integrating them under an overall relationship marketing concept. Such cases can be identified in the financial services sector where relationship marketing is implemented for certain target groups like wealthy private clients. In this area a **strategic lack of orientation** can nevertheless be seen, since there is no strategy to be found for dealing with the currently non-profitable small customers that make up a large share of the total demand in terms of numbers.

One can also find **incognisants** in the field of relationship marketing. This group of corporations focuses primarily on transactions and implements barely any relationship orientation. An example can be found in the telecommunication industry where companies are involved in various countries in a pure pricing competition. Even though the conditions are similar to those in the banking sector (that is, membership type relationships), only few relationship marketing approaches can be recognised in this segment.

Relationship marketing's imperfection is reflected by the **literature**, which offers few relevant comprehensive strategic concepts. The respective discourses are based either on theories such as the correlation between customer satisfaction and their retention, or relate to instrument-based methodologies such as the CLV. Consequently, the development of a strategic relationship marketing concept needs to be addressed as the primary field of research. On the basis of the theoretical knowledge of customer relationships, a framework must be attained to enable structuring of the individual relationship marketing instruments discussed above.

Summary

This chapter has addressed the strategic focus of relationship marketing. After introducing five requirements for developing strategies in relationship marketing, three main strategic areas were covered: strategies on basis of the customer relationship life cycle, business area strategies, and market participant strategies. Strategies that are based on the customer relationship life cycle can be differentiated according to customer acquisition, customer retention, and customer recovery. For each case we developed portfolios which clearly mark specific strategic options for an organisation. When pursuing business area strategies we can differentiate strategic options as follows: market segment strategies and competitive advantage strategies. These two options were described in more detail. Finally, we looked at market participant strategies where we elaborated on five specific strategic options which can be followed for addressing customers, competitors, the sales agent, and the business environment.

Relationship marketing in practice

Overview This chapter deals with the instruments which organisations can use to apply relationship marketing in practice. We first introduce a new systematisation of relationship marketing's operational instruments that differs from the traditional marketing mix. Following our perspective of relationship marketing, we consider the customer relationship life cycle as a new dimension for structuring relationship marketing instruments. Besides these phase-driven instruments we show that organisations also have to apply some phase-overlapping instruments. As these instruments support relationship management independent from the life cycle phases, they have to be planned separately. Thus, we will address the following questions in this chapter:

➤ When structuring the relationship marketing mix according to the understanding of the customer relationship life cycle, what are the specific instruments that can be applied in the initiation, socialisation, growth, maturity, imperilment, termination, and abstinence phase?

➤ Besides these phase-driven instruments which instruments can be applied that are phase-independent?

6.1 New structure of marketing instruments

The classic one-dimensional structuring of marketing instruments according to the marketing mix is applied in practice because it is comprehensible. However, it has some disadvantages because of its undifferentiated treatment of corporate customers. Among these are aspects like marketing's product-oriented focus based on the marketing mix and the isolation of marketing activities in a particular department (see section 1.1 for a detailed discussion).

Structuring marketing instruments for **designing relationship-focused marketing** is possible not only according to the marketing mix but also in terms of the customer relationship life cycle phases as a second dimension. It appears meaningful to use approaches from all the marketing mix areas in the various relationship phases. Accordingly, based on the customer life cycle attributes and requirements, it is necessary to establish specific marketing mix related actions that can be applied to fulfil the tasks in each phase (Figure 6.1). These **phase-driven relationship controlling instruments** can be divided into three core areas:

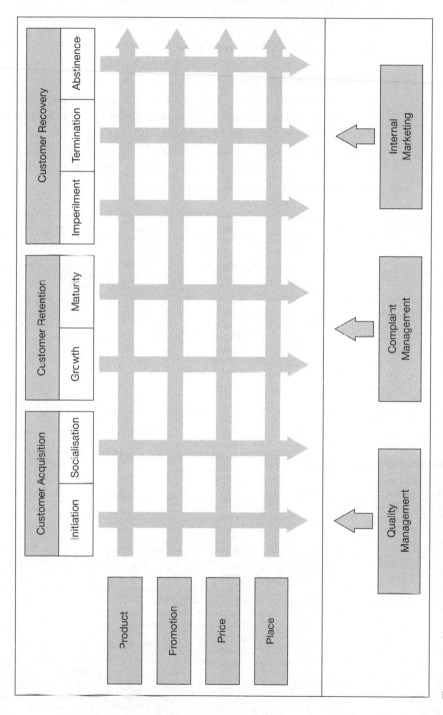

Figure 6.1 Systematisation of relationship marketing's operational instruments

1 Customer acquisition management instruments

2 Customer retention management instruments

3 Customer recovery management instruments

Figure 6.2 depicts an **overview** of typical instruments for the above-referenced areas addressed individually in the following sections.

The intent of relationship marketing in practice is not to replace the traditional marketing mix but instead to **restructure the instruments**. The specific application is dependent on the customer relationship life cycle phases and it attains changes ranging from a minor shift in emphasis through to a high relationship focus. Phase-independent instruments are additionally necessary for developing, designing, and intensifying customer relationships. These **phase-independent relationship-supporting instruments** are currently aimed at the following areas (Figure 6.1):

Attributes	Initiation	Socialisation	Growth	Maturity	Imperilment	Termination	Abstinence
Tasks	● Persuasion ● Stimulation	● Acclimatisation	● Customisation ● Cross selling	● Switching barriers ● Efficiency improvement	● Error rectification ● Restitution	● Persuasion (Creating added value) ● Stimulation (Recovery offer)	
Product	● Quality guarantees ● After sales service ● Product tests ● Product standardisation ● Package deals	● Keeping the same customer representative	● Customer integration ● Value-added services ● Programme palette expansion	● Bundling of products ● Product standardisation	● Product improvement ● Substitute product	● Product customisation ● Taking on the handling of transaction formalities	
Promotion	● Product-based promotion ● Control of direct recommendations ● Public relations ● Promoting communication between customers ● Direct mailings	● Customer training ● Service numbers ● Events	● Customer newletters ● Customer club ● Customer workshops	● Exclusive promotion ● Online promotion	● Customer training ● Gifts	● Exclusive promotion ● Customised promotion	
Price	● Price as a quality indicator ● Special sales ● Pricing transparency ● Discounts	● Constant prices	● Pricing differentiation ● Value-based pricing ● Package deals ● Customer cards linked with discounts	● Customer card linked with discounts ● Taking advantage of willingness to pay	● Price reductions	● Price reductions ● Cash payment	
Place	● Choice of location	● Constancy in distribution	● Flexible distribution systems ● Distribution customisation	● Distribution diversity ● Distribution standardisation	● Distribution improvement ● Distribution presents	● Distribution customisation ● Reimbursement of distribution costs	

Figure 6.2 Relationship marketing instruments in the customer relationship life cycle phases

1 Quality management instruments

2 Complaint management instruments

3 Internal customer orientation instruments

6.2 Phase-driven relationship controlling instruments

6.2.1 Customer acquisition management instruments

To control customer relationships the marketing instruments can be applied on the basis of the customer relationship life cycle phases. The instruments for customer acquisition, retention, and recovery can accordingly be divided broadly as follows. The key customer acquisition phase is divided into the **initiation phase** and the **socialisation phase** such that the marketing instrument applied enables management of both phases.

Initiation phase management

In the **initiation phase** the seller and buyer have had no contact yet with each other. The firm seeks to establish contact to win her or him as a customer and to initiate a relationship. In this phase, marketing consequently is faced with the following main **tasks** from which the measures to be undertaken can be derived:

a **Customer persuasion**: a potential customer probably receives a whole range of information on a particular product from different sellers. Commonly, due to the customer's information asymmetry compared to the seller's, the former often finds it very difficult to comprehend the data received. Hence, the firm should attempt to convince the customer that its products could best satisfy her or his needs.

b **Customer stimulation**: furthermore, it is necessary to stimulate the customer to use the seller's product. If a customer is convinced of the output's pertinence, he or she must be given an incentive to contact the firm and try the products or services at least once.

(a) Customer persuasion

Persuading the customers can be ensured through various product, price, promotion, and place policy related actions. Since the intent of this phase is to prove the firm's capability to satisfy customer needs, the relevant actions relate primarily to the **management of expectations**. Guiding the customers' expectations provides them with a better idea of the outputs offered. In this way, **marketing's 'inside-out' perspective can be converted to an 'outside-in' perspective**. For this purpose, the use of both push and pull promotion is particularly important to persuade the customers. Under push promotion the company voluntarily provides the information, whereas under pull promotion the information is provided if and when the customer requests it. This strongly supports the perspective change mentioned above.

In addition to the promotion policy, tasks have to be addressed in other instrument areas as well (e.g. through bundling of products or price guarantees).

It is feasible to convince the customer either directly or indirectly. For direct persuasion the output is at the core of the company's activities. These activities can be broken down further depending on whether they occur in the form of an assurance by the firm or come as a recommendation more or less from an independent third party. Since recommendations do not originate directly from the firm, appropriate actions are needed to stimulate recommendations by third parties. By comparing the two dimensions the persuasion activities can be structured to enable differentiation of the following four possible **instrument groups** for convincing the customer (Figure 6.3):

1 Direct assurances

2 Indirect assurances

3 Direct substantiation of recommendations

4 Indirect substantiation of recommendations

Organisations utilise direct assurances to inform the customer of product and service related aspects such as **quality guarantees** that are supposed to be convincing evidence of the firm's relevant capabilities (for additional reading, see Ostrom and Hart 2000; Moorthy and Srinivasan 1995; Hart 1993). These guarantees are assurances that the company will make every effort to meet the potential customer's expectations and will provide appropriate reimbursement in case of default. Figure 6.4 illustrates some examples of individual corporate quality guarantees in different segments (for more examples, see Kotler 2000, p. 448). The organisation makes use of guarantees as a means to indicate that it itself is won over by the products and hopes thereby to similarly convince the customer. Generally, customers should find guarantees clearly stated and easy to act upon, and the company's redress should be quick (Kotler 2000, p. 448). Otherwise consumers will be dissatisfied,

Content \ Directness	Direct	Indirect
Assurance	**(1) Direct assurances** Examples: • Quality guarantees • Output-based promotion	**(2) Indirect assurances** Examples: • After sales services • Price as a quality indicator
Recommendation substantiation	**(3) Direct substantiation of recommendations** Example: • Product tests • Recommendations	**(4) Indirect substantiation of recommendations** Example: • Public relations • Promoting communication between customers

Figure 6.3 Persuasion instruments in the initiation phase

Segment	Corporation	Guarantee
Parcel services	FedEx	Next day delivery, absolutely, positively by 10:30 am
Office equipment	XEROX	If a customer is dissatisfied with any Xerox equipment, it is replaced free of charge
Hotel	Hampton Inn Motels	Unconditional 100% Satisfaction Guarantee, that is, if a customer is not completely satisfied with his stay at a Hampton Inn hotel, he does not have to pay
Food services	Domino's Pizza	Guaranteed 30-munute delivery on telephone orders for pizza, late-arriving pizzas are free (later amended to $3 off the order)
Automobile	Rover	If the customer is dissatisfied with a new vehicle purchase, it may be returned within the first 1,000 km for a full refund
Insurance	Delta Dental Plan	Seven separate guarantees are given covering accessibility of personnel, problem-free billing, punctuality of reimbursements, etc.
Machinery	Westinghouse	A project manager's guarantee is issued for the duration, deadlines, costs, and on informing internal customers on project progress

Figure 6.4 Examples of quality guarantees

which can lead to a bad word-of-mouth reputation being spread, or, even worse, a potential lawsuit as in the case of Domino's Pizza. The company had to cancel its guarantee when a St. Louis court awarded $78 million to a woman who had been struck by a speeding Domino driver in 1989 (Kotler 2000, p. 448).

Direct assurances are also possible through **output promotion**. Above all, companies seek to assure the customer of their products and services through advertisements and also through sales channels like representatives, for example, or through a website on the Internet (George and Berry 1981). If the firm succeeds in bringing these promotion activities across as being trustworthy the customer can be persuaded accordingly.

Some companies offer an extraordinary promise setting them apart from their competition. Considering different types of products quality guarantees are easier to formulate and meet for standardised products. For instance, A.T. Cross guarantees its Cross pens and pencils for life. When the pen is posted to A.T. Cross, it is repaired or replaced at no charge (Kotler 2000, p. 448). Conversely, guarantees for complex products or services are often symbolic ones like the 'unconditional 100% Satisfaction Guarantee' given at Hampton Inn Hotels (Figure 6.5). The promotion also depends on the type of product involved. The more intangible the product or service, the greater the difficulty in communicating concrete attributes. In these cases, symbolic assurances like exclusivity of sales channels are frequently utilised just as for services.

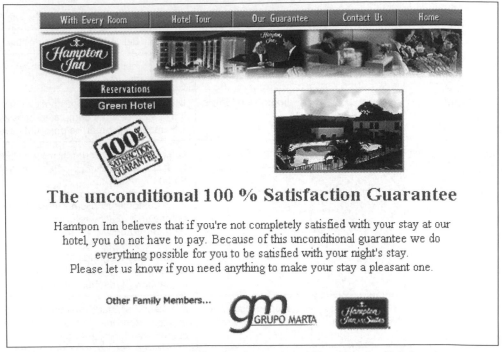

Figure 6.5 Unconditional 100% Satisfaction Guarantee at Hampton Inn Hotels
(*Source*: www.hamptonhotel.co.cr/guarantee.html, accessed on May 22, 2001)

For **indirect assurances** the output itself is not the central facet of persuasion. Hence, the customer must be convinced of the firm's product capability through other aspects of the offer. Indirect assurances can be made in the form of **output-independent promotion** such as the sponsoring of events or use of famous, believable and trustworthy personalities in testimonial advertising to persuade the customers of the firm's exclusivity and its products.

Example 6.1

According to an article from USA Today, the decision of Michael Jordan, who is viewed as one of the world's premiere athletes, to return to the NBA has set off a 'flurry of soul-searching among corporate sponsors, who pay him an estimated $40 million a year to pitch their products' (McCarthy 2001). Sponsors are rolling out new ads to piggyback on the hype surrounding Michael Jordan's return. For instance, MCI, an operating unit of WorldCom, which is a provider of residential voice, advanced messaging and commercial telecommunications services in the USA, scheduled to air a humourous 1-800-COLLECT TV-spot showing Jordan in which he tries out new hairstyles – deciding to stay with his familiar bald-headed look. 'Stick with the original' he tells viewers with a grin (McCarthy 2001). As a result, Jordan's TV-spot might convince customers to keep their relationship with MCI instead of switching to other providers. The box 'Insights 6.1 Marketers jump with Michael Jordan's return' describes some more examples in detail.

Another option for output-independent promotion can be found on the Internet, e.g. companies offering the participation in online computer games (see, for instance, Kellogg's website www.cocopops.co.uk). A corporation also applies **after-sales services** to try and convince the customer of its products with offers such as free delivery or repair services. Just as for quality guarantees, by offering such services the firm attempts to express the fact that – although it anticipates no problems – it would look after its customers if something did happen. Indirect assurances can be articulated also through the price level. As the price itself often represents a standard for the customers to measure the quality expected, a company can use the **price as a quality indicator**.

Insights 6.1

Marketers jump with Michael Jordan's return

Since the news of Michael Jordan's return in the NBA not only "hero-starved" basketball fans are becoming excited. According to an article from Davide Dukcevich, Forbes.com, investors too have a reason to celebrate. While the biggest single beneficiary is likely to be Nike, it is assumed that other companies will see a similar boost, for instance, sports clothing and footwear retailers such as Sports Authority or Foot Locker as well as television. In the case of Nike, Jordan's impact is supposed to add $170 million in sales to the Beaverton-based firm in the next six months (just on U.S. footwear). Nike might even start selling a new Jordan trainer. However, according to John Shanley, Wells Fargo Van Kasper's Nike analyst, retailers would not have a hard time selling it, even though the new Jordan trainer could cost about $200, thus making it the most expensive trainer ever. Similar effects are likely for other sportsgoods retailers. As Dukcevich puts it, 'inspired fans will buy more basketballs, hoops and socks'. Third winner is supposed to be television, as networks might see a boost of attracting new or lost viewers. For instance, ESPN might be able to attract lost fans, turning again into SportsCenter to watch basketball highlights.

Source: based, in parts, on an article from Forbes.com. See for more information Dukcevich, D. (2001): 'The Michael Jordan Portfolio', Forbes.com, September 28, 2001, www.forbes.com/2001/09/28/0928jordan.html (accessed on May 28, 2002).

Owing to **differences in output types**, output-independent promotion is utilised primarily for customised outputs due to the difficulty in assessing and being able to comprehend them. After-sales services are relevant mainly for customised products/services, because of the latter's complexity. Although after-sales services are not needed for standardised products, they are nevertheless included partly to homogenise the products and to gain competitive advantages. Largely due to the great difficulty in judging customised outputs the price becomes the key quality indicator.

Direct substantiation of recommendations refers to the support of direct recommendations of the firm's products to potential customers by third parties, i.e. third parties are called upon directly to emphasise the firm's products. This can, for example, occur through **consumer tests** as seen in articles put out by magazines.

Example 6.2	In the USA, **Consumer Reports** is an example of a comprehensive source for unbiased advice about products and services, personal finance, health and nutrition, and other consumer concerns. Published by Consumers Union, an independent, non-profit testing and information organisation, the print magazine 'Consumer Reports' and the online edition 'Consumer Reports Online' (www.consumerreports.org) have been informing the public about test results since 1936. Their goal is to protect the consumer. In Germany, a similar magazine is published by the independent organisation **Stiftung Warentest** which was founded in 1964. Its goal is to protect market transparency through testing and informing the public about 'objective features' of products and services.

If the company's products and services fare better than those of the competitors, then customers are more likely to become convinced. **Recommendations by actual customers** using word-of-mouth communication with friends, acquaintances, and colleagues achieve the same effect (Haywood 1989; Richins 1983). Hence, firms should request current customers to recommend its products and services to others through promotional measures such as advertising displays in hairdressing salons, direct communication through sales representatives or over the Internet.

Example 6.3	The IT company Novell offers on its homepage a showcase of success stories from its customers worldwide. In the current spotlight, Troy Aswege, Assistant Vice President of Information Systems Noridian Mutual Insurance Company which is the largest healthcare provider in the state of North Dakota, USA, states that '... We have complete confidence in the Novell solution.' Each success story illustrates how Novell's products can help one's own company to succeed. This way, Novell has developed a tool to inform potential customers about the company's products which are also recommended by actual customers. Figure 6.6 illustrates this innovative way of promoting customer success stories online.

Under **indirect substantiation of recommendations** third parties are not called upon directly to recommend the product to others. However, the appropriate conditions are created such that professional or private persons making recommendations have reasons to stress the firm's products and services to potential customers. This could take place through relevant **public relations**, whereby experts affiliated with professional journals are kept updated on the company's activities. Fundamentally, **securing a high level of quality with current customers** ensures positive word-of-mouth communication by them. **Promoting communication between customers** through forums or bulletins on the Internet, for instance, also supports recommendations.

As a result of **differences in output types** tests of standardised products are easier to understand. Nevertheless, recommendations are generally a decisive purchasing decision factor for customised outputs irrespective of whether they come

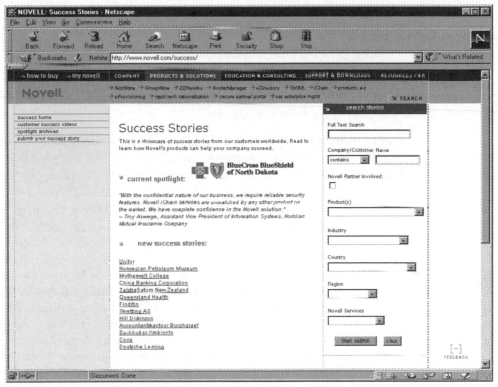

Figure 6.6 Promoting customer success stories over the Internet
(*Source*: www.novell.com/success, accessed on January 11, 2002)

from acquaintances or expert test reports. This is due to the difficulty of judging such outputs, with the result that a potential customer is more likely to follow a recommendation than a promotion by the firm.

Finally, with respect to persuading customers it is worth mentioning that companies should attempt to find out the extent of the persuasion need that exists among various customer groups. This will help to avoid overloading certain customers with corporate promotional activities. Based on these analyses, it is possible to develop a **persuasion strategy** founded on the various dimensions involved.

(b) Customer stimulation

In addition to convincing customers, firms must stimulate them to use their products and services in the initiation phase. The relevant measures for **stimulating customers** could be either short-term or long-term in nature. Short-term ones serve to generate single transactions (e.g. through sales promotion at the point-of-sale). Long-term ones are aimed at multiple transactions between the customer and the firm and are oriented towards developing a customer relationship. The stimulus can be direct or indirect. Direct stimulation means contacting the customer directly on using the product. For indirect stimulation, on the other hand, the necessary conditions are achieved to encourage the customer to buy the product (e.g. assurance of ubiquity). Accordingly, a possible structure of stimulation measures can lead to identification of the following **instrument groups** (Figure 6.7):

1 Direct short-term stimulation

2 Indirect short-term stimulation

3 Direct long-term stimulation

4 Indirect long-term stimulation

Direct short-term stimulation (Field I) involving a single transaction means directly urging the customer to buy the product. This could be accomplished through a **special sale** often covering an offer of good value on the company's products over a limited time. This is seen frequently in the form of short-term stimulation particularly on the internet, for instance, at Amazon.com. **Direct mailings** work similarly in that the customer is specifically encouraged to use certain products.

| Example 6.4 | Direct mailings are becoming increasingly interesting for online retailers (etailers). Several etailers, particularly Buy.com and 800.com, have resorted to significant offline promotions and direct mail campaigns to acquire new customers, while using email and other online forms of advertising for customer retention only. For instance, 800.com is distributing two million cards promising a rebate of $20 for a purchase on its website through its relationship with Heineken and Amstel Light. Furthermore, the etailer is dropping one million 54-page catalogues promoting its products. Buy.com is raising the stakes further, mailing out ten million catalogues, including seven million to non-customers.

(*Source*: Lindsay 2002) |

Indirect short-term stimulation (Field II) does not push the customer to immediately take the output but instead manages to set up the conditions under which the customer can be stimulated to do so at least for certain products. For instance, **output standardisation** is conducive to judgment of the products by the customer

Directness / Duration	Direct	Indirect
Short-term	(1) Direct short-term stimulation Examples: • Special sales • Direct mailings	(2) Indirect short-term stimulation Examples: • Product standardisation • Transparent pricing system
Long-term	(3) Direct long-term stimulation Example: • Discounts • Package deals	(4) Indirect long-term stimulation Example: • Location choice • Customisation potential

Figure 6.7 Stimulation instruments in the initiation phase

and for their marketing. Should the customer be stimulated by the product itself, standardised ones could help move the customer towards using it. The same applies to a **transparent pricing system**. In cases where a customer does not understand the pricing the decision to buy becomes difficult for her or him.

In view of output-related differences it is easier to standardise products with a lower level of complexity and heterogeneity. This also applies to transparent pricing, which is easier to implement for simpler products.

Direct long-term stimulation (Field III) is aimed at urging potential customers to start a relationship with the firm immediately by either using one product several times or by choosing several products. This can be implemented by offering discounts, which means that price reductions will be given for products or services that are used several times. Offering package deals is another way to stimulate customers to enter into a relationship.

Example 6.5	The Swiss Federal Railways, SBB, offers special travel tickets called 'Snow'n'Rail' to 30 ski resorts in the Alps. These tickets include a return train ticket as well as a full-day lift pass. Thus, customers do not have to buy their lift ticket at the destination. Instead of standing in queues at the ticket office, these travellers can take the ski lift straight away. Overall, this type of package deal has been very well received by SBB's passengers.

Differences in types of outputs result in discounts being offered mainly for standardised outputs, because a rebate here is easier to comprehend. On the other hand, package deals for customised products make sense since they often cover a broader spectrum.

Through **indirect long-term stimulation** (Field IV) one manages to set up the requirements that enable the customer to enter into a relationship with the firm by being able to make use of the outputs numerous times. This could be achieved by **location choices** provided in line with the place policy. The chances of a multiple selection of a product by the customer are higher, the better the location suits the customer. A good **internet offer** could be equally relevant. The **potential for customising** the seller's products can also contribute to the seller being sought out. The choice of locations is particularly relevant in the case of customisation because of the **various types of outputs** involved. This applies especially, for example, to services where the customer must be at the seller's location during the delivery process. By the same token customised services have a higher potential for customisation due to their heterogeneity.

Socialisation phase management

The **socialisation phase** commences when the seller and buyer come in contact with each other for the first transaction. The course of the upcoming relationship is set in this phase. The corporation's goal must be to introduce the customers to the products and services so they become familiar with them and are unlikely to defect directly. One task of the socialisation phase is also to **acclimatise the customer**.

Acclimatisation measures ensure that the customer gets used to handling the product, which helps to avoid problems during its use.

The acclimatisation activities could be related more or less directly to the product itself. For actions with a direct relation the output itself is the central acclimatisation aspect. Measures with indirect relevance to the output involve aspects that are tangential to it. As a result, the following two **instrument groups** can be identified in **the socialisation phase**:

1 Acclimatisation directly through the output
2 Acclimatisation indirectly through the output

Acclimatisation directly through the output serves to acclimatise the customer to the firm's products. The intent is to familiarise the customer with them and to help her or him with any possible problems. **Customer training** could be undertaken to explain its use to the customer. On the Internet one often finds similar training-like measures, as in the case of a demo-version of an online banking programme at Home Federal Bank (see Figure 6.8).

Additionally, **personal customer representatives** are deployed to get the customer used to the product, thereby speeding up building familiarity. **Service lines** or hotlines can also help to alleviate problems with products, thus easing their application. Finally, the **Internet** has become a popular tool for companies commonly offering answers to frequently asked questions (FAQs). While Figure 6.9

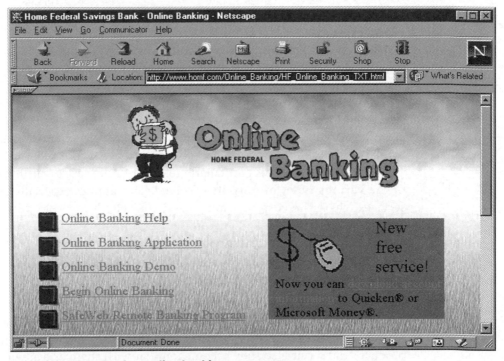

Figure 6.8 Example of an online banking programme

(*Source*: www.homf.com, accessed on May 16, 2002)

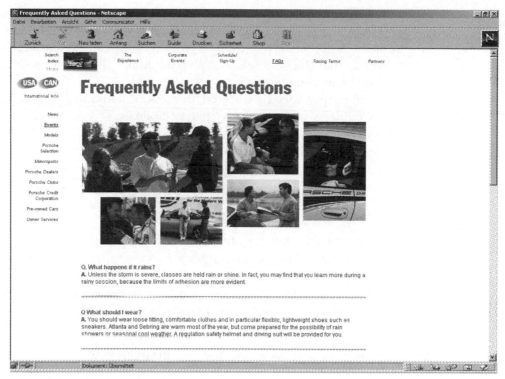

Figure 6.9 Example of FAQs
(*Source*: www.porschedriving.com/faqs.html, accessed on May 16, 2002)

illustrates such an example found on the Porsche website, the following example demonstrates how FAQs on the Internet can increase a company's productivity.

Example 6.6

Cisco Systems which makes products such as routers, switching devices, relays, and internet software, has build up a knowledge base of frequently asked questions. As customers can usually get an answer without talking to anyone on the phone, Cisco reduced the calls it was receiving by 70 per cent or 50,000 calls a months, thus saving $200 a call or $10 million a month. Cisco increased productivity such as reducing the necessary staff for answering calls (now 700 instead of 1,000). Furthermore, each new call and solution goes to a technical writer to be entered into the knowledge base for reducing the number of future calls (Kotler 2000, pp. 445–6).

Under **acclimatisation indirectly through the output** customers are introduced to the company through aspects not directly based on the product. In contrast to acclimatisation directly the customer will not be familiarised with the outputs or the provision of them, but primarily with the firm as her or his business partner by keeping the same customer representatives, etc. This approach supports strengthening of the customer relationship. Such acclimatisation can be achieved through the holding of **events** like an open house at a car dealership, which is a non-output related contact with the customer. The more such contacts the customer has with the firm, the greater the familiarity in dealing with the seller, its employees, and its products. A further acclimatisation possibility lies in maintaining **constant distribution** so that the customer can always acquire the firm's products and services over the same sales channels.

Due to **output-specific differences** the acclimatisation phase is mainly relevant for customised services owing to their complexity. One of many examples would be customer training for software or special machinery. Since close employee–customer contact has been repeatedly observed, having the same employees is also a decision element for the customer particularly in the case of customised services. Service lines are also especially common for customised services, because of their complexity. Such offers from sellers of standardised products typically indicate indirect relevance to the output.

The first contact between the seller and buyer thus occurs during the socialisation phase. Even if the initial impression of the seller represents a significant basis to the customer for the subsequent course of the relationship, it is important from the seller's perspective to set up a transition to the customer retention phase. The development and intensification of the relationship should thus be pushed.

6.2.2 Customer retention management instruments

Growth phase management

From a corporate perspective, rapid execution of the socialisation phase is worth striving for in order to make the customer relationship more profitable during the **growth phase**. The customer must be tied more strongly to the firm such that he or she has not only minimal interest in competitive offers but will also value and make use of the firm's products to a great degree. Relationship marketing thus has the following **tasks** at hand:

a **Customisation of outputs**: To make the outputs attractive for the customer over the long-term they must be modified to match her or his specific needs. Hence, it is necessary to take a key standardised product, turn it into a customised one, and make it available for use.

b **Cross selling**: In order to extend the acceptance of products by the customer, active cross selling is needed on top of customisation, i.e. specific measures need to be undertaken to stimulate the customer to utilise other corporate products or services.

(a) Customisation of outputs

Customisation relates foremost to the product and service policy and can be attained through customer integration on the one hand and value added services on the other. **Customer integration** means involving the customer in the product/service planning and provision activities in the sense of externalisation of provision-related activities. This allows specific customer needs to be matched. The intent here is not on externalising to reduce costs but rather on service customisation. This method builds a basis for trust with the customers. The key requirements for integrating customers are a flexible output programme, production structure, and employees. Figure 6.10 illustrates the choice which the customer has when accessing the website of ewatchfactory. The customer can determine individually the design of the face, the case, or the strap. Even photo uploading and an engraved message is possible.

Customer integration into the innovation process of the firm entails a more complex arrangement. The customer is included in the development of innovative outputs, thereby enabling the company to adjust its products and services entirely to the customer's needs. The respective **integration possibilities** become apparent by considering the innovation processes involved (Scheuing and Johnson 1989; Figure 6.11).

- While generating ideas, discussions can be held with the customer and complaint management information can be applied.

- Findings of customer questionnaires can be included when evaluating ideas.

- For testing the concept, customers selected on the basis of the lead user concept (Urban and v. Hippel 1988; v. Hippel 1986) can be invited to test and rate the product concept.

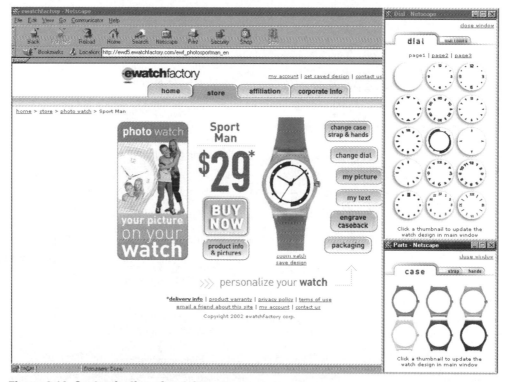

Figure 6.10 Customisation of watches

(*Source*: www.ewatchfactory.com/retail/en/index.htm, accessed on May 22, 2002)

▪ Normally, consumers are used to test the specific product and the market. For market tests, in particular, usually economic evaluations are done (e.g. sales quantities in the test market). Nevertheless, it appears reasonable to enhance these economic evaluations with psychological assessments such as customer satisfaction and benefits by using a large sample of customers.

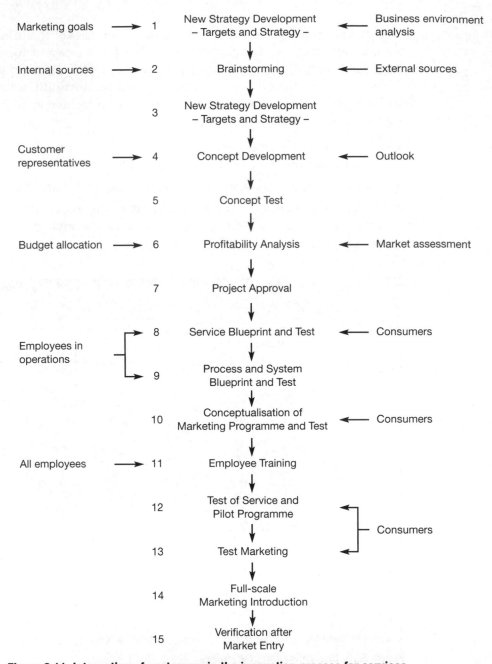

Figure 6.11 Integration of customers in the innovation process for services
(*Source*: Scheuing and Johnson 1989, p. 30)

Customer integration appears to be a reasonable instrument to compare **output types**, especially customised services due to their complexity, heterogeneity, and the relative significance of individual customers (e.g. individualised machinery in the industrial goods field, or management consulting in the services area). For standardised products like screws, chewing gum, and movies, typically cost reasons preclude any customer integration.

Besides customer integration **value-added services** can be applied in the growth phase to tailor the customer relationship. These services can be divided into two dimensions: (1) materialistic and non-materialistic added services can be separated, and (2) in view of the customer's reciprocity, added services are feasible with or without a surcharge. Added services at no extra charge alone represent an additional benefit for the customer. Conversely, added services can be offered at a surcharge only if the customer views them as an additional benefit in spite of the higher charge. This is possible, for example, if an exclusive product can be acquired only from the respective seller or when it is more convenient for the customer, who would otherwise have to obtain the product from another seller. Based on these two dimensions the following four types of value added services can be defined (Figure 6.12):

- **Materialistic added services without a surcharge**: e.g. substitute car during servicing; course material for a continuing education seminar
- **Materialistic added services with a surcharge**: e.g. a high-end CD player from a car dealer
- **Non-materialistic added services without a surcharge**: e.g. insurance protection included with credit cards
- **Non-materialistic added services with a surcharge**: e.g. travel insurance with a plane reservation; employee training by the manufacturer on a new machine

Surcharge Type	Without surcharge	With surcharge
Materialistic	(1) Materialistic added services without a surcharge Examples: • Substitute car during servicing • Course material for a seminar	(2) Materialistic added services with a surcharge Examples: • Car radio from a car dealer • Guide book in travel agency
Non-materialistic	(3) Non-materialistic added services without a surcharge Example: • Insurance protection with credit cards • Guidance on planning a kitchen	(4) Non-materialistic added services with a surcharge Example: • Travel insurance with a booked flight • Employee training on a machine

Figure 6.12 Types of added services

The deployment of value-added services has different functions depending on the **output type**. For customised outputs added services are often necessary to make the product or service useful to the customer (e.g. guidance on planning a kitchen). For standardised outputs, however, added services are usually a way of differentiating oneself from the competition and not absolutely necessary for providing or using the product or service (e.g. coffee shop in a museum). Additionally, many value added services can be classified on the basis of the expected behaviour of the customer and the affinity of the added services to the core product. Figure 6.13 shows such a classification.

Customisation efforts are feasible not just with product policy related actions but more so with actions involving other instrument areas. Customisation is supported within a **promotion policy** through customer magazines, clubs, and workshops. The **pricing policy** can achieve price differentiation based on customer related attributes or benefit associated pricing. Through a **place policy** flexible distribution systems can secure customised distribution.

(b) Cross selling

In the growth phase, **cross selling** is necessary along with customisation to ensure economic development of the customer relationship. The aim of cross selling is primarily to raise the sales level with a customer. This goal can be reached by pure cross selling and by raising the purchasing frequency. **Pure cross selling** activities are those that serve to extend customer demands onto corporate products not yet used. In contrast, a **higher purchasing frequency** means greater quantities and revenues achieved with the customer on currently used products.

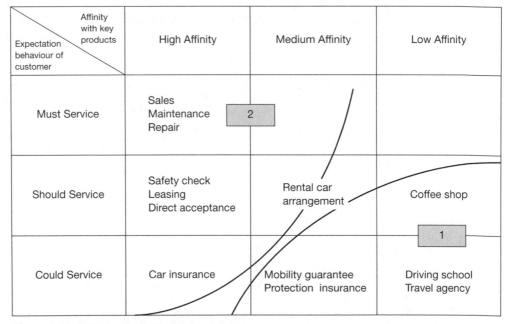

Figure 6.13 Forms of value-added services
(*Source*: Laakmann 1995, p. 19)

Both pure cross selling and higher purchasing frequencies can be aspired for by focusing on the quality and price. With a **quality focus** the outstanding quality and customer satisfaction should urge the customer to utilise these outputs more often and to also take on other products or services. A **pricing focus** offers financial benefits to the customer as one reason for extending the business relationship.

By combining pure cross selling with increased purchasing frequencies and quality and pricing orientation, four alternative types of cross selling activities can be identified:

- **Quality-focused cross selling**: the approach of applying quality related arguments should convince the customer to take on corporate products that are not yet used. An expanded programme palette is a typical example of quality-focused cross selling. The customer receives offers of new products and services that are not yet available from the particular seller but ones that he or she could well use (e.g. in the financial services sector, banks have started to offer new services, such as insurance coverage, besides the traditional products such as savings accounts and loans).

- **Pricing-focused cross selling**: under this approach the goal is to get the customer to ask for products not yet used because of their advantageous pricing. Package pricing is an example of this, whereby two different products/services are offered together at a price lower than that for the two separately (e.g. package price for a flight and a hotel stay). On this basis, a customer probably buys the second output too, although her or his interest was primarily on just the first one.

- **Quality-focused purchasing frequency control**: this involves raising the output quantity taken by the customer as a result of the quality of a product just used by her or him. This is possible with value added services or additional services such as readings in a bookstore. If a customer buys certain products from different sellers, the chances of the customer limiting purchases to a particular seller are higher when the seller offers added services.

- **Pricing-focused purchasing frequency control**: the aim is to raise the buying frequency of a particular product by offering price savings to the customer. Accordingly, customer cards have become quite popular. Often these cards are linked with discounts obtainable on reaching a certain purchased volume.

Figure 6.14 summarises these four alternative types of cross selling activities. Figure 6.15 demonstrates an example of a specific customer card programme at Rocky Mountain Chocolate Factory, a major confectioner with twenty-six locations in Canada and almost 250 throughout North America.

The application of cross selling depends on the **output type** involved. Particularly for customised services that cannot be stored, it becomes necessary for the seller to make use of the cross selling potential (e.g. tourism, airlines, theatre, cinema). These services can be marketed more easily, because of repeated direct contact with the customer. The customer, owing to her or his higher risk compared to standardised outputs, is more likely to go for cross buying (e.g. management consulting).

Type \ Focus	Quality Focus	Pricing Focus
Pure cross selling	**(1) Quality-focused cross selling** Examples: Programme palette extension, such as insurance coverage, besides saving accounts and loans	**(2) Pricing-focused cross selling** Examples: Package deals for a flight and a hotel stay
Purchasing frequency control	**(3) Quality-focused purchasing frequency control** Example: Value added services	**(4) Pricing-focused purchasing frequency control** Example: Customer card linked with discounts

Figure 6.14 Types of cross selling activities

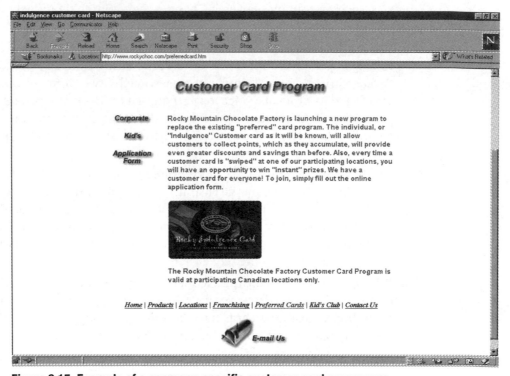

Figure 6.15 Example of a company-specific customer card programme
(*Source*: Rocky Mountain Chocolate Factory, www.rockychoc.com/preferredcard.htm, accessed on May 22, 2002)

Management of the maturity phase

Further intensification of the customer relationship is unlikely in the **maturity phase**, since the customer either uses the seller's products to the required extent or the seller's cost-benefit parameters do not justify additional effort to satisfy the customer. Hence, the relationship should be arranged as efficiently as possible in this phase by taking advantage of the relationship's economic potential without the need for a major effort. In the maturity phase marketing activities thus face the following tasks:

a **Building switching barriers**: the firm can stabilise the relationship over the long term by building barriers to switching. This will ensure that the customer is dependent on the firm and that the related turnover and profits are secured over the time period involved. The switching costs may be created by either the supplier, the consumer or the relationship itself (Egan 2001, p. 64).

b **Efficiency improvement**: the firm can save on transaction costs by utilising its experiences with the customer's recurring analogous use of products. Specific measures have to be implemented in this phase to realise this cost savings potential. These actions must be applied in such a way as to simplify the transactions with the customer from the company's perspective.

(a) Building switching barriers

Customer relationships can be stabilised by **building switching barriers** based on the following three instrument groups which are illustrated in Figure 6.16 (Liljander and Strandvik 1995; for another classification of barriers associated with switching costs, see Egan 2001, pp. 64–6; Shapiro and Varian 1999, p. 117):

1 Contractual switching barriers

2 Economic switching barriers

3 Technical/functional switching barriers

First, legal instruments permit the forming of **contractual switching barriers**. The customer agrees to utilise the seller's products or services over a given period as in the case of a minimum order-size commitment, memberships of fitness clubs, and so forth. A second type are **economic switching barriers** representing

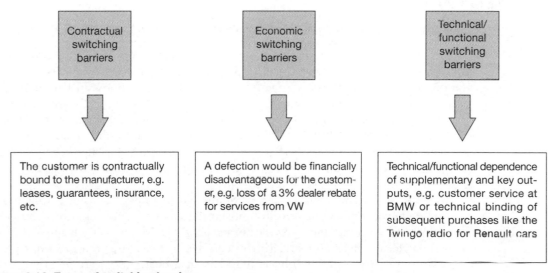

Figure 6.16 Types of switching barriers

a financial disadvantage for the customer in the event of a defection. Examples of such instruments are rebates, customer cards linked to a discount, and subscriptions to magazines. If the customer cancels his relationship with the firm he or she loses the respective advantages. Finally, **technical/functional switching barriers** relate to building technical or functional capabilities of products and services which lead to a lock-in effect, that is, the costs of switching from one brand of technology to another are substantial. These kind of switching barriers can be found mainly in the material goods area, for instance, in the automobile industry where only the manufacturer's navigation software can be used. In the services sector also efforts are increasingly being made to develop such barriers, e.g. in telecommunications or the computer industry (for more information, see the box 'Insights 6.2: The Phenomenon of Switching Barriers: Computers vs. Mobile Phones'). The following are some of the **instruments for building technical/ functional switching barriers**:

■ By **bundling outputs** such that the customer can use a specific product only in combination with another one from the firm.

■ Special customer benefits can also be gained when a firm makes **exclusive promotions** available only to customers or often only to those that are more valuable (e.g. stock market information from the bank's website).

■ Measures can also be undertaken to build technical/functional switching barriers in the **place policy**. The seller's offer of numerous distribution channels could represent an advantage for the customer. If it is not feasible for the competitors to offer the same then relevant barriers could be put up. Additionally, standardising sales could also lead to a switching barrier if the customer cannot receive the same from other sellers.

Insights 6.2

The phenomenon of switching barriers: computers vs. mobile phones

The impending problem of lock-in is especially valid for users of information technology: once you have chosen a technology, switching can be disastrous, that is, data files are unlikely to transfer perfectly and so forth (Shapiro and Varian 1999, p. 11). For instance, when it comes to upgrading the Mac computer you've been using for years, you will think twice about picking a PC or a UNIX machine instead of the new 700MHz CD-RW iMac. As you probably own a collection of Mac software and you are already familiar with using the system, you are facing significant costs if deciding to switch to an IBM technology (Shapiro and Varian 1999, pp. 103–4). Figure 6.17 illustrates the decision problem.

However, the reliance on existing switching barriers might become a source of enormous headaches. While creating substantial profits in the beginning, due to this 'enforced' customer retention, customers might defect instantly if the technological barrier becomes obsolete. This phenomenon can be seen, for example, in the German or Swiss mobile phone market where customers were mostly loyal

Figure 6.17 The choice of different technology: Mac vs. PC

because of the lack of number portability. That is, if a customer decides to switch his provider, he loses his phone number including the prefix. As a result, the technology kept consumers from defecting. Yet, since this restriction has been abolished, there is no compelling reason to choose another service provider instead. Customers can now keep the same phone number, making a defection more dangerous than before.

(*Source*: adapted from Shapiro, C. and Varian, H.R. (1999): *Information Rules. A strategic guide to the network economy.* Boston, pp. 103–34.)

Owing to **differences in output types** the customer senses relatively high switching barriers in the case of customised services, due to the greater risk involved and the decreased ability to judge competitive offers (e.g. medical services are highly customised). Hence, formalisation of such barriers is easier for these services than for standardised products. For customised services like machine building, because of the relative significance of individual customers, a formal customer commitment with the firm is more important. The reduced customer anonymity in this case also makes it easier to strengthen the commitment.

(b) Efficiency improvement

Efficiency improvement for the handling of a customer relationship can involve both the cost and sales elements. On the sales side, efficiency control could relate to either the quantity or the pricing. Three **efficiency improvement approaches** can thus be differentiated for a customer relationship:

- **Cost reduction through standardisation**: cost savings related to a particular customer can be achieved by standardising the marketing activities. The standardisation could involve all marketing areas. At first, products can be standardised for specific elements of little importance to the customer, for example, by making them unchangeable and hence mass-producible as for computer chips.

Communication with the customer can be standardised with online services by the setting-up of newer technologies for communication and information. With respect to pricing policies, methodologies for individual customer pricing could be standardised as done by the airlines. Furthermore, the sales function could also be standardised, for instance, by having the customer select a newspaper subscription instead of buying the paper himself every single day.

■ **Unit cost reduction through increased sales quantities**: the sales volume with a customer could lead to an improvement in efficiency since the unit costs will decrease accordingly. For example, if a customer buys double the volume possibly twice the revenues will be reached without certain costs also increasing linearly (i.e. costs for invoicing, advisory services, and transport).

■ **Taking full advantage of the customer's readiness to pay**: the customer should pay for any price increases as long as he or she is willing to do so without taking defections into consideration. Thus, it is necessary to establish the specific customer's willingness to pay, for example, through a conjoint analysis.

In view of **differences in output types** efficiency improvements are particularly relevant for customised products or services. Even if efficiency improvement considerations are generally important for standardised products they have little to do with specific relationships. Cost reductions through customer-based standardisation, sales quantity increases, and taking full advantage of the customer's willingness to pay are possible mainly for heterogeneous outputs.

The customer retention phase is the key one for relationships. Normally, companies strive for as long a retention phase as possible. From the customers' perspective, however, a certain degree of habitual behaviour can emerge and lead to attractive competitive offers being considered. Customer relationships could be endangered in this way. It is in the interest of the firm to secure the relevant relationships through recovery management measures.

6.2.3 Customer recovery management instruments

Management of the imperilment phase

An **imperilment phase** can occur several times in the course of a customer relationship, whereby the customer mulls over a possible defection and relationship dissolution (Stauss 2000). This happens usually when the customer feels that there have been errors in the seller's provision of products and interactions. The goal of relationship marketing in these imperilled phases is to bring each relationship back to the old satisfaction and retention level. To achieve this goal the following tasks must be carried out in these phases:

a **Error rectification**: the premise for the relationship to return to its old level is a rectification of the errors made by the firm or its employees.

b **Restitution**: in addition to the above, it is necessary for the firm to prove to the customer that it is aware of its mistake and that it was an exception. Therefore, the firm should make amends through appropriate restitution.

Both error rectification and restitution can be accomplished through measures within the four marketing mix areas – product, price, promotion, and place (Figure 6.18). Supporting personnel related actions could be implemented alongside.

Errors can be rectified through product improvements as part of a **product policy**. In retrospect, if the defective product is repairable it can be taken care of (e.g. recalls in the car sector). As a restitution measure the policy could provide for substitutes that serve the purpose of the originally purchased product (e.g. free rental service). Looking at different output types subsequent improvements in products work mainly for standardised ones, since customised services like restaurant food can seldom be repaired following a problem. Substitute products are generally feasible for both types of outputs, although rarely at the time of need for customised ones.

Both corrections and compensations can be achieved with the help of a **promotions policy**. Rectification is possible through customer training, for example, involving subsequent training on a machine if the problematic output usage originated from the customer. Restitution can be executed by promotion policy measures in the form of apologies. These could be done either written or in a personal conversation. Gifts are commonly included with an apology. In contrast to restitution through substitutes, the products that are made available here have no connection with the defective one (e.g. coupons). These gifts could stem from either the firm's product programme or from outside (e.g. a meal ticket for a flight delay).

The **pricing policy** permits both improvements and restitutions to be attained through price reductions such as a rebate following a short-run boxing match. A price reduction for a defective product could be interpreted as an improvement, since the price-benefit ratio then equals the level originally aspired for. As a compensatory measure a rebate also functions as a gift since it is monetary in nature.

Improvements and restitution measures can be implemented through the place policy as well. If the problem relates to this policy, improved distribution could clear it up. For example, if a customer does not receive an item to be delivered a

Instrument \ Task	Error Rectification	Restitution
Product policy	Output improvement Example: Automobile recalls	Substitute output Example: Making a new car available
Promotion policy	Customer training Example: Subsequent training on a machine	Gift/Apology Example: Meal ticket for a flight delay
Pricing policy	Price reductions Example: Rebate following a short-run boxing match	
Place policy	Improved distribution Example: Package search by the post office	Gifts Example: Free shipping by Amazon.com

Figure 6.18 Relationship marketing instruments in the imperilled phases

search can be conducted within the distribution channels to locate the product and expedite its delivery (e.g. online package search by FedEx). Place-policy-related gifts could be used for restitution, for instance, if a customer that normally acquires an output from a store has it delivered several times directly to her or his home (e.g. free shipping by Amazon.com).

Considering the **relative significance** of the various actions, the imperilment of a customer relationship, and suitable recovery activities, it becomes clear that the output itself is of utmost priority. After that comes the price from the customer's perspective, since the perceived value of an output depends on this. Promotional or sales actions are at the next level. For example, an apology will rarely prevent a customer from defecting if nothing changes with the problem itself.

Management of the dissolution and abstinence phase

In the dissolution and abstinence phases too, relationship marketing faces similar tasks. The dissolution phase specifies the point in time or the period when the customer ends the relationship with the corporation. In the abstinence phase he or she is no longer one of the firm's customers. The two phases differ primarily in that in several segments, even after dissolving the relationship the seller and buyer still remain in contact, just as for the remaining period after cancellation of a consulting project. The customer actively contacts the seller during the dissolution phase, so that the seller can respond to the communication. In contrast, communication in the abstinence phase originates typically from the seller. Conceptually, these phases are comparable to the initiation phase only in the sense of a relationship reactivation. Hence, the dissolution and abstinence phases are confronted with two main outstanding **tasks**:

a **Customer persuasion**: if the grounds for the customer defection have been established, he or she must be convinced that these reasons no longer apply. Added value should be achieved for the customer to the point that the business relationship is reactivated.

b **Customer stimulation**: attractive recovery offers can be made to convince the lost customer to spontaneously reinitiate the relationship immediately.

As opposed to the initiation phase, in this phase it is necessary to take into account that contacts between sellers and buyers already existed. On the one hand, one can revert back to the experiences gathered during the relationship. On the other, it must not be forgotten that the defection took place precisely because of these experiences. Besides, there are other correlations in effect than in the initiation phase. For instance, experiences play a big role in the initiation phase, whereas in the abstinence phase a customer will be less likely to rely on word-of-mouth communication due to the past experiences.

A key task of the dissolution and abstinence phase is the identification and analysis of the **reasons for customer defection** (see 'Insights 6.3: Customer Churn' for questions which should be asked when customers leave). These can be divided into three categories:

- **Company-induced reasons for defections** refer to those where the defection occurs primarily due to the firm's defective outputs such as network coverage deficiencies for mobile phones.

- **Competitor-induced reasons for defection** are those where the defection stems from a direct offer to switch made by a competitor to the customers, like a better rate offer in the mobile phone market.

- **Customer-induced reasons for defection** relate to those based on personal reasons or changes in the customer's situation like a move to another city.

Insights 6.3

Customer churn – asking the right questions when customers leave

In the case of customer defections, marketing managers need to identify patterns among customers involved. For instance, when IBM loses a customer, it mounts a thorough effort to learn where it failed (Kotler 2000, p. 38). This analysis should start with internal records, e.g. sales logs, pricing records, and customer survey results. Furthermore, the defection research should be extended to outside resources, such as benchmarking studies and statistics. Here are some key questions to ask yourself in general (Kotler 2000, p. 47):

- Do customers defect at different rates during the year?
- Does retention vary by office, region, sales representative, or distributor?
- What is the relationship between retention rates and changes in prices?
- What happens to lost customers, and where do they usually go?
- What are the retention norms for your industry?
- Which company in your industry retains customers the longest?

Relevant information can also be obtained directly from the defecting customers. Here are some key questions you should ask in an exit interview:

- What is the reason that you have cancelled our relationship?
- What was the main trigger for you to switch to another provider?
- How would you describe the relationship before switching?
- Have you been dissatisfied with any services? If yes, why?
- Have you a complaint about any specific problems?

(a) Customer persuasion

An analysis of the above defection reasons represents the starting point for the recovery management (Chapter 4). **Customer persuasion** becomes necessary up to the point where the events that led to the defection lose their relevance. This can best be accomplished by **creating added value** that could push the customer into reinitiating the relationship. Added value can be created as follows in the four **marketing mix** instrument areas:

- **Added value in products** can be created by adapting the product more closely to customer needs (e.g. engagement of experts by a consulting firm)

- **Added value in promotions** can be realised, for example, by providing the customer with exclusive access such as a personal representative in the banking sector.

- For **added value in pricing** the product itself is not altered. Instead, the customer is offered a lower price with a better price-benefit ratio resulting in the realisation of a higher perceived value as in the case of success based fees for tax consulting.

- **Added value in the place** can be achieved through adjustment of related processes to better match customer needs. An example is giving the customer a choice of an alternative sales channel other than the standard one.

Example 6.7

Added value in distribution:

Home delivery is a good example of giving the consumer the choice of an alternative sales channel. When ordering a pizza, customers generally have the choice between picking up their pizza themselves or getting it delivered. However, pizza delivery is quite common nowadays, so it is not really seen as a value added any more. A newer example for achieving an added value in the sales channel can be found in home delivery of groceries. The Swiss retailer Migros (in Switzerland, two retailers – Migros and Coop – account for about 70 per cent of all retail food sales) has extended its distribution channel, offering consumers the choice of online shopping with the opportunity of home delivery or pick-up at some store. Using technology and the Internet, Migros has found new ways of selling their products, such as groceries. The possibility of choosing the delivery individually can clearly be seen as an added value for customers.

Example 6.8

Customer communication:

The telecommunication company BellSouth addressed the defection drivers directly in carefully designed promotions. However, sending 3,500 switchers a direct mail reactivation offer for free phones, free airtime and credit for dropped calls met with disappointing results: a three per cent response rate from direct mail and a one per cent reconnection rate. Additional customer research then revealed that although respondents rated the recovery offer strong, current contracts with their new network provider, and misplacing or never receiving the direct mail card, prevented lapsed customers from switching back (Griffin 1999).

In developing added value measures it must be kept in mind that all such actions incur extra **costs**. Hence, prior to undertaking the actions it is critical to determine if recovery of the respective customers would be profitable. This applies to only the profitability of relationships that can be evaluated, for instance, on the basis of the customer lifetime value (Chapters 4 and 8).

(b) Customer stimulation

This involves presenting reasons to persuade a customer to reactivate the relationship with the firm. **Customer stimulation** measures are applied over the short term and should induce one to immediately reinitiate the relationship with the company. These include recovery offers to create the motive for a relationship reactivation by the customer. Stimulation measures can also relate to three of the **marketing mix areas** (product, price, and place policies).

- A **product-related recovery offer** could possibly involve taking charge of handling the formalities on reactivation of the relationship and the attendant dissolution of another relationship.

- A simple form of a **pricing-related recovery offer** involves a cash payment. The customer is expected to reinitiate the relationship on receipt of a specific amount.

- A one-off or time-limited reimbursement of sales costs could also be applied as a **place-related recovery offer**.

The promotion policy is for informing the customer about the recovery offer. This can be done in person, by phone, or in writing. A corporate questionnaire of 50 Swiss banks and insurance companies showed that in case of relationship dissolution in practice, primarily personal contacts are undertaken as recovery measures. The banks and insurers sought to find out the precise dissolution reasons by asking questions, for example, directly at the bank counter so as to be able to submit a focused reactivation offer. These were subsequently followed by phone calls and individual letters. With regard to the **suitability of instruments** for reinitiating the business relationship, the study highlighted distinct differences. Whereas personal or phone contacts were rated as being effective to very effective for regaining lost customers, other measures such as letters, contractual changes, special conditions, contact through a call centre, etc. were estimated as having only limited success.

| Example 6.9 | When Wachovia Bank (www.wachovia.com) was looking for ways to increase activation and usage of inactive card members, it turned to Customer Communications Group (CCG) for fresh ideas. After reviewing card member profiles, usage patterns and competitive offers, CCG recommended testing three concepts: a rebate on spending during a promotional period, a limited-time sweepstakes, and a premium (gift) for minimum spending during a fixed period. CCG also designed the direct mail packages for maximum impact in the mailbox. As card members needed to know the benefit at a glance or they would never even open the package, each package had a unique design targeted to the audience and the offer. Fulfilment also had to be easy for the customer as well as the client, Wachovia Bank. CCG coordinated the fulfilment of the sweepstakes and premium. The results show that reactivating existing customers is a profitable strategy for Wachovia. While all promotions were considered successful, one was significantly more profitable and selected for a rollout based on test results. In detail, the premium promotion had the smallest lift in sales but doubled expectations. The rebate netted a double-digit lift in purchases. However, the big winner was the sweepstakes offer resulting in a three-digit increase in purchases.

(Source: www.customer.com/crmpulse/case_studies/wachovia_case.html, accessed on January 12, 2002).

Due to differences in **output types** recovery measures are particularly relevant for customised products and services. Each customer for such outputs is relatively significant for the corporation. Assuming a certain customer profitability level the loss and subsequent recovery of a customer has a major impact on the corpora-

	Phases		Tasks	Instruments
Customer acquisition	Initiation phases		Persuasion	• Direct assurance • Indirect assurance • Direct substantiation of recommendations • Indirect substantiation of recommendations
			Stimulation	• Direct short-term stimulation • Indirect short-term stimulation • Direct long-term stimulation • Indirect long-term stimulation
	Socialisation phase		Acclimatisation	• Acclimatisation directly through the output • Acclimatisation indiretly through the output
Customer retention	Growth phases		Customisation	• Customer integration • Value-added services
			Cross selling	• Quality-focused cross selling • Pricing-focused cross selling • Quality-focused purchasing frequency increase • Pricing-focused purchasing frequency increase
	Maturity phases		Building switching barriers	• Economic switching barriers • Technical switching barriers • Contractual switching barriers
			Efficiency improvement	• Standardisation • Sales volume increase • Taking full advantage of willingness to pay
Customer recovery	Imperilment phases		Error rectification	• Product policy • Promotion policy • Pricing policy • Place policy
			Restitution	• Product policy • Promotion policy • Pricing policy • Place policy
	Termination/ Abstinence phases		Persuasion	• Added value in products • Added value in promotion • Added value in pricing • Added value in the place

			Stimulation	• Recovery offers
				  • Product related
				  • Price related
				  • Place related
				• Informed through promotion

Figure 6.19 Overview of phase-driven relationship marketing instruments

tion's profit situation. An **assessment of recovery measures in practice** has established that the majority of the firms do not conduct this systematically. Although the firms do recognise the value of the recovery measures, they frequently do not undertake any consistent analysis, definition, or control of the recovery effort. Figure 6.19 shows how the phase-driven operational relationship marketing instruments are addressed in practice. This figure provides an overview of the categories of measures that could be applied to fulfil the tasks within the customer relationship life cycle phases.

6.3 Phase-independent instruments for relationship support

In addition to marketing instruments that are the focus of applications in certain phases of the customer relationship life cycle, relationship marketing has elements that have a **phase-overlapping character**. These elements support customer relationship management independent of the life cycle phase, and have to be planned separately from specific customer relationships. Among these are:

- Quality and complaint management for product support of relationships
- Internal customer orientation for personnel support of relationships

The **phase-overlapping significance** of these measures becomes apparent when considering the tasks at hand in the various customer relationship life cycle phases. Thus, high product and service quality is a prime prerequisite for customer acquisition (persuasion through quality), their retention (quality as the main determinant of retention), as well as their recovery (quality problems as reasons for defection). This is achievable through quality management. A functioning complaint management system is a key factor at least for the customer retention and recovery phases. In numerous sectors, internal personnel processes represent a vital success factor for customer acquisition, retention, and recovery.

6.3.1 Output support of relationships

Securing high output quality through quality management

Systematic quality management guarantees corporate products and services with a continuously high quality that is a core prerequisite for the initiation, development, and intensification of customer relationships. Quality management thus covers every quality-related corporate activity and target, i.e. all corporate planning, implementation, and controls that ensure a high level of quality. In the process of pursuing its primary goal of a high service quality, quality management involves the following **sub-goals**:

- **Internal psychographic goals** that comprise the creation of quality awareness, customer orientation, and employee motivation, which are imperative in most sectors for successful development of customer relationships.

■ Included among **internal economic goals** are productivity increases, efficiency improvements within processes, and error avoidance. These factors help to organise efficient customer relationships and thereby influence the relationship profitability from a cost standpoint.

■ Increased customer satisfaction and higher retention, an improved quality image, and the creation of market entry barriers are subsumed under **external psychological goals**. These aspects form the basis for achieving a long-term customer relationship.

■ **External economic goals** comprise profit enhancement, increased sales and market shares, more repeat purchases, and full utilisation of the cross selling potential. In this way, quality management supports the realisation of relationship marketing's prime goals.

Quality management instruments are structured according to the quality management control circle below, in terms of classic management tasks covering planning, implementation, and control in the various phases (Figure 6.20):

■ Strategic quality planning

■ Quality implementation

■ Quality control

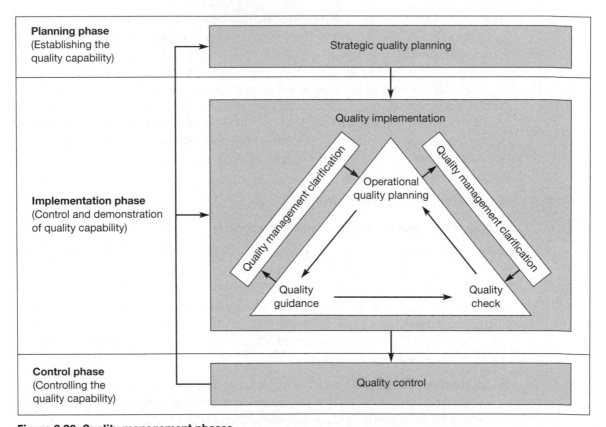

Figure 6.20 Quality management phases

Strategic quality planning involves establishing the fundamental operating framework for quality management and thereby the firm's strategic quality focus in accordance with its strategy. This strategy is fixed by binding quality principles, which form the basis for the execution of related corporate activities. The guidelines should be made transparent to all employees through appropriate communication and provision of, say, a quality handbook. By 'implanting' quality into the minds of all, the company will be able to lay the foundations for developing and intensifying profitable customer relationships.

Quality implementation covers accomplishing the related strategy. The key elements are mainly the requirements stated by customers that are then ascertained for planning the quality operations achieved by quality management, and finally verified through quality control analyses. Clear-cut quality management is one flank of the quality implementation building block that helps to create internal and external trust in the firm's quality capability. This refers to the ability to deliver the products in the quality demanded by customers. **Perspective taking**, which represents an important principle of relationship marketing, is achieved as a part of quality planning. In subsequent quality management phases it is then established that the customer is satisfied with the firm's quality and is interested in continuing her or his business relationship.

Quality control encompasses a firm's strategic controlling activities. It is most important to consider the economic efficiency of quality management activities. The more profitable the quality management system the greater will be the profitability during customer relationship development and intensification.

Quality management is irreplaceable in every **customer relationship life cycle phase**. The purchasing decision factor in the customer acquisition phase is a positive quality image that can be attained only through consistent quality measures. In the retention phase, output quality represents an important determinant of customer satisfaction and retention. Customers often defect due to quality flaws and can be re-acquired only by guaranteeing a higher quality level in the recovery phase. The **relationship marketing success chain** can be initiated in all the customer relationship phases to ensure high service quality.

Reaction of complaint management to product and service defects

Complaint management goes into action if quality management does not manage to avoid defects in quality. The management of complaints (customer voice) is important because they have positive effects for an organisation. Stewart (1998, p. 236) describes them as the means by which 'wayward businesses and organisations respectively, are made aware of their lapses and can begin to right their affairs'. In other words, organisations can improve the chance that customers involved will remain brand loyal and continue to repurchase the company's items if complaints are resolved satisfactorily (Lovelock 2001, p. 166). The complaint management comprises all the analysis, planning, execution, and control measures that a firm undertakes for complaints from customers or other stakeholders. It consequently involves an active corporate process aimed at shaping customer relationships and enhancing customer satisfaction and retention, while ensuring that the development and intensification of customer relationships are not endangered, even in the face of product or service defects. While this generally relates to the Business-to-Consumer environment, it seems that in the Business-to-Business arena the same set of rules apply. That is, companies should try to listen to their customers for finding out any dissatisfactions and resolve those problems (Stephens 2000, p. 294).

The main **goal** of complaint management is to react to any expressed dissatisfaction so as to either defuse the situation or to ensure reinstated customer satisfaction on completion of the complaint handling process. The following **sub-goals** can be derived from the above main target (Stauss and Seidel 1998):

- **Implementation and clarification of a customer-oriented corporate strategy**: The existence of active complaint management is a visible sign of a company's customer orientation. It thus helps to project and maintain an image outside of the firm of one close to customers. Internally, complaint management is aimed at implementing customer-oriented thinking and handling by institutionalising critical customer feedback. Both these aspects are important for developing and intensifying profitable customer relationships.

- **Avoiding other types of reactions from dissatisfied customers**: Since complainers articulate their dissatisfaction directly to the firm, the firm is given a chance to take care of the problem itself. Complaint management should thus be applied to avoid the alternative options open to a complainer such as defection to a competitor, negative word-of-mouth communication, or inclusion of the media. Figure 6.21 illustrates these different options. A functioning complaint management system thus provides the means for not endangering a customer relationship.

- **Achieving additional acquisition and retention effects**: By reinstating customer satisfaction, organisations should be able to not only avoid negative word-of-mouth communication but also manage to initiate positive word-of-mouth communication to influence the attitudes of potential customers. Furthermore, research by Fornell and Wernerfelt (1987, p. 344) supports the notion that customer loyalty can be increased by encouraging customers to complain. Besides supporting current relationships, this then helps to develop additional customer relationships.

- **Gaining information on product deficiencies**: Complaints contain important information on the problems perceived by the customer, including highly valuable ideas and measures for quality and innovation management. These potential ideas also contribute towards the development and intensification of other customer relationships. For instance, the company 3M claims that more than two thirds of its product-improvement ideas come from listening to complaining customers (Kotler 2000, p. 48).

From a process-based viewpoint four **working areas for complaint management** can be identified (Stauss and Seidel 1998; Figure 6.22):

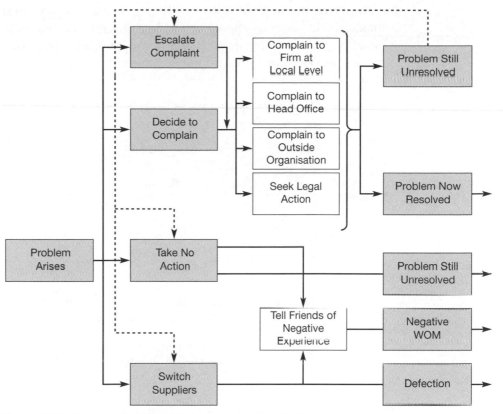

Figure 6.21 Courses of action that are open to dissatisfied customers
(*Source*: Lovelock 2001, p. 165)

1 **Stimulating complaints**: The sub-process of stimulating complaints covers all systematic and targeted corporate activities that urge customers to make complaints in the case of dissatisfaction. The main goal is to manage the complaints in an easy and uncomplicated manner. If a customer can be won over to actively complain, it is an indicator of an intensive business relationship. Examples for stimulating customer complaints and feedback are prominently displayed customer comment cards, toll-free hotlines and the Internet (see also the example below).

2 **Recording complaints**: The goal is to obtain a systematic and complete record of the complaint data along with appropriate behaviour of the employee noting down the verbal statements.

3 **Handling and reacting to complaints**: The main purpose is an analysis of complaints, distribution of the information to the relevant departments or employees, and the setting up of standards for handling the complaints. From a customer's standpoint, an adequate reaction to a complaint is most critical to avoid imperilling the relationship.

4 Complaint management controlling: An economic analysis of complaint management activities should be conducted regularly to look at their costs and benefits. In order to ensure profitable customer relationships complaint management should also focus on profitability aspects.

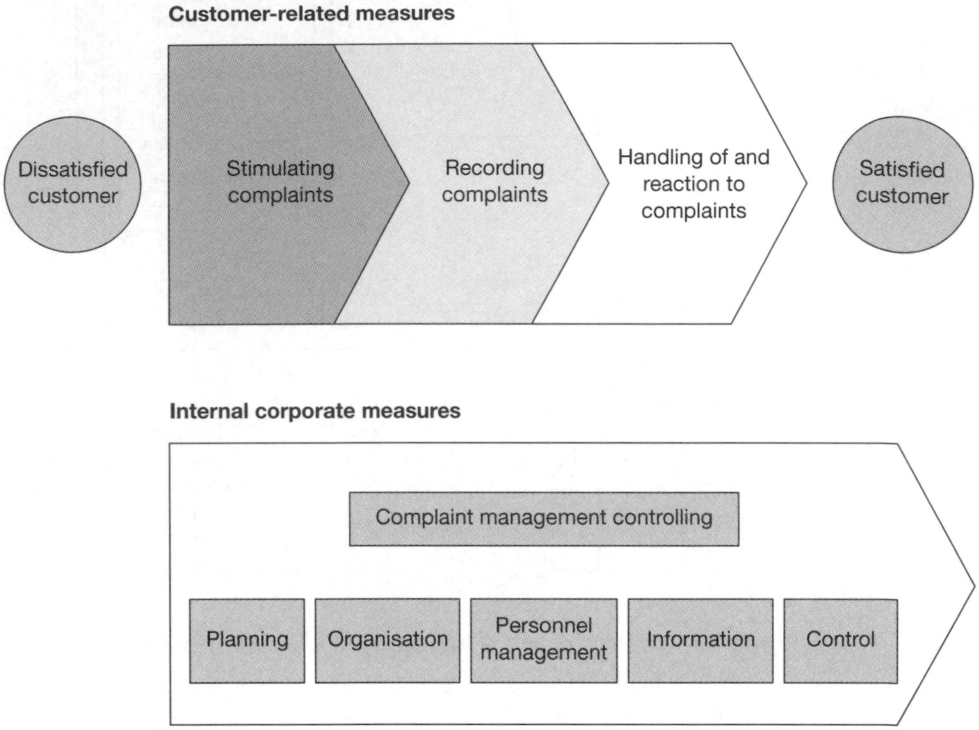

Customer-related measures

Internal corporate measures

Figure 6.22 Phases of a complaint management system
(*Source*: Stauss and Seidel 1998, p. 66)

Example 6.10
On the homepage of the IT-company Novell (www.novell.com) customers have the opportunity of giving systematically positive and negative feedback. On the website for the Premier Program Feedback (Figure 6.23), the type of issue is differentiated between questions about the programme, programme suggestions, programme complaints, and other issues. This way, Novell offers its customers an easy and accessible way to get in touch with the company. The possibility of filing complaints has resulted in a high acceptance by Novell's customers. As customers have to choose a category, Novell can react accordingly to the clients' needs. Furthermore, Novell obtains a systematic and complete record of complaint data.

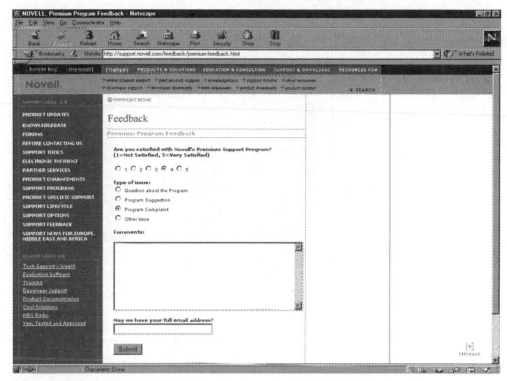

Figure 6.23 Example for stimulating customer complaints and feedback on the worldwide web

(*Source*: www.novell.com, accessed on January 11, 2002)

Although complaint management is valuable in the **customer relationship life cycle phases**, it has little to contribute to the customer acquisition phase. However, it can still have a positive impact on the firm's success through, for example, reduction in negative word-of-mouth communication or by projecting a generous seller image. In the customer retention phase, consistent stimulation and management of complaints is the key requirement to gain customer trust in the corporation. Since the recovery phase is often initiated after problems have occurred, the complaint management's aim here is to re-satisfy the customer. Customers can be satisfied again through complaint management, thereby enabling the relationship management success chain to carry on. For example, research suggests that the recovery of dissatisfied customers can lead to even greater customer satisfaction (e.g. Bejou and Palmer 1998, p. 11). Figure 6.24 illustrates some of the implications of resolving customer complaints, showing that especially quickly resolved complaints (minor and major ones) result in very high customer satisfaction.

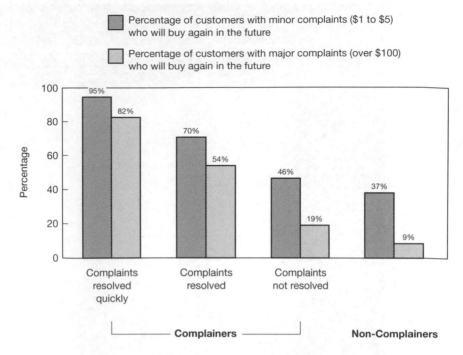

Figure 6.24 Implications of resolving customer complaints
(*Source*: adapted from Clark 2000, p. 213)

6.3.2 Personnel support of relationships through internal customer orientation

In numerous sectors a central influencing factor of the customer's product/service quality perception lies in the quality of the company's internal output processes. This quality in turn depends to a great degree on **internal customer orientation** or the customer orientation of internal suppliers for their internal customers.

This can be demonstrated clearly by the **GAP model of service quality** illustrated by Figure 6.25 (Parasuraman, Zeithaml and Berry 1985, 1988). According to this model the emergence of service quality, defined as Gap 5, between the customer's perception and expectations can be explained by four previously occurring shortfalls or gaps described below. The occurrence of these gaps can be traced back to inadequate internal customer orientation (Figure 6.26):

- **Gap 1** between customer expectations and management's perceptions of these expectations occurs due to defective upward internal communication.
- **Gap 2** between management's perception of customer expectations and the service quality specifications is influenced by faulty considerations of the capabilities and readiness of employees when specifying the service.
- **Gap 3** between the service quality specifications and the actual service delivery is, for example, caused by inappropriate employee motivation.
- **Gap 4** between the actual service delivery and what is externally communicated could be due to deficiencies in the employee's information on the external communication.

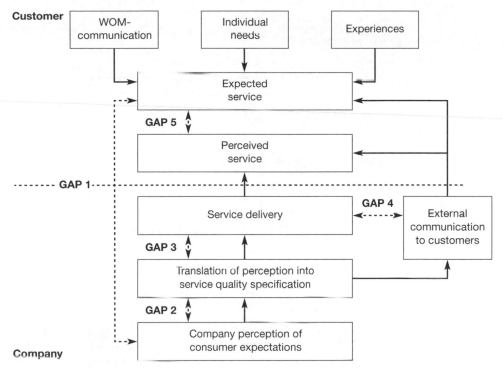

Figure 6.25 GAP-model of service quality
(*Source*: Parasuraman, Zeithaml andBerry 1985, p. 44)

It can be shown that all four internal gaps and as such the external fifth gap that designates the service quality and is influenced by the other four gaps, are dependent to a high degree on internal exchange relationships. In this regard, the following **types of internal customer-supplier relationships** can be identified:

- Interpersonal and inter-organisational exchange relationships can be differentiated depending on the relationship partner. For **interpersonal relationships** the exchange partners are people such as an employee and manager. **Inter-organisational relationships** involve two institutional units each represented by a person, as in the case of the research department and product management.

- Vertical and horizontal relationships can be identified between the relationship partners in terms of the hierarchies present. For **vertical relationships** the partners are located at different vertical hierarchical levels (e.g. manager and employee). Within **horizontal relationships** the partners such as two colleagues are at the same hierarchical level.

A **success chain for internal customer relationships** can be put into effect by guiding internal relationships, establishing internal customer orientation, and adapting the relationship success chain. Ensuring a high service quality level is the prerequisite for satisfying and retaining internal customers. If a firm manages to guarantee internal customer orientation, an external relationship marketing success chain can be indirectly initiated (Figure 6.27).

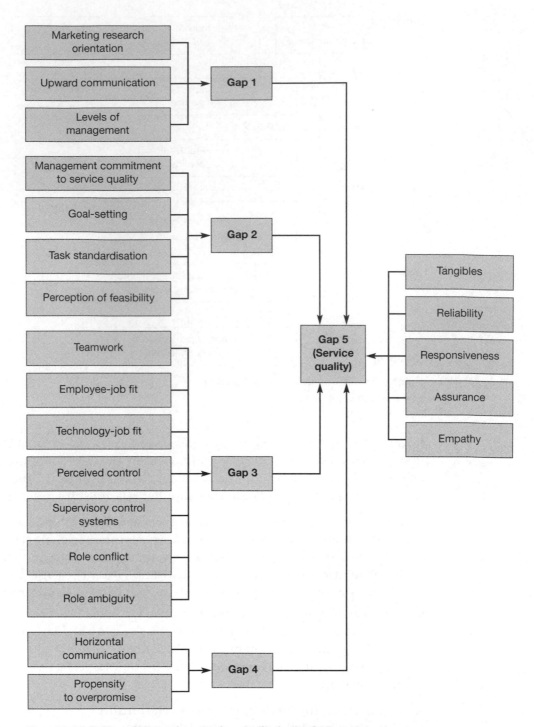

Figure 6.26 Factors influencing service quality in the GAP model
(*Source*: Zeithaml, Berry and Parasuraman 1996, p. 46)

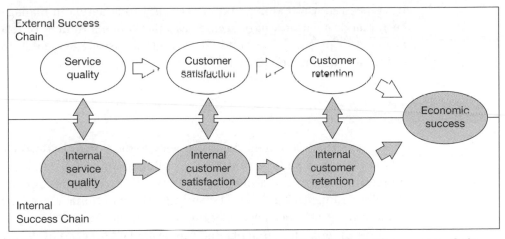

Figure 6.27 Internal customer orientation and the relationship marketing success chain

For instance, the following **internal customer orientation measures** can be applied:

■ **Internal communication** is very important. Customer-focused communication down the ladder can help to inform employees and to motivate them towards customer targeted behaviour. Creation of incentives for communication up the ladder as in the form of suggestion boxes or employee talks can help to ensure that as little as possible of the information held by employees is lost.

■ Another important internal customer orientation element is represented by **empowerment** under which employees are given a relatively wide latitude to manoeuvre. This approach enables an employee dealing directly with a customer to consciously shape the relationship and thereby effectively support its development and intensification.

■ Establishing the prerequisites for **internal relationship management** can contribute towards a relationship-oriented culture throughout the whole firm.

| **Example 6.11** | The case of the Radford Community Hospital in Radford, Illinois, shows how internal and external customer orientation can work together. According to Kotler (2000, p. 435), the organisation has set up a fund of $10,000 out of which patients are paid who have justified complaints ranging from cold food to overlong waits in the emergency room. The 'hook' or the motivation for the hospital's employees is that any money not paid out of the fund by the end of the year is divided among the employees (internal customer orientation). As a result, this plan has added a great incentive for the staff. For instance, with 100 employees in total and no complaints by the end of the year, each employee receives a bonus of $100. Treating patients well (external service quality) thus has improved. The hospital also benefited financially because in the first six months, it had to pay only $300 to patients (Kotler 2000, p. 436). |

It has been shown that in addition to quality and complaint management, internal customer orientation can be secured as a flanking instrument of relationship management in practice. The mind-set of internal customer orientation consequently flows into the implementation phase of relationship marketing.

Summary

This chapter has described the instruments which organisations can use to apply relationship marketing in practice. According to our understanding of relationship marketing we develop a new systematisation of relationship marketing's operational instruments. That is, we believe that the traditional marketing mix has to be enhanced with the perspective of the customer relationship life cycle phases. Thus, we show different instruments that can be applied for each of these phases. Besides these phase-driven instruments we show that organisations also have to apply some phase-overlapping instruments. Quality and complaint management as well as internal customer orientation need to be considered in each of the customer life cycle phases. Thus, these instruments have to be planned separately.

7 The implementation phase of relationship marketing

Overview

The relationship marketing phases covering the analysis, strategy, and actions are all planning-based in nature, whereas the implementation phase transforms the relationship marketing concept within a company. Any concept is worthless without systematic implementation, and to ensure success all employees must be involved. Precisely due to the thinking in relationship marketing, major changes may be required in internal operational processes. In this chapter we will address the following questions:

➤ What targets and phases can be differentiated when implementing relationship marketing strategies?

➤ What are the barriers of implementing relationship marketing?

➤ Which implementation approaches can be differentiated?

➤ Which steps have to be followed to implement relationship marketing?

7.1. Foundations of strategy implementation

7.1.1 An inherent problem of strategy implementation

It has been demonstrated in many cases involving the introduction of marketing concepts and programmes that the expected success level is seldom reached. The same may apply when implementing the concept of relationship marketing. In terms of the **relationship marketing success chain** this means that corporations have developed a concept and measures for improving output quality, customer satisfaction and retention, and, consequently, economic success. Nevertheless, specific intermediate targets are often achieved only to an inadequate degree. Looking across the complete success chain, the individual implementation problems have a catalytic effect. For example, implementation problems in services impact the entire success chain through to the economic success stage. The corporation is thus not in a position to initiate profitable customer relationships and to develop and intensify them as planned.

This situation could have numerous causes because of the complex change processes necessary in a firm to enable relationship marketing to be applied. A key practical problem is the **implementation gap**, which is the lack of a comprehensive and consistent approach for implementing marketing concepts and relationship marketing.

In general the term **implementation** is understood as a process 'that turns marketing plans into action assignments and ensures that such assignments are executed in a manner that accomplishes the plan's stated objectives' (Kotler 2000, p. 695). Applied to relationship marketing, implementation denotes a process for converting the relationship marketing concept and plan into executable tasks. The goal of these tasks is to initiate, develop, and intensify profitable customer relationships.

A key assignment in implementing relationship marketing is achieving an **'outside-in' outlook** in place of the **'inside-out' outlook**. For this it is necessary among other things to open up access to the corporation by offering communication channels for customers to be able to contact the firm so all their needs are met. It is also important to bring about a customer-orientation-related mental change amongst the company employees and staff.

Implementation programmes aimed at successful achievement of tasks are frequently designed and initiated within companies. For instance, the British Airways approach entitled 'Putting People First' (PPF) strives to improve the employee-customer relationship by specifically focusing on helping customer-interacting staff members to better fulfil customer expectations (for more information, see Payne *et al.* 1996). Just as for the relationship marketing's planning phase a systematic approach should be laid down for the implementation phase. To do this it is vital to initially specify the implementation targets and phases involved. The box 'Insights 7.1: Implementing loyalty schemes successfully' describes how the German car manufacturer Porsche and the British retailer Tesco have performed after implementing their loyalty programs.

Insights 7.1

Implementing loyalty schemes successfully

The **Porsche AG** established in 1994–5 the **'Porsche Kundenkontaktprogramm'** (New and Used Car Programme). This loyalty scheme provides different marketing activities such as direct mailing, customer magazines, invitations to events, direct calling, etc. to improve loyalty and increase customer satisfaction. All activities are focused on the customer life cycle, which is called 'Curriculum-Marketing'. Since the loyalty scheme started, the company increased sales by 69 per cent from 19,262 cars in 1994–5 to 32,383 in 1996–7 and reached 36,686 car sales in 1998–9.

The British company **Tesco** started with a **'thank you' loyalty scheme** in 1995 to gain share in the highly competitive retail market. Within one year after the launch of the club card the company gained leadership of the British food retail market. A plastic swipe card allows members to collect points for buying at Tesco, thus participating in sponsored activities with other producers, use of energy from partner suppliers of gas and electricity or using the Tesco Personal Finance VISA Card. When buying at Tesco, 2 points are given for the first £10 of purchases and another point for every additional £5. Every quarter customers receive vouchers about the collected points together with the Club Card Magazine. The collected data educates retailers about which types of products are bought together providing Tesco with information for investing in loyalty-building schemes. Micro-information on customer buying patterns is made available and therefore the ability to target and nurture most valued customers. Tesco also segmented the market to offer different cards. The results were exceptional. More than six million customers signed up by the end of 1997 and profits increased by 16 per cent. By the end of 1999 Tesco had 12 million customers per week. Furthermore, in 1999 Tesco was recognised as the most admired company in Great Britain for the second time in three years.

(*Source*: BBDO Consulting (2001): Customer Relationship Management, Case Studies, Executive Summary, http://www.bbdo.de/bbdo-media/crmcasestudies.pdf, accessed on January 11, 2002. For additional reading see Peck, H., Payne, A., Christopher, M. and Clark, M. (eds.) (1999) *Relationship Marketing. Strategy and Implementation, Case 2.3: Does Tesco hold all the cards?*, case prepared by H. Mitchell and H. Peck, Cranfield School of Management, as a basis for classroom discussion, Oxford, pp. 79–96.)

7.1.2 Strategy implementation targets and phases

For successful implementation of customer-oriented concepts it is necessary to first set down the **strategy implementation targets**. Since raising the relationship orientation of a firm is a multi-stage process, each process phase has different targets (Figure 7.1). The focus in the first phase is on achieving acceptance of the necessity for an enhanced relationship orientation and on informing the employees. The second phase target shifts from initiation to enforcement of relationship orientation. The goal is to work out measures to improve the firm's relationship orientation and to fix specific responsibilities. The third phase is aimed at implementing the actions established for each department or project, making modifications, and controlling the advances made.

Getting the affected employees to **accept and understand** the project is a troublesome task of the process. The necessary sub-tasks to better achieve this target are as follows:

- Communicating the knowledge on the relationship marketing theme and the related implementation project
- Ensuring that the concept is understood by every person involved
- Attaining a high level of enthusiasm at all hierarchical levels

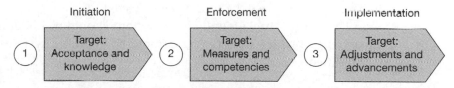

Figure 7.1 Implementation process targets and phases

In the **enforcement phase** the concept building blocks that were globally formulated in the planning phase are defined precisely and the focus is placed on improving the relationship orientation by detailing relationship marketing's focus and measures. This also calls for intensive discussions with the managers on corporate improvement possibilities and on the relevance of the measures from the customer standpoint. Numerous company employees should be involved in **implementing** the relationship marketing concepts. This phase will also require adjustments to corporate targets that could, for example, involve the introduction of a new databank for setting up a complaint management department aimed at guaranteeing a stronger focus on customer relationships.

It is important while setting implementation goals not to overlook the fact that they have associated **cost and time effects**. Hence, questions on the cost-benefit aspects of the planned customer orientation actions should be clarified prior to any implementation. In this regard one aspect could be the possible advantage of engaging external consultants in the implementation process. Additional thoughts should be given to assessing whether a complete restructuring of current information systems is necessary or if changes in selected system elements would suffice. Furthermore, it should be verified which aspects (such as specific quality attributes) provide the greatest benefits when improved.

For successfully implementing and executing strategies in companies, various changes must be made within the firm. This is due to the necessity for a **fit between the strategy and the corporate situation**.

For successful implementation an initial requisite is that a fit exists between the strategy and the corporate structures. For instance, if just a small number of company employees is in contact with customers and are hence aware of the customer situation it is an indicator of a **strategy-structure fit** problem. The implementation could as well be hindered by a problematic fit between the strategy and the company's management system (e.g. MIS). From a relationship marketing perspective, the company lacks a **strategy-system fit** when the corporate information system is not capable of generating, recording, processing, and delivering customer-specific data. In such cases, controlling, developing, and intensifying customer relationships will be problem-bound. Implementation problems could also crop up if a fit cannot be attained between the strategy and the corporate culture. A **strategy-culture fit**, for example, is non-existent if the employees exhibit highly technical or product-focused thinking that contradicts the customer-oriented concept of relationship marketing. If the corporate culture does not reflect customer orientation, difficulties will be encountered in directing corporate activities towards individual customer relationships and the development and intensification of profitable relationships will be accordingly affected.

In light of this background an assessment should be undertaken to determine the extent to which the existing corporate structures, systems, and culture will be modified.

7.2 Relationship-focused structures, systems, and culture

7.2.1 Barriers to implementing relationship marketing

Regarding the aforementioned modification of structures, systems, and the corporate culture, organisations are frequently hindered by implementation barriers. That is, in business there are abundant hurdles to implementing marketing concepts. For instance, Grönroos (2000, p. 383) describes the following five barriers for successful implementation: organisational barriers, systems and regulations-related barriers, management-related barriers, strategy-related barriers, and decision-making barriers. A lot of research has been done to find out weaknesses in strategy implementation. Figure 7.2 illustrates the significance of different barriers for the German market, based on a poll of 340 managers in German industries.

This sector-overlapping study in Germany clearly demonstrates that these circumstances were primarily associated with the structures, systems, and the culture that either hindered implementation of relationship marketing or at least slowed it down (for similar research on barriers to market orientation, see Harris and Piercy 1999; Liu 1995; Rueckert 1992). The implications of these factors have been confirmed by many empirical reports of practical experiences (Reinecke, Sipötz and Wiemann 1998, p. 278). The challenge to be faced is to control and manipulate the specific aspects associated with these key barriers.

Structural barriers, for instance, concern the organisational anchoring of relationship marketing within the firm. Two extremes that are not conducive to systematic guidance of customer relationships can be identified. One: assignment of relationship marketing responsibilities exclusively to one department results in

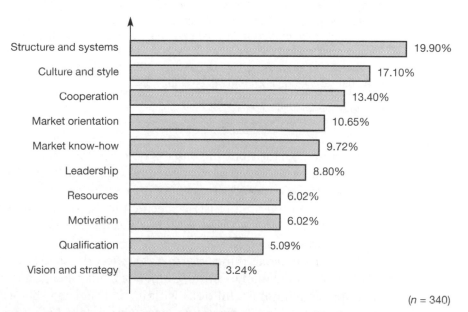

(n = 340)

Figure 7.2 Barriers to implementing customer orientation in Germany
(*Source*: Plinke 1996, p. 50)

other departments not feeling responsible for the customer(s). Two: broadly assigned responsibilities that require everyone to be responsible for a customer and relationship orientation results in a 'pass the buck' phenomenon where each thinks the other will take care of the customer.

System barriers include deficiencies in the information and control systems. For example, it could be the lack of databases or customer-focused control systems for measuring relationship marketing success variables. This often leads to problems in economic evaluations of process optimisations. For instance, the ABB Corporation had already invested heavily to improve customer and relationship orientation, but could not evaluate the related processes within its accounting systems. This was caused by the lack of process cost accounting to enable cost allocation based on its source (Zoller 1998, p. 26).

In the **cultural arena** the typical problems lie in the indifference and insensitivity of employees towards customers or in the employee's perception that the corporation's top management places no value on relationship orientation. Additional problems are the joint activities of partners in the value-added chain or also within the company itself. Agreement problems, fear of losing power, subjective reservation etc. can all hinder the implementation of relationship orientation.

Example 7.1	During the 1980s, British Telecom (BT) went from a bureaucratic, unresponsive public sector organisation to a private company. The management structures were not designed for competition or particularly for customer and relationship-oriented processes. Complaints confirmed how badly customer relationships were managed, such as the inflexibility of employees in implementing customer wishes. By the end of the 1980s, a revolution occurred within BT regarding the way it managed its services to business clients. Account managers were appointed and focused training efforts were employed to improve customer orientation. Through the dedication of named account managers to individual customers, trust and relationships were built up. As more than half of the account managers were external recruits from companies which have already focused on customer needs, their background allowed BT to bring about a cultural change from that as a monopolist. (*Source*: adapted from Palmer 1994, pp. 84–5).

This finding of the study presented is noteworthy, in that the **conceptual design** of relationship marketing or customer orientation was classified as unproblematic in vision or strategy by 3.24 per cent of the respondents as shown in Figure 7.2. The company should recognise these specific problems, or others that appear to be either comments on inadequate business area demarcations or relate to the lack of customer orientation targets.

There are numerous difficulties that can affect the successful implementation of relationship orientation in a firm. Corporate management must take on the task of creating the requisite conditions within the firm such that existing barriers are removed and customer orientation measures can take full effect. Therefore, within the framework of relationship marketing greater attention can be paid to the development of customer-oriented organisational structures, management systems, and an appropriate corporate culture.

7.2.2 Relationship-focused organisational structures

A debate is continuing on the various advantages and disadvantages of organisational forms relevant to the implementation of strategies based on products, segments, or matrices. The ability of traditional organisations to assign clear competencies with low coordination needs is accepted by all as an advantage, but their flexibility and reaction capability are viewed as major drawbacks. Hence, the question in the context of relationship marketing is how firms should be organised to set up, maintain, and improve profitability and sustainable customer relationships.

An answer to this question depends mainly on the demand profiles of internal and external buyers. Nevertheless, four development tendencies for **designing relationship-focused organisational structures** can be recognised:

1 Setting up of decentralised units

2 Intensification of process orientation

3 Encouragement of function-overlapping collaborations

4 Expansion of decision-making competencies

The question of where to embed marketing's organisational concepts is an **area of tension between centralisation and decentralisation**. The key task of complex organisations in this respect is to develop 'smallness' by setting up **decentralised units**. This phenomenon of putting together smaller, decentralised, and normally autonomous units is spreading in the business world, despite growing globalisation tendencies. This entails the removal of hierarchical structures to achieve better information flows and thus greater flexibility in solving customer problems. This removal of hierarchies is not to be equated with the full dissolution of former corporate structures. On the contrary **hybrid organisational forms** are emerging to respond to different organisational situations as required.

Example 7.2

A few years ago, the BMW Group in Germany recognised the necessity of modifying its organisational structures. This was defined in 1991 as the pilot phase called 'Future Working Structures'. The experience gained in this phase led to a specific shop agreement used as the basis for introducing successive organisational forms. Independent teams with clearly defined tasks and their own competence areas thus form the basic new organisation. The employees participate in making strategic and other decisions. Unnecessary interfaces are avoided by supplementing the main team tasks with secondary functions such as logistics and quality assurance. The outcome of these organisational changes is enhanced productivity, greater work satisfaction, and higher product quality that contribute significantly to an increase in the overall customer orientation.

An **intensified focus on processes** can also guarantee increased relationship and customer orientation. This 'new' outlook relates to the value added chain aspect of organisational procedures. All processes starting with the supplier to the various internal corporate stages through to the retailers must be newly defined and optimised. The purpose is to guarantee the best possible cooperation between the individual value-added chain participants such as the suppliers, employees, managers, logistics service providers, and retailers, so as to be able to react quickly and more flexibly to customer wishes.

In the retail and consumer goods area attempts are being made, for example, to introduce the **Efficient Consumer Response (ECR) concept**. Building stronger links between manufacturers and retailers, the implementation of ECR raises the value added chain's flexibility and productivity, and thereby enhances relationship and customer orientation. The concept involves four tools (Kotler 2000, p. 511). 'Activity-based cost accounting' enables the manufacturer to measure and demonstrate the true costs of the resources consumed in meeting the chain's requirements. 'Electronic data interchange' (EDI) improves the manufacturer's ability to manage inventory, shipments, and promotion. The 'continuous replenishment program' (CPR) as the third tool enables manufacturers to replenish products on the basis of actual and forecasted store demand. Finally, 'flow-through cross-dock replenishment' allows larger shipments to retailer distribution centres. Thus, ECR improves the relationship between retailers and their manufacturers as well as the relationship with the consumer. The box 'Insights 7.2: ECR in the food supply industry' shows how ECR and EDI have developed in the retail food industry.

Insights 7.2

ECR in the food supply industry

Retailers are just now beginning to use the large amount of consumer information stored in their computer systems. For example, approximately 50 per cent of all retailers nationwide have implemented some type of frequent shopper or customer loyalty scheme, and a smaller number have worked out how to use their consumer data to reduce costs and increase sales. Since the early 1980s, Wal-Mart has built its business on knowing exactly what its customers were purchasing on a daily basis and on asking its vendors to restock shelves in a timely manner. This way, Wal-Mart avoided tying up cash in inventory and could work with vendors to drive down the cost of goods sold and the cost of moving them from manufacturer to consumer. This enabled Wal-Mart to offer lower prices and capture an ever-increasing share of the market. Wal-Mart is now the largest retailer in the world with over 3,600 stores. It has captured 13 per cent of all the sales in grocery, discount, and supercentre stores in the US (its nearest rival, Kroger, only has six per cent of this market.) Wal-Mart accounts for about five per cent of all food sales in the US, making it the third largest food store in the nation. Because Wal-Mart is large and efficient, it has forced the rest of the industry to become more efficient and more organised. In 1992 the rest of the retail food industry woke up and realised it needed to copy the Wal-Mart model.

Accordingly, the food supply industry developed the ECR system, which shares information between retailers and vendors. It allows for deliveries to be based on sales, lowering storage costs. The system has three main components. A recent development is electronic data interchange (EDI). This allows businesses to order merchandise, slim down the offerings in each food category, streamline delivery, and reduce overall costs. EDI, however, requires that suppliers and retailers use compatible computer systems, which takes capital to install and skilled personnel to operate.

(*Source*: extracted from Kinsey, J.D. (2000) 'The big shift from a food supply to a food demand chain,' Minnesota Agricultural Economist, Fall 1999, No. 698, www.extension.iastate.edu/agdm/articles/others/KinApr00.htm, accessed on May 22, 2002. With the permission of the author)

Due to the fact that some differences in cultures are to be found in every company, one observes the growing **encouragement of cooperative efforts across functional groups**. The goal is to get rid of departmental egoisms and interface conflicts when satisfying customer wishes. To work out these assignments, typical key problem areas such as communication deficiencies must be highlighted in the first stage and suitable measures undertaken to resolve them. Examples of these actions are receiver-relevant communication, informal communication, temporary exchanges of employees between departments in conflict, and the integration of working premises.

| Example 7.3 | The concept of 'Cross Functional Visits' has been applied in practice as an integrated coordination concept for marketing implementation. Its prime goal is to reduce communication deficiencies between the marketing department and other functional units in the firm. This is achieved by having employees jointly responsible for direct customer contacts. For instance, it is feasible that the R&D staff are confronted directly with a customer problem without marketing's involvement. Through this approach, the normal 'translation of customer wishes' into the specific speak of the developer becomes unnecessary. But naturally, function-overlapping project groups like those at ABB or the quality circle can promote such cooperative work. |

Modifications of company structures usually involve changes in the management structures. This shows up in the form of **empowerment** of lower level employees, through an expansion of decision-making competencies to lower hierarchical positions. Empowerment refers to all actions that permit an employee to make her or his own decision in a particular customer contact situation (Egan 2001, p. 145).

| Example 7.4 | The award winning hotel chain Ritz-Carlton is a classic example of implementing a successful empowerment. According to the company's policy employees have a discretionary amount of $2,000 which they can use and spend in the case of a complaint. As it is their own decision, conflicts can be resolved very quickly. Even though this measure could result in cheating by customers, Ritz-Carlton is proud of its empowerment culture. |

With empowerment, the organisational structure changes to the extent that factors such as self-determination, self-control, and independent decision-making become more meaningful. Through this extension of decision-making competence, effective coordination of tasks is achieved and a higher degree of relationship and customer orientation can be assured. Empowerment makes employees more motivated so that they see the relationship not only as one with the firm but also as a personal one. Consequently, they put in even more effort to satisfy the customer. If this leads to a high level of customer satisfaction and resultant retention, then the main requirements for developing and intensifying more profitable customer relationships have been reached. The following box 'Insights 7.3: Empowerment in retailing' demonstrates a successful case at Nordstrom.

Insights 7.3

Empowerment in retailing – the example of Nordstrom

The North American department store chain Nordstrom whose headquarters are in Seattle, Washington State, has a long-established reputation for empowering its sales associates. In turn, the company has also a phenomenal reputation for loyal customers. Regarding the empowerment practice, Nordstrom's sales associates have an 'empowered state of mind' feeling more control over how to perform the job, more awareness of the business context in which they perform their job and more accountability for performance outcomes. This is accomplished through management practices that confer significant amounts of power, information, knowledge and rewards upon them. As regards power, the associates have the discretion to do whatever it takes to please the customer. This is clearly documented in the Nordstrom policy manual consisting of the two sentences: 'Use your good judgment in all situations. There will be no additional rules.' Second, information on products and sales performance is widely shared in the company. As to knowledge, Nordstrom relies on an extensive on-the-job training rather than formal classroom training. Finally, associates can benefit from rewards. That is, the employees can earn well above the industry average through commissions on sales. There are also numerous status rewards such as being elected as 'Employee of the Month' or being nominated to the VIP Club. Assessing the value, industry analysts state that due to its empowerment practice Nordstrom accounts for a high level of employee sales, customer satisfaction and profits that make the company a benchmark in retailing.

(*Source*: based on Grönroos, C. (2000): *Service Management and Marketing. A Customer Relationship Management Approach*, 2nd edn. Chichester: John Wiley and Sons, p. 348. For additional reading and a more extensive discussion of Nordstrom see Peck, H., Payne, A., Christopher, M. and Clark, M. (eds.) (1999) *Relationship Marketing. Strategy and Implementation*, Case 5.3 Nordstrom Inc., case prepared by R.T. Pascale as a basis for classroom discussion, Oxford, pp. 375–401.

7.2.3 Relationship-focused management systems

In addition to structural changes management systems must also be modified simultaneously for successful implementation. The term management system refers to all permanent, partly or completely standardised processes set up to continuously ease the handling of activities in the firm. Management systems are comprised of sub-systems such as those for value, planning, control, personnel, the organisation, and for information. The following systems are the key ones for attaining customer orientation:

- Information system
- Control system

Appropriate changes are needed within the **information system** to enable the firm to collect and process all data on current customers. A relationship-focused information system should, for example, permit the derivation of customer structure analyses, calculations of rates of return for customers, or customer portfolios (Egan 2001, p. 193; Grönroos 2000, p. 31, 171). Guidance and control of individual relationships is possible only through such specific analyses. The individual relationship can be built up and intensified by customised processing of information such as that from customer databases with the application of specific software for customer contacts. Figure 7.3 illustrates how the processing of information influences different service encounters of airlines.

The centralised storage of information in a **data warehouse** is another important aspect of information systems in the sense of profitable relationship marketing. Due to the implementation of data warehousing FedEx reduced its campaign management cycle times and helped increase response rates in campaigns. As a measurable

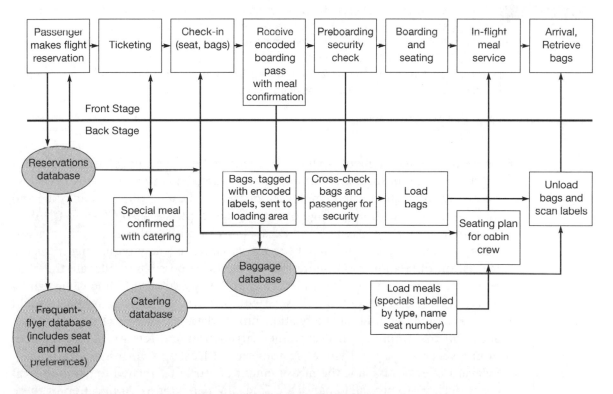

Figure 7.3 Using IT for customisation of service to airline passengers
(*Source*: Lovelock 2001, p. 550)

result, revenues of FedEx's first overnight service increased dramatically (BBDO Consulting 2001). The information system must also secure information exchange over an 'Electronic Data Interchange' (EDI), for example, with prior and subsequent partners. A system should then be developed to fulfil the need for the internal and external customer related information required to achieve buyer-directed strategies founded on a sound information basis.

Example 7.5	The case of USAA which converted from an bureaucratic, product-centric organisation into one of today's most successful icons for customer service and one-to-one marketing illustrates how information systems can contribute to relationship marketing strategies. The company establishes customer loyalty by constantly updating its professional customer database and remembering all the details of an individual customer's history with the firm. And its customer base, which stands at over 3.5 million people, grows by up to eight per cent annually. Meanwhile, the company has become the builder and user of the world's largest automated call distribution system, handling 400,000 voice calls over more than 23,600 phone lines and 16 million computer transactions daily. (*Source*: BBDO Consulting 2001)

Example 7.6	Laura Ashley, the British-based fashion and furnishing retail group, was one of the most successful retail chains in 1980. Laura Ashley had a special electronic point of sale system (EPOS) in each store. This recorded the inventory status and transmitted changes immediately to the group head office, which initiated an automatic replenishment order. The optimal inventory levels were calculated for each season at the head office. In the case of bottlenecks, the system assigned priorities to the bigger stores. (*Source*: adapted from Peck 1995)

There are two requirements that can be identified on this control aspect. One: for enhancing relationship orientation, inwardly directed **control systems** like those for measuring customer and employee satisfaction must be widely established and also integrated in the existing controlling concept (see also Chapter 8). Two: prominence must be given to the expansion of traditional cost accounting systems to include customer-related success variables as a key requirement for the realisation of relationship orientation. It should be possible to allocate the costs and benefits to individual customers so that the customer's lifetime value can be determined (Hart, Heskett and Sasser 1990, p. 148). The control systems should thus be aligned with all of the relationship marketing's success chain variables – above all the output quality, customer satisfaction and retention, and the economic success of an individual customer or at least at a customer group level. Relevant methods include the measurement of attributes related to psychological constructs, customer sales analyses, or the CLV (Chapter 8). Application of these instruments enables one to verify and control the achievement of relationship marketing's success chain. This then secures the development and intensification of more profitable customer relationships.

In this context, stronger future **collaboration between structural and system modifications** will be necessary. This is evident, for example, in the area of processes where simultaneous modifications in the organisational structures (business processes) and in cost accounting (process cost accounting) are needed. If by making the structure more process focused, it appears that the firm's existing systems such as cost-carrier accounting are not suitable for controlling processes, it will become necessary to shift the focus of the control systems to the processes. This can be done, for instance, through the application of process cost accounting that permits process cost analyses within the company, and for customer contacts independent of specific products.

7.2.4 Relationship-focused corporate culture

Among optimally-designed structures and systems, the corporate structure is the critical facet for implementing relationship orientation. This is particularly true in the service sector characterised by extensive customer contact, but is also an important factor in the classic consumer goods sector. The term corporate structure refers to basically all the combined values and expected norms as well as intellectual and behavioural patterns that characterise decisions, actions, and activities of company employees (Egan 2001, p. 144; Grönroos 2000, p. 356). The need to modify the corporate structures arises if the existing corporate values and norms no longer represent the current social requirements with respect to relationship orientation.

A **non-relationship-focused corporate structure** has various indicators. If some of the following indicators are present, it can be assumed that the **relationship and customer orientation** have major deficiencies:

- Management positions are staffed exclusively by individuals with a product-focused outlook
- There is no direct customer contact above a certain management level
- Horizontal and vertical exchange of customer related information does not take place
- The company has many hierarchies that handicap agreements within the company
- The company has extensive bureaucracy
- Service provision does not reflect customer wishes

Example 7.7

Traditionally, customer orientation is not something that comes naturally to many of the existing gas suppliers, given that most have internally-oriented engineering cultures, while their monopoly or near-monopoly status meant that customers had little or no choice of an alternative. However, the organisation of energy companies in terms of relationship and customer orientation is currently being intensely debated in Germany and other European countries. Power producers face the task of expanding their range of services and especially of improving their service quality. For example, in both Europe and the US, companies have emerged to offer utility services – from banking and telecoms to bundled electricity and gas supplies – over the Internet.

In numerous segments company employees take on a key role as the 'culture supporters' for customer and relationship orientation. **Customer and relationship orientation of employees** can be divided into two dimensions (Homburg and Stock 2000):

1 Customer-oriented attitude

2 Customer-oriented behaviour

A **customer-oriented attitude** is the basis for the company's focus as practised through its employees. First of all, the overall employee motivation for customer orientation is relevant. Experiences of individual employees with customers, particularly dissatisfied or even angry ones, and their customer complaints influence the customer orientation attitude. In addition, personality attributes such as the sense of self worth, sociability, and empathy are important drivers for the customer orientation of employees. A customer-oriented attitude is only valuable for developing and intensifying relationships if it leads to **customer-oriented behaviour**. Key factors for such behaviour are the employee's social and professional capabilities and employment satisfaction level.

If companies discover deficiencies in culture within the entire organisation they should seek to make positive changes. In the past, heated debates have been held over the question of whether such a change is possible or not. Presently, it is accepted that a **culture alteration process** is feasible and can be directed within limitations. Nevertheless, it should not be ignored that a corporate culture modification occurs very slowly and numerous internal hurdles must be overcome. Within set limits a three-step approach is required to **effect corporate culture changes**:

1 Analysis of the current corporate culture

2 Culture changing process

3 Monitoring the cultural changes

The first step covers an **analysis of the existing corporate culture** to evaluate the cultural proclivity for the relationship orientation. There are various methodologies that can be utilised. For instance, a written questionnaire with different cultural dimensions can be conducted for all employees (Deshpandé, Farley and Webster 1993). A status quo analysis is the derivation of characteristic attributes of the current corporate culture that make it possible to identify different cultural types. Figure 7.4 illustrates the attributes of four **cultural types**: the clan, adhocracy, market, and hierarchy cultures (refer to Quinn and Rohrbaugh 1983 on the development of cultural types; for the application to marketing see Deshpandé, Farley and Webster 1993).

Research in this field has shown that companies with an adhocracy culture achieve the highest relationship and customer orientation. This is followed by the market and clan culture, while companies with a hierarchical culture exhibit the lowest degree of relationship and customer orientation.

Inclusion of two groups of people can function well for initiating the culture change process. First, the use of **individuals** with leadership personalities can

Organic Processes
(flexibility, spontaneity)

Type: **Clan** Dominant Attributes: Cohesiveness, participation, teamwork, sense of family Leader Style: Mentor, facilitator, parent figure Bonding: Loyalty, tradition, interpersonal cohesion Strategic Emphases: Toward developing human resources, commitment, morale	Type: **Adhocracy** Dominant Attributes: Entrepreneurship, creativity, adaptability Leader Style: Entrepreneur, innovator, risk taker Bonding: Entrepreneurship, flexibility, risk Strategic Emphases: Toward innovation, growth, new resources
Type: **Hierarchy** Dominant Attributes: Order, rules and regulations, uniformity Leader Style: Coordinator, administrator Bonding: Rules, policies and procedures Strategic Emphases: Toward stability, predictability, smooth operations	Type: **Market** Dominant Attributes: Competitiveness, goal achievement Leader Style: Decisive, achievement-oriented Bonding: Goal orientation, production, competition Strategic Emphases: Toward competitive advantage and market superiority

Internal Maintenance (smoothing activities integration) — **External Positioning** (competition, differentiation)

Mechanistic Processes
(control, order, stability)

Figure 7.4 Correlation between the corporate culture and relationship orientation
(*Source*: adapted from Deshpandé, Farley and Webster 1993, p. 25)

initiate the desired cultural change if they have and exemplify strong models with definitive expectations of the corporate culture that one strives for (Mallak 2001, p. 22; St-Amour 2001, p. 21). Second, the change process can also be pushed forward by the participation of **all company employees**. The latter often means creating a new company outlook and implementing corporate identity concepts.

The **employee culture** can be guided in two ways: by hiring new employees or persuading current ones. When **hiring new employees** particular attention should be paid to the candidates' customer-related nature including attributes such as mental flexibility and well-developed communication and contact skills (Figure 7.5).

To **persuade current employees** their attitude and behaviour needs to be focused much more towards the customer. A customer representative, for example, will require training in active listening and observing, recognising the customer type, a customer-oriented speech style, non-verbal communication, and self-organisation (Egan 2001, p. 147; Kotler 2000, p. 636). In all, this involves the key relationship marketing principle of perspective taking (Chapter 3).

Reward systems, too, may play a crucial role in employee development (Egan 2001, p. 148). At present, most compensation systems include a mix of basic salary

Potential Requirements	Process Requirements	Outcome Requirements
• Endurance	• Clear diction	• Reliability
• Stress tolerance	• Empathy	• Preciseness
• Inertia	• Communication capability	• Punctuality
• Mental flexibility	• Contact capability	• Accessibility
• Qualifications	• Self control	• Decision-making capability
• Energy	• Listening capability	• Flexibility
• Impression	• Initiative	• Acceptance of criticism

Figure 7.5 Characteristics of customer-oriented employees

and a variable, performance-related bonus which is based on sales volume and customer acquisition data. However, following a relationship marketing strategy, further criteria have to be considered. Over the long term, employees should be rewarded by customer profitability, account penetration, and customer retention.

Example 7.8

The John Lewis Partnership, Great Britain, is a retail organisation that has always treated its employees as partners. Each employee also participates in the 'partnership benefits' such as dividends and the right of co-determination on strategic and tactical decisions of the store group. However, as times have become more competitive in retailing, the question arises of whether John Lewis will be forced to restructure more in line with other retailers in Great Britain. According to an internal communiqué, this seems not to be the case. In the internal company newsletter (the 'Gazette') of May 22, 1999, the Director of Administration stated, that 'the Partnership is a commercial enterprise, and if it is to survive in an increasingly competitive world, it must balance the interests of "partners" with the expectations of customers'. Thus, there will be no restructuring, but some rebalancing of priorities.

(*Source*: adapted from Egan 2001, p. 149).

The last step of **monitoring the cultural changes** determines if the targeted corporate culture has been accomplished or not. The term monitoring here refers to a continuing assessment process to see if the changes are actually taking effect or are stagnating. The more dynamic the competitive environment and the general corporate situation, the more meaningful the assessment. In case of deviation from the aspired-to path, thought is to be given to corrective measures that could be instituted. These must always take into account that natural limits to the culture changing process exist. Figure 7.6 depicts an overview of the flow of a general culture-changing process.

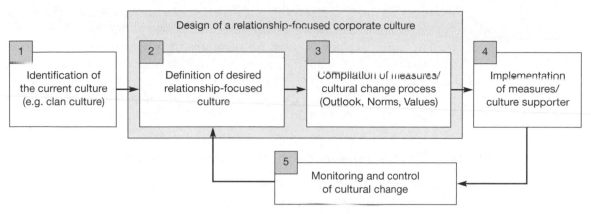

Figure 7.6 Stages involved in the process of culture changing

In summary, it can be confirmed that the corporate culture is a key aspect for the design and improvement of relationships and customer orientation. Limits to changes in the culture must nevertheless be included in the calculations. A **comparative assessment** of the three relationship marketing implementation areas shows that relationship marketing can be successfully implemented only if the structures, systems, and the culture are all handled simultaneously. The priorities should always be placed on the structures and if necessary on the systems, since modifications to them have an impact on the corporate culture changes.

7.3 Implementation process

In order to be able to change the corporate structure, its systems, and culture, it is necessary to initially deliberate systematically on an implementation concept so that the respective measures result in a comprehensive conclusion. A suitable implementation approach needs to be selected followed by the definition of a phase model for ensuring consistent implementation of relationship marketing.

7.3.1 Continuous versus discontinuous implementation approach

The problem of inadequate relationship orientation is not new in most firms wishing to improve the situation. After a certain amount of time developing awareness a discussion is often held on two alternatives. One is on the question as to whether radical **corporate restructuring** should be undertaken, whereby the change process is done top-down by management and introduced successively. The second option is to attain **permanent improvements** by proceeding in small steps with employees participating in the relationship orientation implementation process.

It sometimes becomes necessary to make a choice between a revolutionary and an evolutionary approach. However, this does not appear to be really convincing and, based on corporate practice, not maintainable in that form. It is much more reasonable to combine both approaches to be able to generate the optimal method for enhancing the relationship orientation. At the start it appears to make sense to apply more radical change processes, so that subsequent adjustments of the corporate potential can be done in steps and continuously together with the employees.

7.3.2 Phase model for implementing relationship orientation

The following **phase concept** can be the basis for simple sequential steps to implement relationship marketing (Bruhn 1999b, p. 316):

1 Management commitment

2 Communication with employees

3 Setting-up of a project team to execute the action programmes

4 Employee commitment and transition to a 'learning organisation'

Management commitment is the convincing prerequisite for achieving the prime goal – the successful transformation and execution of a concept for enhancing customer orientation. All building blocks and instruments for relationship orientation would lead to limited success if management's thoughts and actions contradicted the postulated fundamentals of relationship orientation. The focus on customer needs must then be re-examined daily. If management's support is not decisive in the initial implementation phase, then failure is already pre-programmed at this stage.

Example 7.9	One step that management can take here is to commit itself to contacting customers and experiencing for itself the problems involved in implementing relationship and customer orientation. At Henkel KGaA, Gulph Mills, Pennsylvania, the management team held advisory discussions and product presentations in supermarkets.

Based on kick-off events in which the necessity for greater focus on customers becomes clear, the motivation of employees towards implementation of relationship and customer orientation can be increased by **communicating with employees.** Workshops and seminars are possible ways to discuss the targets, contents, and the extent of the change processes. To avoid irritation in the first phase it is essential that the discussions held are open and direct with respect to the corporation's expectations bound within the implementation process. Only open dialogue can help to overcome personnel barriers that often complicate the introduction of new concepts.

Example 7.10

Giving information too early to employees can also have a negative effect, especially if the implementation plans have not yet been thought through and the briefing on the next implementation steps is vague. The German Siemens Group experienced this effect when it informed its employees about a range of implementation data labelled as 'top' without being specific. The consequence was that the employees questioned the whole seriousness of the project.

(*Source*: Zeyer 1995, p. 284).

Implementing action programmes with a project team comprising a small group of employees from different hierarchical levels can help reach the customer orientation targets, and more importantly to identify the barriers involved at an early stage (Reiss 1995, p. 280). This means securing acceptance and getting the knowledge needed to put together concrete action programmes that could be of assistance in raising customer orientation. The measures include aspects such as presenting new management methods, training in quality techniques, or defining the capabilities necessary for appropriate reaction in customer contacts. The impact on performance will be greater with the numbers of employees participating actively in the change programme. Over time, instead of the implementation remaining within the project group confines, it will be successively extended to encompass all the company areas involved.

Example 7.11

In 1995, the car manufacturer Volkswagen founded its own training group in Germany in order to develop suitable managers that could direct and initiate the change process. This group took on the tasks of qualifying employees at an extremely individual level. With this form of care Volkswagen intended to avoid turf wars and to prepare employees for future team jobs.

(*Source*: Henn 1995, p. 306).

Finally, the employees should be committed and should strive for a **transition to a 'learning organisation'**. This refers to the firm's ability to bundle existing knowledge on customer requirements and integrate it into a permanent learning process (Cahill 1995, p. 46). If this process is completed and pursued further, the firm's relationship orientation can be markedly increased.

Example 7.12

Lufthansa, the German airline, installed a worldwide, centralised customer database to generate and continuously improve its 'learning relationship' over the entire customer lifetime cycle (pre pre-flight, pre-flight, flight, post-flight, and post post-flight phase). In addition, continuous improvements are made in the integration of its partners and in the customer contact points such as interfaces, data exchange, and relationship marketing. As a result, derived from the new customer database structure, Lufthansa has developed special acquisition and loyalty activities, e.g. Customer Win Back programme, Top 1000, Berlin programme, Golden Age programme, Junior programme, etc.

(*Source*: adapted from BBDO Consulting 2001, p. 15).

It can be stated that in theory and in practice, numerous problem areas still exist and must be resolved to overcome current gaps in implementation. At the forefront are change processes that have impacts on individuals, groups, and organisations. Only after the structures, systems, and the culture have been sufficiently altered will the prerequisites for the implementation of relationship orientation be truly in place.

Summary

In this chapter we have addressed the implementation phase of relationship marketing. Specifically, we have talked about different targets and phases that can be differentiated and the barriers to implementing relationship marketing. We concluded that within the framework of relationship marketing greater attention has to be paid to the development of customer-oriented organisational structures, management systems, and an appropriate culture. Regarding the implementation process we differed between two approaches: a radical corporate restructuring and permanent improvements. As it is much more reasonable to combine both approaches, we finally introduced a four-step phase concept for implementing relationship marketing successfully.

8 The control phase of relationship marketing

Overview

Developing a strategic relationship marketing concept is fine in theory. However, in practice, organisations are faced with costs of the relationship marketing activities. Therefore, it is vital to include a control phase for monitoring the costs and benefits of relationship marketing. We support that all (pre-economic and economic) monitoring actions should be carried out proactively, so the results can be applied to future planning measures. Elaborating on the control phase we will address the following questions in this chapter:

➤ Which criteria have to be fulfilled for monitoring the impact of relationship marketing?

➤ Which pre-economic impacts can be differentiated, and which control methods can be applied in this case?

➤ Which economic impacts can be differentiated? Which control methods can be applied for monitoring relationship marketing activities in the case of a single period or in the case of multiple periods?

➤ Which integrated control system methods can be applied to monitor the impacts of relationship marketing?

8.1 Control methods and requirements

A strategic relationship marketing concept and its attendant measures can be successful over the medium term only if the activities and their impacts are continuously controlled. Even when the **control phase** is at the end of relationship marketing's planning phase, monitoring actions should be carried out proactively, and the findings applied to future planning measures. The control phase's **relative value** is high because relationship marketing is focused on profitability. Consequently, results of monitoring such as the CLV form the basis for customer segmentation, which in turn enables customer-specific control of relationships.

The impacts of relationship marketing are **monitored** mainly to separate pre-economic and economic monitoring effects (Figure 8.1). Pre-economic monitoring is particularly important because the pre-economic variables enable the determination of economic performance in the context of relationship marketing's success

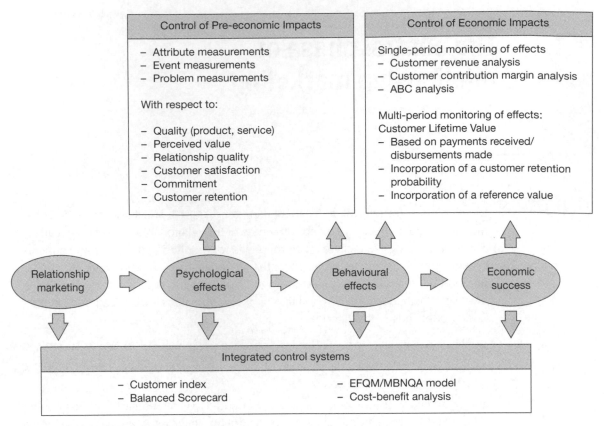

Figure 8.1 Control methods for marketing

chain. Integrated control methods can be used to investigate the effects of pre-economic and economic parameters jointly and interdependently, and also permit consideration of correlations between actions and effects.

To ensure that the implementation of relationship marketing controls is focused, the relevant methods must fulfil various **criteria** that can be sub-divided into either outcome or execution types. The following are the **outcome criteria**:

■ The monitoring results achievable with the method should be **decision-oriented**, i.e. it is necessary to determine if the findings permit derivation of a basis for control.

■ A monitoring instrument should be consistent for high **reliability**, i.e. it must lead to the same result when repeated and thus provide the real value of the control variable.

■ The monitoring method should be **valid**, i.e. it monitors what is to be monitored.

■ The processes and their results should be as **topical** as possible to ensure that the findings of the control instrument are meaningful.

■ The control results should be **comprehensive**, i.e. it should be verified whether all the customer-relationship-relevant aspects can be tested with one control instrument. One should not overlook the fact that incompleteness can possibly have the advantage of being very specific and thus highly decision-oriented.

- The control results should be highly **constituent** due to relationship marketing's focus on individual customers. Only then is it possible to monitor and control relationships with specific customers or customer groups.

Control methods must also fulfil certain **implementation requirements** based on the following aspects:

- The **organisational effort** for the preparation and implementation of single instruments varies considerably.

- The methodologies for specific processes have different **complexity** levels. In many cases this complexity and the meaningfulness of the findings are correlated.

- The **costs** to be estimated for each instrument can at times differ significantly depending on the number of employees, the need for external expert knowledge, the implementation duration, etc.

The above requirements must be taken into account, since the relationship marketing monitoring methods vary greatly in terms of their approach and their outcomes.

8.2 Control of pre-economic impacts

Pre-economic controls are aimed at verifying relationship marketing's pre-economic targets. Hence, it is necessary to conduct various **construct measurements** based on these targets. These include the relationship assessment (product quality, perceived value, relationship quality), the psychological consequences (customer satisfaction, commitment), and the behavioural consequences in the form of customer retention (Chapter 3). These controls can be implemented through three groups of processes:

1 Attribute control
2 Event control
3 Problem control

8.2.1 Attribute control

It is necessary to analyse the features of the constructs in the control phase. A standard measurement of psychological variables represents either single **attribute measurement** or multiple attribute measurement. Single attributes of each variable are measured and aggregated into the overall value for the respective construct. This is done under the assumption that psychological constructs like the perceived product or relationship quality are the results of specific estimates of different **attributes**. Alternatively, a global assessment of a particular construct is the sum of multiple attributes. A customer questionnaire is the main data collection method for determining the attributes and a multi-attribute approach can be adopted as follows:

1 Development of a questionnaire to identify and categorise attributes

2 Application of the questionnaire results to prioritise the attributes, determine construct features, and to derive control measures

Developing a questionnaire

Multi-attribute approaches are implemented by first determining the individual attributes for the relevant construct. **Attribute identification** can be based on many sources including studies in the literature on measurement of the particular construct. The results of verbal customer questionnaires, such as focused group or in-depth single person interviews can be used as an alternative. After completing the initial tests this approach provides a **battery of items** with a range of attributes that can be used for measuring each construct.

Categorising the attributes helps to identify them. This can be done in two ways. One: attributes can be heuristically categorised by allocating them to the relevant logical main attribute. Two: they could be categorised statistically with the help of factor analysis. However, this is only possible on completion of a customer questionnaire to generate the necessary data for the factor analysis.

Marketing literature offers appropriate measurement scales that can be used for laying out the steps to be taken for the relationship assessment, psychological and behavioural consequence constructs, as well as their significance in relationship marketing (refer to Chapter 3 for the conceptualisation of these constructs and their meaning in relationship marketing). A **questionnaire** can be drawn up for determining the constructs by formulating the relevant items. With respect to the **output quality**, which is an important determinant of customer satisfaction and retention, there are classic scales for measuring the **product quality**. The following categories could, for instance, be a part of the product quality (Zeithaml and Bitner 2000, p. 82; Garvin 1988; Figure 8.2): performance, features, reliability, conformance, durability, serviceability, aesthetics, and perceived quality (roughly equivalent to prestige).

It is necessary to apply specific **scales for measuring the service quality**, due to the unique aspects of services such as immateriality and customer integration in the provision of the product process. The **SERVQUAL method** has attained special recognition by defining the discrepancy between the expected and perceived service from the customer's perspective (Parasuraman, Zeithaml and Berry 1988; 1986; 1985). According to this method, service quality is measured on the basis of 22 attributes classified into the following categories (for details about SERVQUAL's structure and definitions of its dimensions, see Parasuraman, Zeithaml and Berry 1988):

■ Tangibles

■ Reliability

■ Responsiveness

■ Assurance

■ Empathy

Quality Criteria	Car	Refrig-erator	Micro-wave	Suit	Stereo system	Bicycle	Yogurt
Technical product features Durability, safety, state of the art, agreeableness, freshness, breakdown frequency	•	•	••	•	••	○	○
Emotional product features Design, brands, company image, innovation, packaging	••	–	–	•	•	•	•
Price Purchase price, price segment, operating costs, re-sale value, financing terms	○	•	•	•	•	○	••
Service Before purchase: product information During purchase: advice, atmosphere After purchase: customer service, guarantee	••	•	•	••	•	•	– –
Delivery capability Prompt delivery, meeting the deadline	–	•	•	••	•	•	••
Environmental friendliness Power consumption, materials, disposal	•	••	•	– –	○	○	○
Customisation Customised planning and design	••	–	–	••	•	•	– –
Product accompanying ambiance Customer clubs, creation of an infrastructure for usage, competition, accompanying information	○	○	•	•	••	○	– –
Handling of complaints Location for filing and handling complaints	•	○	•	–	•	•	–
Purchasing locations Experience centre, advice centre, mail order	•	○	○	•	•	○	–

•• = Extremely important   • = very important   ○ = important   – = not very important   – – = unimportant

Figure 8.2 Product quality attributes

While the original SERVQUAL instrument has been revised and refined, its length, structure, and content have remained the same (Parasuraman, Berry and Zeithaml 1991). Figure 8.3 depicts the revised attribute formulations from a SERVQUAL questionnaire for establishing the **service quality**. The statements are to be answered by the respondents with simultaneous measurement of perception and expectation on a scale ranging from 'absolutely relevant' to 'totally irrelevant'. According to SERVQUAL the service quality dimensions that can be modified or extended depending on the company and sector conditions, are to be taken as the standard.

Reliability
1. Providing services as promised. 2. Dependability in handling customers' service problems. 3. Performing services right the first time. 4. Providing services at the promised time. 5. Maintaining error-free records.
Responsiveness
6. Keeping customers informed about when services will be performed. 7. Prompt service to customers. 8. Willingness to help customers. 9. Readiness to respond to customers' requests.
Assurance
10. Employees who instil confidence in customers. 11. Making customers feel safe in their transactions. 12. Employees who are consistently courteous. 13. Employees who have the knowledge to answer customer questions.
Empathy
14. Giving customers individual attention. 15. Employees who deal with customers in a caring fashion. 16. Having the customers' best interest at heart. 17. Employees who understand the needs of their customers. 18. Convenient business hours.
Tangibles
19. Modern equipment. 20. Visually appealing facilities. 21. Employees who have a neat, professional appearance. 22. Visually appealing materials associated with the service.

Figure 8.3 SERVQUAL questionnaire
(*Source*: Parasuraman, Zeithaml and Berry 1994, p. 207)

Customer expectations that either represent the quality or influence it, depending on the definition of product quality, are often measured on the basis of the service attributes as per the SERVQUAL method (for additional reading, see Bruhn 2000). The questionnaire formulation depends on the type of expectation (Chapter 3). The statement 'attribute X of product Y will be excellent' is measured under **predictive expectations**, while 'attribute X should be excellent with products of type Z' falls under **normative expectations**.

The SERVQUAL method can be very useful for relationship marketing, due to the relevance of service quality and customer expectations. This method offers the appropriate basis for systematic control of relationship marketing's pre-economic success variables.

With regard to **perceived value** in practice, specific attributes questioned often do not relate to those of a particular object such as an output or a relationship, but rather to aspects with which the construct can be described. This could include the price-benefit ratio or the price sensitivity depending on the definition of perceived value. The following sample questionnaire formulations should be scaled to determine the perceived value (Zeithaml 1988):

- 'Service X has a good price-benefit ratio'
- 'Service X has a high quality for its price'
- 'Service X is a good buy'
- 'Service X is fairly priced'

When measuring the **relationship quality** only those dimensions are applied that can be used as a basis for its conceptualisation. In this context, Figure 8.4 shows six attributes of relationship quality that could be allocated to the dimensions familiarity and trust.

The **customer proximity** construct, based on differentiating between the corporation's product offer and interaction behaviour, is closely connected with the two constructs – output and relationship quality (Homburg 1998a). The related measurement approach is based on a study from the industrial goods segment, with the view that the two dimensions can be applied in principle to both the consumer goods and service sectors. The prime dimensions of customer proximity depicted in Figure 8.5 are described in terms of eight factors with 28 indicators (Homburg 1998a).

Customer satisfaction is frequently monitored by measuring it in terms of various attributes and then aggregating them into a combined value (Oliver 1996). This

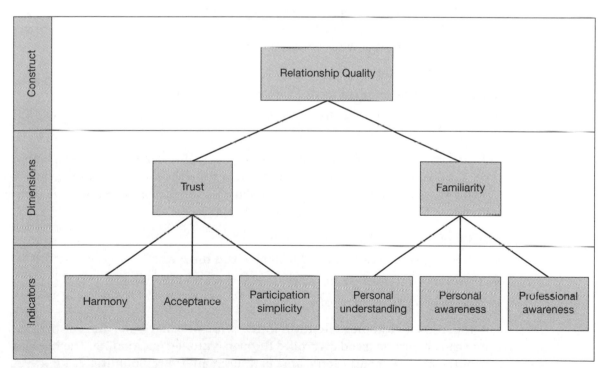

Figure 8.4 Relationship quality dimensions and attributes
(*Source*: Georgi 2000, p. 104)

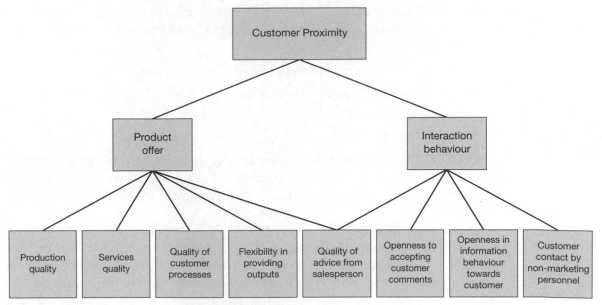

Figure 8.5 Customer proximity factors and dimensions
(*Source*: Homburg 1998a)

approach strongly parallels the determination of product and service quality – with the result that these two variables end up with faulty differentiation. Another customer satisfaction measurement scale is often applied as a national customer index (Fornell 1992). This scale explicitly accounts for customer expectations of satisfaction and covers the following three attributes:

■ Global satisfaction

■ Comparison of delivered service with expectations prior to its usage

■ Comparison of service delivered with an ideally expected service of a relevant category

The attributes of the **commitment** construct are highly dependent on the output type. Customers are thus committed differently to sellers such as a football club or a public transport firm. The following statements were cited to measure the commitment of theatregoers (Garbarino and Johnson 1999):

■ 'I am proud to belong to this theatre'

■ 'I believe that in a certain way I belong to this theatre'

■ 'I am very concerned about the long-term success of this theatre'

■ 'I am very loyal to this theatre'

The intentional **customer retention** in the sense of behavioural aims of the customer can be measured and controlled through customer questioning. The relevant attributes are (Zeithaml, Berry and Parasuraman 1996; Boulding *et al.* 1993; Parasuraman, Berry and Zeithaml 1991):

- Likelihood of repeat purchases
- Cross buying intention
- Intention to make recommendations

The **customer questionnaires** developed for measuring the attributes of one or more constructs are usually conducted in writing, to be able to determine the respective construct from the customers' standpoint.

Applying the questionnaire findings

Developing and conducting the customer questionnaire is aimed at generating results that can be applied in the context of relationship marketing's control phase. The findings could be applied to:

- Set attribute priorities
- Determine features of constructs
- Derive control measures

Setting attribute priorities helps to classify the attributes according to their significance for the particular construct. A classic example of a hierarchy of attributes based on the product quality is the Kano model that differentiates three types of output attributes (Kano 1984; Figure 8.6):

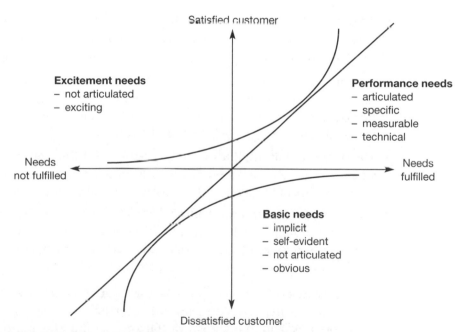

Figure 8.6 Kano model classification of quality attributes
(*Source*: Bailom *et al.* 1996, p. 118; based on Berger *et al.* 1993)

1 **Basic needs** are always expected by the customer. They represent **must factors** not judged positively by the customer and thus have no major impact on subsequent factors like customer retention.

2 **Performance needs** that should be present are called **should factors**. Their impacts on subsequent factors could be positive if present, but negative if missing.

3 **Excitement needs** that are not necessarily expected by customers represent **could factors**. If present they have positive consequences, but are not noticed if missing.

Statistical methods such as factor analysis need to be applied to rank the attributes of a construct based on empirical data. The construct is taken as a factor, and the factor load from the analysis indicates the significance of each attribute in the overall construct. A differentiated attribute ranking can be derived by applying customer indices (section 8.4.2), which consider the correlation between the construct analysed and the remaining constructs.

The **characteristics of the constructs analysed** can be determined from the questionnaire findings by aggregating the attribute features in two ways:

1 The average value of the construct is calculated through **simple aggregation**.

2 Since the significance of each attribute in the overall value of the construct often differs greatly, however, it makes more sense to conduct it a second way with a **weighted aggregation**, where the values taken for the weighting could be the ones calculated for attribute rankings (Figure 8.7).

Deriving actions for improvements is the main construct measurement task in relationship marketing's control phase. The basis is provided by both the features of the construct and the weighting and characteristics of the attributes:

■ The level of a **construct's characteristic** indicates the extent to which the target represented by the construct could be reached (e.g. enhancing customer satisfaction). If the construct's characteristic is below the target it is an indication that the respective variable represents the basis for applying the measures.

■ The **weighting of attributes** can be used to identify levers for adjusting a construct. The greater the importance of an attribute in the main construct the greater the possibility of influencing the construct by controlling the particular attribute.

■ The **characteristic of an attribute** is thus the means for determining the measures. The more positive an attribute's assessment the lower the effect of any further improvement in the attribute. Hence, any attribute with a high weighting and weak characteristics should be monitored.

To **critically assess** relationship marketing's **outcome criteria** for control instruments, it is first necessary to find out if attribute measurements are strongly decision-oriented and to highlight the factors that must be improved to reach relationship marketing goals. However, this is limited to pre-economic targets since economic targets cannot be determined from customer questionnaires.

There could be reliability and validity related problems in the attribute measurements, because of the complexity of the constructs involved. The topicality is

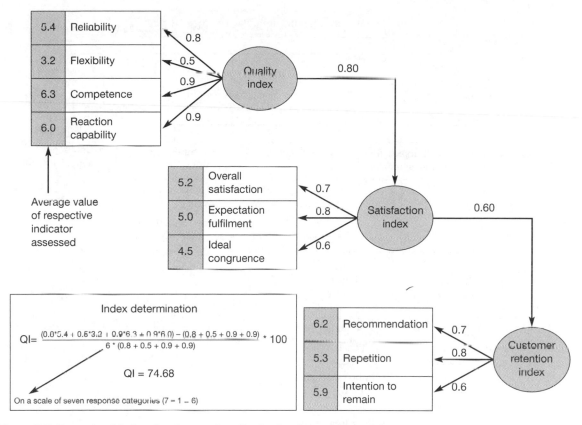

Figure 8.7 Example of index development on the basis of a causal model

highly dependent on the questionnaire's time period. Yet, when evaluating a customer at a particular time very old experiences could also have an influence. During the design of the respective questionnaire the relevant attributes for measuring the particular construct can be comprehensively reached. The outcomes of the attribute measurements could be recorded in terms of a constituent customer level. Certain analyses like statistical ranking of attributes are, however, not possible for specific customers.

The organisational requirements to implement attribute measurements are relatively significant, since the preparation of a questionnaire and the ongoing evaluations of the findings require a considerable amount of time. The evaluation, in particular, is somewhat complex and places high demands on those responsible for the monitoring. Consequently, these processes are very costly.

Determining relationship marketing's target variables requires the respondents to have a certain level of understanding of the products used. Only then can the customers judge an output in a written form. When different **output types** are involved it leads to two conflicting consequences. On the one hand, it can be argued that attribute measurements are preferred for customised products and services, since those customers tend to be more rational (e.g. purchase of a machine in the capital goods area). On the other hand, many customised outputs such as legal

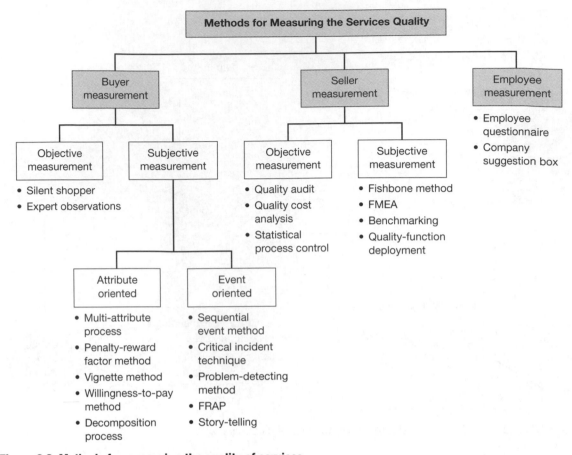

Figure 8.8 Methods for measuring the quality of services

services are more difficult to judge and the measurement of attributes can be problematic. It is hence necessary to modify the questionnaire to match the expertise and ability of the customer to make the assessment. In any case, attribute measurements are a valuable instrument for pre-economic monitoring of standard products.

In addition to attribute measurement event and problem methods can also be applied as key constructs of relationship marketing, particularly for monitoring the quality of services. Figure 8.8 provides an overview of the methods for measuring the services quality.

8.2.2 Event control

Event methodologies, in contrast to those for attributes, address concrete output provision situations from the customer's standpoint. These approaches include two primary types: the **sequential event method** and the critical incident technique. Under the sequential event method respondents are presented with a blueprint in personal interviews that reflects the typical course of a service provided (Shostack 1985; 1984; Figure 8.9). On this blueprint showing elements of the service process,

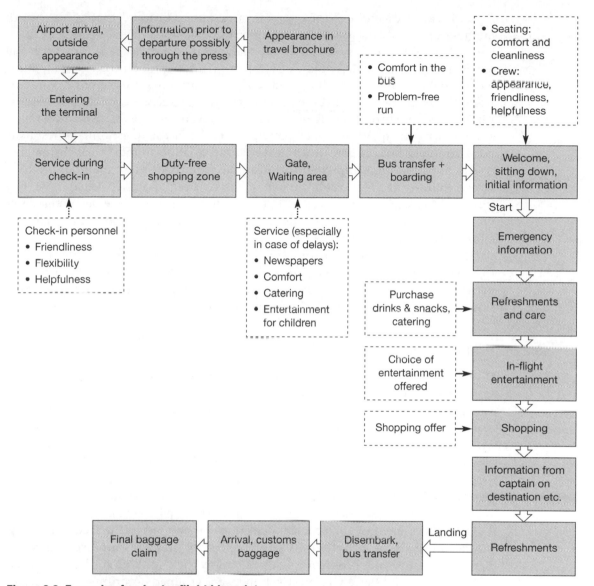

Figure 8.9 Example of a charter flight blueprint

the customers should be asked to think over emotional service experiences and state both the positive and negative ones.

The critical incident technique highlights the strengths and weaknesses of the service provision process at a more differentiated level. Critical incidents are those that the customer designates as particularly satisfying or dissatisfying contacts with the seller (Bitner, Booms and Tetreault 1990, p. 73). This technique attempts to record particular events with the help of questions to assist the customer in recalling the incidents (Mudie and Cottam 1993). This approach enables consistent implementation of the key perspective taking principle of relationship marketing.

A **critical assessment** of the outcome criteria demonstrates that event control methods are highly decision-oriented, since they record concrete customer experiences. The events, however, cannot be analysed in a standardised form with the result that systematic derivation of measures is problem-bound. These methods have reliability problems since each customer presents a different argument. Nonetheless, in specific situations one can assume an adequate amount of validity. A high level of currentness is not necessarily given but the status can be noted easily during the questioning. Comprehensiveness of the questionnaire results is not guaranteed but the constituent level permits analysis of individual customers.

The organisational **implementation requirements** of these methods are relatively significant since each customer has to be questioned separately. The interviews can be executed easily, but the interpretation of the customer statements is quite complex, with the result that event-related methods require a major effort for the assessment.

Due to **differences in output types** event methods are best suited for customised products and services, since these cover several phases of close contact between the seller and buyer. The customer's perception in the course of the provision process is thus of particular significance.

8.2.3 Problem control

Problem-related methods address quality relevant problems from the customer's standpoint. Among these are the problem detection method, the frequency relevance analysis of problems (FRAP), and measurement of complaints.

The **problem detection method** involves questioning customers about specific problems. The aim is to establish the occurrence frequency of a problem in the services provided and the severity of the problem from the customer's perspective. This approach can be applied only to situations where the relevant problem classes have already been defined. These must be determined in advance with suitable methods such as the critical incident technique (Lindqvist 1987).

The development of the problem detection method led to the **frequency relevance analysis of problems (FRAP)** approach that encompasses both the determination of the problem classes as well as their ranking on an evaluation raster (Brandt and Reffett 1989). Customers are grouped according to the occurrence of specific problems and are questioned on the degree of their annoyance and subsequent behavioural reaction. It is assumed that the more frequent the occurrence and significance appears to be for the customer the more urgently the service provider should deal with the particular problem. Figure 8.10 is a condensed scale illustration of a two-dimensional matrix with various fictitious problem relevance and frequency values from a banking services example. In this case the organisation can easily figure out that the most relevant problem occurs in long delays at the counter. While this problem has to be treated first, the delays of sending new checks are not so important for improving service quality.

Complaint measurement delivers information on problem areas within the service provision process. The measurement basis is the stimulation of customers who are urged to take the lead in filing complaints (Tax, Brown and Chandrashekaran

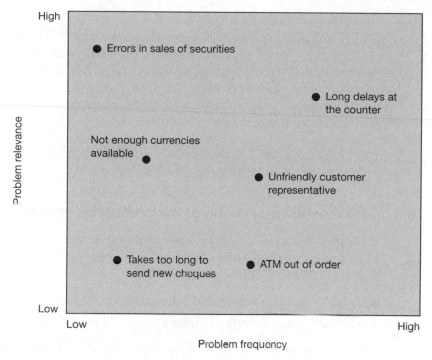

Figure 8.10 Example of a Problem Relevance/Problem Frequency matrix in retail banking

1998). Since customer problems in the service provision process are important reasons for defections, problem methods can be used as an **early warning system for relationship marketing.** By identifying problems, defections can be avoided and customer retention enhanced.

A **critical assessment** of the outcome criteria confirms that problem-methods are highly decision-focused. They identify provision problems of products from the customer perspective and thereby clearly highlight the basis for improvements. However, even though the results can lack reliability, they are regarded as being valid. Complaint measurement in particular exhibits high topicality, since customers normally speak out shortly after occurrence of a problem. However, complaint measurement is not comprehensive since a majority of the unhappy customers tend not to complain. Data collection for individual customers is possible at a constituent level.

The **requirements for implementation** show that the problem detection and the FRAP methods need roughly the same organisational effort and have the same complexity as attribute measurement. These methods thus incur comparative costs. In contrast, complaint measurement is relatively easy and cost effective, but it nevertheless requires the creation of the necessary conditions in the corporation such as motivating employees to proactively stimulate complaints.

Even though problem measurements stem from the services area, they can generate meaningful results for all **output types.** Since customised products and services are problem-bound because of their complexity, the respective methodologies are extremely relevant here.

8.3 Control of economic impacts

Control of pre-economic parameters within relationship marketing's success chain helps to optimise the economic variables, which have to be verified within the economic control framework of relationship marketing. As asserted by the customer relationship life cycle, customer relationships have a dynamic character so that two forms of economic control can be differentiated:

1 Single-period monitoring of customer relationships

2 Multi-period monitoring of customer relationships

8.3.1 Single-period monitoring of customer relationships

Customer relationships can be supervised over a period mainly through an analysis of **customer revenues and contribution margins**, which can be divided into the following (Figure 8.11):

■ Actual value versus potential value analyses

■ Absolute versus relative analyses

Customer revenue analysis looks at the turnover of individual customers. In addition to the current sales (actual value) this could include factors such as the expected or maximum revenues for that customer, i.e. the potential value of revenues. Absolute sales levels often tell little about a customer's relationship. Hence, a relative customer analysis should be conducted, for instance, to determine the following key figures:

■ A customer's **proportion of sales** versus total corporate sales indicates the value of that customer for the particular firm.

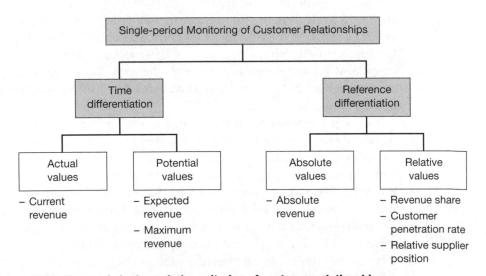

Figure 8.11 Types of single-period monitoring of customer relationships

- The **customer penetration rate** is based on a definition of the absolute market share and gives the customer's share of sales compared with her or his total needs for that product.

- The **relative supplier position** is derived from the relative market share and designates the ratio of sales achieved by the respective seller with a customer to the biggest competitor's sales with the same customer.

An **ABC analysis** can **compare key turnover levels between various customers** (Peck *et al.* 1999, p. 412). This analysis ranks the customers according to the sales level with the seller. The data are entered on an x-y plot with the axes 'cumulative share of customers' and 'cumulative turnover'. Starting with the largest customers on the basis of sales, the value is located on the y-axis and plotted versus the sales contribution along the x-axis. This often demonstrates that a relatively small number of customers make up the largest proportion of sales. In this connection, the 20:80 rule states that 20 per cent of the customers account for 80 per cent of sales. On the basis of the resulting curve the customers can be divided into A, B, or C customers. The A-customers are the largest sales generators and should thus be the first ones to be invested in (Figure 8.12).

A customer revenue analysis directed at the future should also include the **cross selling potential** in the analysis. This will indicate if the customer has needs for a product offered by the firm that has not yet been used. The cross selling potential is highly variable depending on the sector involved. The cross selling potential also varies depending on the significance of the potentially usable products and services in the firm's programme palette. In this context, a differentiation between main versus secondary or profitable versus unprofitable outputs could be relevant.

It is not easy to identify the specific revenues of a customer for all product types due to differences in **output types**. For standard products such as bubble gum the contact between the seller and buyer is often not too close. Hence, the

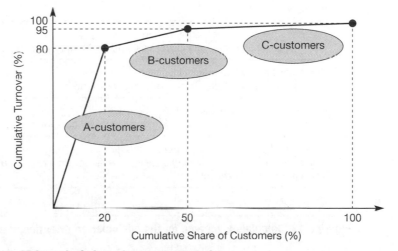

Figure 8.12 ABC-analysis based on customer sales

firm does not know the behaviour of each customer and can thus not specify the related sales amount.

The sales level reveals nothing on the profitability of a customer relationship. Customer sales is thus just an initial benchmark to monitor an economic relationship. The **customer contribution margin analysis** extends the customer revenue analysis by considering the costs involved in addition to the sales level of a relationship (Figure 8.13). Determining the associated costs for customers is partly problematic, since ascertaining the customer contribution margin requires eliciting which costs caused by the relationship apply to a particular customer and which would not apply if the relationship no longer existed (Berger and Nasr 1998).

A **critical assessment** of the outcome criteria over a single period of economic monitoring demonstrates that the relevant processes exhibit a low decision-orientation. These processes do not identify the causes or possible approaches for controlling revenues and contribution margins. The findings are highly reliable and valid. The currentness depends on the underlying calculation update interval. Comprehensive measurement of the target variables is feasible. Looking at the constituent level, the revenue and contribution margin determination is easier to conduct for individual customers, just as for behaviour measurement, in certain segments such as financial services and telecommunications.

The **implementation requirements** are sector-specific dependent. The closer the contact between the seller and buyer and the greater the amount of information held by the seller on the buyer, the lower the effort and the cheaper it is to achieve sales and calculate contribution margins for individual customers. The simplicity of these approaches makes them extremely popular in practice. However, when applying them, it should not be overlooked that these processes show only the profitability tendencies in a customer relationship. Multi-period monitoring, on the other hand, permits a sound analysis of relationship profitability.

Customer gross sales revenue per period − Reduction of sales revenue
= Customer net sales revenue per period − Costs of goods/services sold (direct costs per unit multiplied by sold units)
= Customer contribution margin I − Customer-driven cost per order (e.g. cost of reservation)
= Customer contribution margin II − Customer-driven cost per period (e.g. travel cost for customer calls)
− Other direct costs of customer per period (e.g. salary of an account manager exclusively responsible for the customer, mailing expenses, interest on overdue accounts)
= Customer contribution margin III

Figure 8.13 Calculation scheme for the customer contribution margin

8.3.2 Multi-period monitoring of customer relationships

Multi-period monitoring computes the CLV in three different customer evaluation steps (Figure 8.14):

1 Customer evaluation based on payments received and disbursements made
2 Incorporation of a customer retention probability
3 Incorporation of a reference value

Customer evaluation based on payments received and disbursements made is a classic investment computation that can be enhanced by incorporating a customer retention probability and a reference value. The first variant forms the basis for systematic analysis of relationship profit levels. The second and/or third variants are nevertheless meaningful extensions covering the relationship profitability comprehensively, thereby reflecting the high relevance of customer retention in relationship marketing.

(1) Customer evaluation based on payments received and disbursements made

The CLV method is, simply put, a computation methodology that translates the principles of dynamic capital investment analysis to customer relationships. The CLV is usually defined as the **present CLV** determined by discounting the payment stream to derive the present value. This approach is based on the principle that future payments are less valuable than current ones (Berger and Nasr 1998). The customer's present value is of interest since all the strategic decisions can be made only on the basis of the present value.

A **sample calculation** of the CLV is presented in Figures 8.15 and 8.16 (for more numerical examples refer to Berger and Nasr 1998). In this case, the customer relationship is evaluated over an average duration of eight years at a discount rate of ten percent. The customer specific acquisitions (investment) costs of 50 units are deducted in the first year. Figure 8.15 illustrates how the numbers are accumulated for each period. Figure 8.16 demonstrates how the CLV is calculated when using the

Step	References
Customer evaluation based on payments received and disbursements made	• Mulhern 1999
Incorporation of a customer retention probability	• Andon, Bradley and Baxter 1998 • Berger and Nasr 1998 • Wang and Spiegel 1994 • Keane and Wang 1995 • Dwyer 1997
Incorporation of a reference value	• Andon, Bradley and Baxter 1998

Figure 8.14 Customer evaluation steps based on the CLV

	t = 0	t = 1	t = 2	t = 3	t = 4	t = 5	t = 6	t = 7	
Predicted sales	4	6	10	16	20	20	20	20	
Product price	10	10	10	10	10	10	10	10	
Piece costs	3	3	3	3	3	3	3	3	
Marketing expenditures	20	30	40	40	30	30	20	20	
Acquisition costs	50	–	–	–	–	–	–	–	
Revenue	– 42.00	12.00	30.00	73.00	110.00	110.00	120.00	120.00	
Discount factor (r = 0.1)	1.00	1.20	1.44	1.73	2.07	2.49	2.99	3.58	**Present CLV**
Revenue (discounted)	– 42.00	10.91	24.79	54.09	75.13	68.30	67.74	61.58	Σ = $ 320.55
Customer retention probability (R = 0.75) and discounting (r = 0.1)	1.00	0.63	0.39	0.24	0.15	0.10	0.06	0.04	**Present CLV with customer retention probability**
Revenue (discounted, including retention rate)	– 42.00	8.18	13.95	22.82	23.77	16.21	12.06	8.22	Σ = $ 63.21

Figure 8.15 Calculation example of a CLV as an investment

Customer Lifetime Value (Present value)	$$CLV = -I_0 + \sum_{t=0}^{T} \frac{x_t \cdot (p - k) - M_t}{(1 + r)^t} = \boxed{\$ 320.55}$$
Customer Lifetime Value (Present value with customer retention probability)	$$CLV = -I_0 + \sum_{t=0}^{T} x_t \cdot (p - k) - M_t \frac{R_t}{(1 + r)^t} = \boxed{\$ 63.21}$$

t = Year
T = Anticipated number of years that the wooed customer remains
x_t = Predicted sales for year t
p = Customer specific product price
k = Piece costs
M_t = Customer specific marketing expenditures in year t
r = Computation interest rate
R = Retention rate
I_0 = Acquisition costs at time t = 0

Figure 8.16 Formulae for calculating the CLV as an investment

formulae. While both figures exhibit the calculation of the CLV in detail from a theoretical standpoint, organisations often face difficulties in practice when trying to implement the CLV method. However, if the calculation of a complete present CLV proves to be too cumbersome because of the lack of information, statistical models and so forth, organisations should at least try to calculate an average customer's lifetime value in a rather simplified manner (e.g. by customer segments).

(2) Incorporation of a customer retention probability

The **customer retention probability** is taken into account on the premise that integrating the uncertainty of retaining the relationship into the CLV computation also incorporates the risk in a relationship. Assuming the differences between markets based on the always-a-share and lost-for-good models (Jackson 1985; section 1.3), this uncertainty can be conceived through a migration model and a retention model (Dwyer 1997). The **migration model** is based on the always-a-share model and makes the assumption that the likelihood of a firm's renewed consideration by a customer is lower the greater the lapsed time since the last purchase. A probability tree is built up on this basis to determine the customer value in terms of an expected value. This value should be applied with caution due to the very high level of uncertainty in the relationship, particularly in transaction marketing. The **retention model** can compute the CLV in the lost-for-good model. Under the assumption that the customer relationship should be a long-term one, the payments received and disbursements made are adjusted by a customer retention probability determined on the basis that the relationship continues for the next period. These values lie between zero for relationship termination and one for definite relationship continuation.

The sample calculation as shown in figures 8.15 and 8.16 illustrates how the **CLV with the customer retention probability** is calculated. Ideally the retention probability is calculated for each customer to provide the likelihood of a repeat purchase within the upcoming year. In the example, the assumed probability of 0.75 suggests there is a 75 per cent chance that the customer's next purchase over the next period will be from this firm. This probability reduces the CLV by also considering the customer's specific risk.

The customer retention probability is an underlying element in the CLV computation, since it is the only one that can assess the customer-company relationship and the attendant risks in an extended investment analysis. Efforts have hence been made to analyse this probability more precisely, especially for individual customers. The **basic aim** of this analysis is to understand why a customer utilises the company's offer again. If one assumes that retention is influenced primarily by the relationship with the firm, then the likelihood of a repeat purchase or continuation of the relationship is dependent on the degree of retention.

A large number of possible indicators could be retention **influencing factors** (Figure 8.17). It is the firm's task to identify influencing factors that are significant for calculating the customer value. As an example, a study of automobile dealers analysed such factors to show the influence of various customer characteristics on the customer value (Reinartz and Kumar 2000).

The **computation of a specific customer retention probability** can be determined with a scoring model in which the various factors can be weighted. It is also possible to identify customer value factors on the basis of factor or structural equation models. Furthermore, to incorporate the customer relationship into the CLV calculation, one can develop buyer- and seller-specific quality and potential values using various relationship specific determinants (Hoekstra and Huizingh 1999; Figure 8.18). The first summand furnishes the past value of a customer based on the buyer's quality. This is then enhanced by the future value potential (seller quality, seller and customer potential) of the customer.

Economic determinants	Purchase related	• Order frequency • Sales volume • Cross selling rate • Customer duration
	Contractual	• Contracts • Club • Customer card
	Situational	• Competition • Switching barriers
	Technical/functional	• Technical dependence
Pre-economic determinants	Affective	• Satisfaction • Acceptance • Trust • Loyalty • Seller image
	Cognitive	• Willingness to take risks • Degree of publicity • Quality awareness • Price sensitivity

	Conative	• Cross buying intention
		• Intention to repeat a purchase
		• Acquisition/communication behaviour:
		  • Option leadership
		  • Recommendation behaviour
		• Information behaviour
		• Complaint behaviour

Figure 8.17 Customer retention influencing factors

(3) Incorporation of a reference value

The **reference value model** considers a customer recommendation as a part of the customer value (Andon, Bradley and Baxter 1998). The value computed is that which arises through the interpersonal communication between consumers about a seller and its products or services. The base assumption of this approach here is that customers communicate with each other both in the pre-purchase and the post-purchase phases (suggestions, trading experiences, etc.), in which positive or negative data (references) are noted or proposed. The reference value is a combination of the segment specific reference rate, the opinion leader proclivity, the size of the social net, and the satisfaction level (Figure 8.19). The factors are analysed empirically and converted algorithmically to a monetary customer reference value (Figure 8.20).

A **critical assessment** of the CLV based on outcome criteria demonstrates that the approach has a high level of decision-orientation, in particular when computing the specific customer retention probability by considering factors that influence retention. As more and more pre-economic factors are taken into

$$LTV_j - \sum_{t=0}^{p} CQ_{jt} \cdot (1 + r)^{p-t} + \sum_{t=p+1}^{n} (CS_{jt} \cdot CP_{jt}) \cdot (1 + r)^{p-t}$$

LTV_j = Lifetime value for customer j at time t = p
CQ_{jt} = Customer quality = I(Sales per period, profit contribution, number of different products,...)
CS_{jt} = Customer share = I(SQ_{jt}, SP_{jt})
SQ_{jt} = Seller quality – I(customer satisfaction, commitment, trust,...)
SP_{jt} = Seller potential = I(Purchase intention, anticipated customer share, product line budget,...)
CP_{jt} = Customer potential = I(Projected sales volume, projected profit,...)
r = Discount rate
p = Number of periods since the first transaction (present)

	Customer quality	Seller quality
Past	<ul><li>Customer duration</li><li>Number of products sold per period</li><li>Number of different products sold</li><li>Sales per period</li><li>Total number of products sold since the first transaction</li><li>Total sales since the first transaction</li><li>Profit contribution per period</li><li>Profit contribution since first transaction</li></ul>	<ul><li>Customer satisfaction with product specific services</li><li>Customer satisfaction with products purchased in the last year</li><li>Customer budget amount</li><li>Recommendation by customer</li><li>Share of customer budget within the corporation</li><li>Switching costs (perceived by customer)</li></ul>
	Customer potential	**Seller potential**
Future	<ul><li>Sales forecasts</li><li>Projected customer duration</li><li>Sales trends</li><li>Profit projections</li></ul>	<ul><li>Repurchasing intention</li><li>Intention to recommend</li><li>Changes in customer budget used</li><li>Changes in total customer budget</li></ul>

Figure 8.18 CLV process of Hoekstra and Huizingh
(*Source*: Hoekstra and Huizingh 1999, p. 268, 270)

account, the reliability and validity of the findings, however, falls. The topicality of the results depends, as in the case of the revenue and contribution margin analyses, on the underlying computation period. The complex definition of customer value implies difficulties in ensuring a comprehensive analysis. In terms of the constituent level, individual customer analysis is easier the closer the contact between the customer and the firm.

The **implementation requirements** call for a significant organisational effort with high application costs, since each of the three CLV stages is complex. A **data problem** should definitely be mentioned in this context. The data quality is especially important for a sound CLV computation, given that poor data lead to unexpected customer management consequences. Another problem involves the aggregation of the data in the accounting systems and customer databanks since only constituent data can be properly applied to compute the CLV. For many firms this means a change in data storage methods. An outlying danger to the quality of data is related to data security and customer objections to releasing the information. Increased fear of data misuse and legal regulations also hinder firms from being able to collect customer specific data.

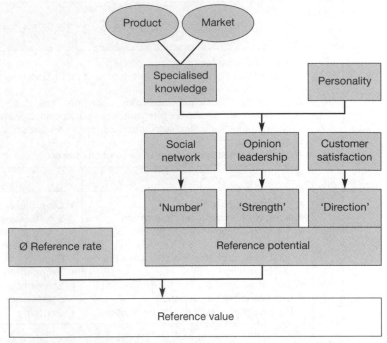

Figure 8.19 Reference value model components
(*Source*: Cornelsen 1998, p. 10)

$$RW_k = \left[\sum_{i-1}^{I} (P_i \cdot G_i)\right]_k \cdot MF_k \cdot KZ_k \cdot RR_b$$

RW_k = Periodic reference value of customer k
P_i = Number of persons in personnel group i
G_i = Weighting index for discussion intensity in personnel group i
MF_k = Opinion leadership index of customer k
KZ_k = Customer satisfaction index of customer k
RR_b = Average segment specific reference rate in segment b

Figure 8.20 Computing the reference value
(*Source*: Cornelsen 1998, p. 29)

The CLV is important in relationship marketing, since it is a monitoring factor that enables the dynamics and long-term characteristics of customer relationships to be taken into account. It is not only the customer related success elements that are considered, but especially the potential success that the firm could achieve with a particular relationship. Because of these features, the CLV is often utilised. It is, hence, viewed as a key economic control variable for relationship marketing and thereby as the target factor in the latter's success chain.

8.4 Integrated control systems for relationship marketing

8.4.1 Integrated control system methods

Pre-economic monitoring of customer relationships measures the characteristics of pre-economic variables of relationship marketing, while economic controls investigate the financial effects within the customer relationship. It is necessary **to link the pre-economic and economic planes** to be able to derive systematic control measures for relationship marketing. Only then is it feasible to identify the pre-economic levers for economic performance within a relationship, whereby the levers also offer an approach to derive control measures.

This linkage forms the **integrated control system** for relationship marketing, and should enable comprehensive monitoring of the pre-economic and economic parameters of relationship marketing and their interdependencies. The **necessity of interdependency analyses** argues that specific variables such as customer satisfaction are of no special importance for a firm. Instead, the interdependencies within the success chain are relevant for relationship marketing. An example of interdependencies is the indirect influence of customer satisfaction on economic performance, which can occur through the impact on either customer retention or recommendations.

Three types of **integrated control system methods** can be identified in one, two, or three dimensions (Figure 8.21). Scoring tables as one-dimensional and customer portfolios as two-dimensional methods are simple ways of linking pre-economic and economic data. **Scoring tables** enable an integrated evaluation of customer relationships through the appropriate evaluation and weighting of pre-economic and economic criteria. With respect to **customer portfolios** (details on customer segmentation can be found in Chapter 4), the pre-economic and economic dimensions can be plotted against each other. For instance, this can show the customers for whom satisfaction and retention (pre-economic variables) result

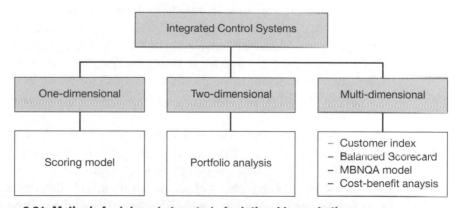

Figure 8.21 Methods for integrated control of relationship marketing

in profits (economic variables). The disadvantage of both methods mentioned above is that it is not possible to consider the impact of correlations between relationship marketing's various parameters. Under the following four **multi-dimensional approaches**, on the other hand, variable interdependencies are included fully in the assessment (Figure 8.21):

1 Customer index
2 Balanced Scorecard
3 MBNQA quality model
4 Cost-benefit analysis

8.4.2 Customer indices

For the **customer index** various effects of relationship marketing are measured simultaneously in line with the success chain. Both the correlations between the respective factors and the construct features are monitored. The customer index methodology stems from research on the **national customer satisfaction index** (Anderson and Fornell 2000; Bruhn and Murmann 1998; Fornell 1992), in which measurements of various consumer-based success factors for firms and institutions are made across segments and companies. Besides customer indices that are already established, such as the national indices in Sweden, Germany, and the US, numerous other countries such as Norway (Andreassen and Lindestad 1996), Switzerland (Bruhn and Grund 2000), and Russia (Murgulez *et al.* 2000) have also implemented similar projects. In addition, Brazil, Korea, New Zealand, and Taiwan have ongoing pilot programmes.

A **national customer satisfaction index** refers to a segment-encompassing study done by a neutral institution that periodically collects data to measure consumer satisfaction and the relevant situation in many sectors, branches, and firms within a country or an economic region (Fornell 1992). In other words, a national index is a cross-sectional study that measures the level of satisfaction and the ranges within it, in order to assess the national consumer satisfaction climate. These results can be used to make different types of comparisons between, for example, companies, segments, and countries over a long time-period.

This approach can be applied to **company-specific customer indices** for conducting related measurements. Figure 8.22 illustrates a model of such a customer index.

Most of the customer indices have an underlying **causal model** in which the correlation between pre-economic and economic parameters is fully displayed. Within this model the **structural variables** are recorded as latent constructs and the multi-dimensional ones are based on **indicator variables** (e.g. attributes of a service as an indicator of the perceived service quality).

Depending on the features of an indicator variable determined by the customer one such model is estimated with the help of **causal analysis**, which carries out numerous iterations to identify the best possible correlation between the parameters in the model. Appropriate statistical programs like LISREL or Amos

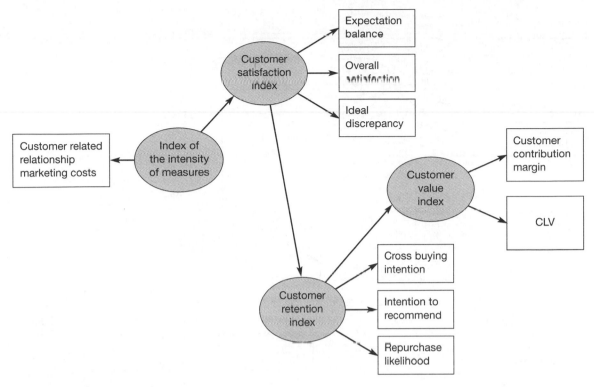

Figure 8.22 Model of a customer index

(www.smallwaters.com/amos) are applied to determine the degree of correlation between the model parameters. The degree of the correlation between the structural variables such as the influence of customer satisfaction on retention is expressed through measurement parameters. The causal analysis results can be applied to monitor the effects through:

- Correlation analysis
- Simulation
- Index development
- Index comparison

First, a **correlation analysis** can be conducted between the success chain parameters. This will not only show the extent to which the pre-economic target variables influence achievement of the economic targets, but the correlations between the pre-economic variables can also be estimated. In doing this, both the direct and indirect effects can be investigated.

The findings enable the impacts of changes in each variable to be **simulated** as exemplified by Figure 8.23. If the firm involved is able to raise its responsiveness to between 6 and 6.5 on a scale of 1 to 7, noticeable improvements will be reached in the quality, satisfaction, and customer retention indices.

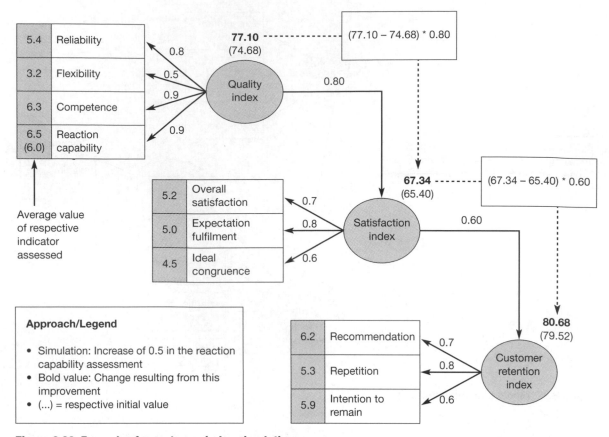

Figure 8.23 Example of a customer index simulation

Furthermore, **indices** for satisfaction or customer retention, etc. can be developed by weighting the median value of a structural variable with a measurement parameter. Weighting factors are determined through overall model estimates. This then provides not only the correlation between two constructs (e.g. customer satisfaction and retention), but also between the construct and its specific attributes (e.g. reliability as a service quality attribute). These values can then be used as weightings for computation of the index.

The development of indices enables a comparison of relevant constructs in terms of similar objects. For example, customer satisfaction can be analysed over time or compared by benchmarking different sellers. The following types of **index comparisons** can be conducted:

■ Comparison over time

■ Subsidiary comparison

■ Regional comparison

■ Comparison of firms (using the national consumer index results)

A **critical evaluation** of customer indices shows that the outcome criteria have a high decision orientation, due to the inclusion of the correlations between all of relationship marketing's impacts. Since many factors are considered in the various analyses the reliability and validity of the approach depends on the method used for measuring each variable. This also applies to the topicality. The approaches are broadly conceived and hence comprehensive. In terms of the constituent level, no attempt is made to implement customer indices for individual customers. Instead, fundamental effects of relationship marketing should be revealed. The **implementation requirements** for customer indices are significant, highly complex, and costly.

Customer indices enable continuous monitoring of relationship marketing's target variables and their interdependencies through **tracking**. As such, these indices account for the customer success variables and can form the basis for a Balanced Scorecard assessment.

8.4.3 Balanced Scorecard

The Balanced Scorecard can coordinate relationship marketing's pre-economic and economic target parameters (Kaplan and Norton 1996a; 1996b; 1993; 1992). The base concept behind this is to classify the firm from financial, customer, process, and potential-oriented perspectives. Figure 8.24 displays an overview of these four Balanced Scorecard perspectives. In practice, the perspectives can be adapted to the

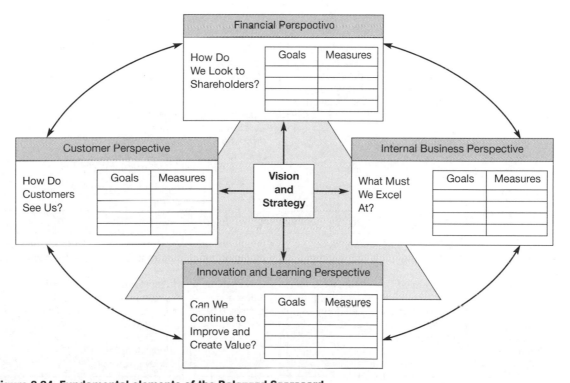

Figure 8.24 Fundamental elements of the Balanced Scorecard

(*Source*: Kaplan and Norton 1992, p.)

individual needs of an organisation. Figure 8.25 shows the Balanced Scorecard for the firm Systor AG, Switzerland, in terms of its base elements. Generally, a balance is supposed to be achieved between the four perspectives by linking them through a comprehensive set of indicators:

- External and internal key indicators
- Past and future key indices
- Key indicators easy or difficult to quantify

The Balanced Scorecard is thus more than just an instrument to improve the **transparency among key corporate indicators**. Especially firms whose business areas are highly autonomous prefer the Balanced Scorecard as a management system for

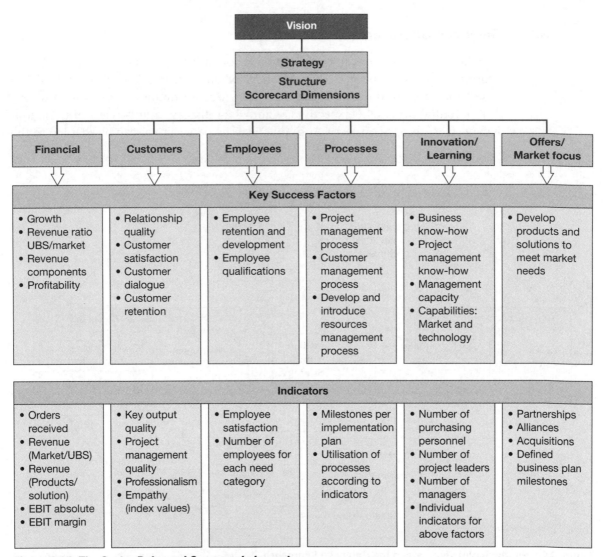

Figure 8.25 The Systor Balanced Scorecard elements

(*Source*: Bütikofer 1999, p. 327)

strategic controls and for implementation of tasks: e.g. ABB of Sweden is one firm that has successfully applied the Balanced Scorecard since 1996 (Ewing and Lundahl 1996).

Fulfilment of controlling and implementation activities complies with the base concept of the Balanced Scorecard, which includes the following four key tasks (Kaplan and Norton 1996b):

1 Explanation and breakdown of vision and strategy (linking of strategic and operative management)

2 Communication and linking of strategic goals and actions

3 Planning or setting of targets and coordination of strategic initiatives

4 Improvement of strategic feedback and learning

Although these tasks must be detailed and clearly separated, the fundamental Balanced Scorecard success chain can be described as follows: Mission/vision → strategy establishment → identification and linking of value drivers (finance, customers, processes, potential) → conversion of value drivers into operational key indicators, such that each indicator reflects a particular cause-effect correlation (e.g. customer satisfaction results in customer retention).

A **critical assessment** confirms that the Balanced Scorecard concept, especially through its attempt to gain a comprehensive look at various value perspectives, is a possible method for developing corporate strategies and to transform these into executable tasks. Hence, the Balanced Scorecard reflects the thinking within the context of **relationship marketing**. The contribution of customer relationships to success, in particular, can be achieved by considering different target variables. With regard to controls, the Balanced Scorecard is comparable with the customer indices, since it also permits consistent implementation of interdependency analyses.

8.4.4 MBNQA Quality Model

An analysis of whether relationship marketing can be consistently implemented in a firm is possible with the **Malcolm Baldrige National Quality Award's (MBNQA) Quality Model**, which emphasises relationship marketing's target activities and variables. The quality model structures the judgment criteria according to the MBNQA. The MBNQA utilises the following seven quality categories to judge a firm in order to assess the fulfilment of these base principles by a firm (NIST 2002):

1 Leadership

2 Strategic planning

3 Customer and market focus

4 Information and analysis

5 Human resource focus

6 Process management

7 Business results

These categories and their individual sub-elements are dynamically correlated in the MBNQA quality model, which is focused on the attainment of customer satisfaction. This is shown schematically in Figure 8.26. For each category the maximum possible points are stated in brackets and the overall total is 1,000 points.

The original purpose of the MBNQA Quality Model was to issue the Malcolm Baldrige National Quality Award, but an increasing number of firms have been undertaking a **self-assessment** on the basis of this model. This approach also permits an audit of the relationship marketing measures.

A **critical assessment** of the MBNQA model in terms of the outcome criteria leads to the conclusion that a certain decision orientation exists. The model verifies the relationship marketing measures the firm has implemented, although certain measures are idealised. Since each measure could be implemented in a different way the MBNQA model has reliability and validity problems. Additionally, it is not necessarily up-to-date. It can be assumed to be highly comprehensive due to the broad underlying framework of the model. With regard to the constituent level, individual customer analysis is neither possible nor desired.

The MBNQA model has major **implementation requirements**, while it is very complex and involves high costs. The MBNQA model offers the advantage for **relationship marketing** that the possible actions to control the corporation's relationships with its stakeholders are comprehensively considered. The activities and their impacts can be compared in the framework of the cost-benefit analysis addressed below.

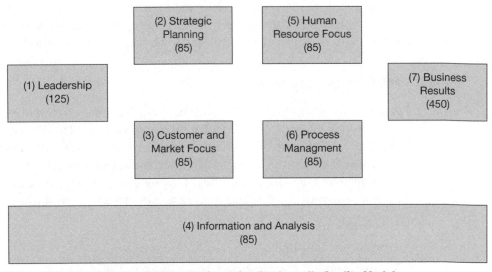

Figure 8.26 The Malcolm Baldrige National Quality Award's Quality Model

(*Source*: Developed from Criteria for Performance Excellence, Baldrige National Quality Program, National Institute of Standards and Technology, 2002. Not copyrightable in the United States)

8.4.5 Cost-benefit analysis

Relationship marketing's cost-benefit analysis assigns success effects to its set of actions. Linking of actions and effects allows an assessment of the **economics** of implementation measures.

Cost-benefit analysis of relationship marketing is the main instrument that monitors performance by comparing the costs against the benefits. This generates **cost-benefit key indicators** that enable differentiation of static and dynamic factors (Figure 8.27). The primary static indicator is relationship marketing's profit that arises from the difference between its benefits and costs. Dividing the profit by the costs gives the rate of return for relationship marketing. The primary dynamic indicator is the value of relationship marketing, which is the present value of the sum of its yearly profits and losses. The dynamic rate of return is derived by dividing the value of relationship marketing by its cumulative discounted costs. For a cost-benefit analysis, the costs and benefits of relationship marketing are thus determined and reallocated to each other.

Determining costs means first defining the costs generated by relationship marketing activities. One problem with this is that numerous relationship marketing actions cannot be recorded in isolation from output provision activities. Thus cost allocation computations can be conducted only in a few relevant instances. It is rather important to identify all the activities that can be assigned directly to relationship marketing, since the costs incurred then apply solely to it.

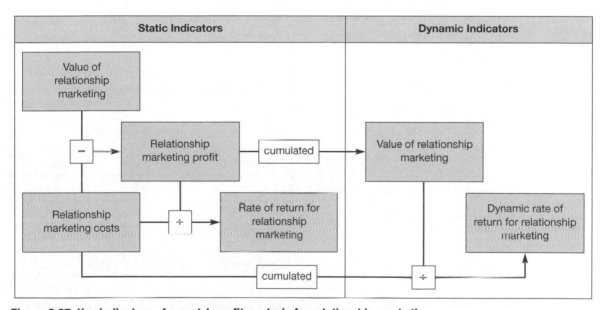

Figure 8.27 Key indicators of a cost-benefit analysis for relationship marketing

The value of relationship marketing is established on the basis of its success chain. The results of the impact analysis can be used to **determine the benefits**. The monetary value consists of the economic performance that can be traced back to relationship marketing by linking the success chain's elements. For example, the value of relationship marketing is simply the economic performance that comes from the particular retained customer whose retention results from her or his satisfaction. The retention of all customers cannot be traced back to their satisfaction. Likewise, the entire economic performance with retained customers cannot be allocated to their satisfaction. Hence, it is necessary to appropriately **assign success to relationship marketing** by applying the results of the customer indices. Through simple multiplication, the value of relationship marketing is specified as a proportion of the economic performance that originates from relationship marketing itself (Figure 8.28).

The **problem in value determination** is that behavioural intentions do not always represent the purchasing behaviour in reality. Moreover, in choosing a method for measuring the profit per customer the heterogeneity among the core customers of the particular firm must be considered. Effects of other aspects such as other actions or competitor activities can also surface when determining the benefits and should be isolated through appropriate operational measures.

A **critical assessment** of cost-benefit analysis demonstrates that its outcome criteria are highly decision-oriented, since the entire relationship marketing success chain is considered. Reliability and validity problems are to be expected because of the large number of variables included. This applies especially to the determination of benefits, which is based to a high degree on pre-economic data. Additionally, the breadth of the approach makes it difficult to ensure its topicality. The method's comprehensiveness is implicit. Analysis at the constitutive individual customer level is not feasible.

Just as for the other integrated control approaches, the **implementation requirements** for cost-benefit analyses of relationship marketing call for a major effort, involve high complexity, and thus incur high costs.

Computation Steps	Value
Value of customer retention for economic success	80.0%
* Value of customer satisfaction for customer retention	70.0%
* Value of relationship marketing for customer satisfaction	60.0%
= Proportion of economic success resulting from relationship marketing	33.6%
* Economic success (e.g. revenue)	$ 1,000,000
= Economic success resulting from relationship marketing (value of relationship marketing)	$ 336,000

Figure 8.28 Stepwise computation of the value of relationship marketing in economic categories

In view of its **significance for relationship marketing**, cost-benefit analysis enables the complete linking of relationship marketing's various target variables based on the success chain. However, it is particularly difficult to determine the benefits and to allocate them to specific relationship marketing measures. Hence, there are still unanswered questions on the relationship marketing concept for researchers to grapple with further.

The control phase delivers the basis for future decisions in the remaining planning phases of relationship marketing. Consequently, as in the case of deterministic planning, this control is not to be viewed as the isolated end of the planning process. On the contrary, the planning process is a continuous one centred on the monitoring and control. Verification of the characteristics of relationship marketing's target variables through control instruments delivers new bases for revised target planning, which permit a new planning process run to go into action.

Summary

In this chapter, we have described the control phase of relationship marketing. When developing a strategic relationship marketing concept, it is vital to monitor the costs and benefits of relationship marketing. After introducing some important controlling criteria which can be differentiated with respect to the company's outcome on the one hand and to the implementation process on the other hand, we elaborated on the pre-economic and economic monitoring actions that should be carried out proactively. With regard to pre-economic controlling actions we differentiated between three groups of processes: attribute control, event control, and problem control. With respect to economic monitoring activities we took a closer look at two cases: single-period and multi-period controlling of relationships. Finally, we introduced several integrated control system methods which are structured according to their dimensions.

9 Multi-faceted characteristics of relationship marketing

Overview

So far we have introduced a general concept of relationship marketing that is based on a fundamental theoretical foundation. However, the focus can differ depending on the specific business segment. In this chapter we will take a closer look at relationship marketing from an institutional standpoint. Under the heading of the multi-faceted features of relationship marketing, we talk about characteristics of consumer goods (B2C), industrial goods (B2B), and services and their impact on the conceptualisation as well as the planning process of relationship marketing. Specifically, we will address the following questions:

➤ What are the attributes of consumer goods, and how do they influence the conceptualisation and the planning process of relationship marketing for consumer goods (B2C) markets?

➤ What are the attributes of industrial goods, and how do they influence the conceptualisation and the planning process of relationship marketing for Business-to-Business (B2B) markets?

➤ What are the attributes of services, and how do they influence the conceptualisation and the planning process of relationship marketing for services markets?

9.1 Goals and issues from an institutional standpoint

Relationship marketing's focus differs greatly depending on the segment in which the corporation is active. This situation was addressed previously in Chapter 1 by differentiating between customised and standardised products and services based on the output typology. This classification can be applied to the **multi-faceted features of relationship marketing** covering consumer goods, industrial goods, and services (Figure 9.1 shows the differences between the three segments). It should be mentioned that an explicit treatment of the non-profit segment has been dispensed with for two reasons. First, this entire book concentrates on commercial products and services. Second, most of the unique features of services can be applied directly to the non-profit sector, making special handling of this area unnecessary.

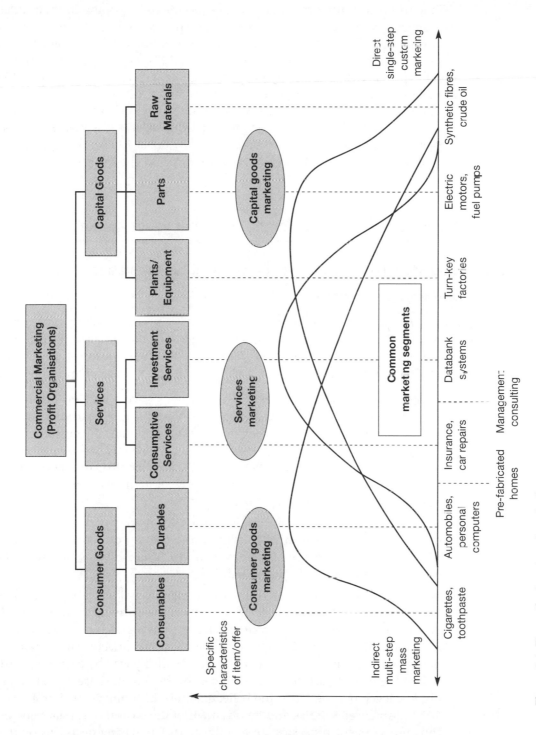

Figure 9.1 Theoretical cycles of marketing segments

Even if relationship marketing's fundamental principles are generally relevant for all three segments, there are differences between the segments in terms of their **values and possibilities** for application of specific concepts and in their differences in emphasis on particular instruments. In the three segments variations often occur in the interpretation of similar relationship situations. This chapter will predict trends due to these differences, although it should be noted that for each predicted trend a specific example with an opposing argument can always be found. However, the following appear to be typical trends in each of the product and service areas.

These unique features are addressed for each segment on the basis of prior chapters of this book covering conceptualisation, analysis, strategies, measures, implementation, and control, complemented by the attributes of each output type. A sample argumentation is usually made to highlight the main characteristics.

9.2 Relationship marketing for the consumer goods market

9.2.1 Foundations of relationship marketing for consumer goods

Attributes of consumer goods

Consumer goods encompass a broad spectrum of products that can be fundamentally separated into durable goods like cars and into consumables like erasers. Based on output typologies addressed in Chapter 1, **consumer goods** can be compared as follows with industrial goods and services (Kotler 2000; Palmer and Cole 1995):

■ In terms of **contact attributes** consumer goods have a low level of integration since they can basically be manufactured without any customer integration. Even though the degree of interaction is often minimal, the customers are relatively well informed on the particular product (low customer-end information asymmetry), and the contact between the customer and supplier is quite indirect. Furthermore, the customers are basically anonymous from the firm and the significance of individual customers is low.

■ In view of the **output attributes**, from the customer's perspective the provision of consumer goods is relatively insignificant. Certain categories of products are highly homogeneous and often less complex than services, whereas material goods can be stored and transported.

■ With regard to **customer attributes** it is critical to classify the customers into two groups from the producers' perspective: the **consumers** as end-users and **commercial traders** as sales agents. Relationships for each of these groups differ fundamentally and should be taken into account in conceptualising relationship marketing. Consumer goods can be judged relatively well by customers, irrespective of the type of customer, since each possesses a high share of search qualities but low levels of experience and belief qualities (Zeithaml 1991; Darbi and Karny 1973). Moreover, the risk and involvement of the customer is relatively low and thus procurement processes are mainly short. Purchasing decisions by the consumers tend to be emotional and barriers to switching seldom exist.

Even if these characteristics do not apply wholly to all consumer goods, particularly for concentrated mass-produced items they tend to be as described instead of being similar to those for industrial goods or services. These attributes of the goods result in unique aspects when conceiving relationship marketing for this segment.

Conceptualisation of relationship marketing for consumer goods

The **customer life cycle** is the basis for conceptualising relationship marketing, whereby the customer life cycles for needs and relationships can be differentiated from each other. The **customer needs life cycle** for **consumers** can vary over time at the product category, product, and brand level. The needs for certain product categories can shift over a period of time. For instance, cosmetics clients in their youth require products against acne but later in life need more items for wrinkles. Needs can change at the product level too – young people desire good deals on small cars, whereas parents possibly prefer comfortable family vehicles. The need for particular brands can also change over time because of the image. The customer needs life cycle for **commercial traders** is dependent on competition dynamics: e.g. retailing needs typically change when a new positioning of the traders takes place.

Through the **customer relationship life cycle** it can be shown that some of the phases in the consumer goods sector are of little or no significance for **consumers**. The initiation phase is one that frequently tends to be relatively short due to the ease in evaluating consumer goods (Zeithaml 1991). The socialisation phase is typically short since these goods tend not to be complex. During the growth phase consumer goods manufacturers often manage cross selling actively. This is achieved to some extent by product differentiations or line extensions (e.g. Nivea, Marlboro). The customer relationship life cycles for **commercial trading**, like the initiation and growth phases, are quite distinct.

Perspective taking is also an important relationship marketing principle that urges companies to put themselves in the place of the customer when designing their relationship programme. For the consumer goods segment, as a result of indirect contact with the consumers (e.g. purchase of washing powder at a store and not from the manufacturer) firms experience much greater problems in perspective taking than in relationships with traders or in the area of services. This does not, however, imply that perspective taking for consumer goods is impossible. In this segment it is necessary to see how one can apply indirect methods like the 'Means-End Analysis' (Gutman 1982) or 'Laddering' to account for customer expectations.

Laddering refers to an in-depth, one-on-one interviewing technique used to develop an understanding of how consumers translate the attributes of products into meaningful associations (the technique is described in depth in Rugg and McGeorge 1995; for its application in advertising, see Reynolds and Gutman 1988). The method involves a tailored interviewing format using primarily a series of directed probes typified by questions like 'Why is that important to you?'. This is done with the purpose of determining sets of linkages between the key perceptual elements across a range of attributes, consequences and values.

With respect to **relationships from the customer standpoint** in line with relationship marketing's success chain, the homogeneity of products for **consumers** often results in parameters other than the output quality that take on a needs fulfilment function for consumer goods. The quality of the relationship with the seller (company, employee) is often not very clear. These consumers tend instead to develop **relationships to brands** (Fournier 1998). Accordingly, emotional aspects such as the brand image become more important for controlling relationships. Relationships with **commercial traders** are hence similar to the close relationships between employees of both companies, as in the industrial goods segment. Based on its conceptualisation, the uniqueness of relationship marketing for consumer goods can be demonstrated by the **planning process**.

9.2.2 Unique planning process features of relationship marketing

Analysis phase for the consumer goods market

The analysis phase tasks include a SWOT-analysis, target planning, and customer segmentation. The predominant aspect of a **SWOT-analysis** is an aggregated analysis of consumer goods related to the **consumers**. As a consequence of the relatively low significance of individual customers in this segment an analysis covering a complete investigation of each customer's satisfaction, for instance, would require an enormous effort. In any case, analysis of individual customers is problematic because of their anonymity and the indirect nature of the contact between the seller and buyer. Hence, in the consumer goods segment, studies are done mainly at an aggregated level of pre-economic parameters (e.g. the image) and economic aspects like the customer contribution margin. Since a firm has relatively few **commercial traders** as sales agents, analyses covering aspects such as the contribution margin or ABC-analysis can be conducted in-depth for each customer.

The anonymity of consumers and the indirect seller-buyer contact also lead to unique aspects in relationship marketing's **target planning** for consumer goods. The profit and the contribution margin per transaction (unit output) are very important economic variables, especially since the sales or costs per customer barely change in the course of a relationship. A strong image or position in the mass market is the often sought after external psychological goal. For **commercial traders** specific targets like the sales or contribution margins per customer can be relevant, since the variables could vary considerably depending on the trading firm's target group or regional coverage.

Problems with data availability from customer analyses impact **customer segmentation** methods for consumer goods. Economic data on a customer basis in particular are often not considered for segmenting customers. For consistent control of relationships based on the success chain of relationship marketing, consumer goods producers should thus seek to use all the chain links at as low a constituent level as possible when conducting the segmentation. **Retailers and wholesalers** can be segmented relatively easily at an individual customer level, for instance in the form of sales agent portfolios. The relationship strategies in retailing are developed on the basis of customer specific targets and segmentation. For instance, consumers can be segmented according to their usage rate. Marketers then vary their promotional efforts accordingly.

Example 0.1

According to Kotlor (2000, p. 208), Repp's Big & Tall Stores, a catalogue and retail outfit, which is the largest provider of clothing for today's big and tall man with over 400 stores across the US, slices its customers into 12 segments according to response rates, average sales, and so forth. While some receive six to eight mailings a year, others receive only three to five, or only one to three. Infrequent store shoppers are offered an extra incentive, such as a 15 per cent discount, for particular days. This type of segmentation has proved successful, as Repp gets a six per cent response rate of its segmented mailing which is far superior to the huge non-segmented mailing of 750,000 pieces that have a response rate of just 0.5 per cent.

Strategy development for consumer goods

Relationship strategy development involves decision-making at several levels. Particularly relevant for a stronger relationship focus is the determination of phase-driven strategies and the creation of competitive advantages in the area of relationships.

There are various grounds for developing **phase-driven strategies** covering the acquisition, retention, or recovery of consumers in the consumer goods segment. Typical conditions for an acquisition strategy are the introduction of a new product like a unique chocolate bar, and disregarding a significant customer segment (e.g. exclusive handling of the female market by perfume manufacturers in earlier times). Input conditions for a retention strategy should include aspects like the use of products such as a washing machine and tumbledrier from different firms, or the ability to make a new decision before each purchase of, say, ice cream. A recovery strategy in the consumer goods area should cover aspects such as customers defecting due to performance problems with a particular product like the failure rate of a DVD player, or being enticed away by competitors. Mainly transaction strategies directed at only winning new customers are developed in this segment due to the anonymity of consumers (Jackson 1985), with the result that firms pay too little attention to brand retention. The phase-driven strategies for **commercial traders** are comparable with those for the industrial goods segment.

The **relation leadership strategy** for consumer goods often has little to do with the relationship between the firm or its customer representative and the consumers, but is instead a 'brand relationship' (Fournier 1998; see Figure 9.2 for customer-brand relationship types). Accordingly, this strategy focuses on developing the relationship between the brand and the customer as exemplified by the following cases:

- Separate Coca Cola campaigns that refer to 'old times' as with the introduction of Cherry Coke by referring to Classic Coke

- Ensuring familiarity or a re-recognition effect in the annual announcements by McDonalds' advertisements that certain products are again available
- Trust-oriented extension of an offer like that of bags or watches by designers

The relationships with **commercial traders** in the consumer goods segment, on the contrary, are personal ones between the employees of the manufacturer and the traders. Hence, strategic aspects similar with those in the industrial goods segment are much more relevant (section 9.3). The strategy established provides the framework for concrete measures with which it is supposed to be put into effect.

Relationship form	Definition
Arranged marriages	Non-voluntary union imposed by preferences of third party. Intended for long-term, exclusive commitment, although at low levels of affective attachment.
Casual friends/buddies	Friendship low in affect and intimacy, characterised by infrequent or sporadic engagement, and few expectations for reciprocity or reward.
Marriages of convenience	Long-term, committed relationship precipitated by environmental influence versus deliberate choice, and governed by satisficing rules.
Committed partnerships	Long-term, voluntarily imposed, socially supported union high in love, intimacy, trust and a commitment to stay together despite adverse circumstances. Adherence to exclusivity rules expected.
Best friendships	Voluntary union based on reciprocity principle, the endurance or which is ensured through continued provision of positive rewards. Characterised by revelation of true self, honesty, and intimacy. Congruity in partner images and personal interests common.
Compartmentalised friendships	Highly specialised, situationally confined, enduring friendships characterised by lower intimacy than other friendship forms but higher socio-emotional rewards and interdependence. Easy entry and exit attained.
Kinships	Non-voluntary union with lineage ties.
Rebounds/avoidance-driven relationships	Union precipitated by desire to move away from prior or available partner, as opposed to attraction to chosen partner per se.
Childhood friendships	Infrequently engaged, affectively laden relation reminiscent of earlier times. Yields comfort and security of past self.
Courtships	Interim relationship state on the road to committed partnership contract.
Flings	Short-term, time-bounded engagements of high emotional reward, but devoid of commitment and reciprocity demands.
Enmities	Intensely involving relationship characterised by negative affect and desire to avoid or inflict pain on the other.
Secret affairs	Highly emotive, privately-held relationship considered risky if exposed to others.
Enslavements	Non-voluntary union governed entirely by desires of the relationship partner. Involves negative feelings but persists because of circumstances.

Figure 9.2 Typology of forms of customer-brand relationship
(*Source*: Fournier 1998, p.13)

Relationship marketing programmes for consumer goods

Relationship marketing in practice entails fixing the corporation's related strategy. Various measures can be undertaken in the relationship life cycle phases for consumers in the consumer goods segment. The **customer acquisition phase** encompasses the initiation and socialisation phases. The customer must be persuaded and/or stimulated in the **initiation phase** to want to enter into a relationship with the firm. Examples of convincing activities for consumer goods are providing product samples in pharmacies or cosmetic stores, or publicising product tests through magazines like Consumer Reports. Examples of stimulation are special offers at the point of sale or image building through mass communication. The role of the **socialisation phase** is to acclimatise the customer, something that is seldom done for consumer goods. Examples of appropriate activities are events like a festival at a car dealership to attract consumers who have already shown interest in the dealership's cars.

The second key phase of the relationship life cycle, the **customer retention phase**, comprises the growth and maturity phases combined. The relationship should be developed in the **growth phase** through customisation and cross selling. For consumer goods, customisation is traditionally impersonal, since the contact between the seller and buyer is indirect. An attempt is made here to satisfy the customer needs with the seller's mainly impersonal offer, as with a chocolate flavour based on explicit studies conducted prior to its development and production. However, with the increase of information technology and the internet, consumer goods companies can step into new business opportunities offering customised products as well (see 'Insights 9.1: Customisation in the 21st century – anything from notebooks to trainers'. The potential for cross selling, for example, comes from product differentiations or line extensions.

Insights 9.1

Customisation in the 21st century – anything from notebooks to trainers

One excellent example of applying the approach of mass customisation in the consumer world is Dell Computer Corporation (www.dell.com). Dell's story is by now a familiar one. Beginning with a radically different business model for a high-tech company, Dell is selling computers directly to customers over the phone or via the world wide web and offering them direct technical support. The company's most striking feature is a website that allows the customer to design an individual computer and then track it through to delivery. As Core-e-spondent Michael Chanover, VP, Business & Production at frogdesign, puts it: 'Want more RAM? No problem, add more RAM. Need a DVD instead of a CD-ROM? Not a worry. Got to have that extra disk space for all those MP3s? Not a concern, the online shopper just chooses it.' Figure 9.3 shows how the customer has to decide when choosing from a notebook line. However, while customers can select what they want from hundreds of different components to configure the computer of their own choice, Dell does not begin building until it has received the money for it. With a production process 'build-to-order', inventories at Dell have fallen sharply.

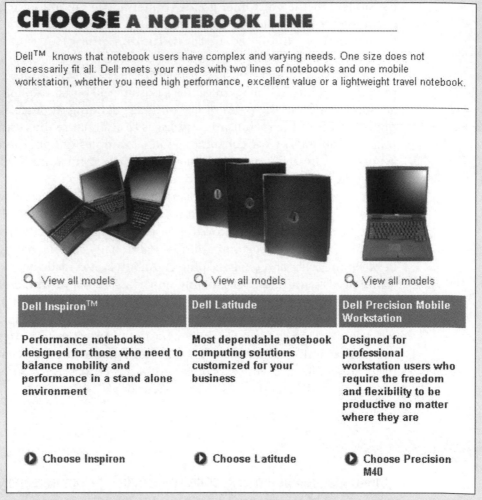

CHOOSE A NOTEBOOK LINE

Dell™ knows that notebook users have complex and varying needs. One size does not necessarily fit all. Dell meets your needs with two lines of notebooks and one mobile workstation, whether you need high performance, excellent value or a lightweight travel notebook.

🔍 View all models   🔍 View all models   🔍 View all models

Dell Inspiron™	Dell Latitude	Dell Precision Mobile Workstation
Performance notebooks designed for those who need to balance mobility and performance in a stand alone environment	Most dependable notebook computing solutions customized for your business	Designed for professional workstation users who require the freedom and flexibility to be productive no matter where they are
▶ Choose Inspiron	▶ Choose Latitude	▶ Choose Precision M40

Figure 9.3 Customisation of consumer goods on the Internet

The success enjoyed by Dell Computer has given the prospects for applying mass customisation to trainers, clothes, vitamins, cosmetics, and cars. For example, at Nike's website, customers can choose from a handful of 'uppers' and 'soles' to create one's own combination. And if that were not enough, Nike even offers to get one's name embroidered on the back of each trainer. This just gives an impression which new possibilities arise for relationship marketing in the consumer goods market.

Source: based, in parts, on Chanover, M. (2002), www.core77.com/reactor/mass_customisation.html, accessed on May 22, 2002.

Individual customer relationships often cannot be developed further in the **maturity phase**, since the customer's needs are met by the product offered. Relationship marketing's role thus is to take the most efficient advantage of the success potential of a relationship by building switching barriers and by raising the efficiency. Because of the indirectness of the contact and the anonymity of individual customers, relatively few barriers to switching exist in the consumer goods segment. With the help of club membership programmes organisations can learn more about their customers (for the application of a club programme in the automobile industry, see 'Insights 9.2: Club membership programme at Volkswagen'). Nevertheless, one can partly put up some primarily economic barriers like price leadership, or technical/functional barriers like a car in which only the manufacturer's radios can be installed. For consumer goods particularly, sellers have to reckon with the barriers holding for a limited time only, because of the large number of imitations. Raising the efficiency of individual relationships in this segment is also problematic as many processes are already standardised. One possibility to enhance the efficiency lies in taking advantage of consumers' readiness to pay a premium for goods like luxury items or pharmaceuticals.

Insights 9.2

Club membership programme at Volkswagen

The Volkswagen AG has created a successful club membership programme (www.vw-club.de). Upon submitting a fee, the Volkswagen Club offers several benefits. First, according to Stauss et al. (2001, p. 14), the club operates an individual customer contact programme which offers a welcome package, four seasonal mailings with seasonal offers and one product-related mailing. In the US, for instance, new members joining the club receive the first issue of a club magazine, a T-shirt, a road atlas, a phone card, and discount offers. Second, the club sends the 'Volkswagen magazine' regularly to its customers. This 100-page journal provides up-to-date news about Volkswagen. A third component is the Service Centre which offers a wide range of single benefits, such as route-planning, dial-up traffic news, and a ticket agency. In addition, a number of specific products, such as miniature models and accessories, are offered to the members in the club shop. The most important part is the bonus programme. Here the club offers its members the opportunity to collect bonus points every time he or she purchases something from Volkswagen or from a cooperating partner. These points can then be either exchanged for gifts or can be added as discounts on the invoices of a local Volkswagen dealer. Figure 9.4 summarises the Volkswagen Customer Club Programme (for more examples of successful clubs, see Kotler 2000, p. 53).

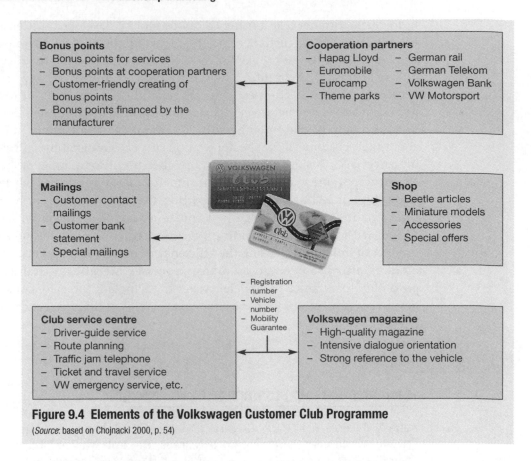

Figure 9.4 Elements of the Volkswagen Customer Club Programme
(*Source*: based on Chojnacki 2000, p. 54)

The imperilment and the termination/abstinence phases have to be organised in the **recovery phase**. The problem in these phases is the identification of endangered relationships or lost customers. Since the firm does not know the customers through the relationship, owing to the indirect seller-buyer contact and their anonymity, it must undertake special activities such as market research to identify defecting and lost customers. The low degree of integration of these customers in the provision of the output and the storage ability of consumer goods, on the other hand, helps ease the management requirements for both phases. Consequently, in the **imperilment phase**, rectifying defects (e.g. repairing a malfunctioning computer) as well as undertaking restitutions (e.g. car recalls in the automobile industry) are easy to accomplish for the product itself. As a consequence of the low barriers to switching, management of the termination/ restitution phase cannot be based on the product. Recovery offers need to consist instead of pricing offers such as discounts for car repairs. In addition to the above, the high significance of sales agents for consumer goods calls for measures to address the relationship with **commercial traders** in a way similar to those in the industrial goods segment (section 9.3).

Implementation phase for the consumer goods market

Relationship marketing strategies and measures can be successful only if thought is given in the **implementation phase** to the implementation and transformation of the concept within the firm. Specifically, the management systems and organisational and corporate structures need to be focused on relationships.

The **organisational structures** for consumer goods should initially be set up with decentralised units. Due to past standardisation in the consumer goods segment, many of the activities related to consumers have been centralised (e.g. production of an advertisement by consumer goods manufacturers for all markets worldwide). At this overall level it is hence not possible to act on specific customer needs. In this segment there is frequently more focus on processes such as the ECR-concept that play a big role (Pearce 1996; Salmon 1993). In this segment it is necessary to shift the outlook from primarily products to customers and relationships. This has already been done for some relationships with **sales agents** through the deployment of Key Account Managers functioning as relationship managers for the commercial traders (Pardo 1997).

Modifications to **management systems** for consumer goods involve both information and control systems. Consumer goods producers should seek to set up their information system on consumers, if not at an individual level, at least for groups. Only then would customer-specific relationship control become feasible. For this it is essential to record additional customer-specific data in the respective information system. The company's existing primarily product-oriented control systems should likewise be coordinated with the customer-related monitoring instruments. In **commercial trading**, such systems are usually standard due to the relative importance of a sales agent to the manufacturer.

The product-focused outlook mentioned for consumer goods is also prevalent in the seller's **corporate culture**. This makes it imperative to initiate modifications towards greater customer or relationship orientation in the corporate culture, as is sometimes currently achieved through the introduction of a Key Account Management system.

Control phase in the consumer goods market

The secret behind successful implementation of relationship marketing is to proactively **control** its strategies and actions covering pre-economic, economic, and integrated controls. **Pre-economic controls** encompass the investigation of parameters representing the preliminary stages of purchasing behaviour for consumer goods. Processes focused on attributes should be set up so that the consumer goods producer can collect information on the perceptions of the anonymous consumers. Despite the indirect contact between the seller and buyer, in this way it becomes possible to guarantee perspective taking from the standpoint of the customer. Furthermore, in this segment the problem-related methods such as complaint management are of value since the seller has no other opportunity to learn about possible customer problems. With commercial traders, mainly due to the direct relationship between the manufacturer and trader, both problem and event related methods could be applied.

For **economic** monitoring the producer of consumer goods should seek to analyse customer sales, contribution margins, and the CLV. The main problem here is generating the necessary data on individual consumers. For example, it is almost impossible for a beverage manufacturer to measure sales per customer. An attempt should at least be made in such instances to arrive at estimates for specific customer segments. For **commercial traders** on the contrary, it is relatively simple to calculate contribution margins etc. at an individual customer level and to permit profitability-focused analyses of customer relationships.

Integrated control is designed for looking at interdependencies between pre-economic and economic parameters during the control phase. The Balanced Scorecard offers the best possible means for a consumer goods producer striving for a balance between pre-economic and economic targets to integrate the pre-economic indicators into the previously mainly economics-based monitoring. These dual groups, comprising customers on the one side and commercial traders on the other, should be the focus of a Balanced Scorecard analysis.

9.2.3 Critical assessment of relationship marketing for consumer goods

In the **consumer goods segment**, relationships with the consumers are characterised by a low level of integration on the part of the customers in product provision and the resulting indirect seller-buyer contact. Relationships with **commercial traders** are quite the opposite since each sales agent is relatively significant for the manufacturer and the two are in direct contact with each other.

With respect to the **consumers**, the reasons why customer relationships in this segment are rarely addressed in practice are as follows. Corporations are still focused primarily on transactions and generally seek to sell as many of their products as possible – in contrast to efforts in relationship marketing aimed at building up the most profitable relationship feasible with a particular customer. The outcome is that both these paths lead to maximisation of sales and profits, although the one with profitable customer relationships reaches the target sooner with fewer customers. A firm could reach its economic targets more efficiently, but the implementation of relationship marketing for consumer goods is problematic mainly due to a lack of the necessary information systems. In contrast to the situation with banking, business activity information on individual relationships is usually unavailable because of the indirect contacts. Companies must therefore generate these data through primary research. Many firms shy away from customer specific relationships, since this could involve a major data collection effort. With respect to relationships with **commercial traders**, though, comprehensive relationship concepts such as the ECR or Key Account Management are already being utilised.

Science has so far also not offered an all-encompassing concept on consumer-goods-specific relationship marketing. The concept of relationship marketing was developed in the industrial goods and services segments and intentionally kept separate from classical consumer goods marketing while being expanded further as an independent field. Only in very recent times have methods emerged for conceiving and controlling the relationships of consumers to brands (Fournier 1998).

This school of thought and deliberations on how consumer goods producers could systematically manage the indirect relationships with their customers are the future challenges facing marketing research. Relationship marketing for commercial traders is conducted in many ways including Key Account Management, but addressed only sometimes by the scientific world. Here too there is enormous room for further research.

9.3 Relationship marketing in the Business-to-Business market

9.3.1 Foundations of relationship marketing for industrial goods

Attributes of industrial goods

The industrial goods segment has many different types of outputs, among which the following four **kinds of industrial goods** can be identified (Backhaus 1999; 1986; Backhaus and Büschken 1997):

1 In the **products business**, products are offered to an anonymous market and the buyer can utilise them in isolation to solve her or his problems with a copying machine or batteries, for instance.

2 In the **OEM business** (original equipment manufacturing), products are mass-produced but developed specifically for particular customers as in the case of special taillights made by the firm Hella for specific manufacturers.

3 In the **systems business**, products are utilised in combination with other technologies and the majority is sold to an anonymous market.

4 In the **industrial plant business**, products are marketed through closed bids. This applies to complex customer-specific hardware or software packages required for the fabrication of other plant such as refineries or rolling mills.

Industrial goods have **commonalities with other types of goods** to some extent. Depending on the buyer they could parallel consumer goods: e.g. a lawn mower is a consumer item for an end user's garden but an industrial product for a farmer. Parallels can also be found for services as in the case of investments in management consulting or R&D services.

In spite of this the majority of industrial goods generally have a certain attribute that differentiates them from consumer goods. Technical industrial goods like equipment will be primarily considered here as opposed to raw materials and replacement parts etc. Industrial goods can be described as follows in terms of the **output attributes** from Chapter 1:

■ Contact attributes have a relatively high degree of integration and interaction for industrial goods. The seller and buyer are in direct contact such that the customer is not anonymous. The importance of individual customers is high but one person seldom makes the purchasing decision, which is normally taken by a buying centre (Thanner 1999). The result is that information asymmetries exist on both the seller and customer ends.

- The provision potential of products is very important in terms of output attributes. Industrial goods could be very heterogeneous and complex. They are primarily storable and transportable once they have been disassembled into parts.

- Customer attributes indicate that industrial goods can be evaluated at least on being used, since they have a high share of search and experience qualities (Darby and Karni 1973). Moreover, the risk and involvement of customers is relatively high (Webster 1990; Choffray and Lilien 1980), such that procurement processes tend to be long. Purchasing decisions are usually made rationally and switching barriers are relatively high.

Relationship marketing can be conceived for industrial goods on the basis of the above characterisations.

Conceptualisation of relationship marketing for the Business-to-Business market

The **customer life cycle** concept provides the basis for conceptualising relationship marketing for industrial goods (Thanner 1999; Håkansson and Snehota 1995), while enabling differentiation between elements of the customer needs and relationship life cycles. In contrast to the customer goods segment the **customer needs life cycle** can fluctuate significantly, since the demand for certain industrial items can change drastically within the lifespan represented by the offering firm's customer. This is caused by the heterogeneity of products in this segment that becomes particularly apparent on changes in the output programme and the resultant alterations in needs. Figure 9.5 illustrates examples of the needs cycle durations in various segments.

The **customer relationship life cycle** phases can be quite well developed for industrial goods. For example, the initiation phase could be relatively intensive due to the typically long procurement processes involved (Håkansson and Snehota 1995). The heterogeneity in the output spectrum can lead to definitive growth phases. The recovery phase could also turn out to be intensive, because of the high value of a customer to the seller.

Product planning and provision for industrial goods often involves direct contact between the seller and buyer. Hence, the **perspective taking** concept is not only possible here but of key significance. Owing to the complexity involved, one

Item	Purchase cycle in years
Weapons system	20 to 30
Oil field installation	15 to 20
Chemical plant	10 to 15
Major components of steel plant	5 to 10
Paper supply contract	5

Figure 9.5 Durations of the needs cycles for industrial goods
(*Source*: Levitt 1983, p. 88)

success factor lies in the machine manufacturer's ability to incorporate customer needs when developing and fabricating the equipment.

In a **customer relationship from the customer's perspective**, in view of relationship marketing's success chain, an important and often encountered factor is the rationality in purchasing decisions involving industrial goods (Sheth 1996) This impacts the customer's buying decisions by focusing them on perceived value (Anderson 1995), which is the cost-benefit variable from the customer's viewpoint. The risk and involvement in a purchase decision moreover imply an emphasis by the customer on perceived relationship quality (Sheth 1996). A long-term relationship will develop only if the customer trusts the seller and perceives a certain amount of familiarity (Dwyer, Schurr and Oh 1987; Ford 1980). Relationship marketing's planning phases can be designed on the basis of it being appropriately conceptualised for industrial goods.

9.3.2 Unique planning process features of relationship marketing

Analysis phase for the Business-to-Business market

The basis for planning relationship marketing is a SWOT-analysis, target planning, and customer segmentation. A constituent customer analysis for industrial goods is appropriate and can be conducted as the component of a **SWOT-analysis**, due to the contact directness and the high significance of individual customers. Since the seller and buyer frequently come into contact with each other, an appropriately trained customer representative can perform a majority of this analysis without any serious analytical effort.

Example 9.2

The MicroScan division of Baxter Diagnostics Inc. conducts customer specific analyses. This firm manufactures highly sensitive equipment to identify microbes in patient cultures, and medical laboratories use the findings to select appropriate antibiotics. In the mid-nineties, this firm battled over market leadership against its main competitor Vitek Systems Inc. Interviews held with lost and existing customers highlighted that MicroScan's customer penetration was way below its potential. These interviews helped identify the reasons for defections, such as concerns about instrument features, reliability, reaction speed, and understanding problems. This knowledge was applied to develop new services and introduce new tools such as customer service reports. Two years later, the firm became the clear market leader.

(Source: adapted from Reichheld 1994).

For the reasons mentioned even **goal planning** for industrial goods is often aimed at individual customers. Specific targets can be set precisely for each customer relationship as a result of their highly heterogeneous sales and cost situations, including the especially important parameters such as profit per customer. Cross selling, for instance, can accordingly be very successful when based on the customer behavioural goals, (Bergheimer 1991). Internal goals should be aimed more at innovativeness and at employee qualifications, while the relationship quality and commitment represent important customer target variables for successfully controlling a relationship.

With respect to **customer segmentation**, a description of the segments is often not required because of the relative significance of individual customers and their prominence, since that makes them easy to identify and account for in the segmentation. Each customer relationship can be directed along the set targets in line with its attractiveness (e.g. standing, loyalty) or the supplier position (e.g. relationship duration).

Strategy development for industrial goods

The relationship marketing strategy should specify the competitive advantage through relationship orientation in phases. Various arguments justify the need for each of the **phase-driven strategy types** for customer acquisition, retention, and recovery in the industrial goods segment. The grounds for an acquisition strategy are, for example, the entry of new sellers into the market as in the case of a beverage bottler as a potential customer of a filling machine producer, or the development of innovative equipment like a new type of recycling plant by the firm involved. A retention strategy is necessary, for example, when the success potential of a customer is inadequately utilised as in the case of not outsourcing maintenance and repairs to the manufacturer of a machine, or when a shipbuilding customer buys engines from different suppliers (Backhaus 1986). In this segment the firm should consider a recovery strategy when it knows that its products often have systematic defects (e.g. very short repair frequency for a machine), or if there are early warning signs of customer defections (e.g. the firm's customers begin to request competitors' offers).

A **relation leadership strategy** for industrial goods could involve the relationship with both the seller and the employees due to the direct seller-buyer contact. Such a relationship strategy becomes apparent, among others, from the following examples:

■ Regular visits by the manufacturer's experts to the customer's firm without any specific sales intentions

■ Invitations for customers to exhibitions and special treatment at the events

■ Advertising the offers of the customer's firm, for instance, through a link between the websites of the customer and the manufacturer

■ Provision of advertising and sales promotion materials for the customer's firm

Phase-driven strategies and the affirmation of relationship orientation as a competitive advantage form the core of strategic relationship marketing based on modified classic marketing strategies. The strategies developed beyond this should be bolstered by appropriate actions.

Relationship marketing programmes for industrial goods

Relationship marketing strategies can be implemented through appropriate **operating measures** based on the customer relationship life cycle phases embodying customer acquisition, retention, and recovery.

The **customer acquisition phase** task facing the industrial goods firm is to commence a relationship with the customer through initiation followed by socialisation. The **initiation phase** involves generating grounds for the customer to enter into a relationship with the company, whereby he or she is persuaded or stimulated to do so. Since industrial goods are complex, have predominant experience qualities, and are a high risk for the customer's firm, the focus of the initiation phase lies on customer persuasion. This is achieved largely through personal communication that helps to explain the seller's outputs to the customer, as done at exhibitions. For industrial goods, stimulation is used less often than for consumer goods, but nevertheless for certain sub-segments like materials it is common in the form of volume discounts. The complexity of industrial goods and the attendant for necessity clarification requires the customer to become used to the seller and its outputs during the **socialisation phase** (Dwyer, Schurr and Oh 1987). Examples of socialisation measures are customer training and keeping the same customer representatives.

Having initiated a customer relationship, it must be developed and intensified in the **customer retention phase**. This necessitates different approaches in the growth and maturity phases. During the **growth phase** an effort is made to intensify the relationship through the application of customisation and cross selling instruments. The heterogeneity of industrial goods necessitates customisation per se, making it the key aspect of the phase. Aligning output provision with the customer's specific needs in order to integrate the customer can evoke customer dependence on the firm. Value added services such as maintenance and repairs can likewise be utilised for this purpose. If these services are offered at a charge, this approach then achieves some cross selling potential too.

A relationship is maintained in the **maturity phase** by creating barriers with contractual, technological, institutional, or psychological bonds or by raising the efficiency. Switching barriers apply to only a few industrial items such as raw materials. The pricing policy permits barriers to be created, for instance, through the achievement of price leadership. Efficiency improvements are usually necessary for customised industrial goods such as machinery, where an attempt must be made to standardise the maximum possible processes including some development and fabrication activities. Another possibility for improving customer retention is the use of business clubs. While commonly used in consumer goods marketing, club schemes are also becoming popular in the Business-to-Business area. Specialised schemes offering exclusive services for its business members can be found in the German electric power industry.

Example 9.3

The German electric power corporation RWE offers its business customers an exclusive membership in a business club. Some of the services in this scheme include, for instance, training with the German soccer team Bayer Leverkusen, the sponsoring partner of RWE, for the members' children, Porsche driving training on the German racing circuit at Nürburgring, and a special seminar programme. The club already has 400 members and RWE wants to increase the number up to 5,000 in the next 18 months (Kleine 2001, p. 31).

The aim of the **customer recovery phase** is to re-intensify endangered relationships in the imperilment phase, and to regain lost customers in the termination/abstinence phase. Problems in the imperilment phase from a customer's perspective could lead to defection. Since the seller-buyer contact is direct and the market is often tight with few sellers and few buyers, it is frequently straightforward to identify these problems and the affected relationships. Corrective measures involve the rectification of defects (e.g. subsequent machine repairs) and restitution (e.g. reimbursement for production stoppages due to equipment failures). In the **termination/abstinence phase** the customer prominence that stems from the direct seller-buyer contact can also be utilised for recovery measures. For standardised products such as raw materials pricing related offers like a new volume discount come into play. For customised ones such as machinery and industrial plants, on the other hand, value added recovery offers such as the joint development of equipment are more appropriate.

Implementation phase for the Business-to-Business market

To transform and implement relationship marketing's concept and actions in a corporation it is necessary to design the **implementation** systematically. In this context it is reasonable to modify the organisational structures, management systems, and the corporate culture to comply with the maxims of customer and relationship orientation.

It is imperative in the industrial goods segment to first promote cooperative work stretching across functions within the seller's organisational structures. Different corporate groups such as the technical or marketing departments face extremely different tasks owing to the complexity of industrial goods. In order to organise company activities to uniformly meet customer needs, it is helpful to set up coordination teams of employees from the different areas involved. In addition, because of the direct contact between the buyer and employees (Håkansson and Snehota 1995), empowerment of customer representatives can also contribute towards raising their relationship orientation. **Relationship promoters** are particularly important for initiating, organising, and accelerating inter-organisational exchange processes (Walter 1999). Industrial goods producers also tend to be more customer- and relationship-oriented, the higher the degree of specialisation and formalisation as well as the greater the degree of decision delegation (Homburg 1998b).

Management systems or especially the information and control systems must also be matched to the relationships. Frequent direct contacts and the relatively high value of individual customers provide industrial goods companies with the chance of managing information and control systems at the individual level with the help of databases. This offers a basis for customer specific relationship control.

In the industrial goods segment **corporate cultures** tend to be highly technically oriented, which can partly hinder the transformation of customer and relationship orientation. It is hence important to strive for appropriate communication to achieve a customer-focused culture within the firm. It is especially critical to attain cooperation between the R&D, marketing, and sales departments to be able to comprehensively develop and intensify customer relationships.

Control phase for the Business-to-Business market

For an industrial goods producer to implement its strategic relationship marketing concept and the relevant profitability-focused measures, it is essential to consistently **control** the pre-economic, economic, and integrated aspects of relationship marketing. **Pre-economic controls** that have to be determined are the features of relationship marketing's pre-economic target parameters such as relationship quality or customer satisfaction. For deploying attribute-related methods the sample sizes for the relevant analyses could sometimes be too low, typically because of the few buyers. In such cases it is not feasible to statistically determine the significance of single-quality attributes in the overall quality. In contrast, event- and problem-related methods could be applied meaningfully due to the directness of the customer contacts and the frequent integration of customers in the output provision process. The firm can utilise the results to control its outputs and relationships with customers from their perspective.

Economic controls should also be conducted around customer-related parameters like sales, contribution margins, and the CLV. Due to the firm's familiarity with the customer, it is possible to analyse data at an individual customer level. This permits conclusions to be drawn on the profitability of specific customers and its implications for controlling the relationship.

Integrated control methods combine the features of various pre-economic and economic variables in line with relationship marketing's success chain, and thereby permit interdependency analyses in addition to feature analyses. For example, developing a corporate-specific Balanced Scorecard enables corporate and customer-related target parameters to be controlled in an integrated manner.

9.3.3 Critical assessment of relationship marketing in the Business-to-Business market

The **industrial goods segment** represents the original and classic area for applying relationship marketing. This situation arose because the direct contact to customers and above all the importance of individual customers forced industrial goods producers to put in an intensive effort on specific customer relationships, with the aim of becoming successful in the market.

The industrial goods segment in **practice** has the advantage over the consumer goods segment that the company culture often incorporates thinking along the lines of customer relationships. However, industrial goods firms typically have no systematic approach for relationship marketing. Even though many customer representatives think and behave in a customer-oriented manner in that they take considerable care of the customers assigned to them, they do so typically without any formal structure. Customers are consequently seldom classified according to their profitability, relationship marketing is often only conducted at each customer representative level, and it involves no planning, control, and monitoring of related activities in terms of economic parameters. Industrial goods companies are thus more technically-oriented in the sense of their emphasis on the potential and results, and less customer-oriented in the sense of their focus on processes. These companies should therefore seek to take advantage of their basic relationship-focused cultural foundation to build up systematic and structured relationship marketing throughout the whole firm.

This conceptual deficit is also found in practice partly in the relevant **marketing science** literature. On the one hand, one hears much on the relationship focus for industrial goods marketing. On the other hand, much of the relevant literature is an adaptation of primarily consumer goods and transaction-based classic marketing with the result that a comprehensive relationship marketing concept for this segment still does not exist. For this reason, the key task of marketing researchers is to develop a holistic relationship marketing concept for industrial goods companies.

9.4 Relationship marketing for the service industry

9.4.1 Foundations of relationship marketing for services

Attributes of services

Just as in other segments the services sector also has a range of different output solutions. One can differentiate between consumer and investment services like those from a bank versus management consulting, respectively. Nevertheless, in this sector also, the following constitutive attributes of services can be identified (Lovelock 2001; Zeithaml and Bitner 2000; Meffert and Bruhn 2000; Palmer and Cole 1995; Gabbott and Hogg 1994):

- Services have a high degree of integration and interaction in terms of their **contact attributes**. Services are often characterised by information asymmetries to the disadvantage of the customer. The contact between the seller and buyer is usually direct so that the customer is not anonymous from the firm. For most services the value of one customer is quite low.

- In terms of **output attributes** the significance of the potential for providing services as perceived by customers is relatively high. Even within one category services can be relatively heterogeneous. They also tend to be complex and are neither storable nor transportable.

- In the context of **customer attributes** services are usually difficult to assess due to their high share of experience and credence qualities (Darbi and Karni 1973). The risk and involvement of the customer is often high. However, procurement processes do not need to be as long as for industrial goods. The decisions can be emotional or rational. Barriers to switching are higher than in the consumer goods sector.

The selection of services on the basis of attributes mentioned leads to unique aspects of relationship marketing in this segment that may apply to its conceptualisation. This tends to result in a concentration of consumer services, since investment services are significantly more relevant for the marketing of industrial goods (section 9.3).

Conceptualisation of relationship marketing for the service industry

The **customer life cycle concept** represents the basis for conceiving relationship marketing for the services sector (Berry 1995; Bitner 1995; Crosby and Stephens 1987), because of the dynamics of a customer relationship. The elements of the customer needs and relationship life cycles can be differentiated within this concept. The **customer needs life cycle** can vary to a great degree for numerous services. These variations are related to the changing needs and interests of consumers in the course of their life. For instance, travel and leisure services have to be adapted according to customers' preferences which continue to evolve (Lovelock 2001, p. 112). The box 'Insights 9.3: Customer needs life cycle in the hotel industry' describes how changing customer needs have affected the business of Club Med.

Insights 9.3

Customer needs life cycle in the hotel industry – the Club Med experience

When Gilbert Trigano launched Club Med (www.clubmed.com) in the 1950s, the concept of holiday villages offering limitless food and innumerable sporting activities in splendid natural surroundings at a single price was unique. The atmosphere attracted a crowd that was primarily young, affluent, educated, and single. These people enjoyed sports, travel and exotic locations. In the late 1960s, Club Med, with its communal lifestyle – which included shared huts, group activities and large dining tables designed to break down social barriers between guests – had captured the spirit of the times. During a burgeoning market in the 1970s and 1980s, Club Med opened villages around the world and epitomised the ultimate leisure experience: a relatively expensive holiday, either at the beach or (later) at winter ski villages in the mountains. However, ten years later, problems began to emerge. The group's financial situation weakened and there was widespread criticism that the Club Med concept had become outmoded. Younger people were now more individualistic and no longer keen on the kinds of sybaritic, group activities for which Club Med was renowned. While finding young new customers was becoming harder and harder, the club's most loyal customers had grown older and considered new criteria for leisure opportunities. Rather than seeking ways to have fun as swinging singles, these guests were concerned about what to do with their children on vacation and how to achieve a healthy lifestyle, including nutritious food, low-impact exercises, and other ways to restore physical and emotional well-being. By 1990, the emergence of low-price, all-inclusive holiday package tours was eroding Club Med's traditional customer base, yet the club had not lowered its own prices in response. After huge losses in 1996, the Trigano family was ousted from the daily running of the company, and Philippe Bourguignon – who had turned Disneyland Paris around – was brought in to revive the club. His approach was aimed at meeting the needs of two very different kinds of segments – the younger, value-conscious market that Club Med had not yet succeeded in winning over and the mature group of customers who had been the backbone of Club Med's past success but whose loyalty was now at risk. To meet the needs of the former group, Bourguignon immediately closed several loss-making villages and converted a number of others into lower-priced camps, rebranded as Club Aquarius. Plans were also made to transform the traditional Club Med concept by catering more to the creature-comfort requirements of older, existing customers. Taking these measures, Club Med recognised the importance of changing needs and preferences of its customers. Now, Club Med differentiates even more life cycle needs. That's why they have designed, for instance, four clubs specifically for children: Baby Club Med™, Petit Club Med™, Mini Club Med™ and Junior Club Med. Divided into different age groups, these clubs will take care of and entertain the little ones from dusk until dawn.

(*Source*: adapted from Lovelock, C. (2001): *Services Marketing. People, Technology, Strategy*, 4th edn, New Jersey, p. 113 (Service Perspectives 4.1); based, in parts, on articles in the Financial Times, February 24, 1997, and October 7, 1997.)

The **customer relationship life cycle phases** could also be highly developed. As such, owing to the complexity of the outputs and the customer integration in the service provision process, the socialisation phase can be especially important for the subsequent course of the relationship. The growth phase is also well developed due to the multifarious cross selling potential of numerous segments (Figure 9.6). The relatively long socialisation phase and the high attendant costs at the start of a customer relationship in this sector (Reichheld and Sasser 1990) result in companies generally focusing on customer recovery activities.

Integration of external factors into the output provision process leads to highly heterogeneous services within one category. Service companies must accordingly place more emphasis on **perspective taking**. Applicable training programmes must be undertaken for the many customer representatives in the firm, who are in direct and frequent contact with the customers due to customer integration and the 'unoactu' principle of a two-way street (Davis 1983).

The difficulty in assessing services should be accounted for by considering **relationships from a customer's standpoint**, since it is very important to measure and control the service quality. The immateriality of these services also ensures that in

Type of service	Entry-level products (Base products)	Cross selling potential	
		Supplementary products	Trading up
Insurance	Base coverage, e.g. household, car liability	Accident/Legal coverage	Term life/disability insurance
Banking	Checking account	Savings account, general loan	Investment counselling, home financing
Credit card businesses	Credit card	Insurance package	Tour offer
Commercial trade	Base products	In addition to daily needs	High value products
Tourism	Rail/air travel, accommodation	Package tours	Club travel

Figure 9.6 Cross selling potential of different service companies

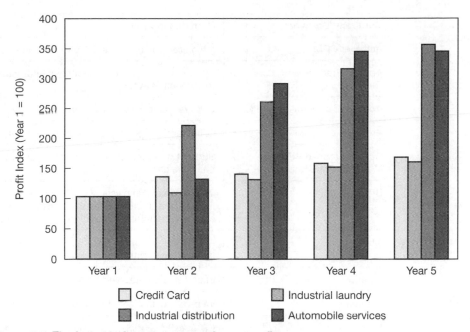

Figure 9.7 The impact of customer retention on profits
(*Source*: Lovelock 2001, p. 152; based on data in Reichheld and Sasser 1990, pp. 105–11)

an abundant number of service areas mainly emotional aspects comprise decision-making factors expressed through the relationship quality, customer satisfaction, or commitment (Moorman, Zaltman and Deshpandé 1992). Furthermore, customer retention is a key factor for profitability (see Figure 9.7 which illustrates how profits are influenced by the duration of a customer relationship). The whole success chain of relationship marketing in the services sector thus takes on extreme relevance. These conceptually unique aspects must be given due consideration in designing relationship marketing's planning process.

9.4.2   Unique planning process features of relationship marketing

Analysis phase for the service sector

As a part of relationship marketing's analysis phase a SWOT-analysis, target planning, and customer segmentation need to be conducted prior to developing the strategies to implement them. A **SWOT-analysis** focuses on customers, because of the importance of customer orientation within relationship marketing. A constituent level analysis of the services can be conducted. The high frequency of the direct seller-buyer contact combined with the availability of data within the firm (e.g. membership like relationships in financial services or in telecommunications), enable an analysis of individual customers or at least customer groups. However, firms still do incur difficulties in data evaluations, even though an increasing number of software programmes like CRM from Data Mining are being developed for this purpose (see Figure 9.8 for an overview of relevant offers).

Company/Software	Brief description
Achiever CRM	Integrated solution for small and medium-sized firms
Applied Predictive Technologies (APT)	Supports direct communication with customers and optimises the branch network
Applix iCustomer Advantage	CRM real time information systems
Ardexus	CRM software geared for the small to mid-market
Baan Enterprise Resource Management System	Support of customer retention management and optimisation of the value chain
Broadbase	Integration and analysis of customer information from the Internet and traditional sales channels, targeted at improved customer acquisition, retention, and profitability
Chordiant	Analysis of customer interactions by integrating data from the Internet, call centres, and field services
Delano	Enables automated and personalised electronic interactions
E.piphany	Web-based analysis of customer relationships
Hyperion	CRM Analysis Applications such as Customer Interaction Centre for measuring and call centre/customer service operations
KnowledgeSync 2000 from Vineyrdsoft	Identification and reporting of certain customer relationship events
Manna FrontMind for Marketing	Web-based prediction of and reaction to customer behaviour
MarketMiner	Direct marketing applications, i.e. response to and evaluation of customer questions, customer relationship modelling
NCR Relationship Optimiser	Control of one-on-one relationships by banks
Norkom Technologies	Prediction of customer and market behaviour
OpenSourceCRM	Diverse CRM applications
Pivotal	Control of marketing activities for managing relationships between employees, business partners, and customers
SPSS CustomerCentric	Good, easy-to-follow CRM software
thinkAnalytics	Analysis of customer relationships
Trajecta	Optimisation of CRM during the course of the customer life cycle
Unica Affinium	Data Mining, projection of customer behaviour and measures management
Update.com	Electronic CRM solutions
Vantive	Electronic CRM solutions
Xchange	Electronic CRM solutions
YOUcentric	Electronic CRM solutions

Figure 9.8 Examples of CRM Software offers

(*Source*: based on KDnuggets 2002, www.kdnuggets.com/solutions/crm.html#W, accessed on May 3, 2002)

Goal planning is possible at the base constituent level. Customer integration into service provision and the heterogeneity of the service programme imply major variations in revenues and costs among different customer relationships. Cross selling and the purchasing frequency are thus very significant behavioural targets. The immateriality of experience and credence goals such as perceived service quality, customer satisfaction, and relationship quality makes these customer-related psychological goals important. Employee-related targets like satisfaction and retention become very critical preliminary stages of the customer-related targets because of the direct contacts involved.

The possibility of high heterogeneity in the profitability and intensity of customer relationships also gives great importance to **customer segmentation** for the services sector. An attempt should be made to apply the success chain parameters relevant for a service provider's success as a segmentation criterion. Figure 9.9 depicts an example of customer segmentation in the power generation sector based on both pre-economic and economic aspects.

Strategy development for services

Strategy development for relationship marketing involves establishing phase-driven strategies and materialising relationship orientation as a competitive advantage.

Phase-driven strategies in the services field covering customer acquisition, retention, and recovery can also be based on the customer relationship life cycle phases. Arguments for an acquisition strategy could be a low market share in a particular segment as with a bank in the insurance business after entering the market, or the low profitability of existing customers. A retention strategy is needed when the sales figures with a customer are low, as in the case of mobile phone customers that obviously sign up only because of a promotional offer from the company, or when customers keep switching their pizza delivery in response to volume discounts offered by the suppliers. A recovery strategy could be necessary when a

Segment	Number of Customers	Customers targeted for acquisition 1996/97	Acquisition costs	Annual customer retention rate	Annual profit per customer
Unprofitable, extremely loyal	421,300	500	£110	99%	£6
Elderly couples	618,000	66,000	£70	97%	£9
Ready for a mid-life change	497,900	110,000	£55	94%	£18
Unfaithful average customers	459,600	220,000	£30	90%	£22

Figure 9.9 Relationship-oriented customer segmentation for a power producer

(*Source*: Payne and Frow 1997, p.69)

seller loses many customers, as has happened with big banks following a merger, merger rumours, or with airlines after an accident.

A services provider should seek to consequently implement relationship marketing to demonstrate its **relation leadership**. The following are examples found in the services segment:

- 'Trust is everything' – the Deutsche Bank campaign
- 'Our most important asset is our customer's trust' – a Citibank slogan (www.citibank.com, accessed July 10, 2001)
- Offer of a range of related services by Sears (e.g. food retailing, financial services, home service)
- Exclusive treatment of frequent-flyer programme members by airlines

Within the framework of relationship marketing that has been enhanced by the phase-driven strategies and competitive advantage of relationship orientation, the classic marketing strategies can be adjusted to the requirements of relationship marketing. Appropriate relationship actions also need to be developed.

Relationship marketing programmes for services

Having set the strategy, it must then be implemented by **operational measures**. The dynamics of customer relationships call for an alignment with the related life cycle phases. A service provider needs to establish measures for customer acquisition, retention, and recovery.

An attempt is made in the **customer acquisition phase** to start a relationship with potential customers. This requires initiation and socialisation of the relationship with the customer. Relationship marketing's task in the **initiation phase** is to persuade and stimulate a customer into starting a relationship with the seller. Since services are of an immaterial nature and it is necessary to integrate the customer in the provision of services, persuasion is feasible primarily through materialisation with a before-and-after presentation, while personification is achieved through the use of testimonials in advertising for services as shown in Figure 9.10. Stimulation through the pricing policy is possible only for lower risk services such as reduced prices for mobile phones from telecommunication companies.

Factors \ Design Target	Materialisation	Personification
External Factors	• Before and after presentation • Service item packaging • Presentation of needs satisfaction	• Reference customers • Testimonials • Public figures/celebrities
Internal Factors	• Material (factual) internal factors • Sample items • Use of symbols • Providing the carrier medium	• Managers • Employees (with or without customer contact) • Presentation of the service process

Figure 9.10 Materialisation and personification for promotional services

The non-transportability of services makes the choice of location a very significant stimulation instrument: e.g. for a long time banks were able to acquire customers only by having a broad network of branches. Nowadays, with the rise of technology and the Internet, banks can offer their services online to anyone at anytime without the need of expanding into new locations.

The need to clarify many of the services lays particular value on the **socialisation phase**, which is relatively easy to control due to the direct seller-buyer contact. Relevant measures in this phase have shown the sellers' continuity to the customer, e.g. in the banking sector having the same customer representative as a contact person is especially important for wealthy private clients. However, innovative instruments can also improve the existing relationship. For instance, in the telecommunications sector providers offer their customers a choice in billing. That is, they can either pay their bill traditionally or they can choose to pay online.

The task for relationship marketing's **customer retention phase** is to intensify and maintain the relationship. This is accomplished in the growth and maturity sub-phases. An effort is made to extend the customer relationship in the **growth phase** through customisation and cross selling. The necessity to integrate the customer in output provision offers multiple options for customising the relationship. In numerous service sectors such as management consulting and supplementary education, modification of the corporate output to meet customer needs is not just possible but quite important. In addition, the heterogeneity and complexity of services offer the opportunity to take full advantage of the cross selling potential. For instance, management consulting projects often help identify other problems that form the basis for follow-on projects.

Since strengthening the customer relationship is unlikely in the **maturity phase**, service providers should strive instead to raise the efficiency of individual relationships. Reinforcing the switching barriers is one way to achieve this, for example, by making it difficult for a customer to transfer stocks to an account with another bank. Such barriers already exist in the services sector due to the customer risk involved (Murray 1991; Lutz and Reilly 1973). Even if the customer risk is low for certain services, barriers such as contracts with telecommunications firms or customer cards with rebates can be set up. Customer cards including a payment function are widely used in retailing (Figure 9.11). Another approach is to lower customer relationship costs. This can be seen in the financial services sector. For instance, Deutsche Bank, Germany, tried to convince their less profitable customers to do business with their group Deutsche Bank 24 or just over the Internet while the more profitable ones were dealt with directly with customer representatives.

To **manage customer recovery** service firms seek to control the imperilment and termination/abstinence phases. If the customer has problems with the seller and its outputs, the relationship is in the **imperilment phase** because the customer reflects on a possible switch to another seller. This leaves the options of error rectification and restitution as a means for the service provider to re-acquire the customer. The non-storability of services often makes it impossible to rectify problems with the output itself, as in the case of a delayed flight that cannot be made retroactively punctual. Error correction here is feasible over the price, whereby the

Customer Card with payment/rebate function	Description
Wal-Mart Credit Card	• No annual fee • Exclusive finance offers for cardholders • No finance charges when paying balance in full each month • Additional cards for family members at no extra cost
Nordstrom Visa Card	• For every net dollar charged on products and services at Nordstrom stores, the customer earns 2 points • For every 2,000 points the customer accumulates, he'll receive a $20 Merchandise Certificate that may be redeemed at any store, including catalogues
Target Visa Card	• Every time a customer uses Target Visa at a Target store or target.com, he earns one point for every dollar he spends, minus returns • On accumulating 1,000 points, he receives a target rewards certificate good for 10% savings on a full day of shopping at any Target store when using Target Visa

Figure 9.11 Examples of customer cards with payment or rebate function

price-benefit ratio can be subsequently improved by reducing the cost of the delayed flight. Since the non-storability also precludes direct restitution of the defective output, this can instead be achieved simply with another form of output like a free ticket for another flight.

In the event the customer has already been lost but is still attractive, it could make sense for the firm to assess how to arrange her or his recovery in this **termination/abstinence phase**. Recovery offers could be made to the customer (e.g. taking care of formalities caused by switching the provider; cancellation of initiation fees in the mobile phone market) or added value created through service customisation. In the services sector, recovery during a termination de-briefing is particularly important due to the direct contact between the seller and buyer.

Implementation phase for the service sector

Systematic execution and implementation of relationship marketing in the services sector calls for consistent actions during the **implementation phase**. It is necessary to evaluate the impact that modifications to the service firm's organisational structures, management systems, and the culture could have on better customer and relationship orientation.

The **organisational structure** should first be assessed to determine if setting up de-centralised units would help to better control customer relationships. The direct contact between the seller and buyer and the need to integrate the customer in output provision could be the grounds for having de-centralised organisational units in proximity to the customers to guarantee meeting the needs of individual or specific groups of them (Schlesinger and Heskett 1992). Empowerment can be an additional helpful instrument for successful control of individual relationships (Zeithaml, Parasuraman and Berry 1990; Swartz, Bowen and Brown 1992; Mudie and Cottam 1993). The customer representative probably knows the solution that would help the customer the most. If one leaves the decision on the measures to be undertaken partly in the representative's hands, he or she will be more motivated and more committed towards the company's success over the medium-term.

It is reasonable to match the service provider's **management systems** to the customer and relationship orientation needs as well. Relationship marketing's success chain could be used as the basis for developing customer and relationship targeted information and control systems. This permits identification of the parameters and their correlations that are relevant for the success of a customer relationship and relationship marketing. Above all, the mainly financial success computations conducted so far need to be extended to pre-economic parameters by applying, for example, the CLV or the Balanced Scorecard.

Particularly in the services sector it is essential to enable the **corporate culture** to become customer- and relationship-focused. Since the customer is in direct contact and also integrated into output provision, he or she frequently gains insight into internal company processes. If cultural deficiencies exist, they alone could lead to negative perceptions by the customer. This refers especially to the employees' attitudes and behaviour towards the customer. It is hence critical to pay due attention to the customer orientation characteristics of new employees and to the development of personnel.

Control phase for the service sector

Customer relationships must be consistently **controlled** in order to guarantee profitable implementation of relationship marketing's strategies and actions. For this a service provider can make use of pre-economic, economic, and integrated control methods. **Pre-economic controls** include the analysis of relevant relationship marketing parameters such as the service and relationship quality and customer satisfaction. The service provider can utilise standardised attribute processes to obtain statements on the customer's perception of the company. Figure 9.12 is an example of a relevant customer questionnaire that could be used in banks. Event- and problem-related methods could also be valuable in this sector, because of the customer integration in the output provision process and the characteristics of the seller-buyer process.

Economic analyses cover customer sales, contribution margins, and the CLV as the control parameters. Recommendations are a major decision-making factor in the services sector as a result of the risk that customers undergo on using a service. A broad-based CLV could make sense here. In addition to considering only payments received and disbursements made as a reference value, the effects of customer recommendations should also be taken into account.

Integrated controls should be undertaken by combining the analysis of pre-economic and economic parameters. Such an analysis includes not just the parameters themselves but also their interdependencies, which can be accomplished using customer indices or the Balanced Scorecard.

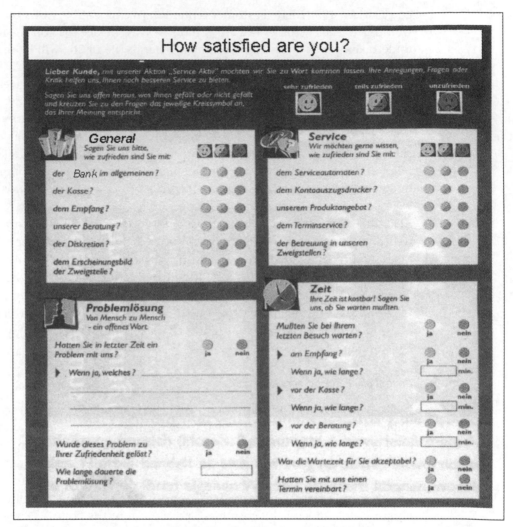

Figure 9.12 Example of a customer questionnaire in a German bank

9.4.3 Critical assessment of relationship marketing for the service industry

The **service sector**, just like the industrial goods segment, is one of the original areas where most of the applications of relationship marketing were made. This development can be explained by the fact that a transfer of the relationship marketing concepts from the consumer goods segment cannot be made without modifications of the problems involved in the marketing of services.

Customer-related instruments have been in use **in the field** for a long time for marketing services. Mention is most often made of customer satisfaction analyses, complaint management measures, customer retention instruments, and CLV methods. Corporations frequently use many isolated instruments that are seldom within a conceptual framework to structure and coordinate their application, as in the case of customer polls to measure their satisfaction but without combining the findings into financial indicators. An abundant number of measures with the same target are consequently implemented, often without coordinating application of the instruments.

This situation also applies partly to the **services marketing science**. Many applications relate to single instruments like the method for measuring the service quality or the control of customer retention. Rarely can one identify relationship marketing concepts that permit corporate thinking along the lines of customer relationships. Researchers thus face the key task of providing a foundation for corporations to be able to focus their customer relationships effectively.

Summary

This chapter has dealt with relationship marketing from an institutional standpoint. So far, the conceptualisation and the planning process has been applied to every organisation. However, the focus can differ depending on the specific business segment, such as consumer goods, industrial goods, and services. When developing a relationship marketing concept the attributes of these markets have to be considered. Therefore, we first looked at the characteristics of consumer and industrial goods as well as services. Then, we elaborated on the consequences for the conceptualisation as well as the planning process of relationship marketing. We concluded each institutional perspective with a critical evaluation.

10 The future outlook for relationship marketing

Overview

In this chapter we will give a future outlook for relationship marketing. In the previous nine chapters existing methods and instruments for relationship marketing were presented and evaluated in terms of the needs of different segments. The relevant observations highlighted the fact that many branches still have barriers that prevent consistent implementation of relationship marketing. Its progress in numerous segments, on the one hand, is characterised by the repeated implementation of isolated relationship orientation elements. On the other hand, there is still enormous potential for advancement in many sectors. Since the initial experiences with relationship marketing were gathered just in the last 10 to 15 years, the relationship activities still tend to be partly rudimentary. In spite of all this, the underlying concepts of relationship marketing are recognisable though they definitely need to be developed further. This advancement must take place not only in practice but also at the scientific level on theoretical, methodological, and empirical fronts. Regarding the outlook, we will address the following questions in this chapter:

➤ What are the future prospects for relationship marketing in practice?

➤ What are the future research prospects for relationship marketing?

10.1 Future prospects for relationship marketing in practice

In many areas of corporate practice relationship marketing represents a new type of problem that the management of most companies have not yet had consistently to deal with. This state of affairs can be seen in the following **problem areas** that present challenges for relationship marketing in the field, and which are an outcome of this book's structure:

- Conceptualisation problem
- Analysis and control problem
- Strategy problem
- Measures problem
- Implementation problem

The **conceptualisation problem** blocks the advancement of thinking along customer relationship lines in practice. Various fundamental ideas of relationship marketing call for basic reforms of marketing's mindset within corporations: e.g. the focus on customer relationships in place of sales volumes and revenues for products, or the satisfaction of stakeholders' needs as the role of relationship marketing, or the somewhat conflicting and often sought after cost or growth targets for the entire firm. Companies find it especially difficult in the consumer goods segment to detach themselves from this conventional mindset and to seek, at least conceptually, to focus on relationship marketing.

Intensive occupation with 'thinking along customer relationship lines' represents a **challenge** for corporate practice. This implies at first an aptness check of the existing methods for one's own segment and firm. The firms should then involve themselves in achieving the possible potential success of relationship marketing and comparing its advantages with prior corporate concepts. Several corporate cases demonstrate the success potential of controlled relationships. In numerous segments companies can realise the wide-ranging potential value of core customers, the firm, and consequently the shareholders.

There is also an **analysis and control problem** among corporations. Customers are in part neither analysed nor monitored; firms set no customer or relationship-oriented goals, nor do they segment customers based on their profitability. One reason for this deficit is the lack of the necessary data, since it is seldom feasible to carry out an analysis at an individual customer level in many branches, possibly due to the data collection effort or privacy problems involved. To some extent firms do not even evaluate existing data, since they are not aware of their usefulness for relationship marketing. Besides, no use is made of current methodologies such as customer lifetime value, either because they are not convinced by them or are short on know-how. Furthermore, customer analyses or the setting of customer goals often oppose management's way of thinking and the incentive system in a firm.

For these reasons, the initial **challenge** for corporations is to establish the data currently available within the firm that can be applied to relationship analyses and control. Here it is necessary that the marketing head and controller show a certain amount of creativity in utilising these data to obtain at least an indication of the relationship tendencies. The relationship goals should also be given more prominence for goal planning. It serves no purpose if just lip service is paid to the customer and relationship orientation, or if they are recited as an adage in the corporate guidelines. These parameters must be formulated as targets, put into practice, and constantly controlled. This is especially critical since the relationship goals, instead of countering the traditionally stated variables like revenues or profits, function as pre-economic parameters according to relationship marketing's success chain to contribute to the achievement of these very prime goals. In addition, it is easy to understand that different goals are needed for different customer relationship life cycle phases. To resolve the analysis problem each case should be assessed for the extent to which the application of IT systems could help attain better data. For example, retail firms have gained access to a broad database at the individual customer level through an appropriate information system and the issuing of customer cards.

A **strategy problem** also exists in practice in addition to the conceptualisation and analysis/control problems. Customer and relationship targets are frequently not translated into respective strategies. Sometimes companies claim to follow a strategy that on closer examination turns out to be typical empty marketing slogans. Often the key attribute of relationship marketing, namely the control of customer relationships in line with individual standards, is not specifically addressed. Rather strategies that sound like relationship marketing are defined for the whole market, leading to inefficient ones that cannot be expected to deliver. There are only a limited number of cases of consistent implementation of the competitive advantages of relationship orientation. Corporations appear to find it hard to disengage themselves from the isolated pursuit of classic competitive advantages like costs or output quality.

The strategy problem offers many approaches for a stronger relationship focus for corporate activities. The **challenge** lies in developing original relationship-oriented strategies. Firms can make use of existing frameworks such as the customer relationship life cycle for deriving the basis for the strategy. Firms could also attempt to redo their whole strategy and conceive specific relationship strategies, possibly in cooperation with important customers. In this context, it is particularly important to define the competitive advantages of relationship orientation. In a real market situation, cost and quality leadership are to some extent not adequate for customer acquisition, retention, and re-acquisition. Therefore, those companies able to achieve relation leadership in their market could benefit from the additional success potential. Materialisation of relation leadership thus is the core task of relationship marketing in practice.

Closely associated with the strategy problem is the **measures problem**, which refers to the fact that companies seldom undertake any relationship planning and implementation of measures. One reason for this is the emphasis placed by the firm on its day-to-day business. Employees in various departments have lists of essential activities to accomplish, which leave no room for innovative actions. On top of this one often encounters departmental thinking that hinders the transformation to relationship-focused measures. The success of complaint management, for instance, depends on the promotion and product policy. If the employees do not cooperate, the actions are either not at all implemented or only half-heartedly. A phenomenon that has also been observed in many segments and corporations is that the majority of initiated activities tend to be imitations introduced in reaction to a competitor's actions.

The **challenge** for relationship marketing in practice is the promotion of employee creativity in deriving the measures. Slack periods during daily activities could help give the employees the time and leisure to search for innovative solutions when controlling a customer relationship. A firm could additionally benefit by differentiating itself from its competitors with respect to relationship marketing activity. A look across segment boundaries could also help to identify innovative ways to implement relationship orientation.

A key deficiency in relationship marketing in practice is defined by the **implementation problem**, which relates to the organisational structure, management systems, and the corporate culture. Most corporate organisations are not suited for a relationship-targeted modification of their activities. Marketing activities are typically bundled together in an isolated marketing department such that company-wide customer and relationship orientation cannot be accomplished. Relationship marketing is also precluded by other additional activities. e.g. a firm often conducts no customer evaluations because the desired data are kept by other departments such as quality control or market research, and neither the marketing department requests the data nor the other unit proactively provides the information. In this situation systematic customer assessment, and with it customer-specific relationship control, is impossible to conduct because there are no comprehensive information and control systems in place. Besides, firms frequently suffer from a highly product-focused mindset so strongly embedded in their culture that a mental change to relationship orientation is currently not feasible.

These problems generate different **challenges** for implementation-related problems of relationship marketing. Companies must reflect on which corporate structure would promote greater customer and relationship orientation. It may become necessary to break down existing organisational barriers in order to remove hurdles along the path towards relationship orientation. The company's information and control systems as well must be aligned with relationship marketing possibly through the use of IT systems. This requires integration into the existing customer control parameters in line with relationship marketing's success chain. It could also be critical to launch initiatives to change the corporate culture, by embedding customer and relationship orientation in the firm to force relationship-driven behaviour by both the firm and its staff members. Internal customer orientation can be a useful concept for this purpose. In companies where cooperation with employees, colleagues, and superiors is integrated in the sense of a customer-supplier relationship, they will likely find it easier to transfer the relationship mindset to external markets.

This book represents the forefront of relationship marketing and thereby offers the initial basis for putting it into practice. However, the state of the art in the literature and science has shortfalls that enable the challenges for advancing relationship marketing to be identified.

10.2 Future research prospects for relationship marketing

A review of the literature on relationship marketing and closely related concepts and problems shows that the concept of relationship marketing is not the only one with shortfalls. This deficit also applies to the academic field, where the following **problem layers** and the resulting **challenges for the scientists** can be identified:

- Theory problem
- Method problem
- Empiricism problem

A **theory problem** of relevance to the academic field is related to the development of a comprehensive concept, a foundation for relationship marketing strategies, and the structure of marketing instruments.

A reader's examination of the literature leads her or him to the conclusion that an **overall concept** for relationship marketing has yet to be discovered. Numerous presentations exhaust themselves with isolated single concepts. The treatments usually do not even reach the conceptual plane but rather deal simply with individual instruments associated with relationship marketing. The discussions consequently get bogged down in the details and research is often pursued at cross-purposes.

The **challenge** for further research on relationship marketing thus lies in creating a conceptual framework for future investigations. The relevant structuring approach should be set at the highest possible plane to satisfy any claim of comprehensive validity. This does not necessarily mean an obsessive effort to discover new ideas, since current structuring methods such as the planning process for decision theories can be fully utilised to develop a relevant concept. Nevertheless, customer and relationship orientation should be more deeply embedded in relevant postulations.

The field of marketing science also faces a strategy problem. Within the literature on relationship marketing, there are hardly any **roots for relationship marketing strategies**. Related publications occupy themselves with theoretical discussions such as the conceptualisation of relationship constructs, the theoretical advantages of relationship marketing, or with providing specific instruments like the CLV. The outcome is that recommendations are seldom made on the strategic thrust for relationship marketing.

In view of this background the **challenge** for academia is the development of strategic options for relationship marketing, with the goal of providing companies with a system for selecting possible strategies with appropriate methods. As a result of the customisation of corporate activities within relationship marketing, it may be reasonable to provide an augmented framework for deriving a strategy instead of presenting 'packaged' strategies. In developing a strategy, companies must account for the special conditions in their own segment with particular emphasis on each individual customer relationship. Hence, the mission for science is to create practical concepts that support firms in developing creative and customised strategies.

Science also faces a problem involving appropriate measures. **Restructuring of relationship marketing measures** is usually undertaken inadequately. In relevant publications specific control measures like communication or quality management instruments are typically treated only peripherally. Moreover, the respective actions are rarely directed at the requirements of relationship marketing, as called for in the various phases of a relationship based on the customer life cycle.

Hence, academics should view it as a **challenge** to derive measures by integrating the following three areas. One: the classic marketing measures for the product, price, promotion, and place policies need to be interpreted and deployed in terms of relationship orientation. Two: thought should be given to deciphering how classic marketing actions can be integrated more intricately with customer and relationship orientation measures like quality and complaint management. Three: an investigation is required to determine if the integration of actions involving other stakeholders with those involving customers could support effective implementation of relationship marketing.

Besides the theory problem researchers are confronted with a **method problem**, that is, **providing analysis and control methods** for relationship marketing. These methods are often not particularly practical. On the one hand, they do not take into account that companies offer resistance by holding on to their existing control systems. Frequently, no integration possibilities exist for such situations. On the other hand, the data status in practice is barely considered. Although the particular methods are theoretically stringent and comprehensively developed, they cannot be deployed in practice due to the lack of suitable data.

Resolving this problem is a key **challenge** for researchers, because of the importance of relationship analysis and control within relationship marketing. The first task is to enable more consistent integration of relationship indices in current key indicator systems. As shown by the success chain, relationship marketing's mechanisms like customer satisfaction and retention are the preliminary stage for the economic success of a company. To be able to analyse their contribution to success it is imperative to integrate them into key financial indicators. The customer index idea could also offer the basis for addressing this task, mainly because the various success parameters are interdependent.

Marketing science also has an **empiricism problem**. There are still unanswered multifarious questions regarding the effects of relationship marketing measures on relationship orientation and on the degree of fulfilment of its goals. Besides, the correlations between the success chain variables of relationship marketing have not yet been thoroughly analysed. On the one hand, it is true that the correlation between customer satisfaction and retention has often been analysed. On the other, a few associations within the chain on the linkage between customer and corporate facets are frequently overlooked. Additionally, little empirical knowledge exists with respect to the significance of the various moderating factors in the success chain.

This leads to the vital **challenge** for scientists to empirically look into these questions. It is a crucial step since an empirical verification of theoretically derived hypotheses is a critical condition for developing a relationship marketing theory.

In addition to the classic theoretical, methodological, and empirical problems, academia also has a **problem implementing education and training**. New marketing methods diffuse slowly through programmes at universities, professional schools, and similar institutions. This state of affairs represents the 'missing link' in putting new marketing concepts into practice: university students trained for their jobs either in research or in the field do not learn about the latest marketing research. If graduates continue their academic studies they need to have the prerequisite high-level basic education. As entry-level employees they tend to focus more on their new colleagues or superiors, rather than on the knowledge gained during their studies. As a result, new concepts take a long time to enter the corporate world. Academics should take on the **challenge** of applying innovative approaches to force the diffusion of the concepts through the students into the practical arena. This would provide companies with the means to consistently introduce new concepts. Relationship marketing embodies a fundamental idea that can, without any doubt, demonstrate its theoretical advantages for corporations. Now it is up to the researchers and practitioners to find the hidden treasure in relationship marketing.

References

Aaker, D.A. (1996) *Building Strong Brands.* New York: Free Press.

Abell, D.F. (1980) *Defining the Business. The Starting Point of Strategic Planning.* Englewood Cliffs: Prentice Hall.

Achrol, R.S. (1997) 'Changes in the Theory of Interorganizational Relations in Marketing: Toward a Network Paradigm', *Journal of the Academy of Marketing Science*, 25, Winter, 56–71.

Adler, J. (1996) *Informationsökonomische Fundierung von Austauschprozessen: Eine nachfrageroientierte Betrachtung.* Wiesbaden: Gabler.

Agrawal, M., Kumaresh, T.V. and Mercer, G.A. (2001) 'The false promise of mass customization', *The McKinsey Quarterly*, 3, 62–72.

Ahlert, D., Kenning, P. von and Petermann, F. (2001) 'Die Bedeutung von Vertrauen für die Interaktionsbeziehungen zwischen Dienstleistungsanbietern und Nachfragern' in Bruhn, M. and Stauss, B. (eds.) *Dienstleistungsmanagement. Jahrbuch 2001. Interaktionen im Dienstleistungsbereich.* Wiesbaden: Gabler, 299–318.

Alderson, W. (1965) *Dynamic Marketing Behavior: A Functionalist Theory of Marketing.* Homewood, IL: Richard D. Irwin.

Allen, N.J. and Meyer, J.P. (1990) 'The Measurement and Antecedents of Affective, Continuance and Normative Commitment to the Organization', *Journal of Occupational Psychology*, 63, March, 1–18.

Alpert, F.H. and Kamins, M.A. (1995) 'An Empirical Investigation of Consumer Memory, Attitude and Perceptions towards Pioneer and Follower Brands', *Journal of Marketing*, 59 (4), 34–45.

Altman, I. and Taylor, D.A. (1973) *Social Penetration. The Development of Interpersonal Relationships.* New York: Holt, Rhinehart and Winston.

Anderson, E.W. and Fornell, C. (2000) 'Foundations of the American Customer Satisfaction Index', *Total Quality Management*, 11 (7), 869–882.

Anderson, E.W. and Mittal, V. (2000) 'Strengthening the Satisfaction-Profit-Chain', *Journal of Service Research*, 3 (2), 107–120.

Anderson, E.W., Fornell, C. and Rust, R.T. (1997) 'Customer Satisfaction, Productivity and Profitability. Differences between Goods and Services', *Marketing Science*, 16 (2), 129–145.

Anderson, J.C. (1995) 'Relationships in Business Markets. Exchange Episodes, Value Creation and Their Empirical Assessment', *Journal of the Academy of Marketing Science*, 23 (4), 346–350.

Anderson, J.C., Håkansson, H. and Johanson, J. (1994) 'Dyadic business relationships within a business network context', *Journal of Marketing*, 58, 1–15.

Andon, P., Bradley, G. and Baxter, J. (1998) 'The Calculation of Customer Lifetime Value (CLV) Theory and Practice', paper, presented at the Workshop on Quality Management in Services VIII, Ingolstadt, Germany, April 1998.

Andreassen, T.W. and Lindestad, B. (1998) 'Repurchasing complex services. The Significance of Quality, Image and Satisfaction on Customer Loyalty', *International Journal of Service Industry Management*, 9 (1), 7–23.

Ansoff, H.I. (1966) *Management-Strategie.* Munich: verl. moderne industrie.

References

Auld, D.D. (1993) *Customer Retention Through Quality Leadership. The Baxter Approach*, Milwaukee.

Babin, B.J. and Griffin, M. (1998) 'The nature of satisfaction: an updated examination and analysis', *Journal of Business Research*, 41 (2), 127–136.

Backhaus, K. (1986) 'Industrial Marketing – State of the Art in Germany' in Backhaus, K. and Wilson, D.T. (eds.), *Industrial Marketing – A German-American Perspective*. Berlin: Springer, pp. 3–14.

Backhaus, K. (1999) *Industriegütermarketing*, 6th edn. Munich: Vahlen.

Backhaus, K. and Büschken J. (1997) 'What do we know about Business-to-Business Interactions? – A Synopsis of Empirical Research on Buyer-seller Interactions' in Gemünden, H., Ritter, T. and Walter, A. (eds.), *Relationships and Networks in International Markets*. Oxford: Pergamon, 13–36.

Bailom, F., Hinterhuber, H.H., Matzler, K. and Sauerwein, E. (1996) 'Das Kano-Modell der Kundenzufriedenheit', *Marketing ZFP*, 18 (2), 117–126.

Bagozzi, R.P. (1974) 'Marketing as an Organized Behavioral System of Exchange', *Journal of Marketing*, 38, October, 77–81.

Bagozzi, R.P. (1975) 'Marketing as Exchange', *Journal of Marketing*, 39 (3), 32–9.

Baker, M.J., Buttery, E.A. and Richter-Buttery, E.M. (1998) 'Relationship Marketing in three Dimensions', *Journal of Interactive Marketing*, 12 (4), 47–62.

Bauer, R. (1960) 'Consumer Behavior as Risk-Taking' in Hancock, R. (ed.), *Proceedings of the 43rd Conference of the American Marketing Association*, Chicago, 389–398.

Bauer, R.A. (1967) 'Consumer behaviour as risk taking' in Cox, D.F. (ed.), *Risk Taking and Information Handling on Consumer Behavior*. Boston, MA: Harvard University Press, 23–33.

BBDO Consulting (2001) *Customer Relationship Management, Case Studies, Executive Summary*, http://www.bbdo.de/bbdo-media/crmcasestudies.pdf, accessed on January 11, 2002.

Beane, T.P. and Ennis, D.M. (1987) 'Market Segmentation: A Review', *European Journal of Marketing*, 21 (5), 20–42.

Becker, J. (1998) *Marketing-Konzeption. Grundlagen des strategischen und operativen Marketing-Managements* (6th edn.) Munich: Vahlen.

Bejou, D. and Palmer, A. (1998) 'Service failure and loyalty: an exploratory empirical study of airline customers', *Journal of Services Marketing*, 12 (1), 7–22.

Bejou, D., Wray, B. and Ingram, T.N. (1996) Determinants of Relationship Quality. An Artificial Neural Network Analysis, *Journal of Business Research*, 36 (2), 137–43.

Benölken, H. and Greipel, P. (1994) *Dienstleistungsmanagement. Service als strategische Erfolgsposition*, (2nd edn). Wiesbaden: Gabler.

Benson, J.K. (1975) 'The Interorganizational Network as Political Economy', *Administrative Science Quarterly*, 20, June, 229–249.

Bergen, U., Dutta, S. and Walker, O.C. Jr. (1992) 'Agency Relationships in Marketing. A Review of the Implications and Applications of Agency and Related Theories', *Journal of Marketing*, 56 (2), 1–24.

Berger *et al.* (1993) 'Kano's Methods for Understanding Customer-defined Quality', *The Journal of the Japanese Society for Quality Control*, Fall, 3–35.

Berger, P.D. and Nasr, N.I. (1998) 'Customer Lifetime Value. Marketing Models and Applications', *Journal of Interactive Marketing*, 12 (1), 17–30.

Bergheimer, M. (1991) 'Cross-Selling', *Marketing Journal*, 3, 226–9.

Berry, L.L. (1983) 'Relationship Marketing', in AMA (ed.) *Emerging Perspectives on Services Marketing*. Chicago: AMA, 25–8.

Berry, L.L. (1986) 'Big Ideas in Services Marketing', in Venkatesan, M., Schmalensee, D.M. and Marshall, C. (eds.), *Creativity in Services Marketing. What's new, what works, what's developing.* Chicago: AMA, 6–8.

Berry, L.L. (1995) 'Relationship Marketing of Services. Growing Interest, Emerging Perspectives', *Journal of the Academy of Marketing Science*, 23 (4), 236–45.

Bettman, J.R. (1973) 'Perceived risk and its components: a model and empirical tests', *Journal of Marketing Research*, 10, May, 184–90.

Bitner, M.J. (1995) 'Building Service Relationships. It's All About Promises', *Journal of the Academy of Marketing Science*, 23 (4), 246–53.

Bitner, M.J. and Hubbert, A.R. (1994) 'Encounter Satisfaction versus Overall Satisfaction versus Quality. The Customer's Voice', in Rust, R.T. and Oliver, R.L. (eds.), *Service Quality. New Directions in Theory and Practice.* Thousand Oaks, CA: Sage Publications, 72–94.

Bitner, M.J., Booms, B.H. and Tetreault, M.S. (1990) 'The Service Encounter. Diagnosing Favorable and Unfavorable Incidents', *Journal of Marketing*, 54 (1), 71–84.

Blattberg, R.C. and Deighton, J. (1996) 'Manage Marketing by the Customer Equity Test', *Harvard Business Review*, 74 (4), 136–44.

Blau, P.M. (1964) *Exchange and Power in Social Life.* New York: Wiley.

Bonoma, T.V. and Shapiro, B.P. (1983) *Segmenting the Industrial Market.* Lexington, MA: Lexington Books.

Boulding, W., Kalra, A., Staelin, R. and Zeithaml, V.A. (1993) 'A Dynamic Process Model of Service Quality. From Expectations to Behavioral Intentions', *Journal of Marketing Research*, 30, (1), 7–27.

Bower, G. and Hilgard, E. (1984) *Theories of Learning*, (3rd edn). Englewood Cliffs: Prentice Hall.

Brandt, D.R. and Reffett, K.L. (1989) 'Focusing on Consumer Problems to Improve Service Quality' in Bitner, M.J. and Crosby, L.A. (eds.), *Designing a Winning Service Strategy*, Proceedings Series. Chicago: AMA, 92–7.

Brodie, R.J., Coviello, N.E., Brookes, R.W. and Little, V. (1997) 'Towards a Paradigm Shift in Marketing? An Examination of Current Marketing Practices', *Journal of Marketing Management*, 13 (5), 383–406.

Bromme, R. and Nückles, M. (1998) 'Perspective-taking between doctors and nurses: A study on multiple representations of different experts with common tasks' in van Someren, M.W., Boshuizen, H.P.A., deJong, T. and Reimann, P. (eds.), *Learning with multiple representations.* Oxford: Elsevier, 175–196.

Brueckner, J.K. (2000) 'The Benefits of Codesharing and Antitrust Immunity for International Passengers, with an Application to the Star Alliance', unpublished study, University of Illinois at Urbana-Champaign, www.brueckner-report.com/bruecknerreport.pdf, accessed on January 17. 2002.

Bruhn, M. (1999a) 'Relationship Marketing – Neustrukturierung der klassischen Marketinginstrumente durch eine Orientierung an Kundenbeziehungen' in Grünig, R. and Pasquier, M. (eds.), *Strategisches Management und Marketing.* Bern/Stuttgart/Wien: Haupt, 189–218.

Bruhn, M. (1999b) *Kundenorientierung. Bausteine einez excellenten Unternehmens.* Munich: C.H. Beck.

Bruhn, M. (2000) 'Kundenerwartungen. Theoretische Grundlagen, Messung und Managementkonzept', *Zeitschrift für Betriebswirtschaft*, 70 (3), 1031–53.

Bruhn, M. (2001) *Marketing. Grundlagen für Studium und Praxis*, (5th edn). Wiesbaden: Gabler.

Bruhn, M. and Grund, M.A. (2000) 'Theory, Development and Implementation of National Customer Satisfaction Indices: The Swiss Index of Customer Satisfaction', *Total Quality Management*, 11 (7), 1017–28.

Bruhn, M. and Murmann, B. (1998) *Nationale Kundenbarometer: Messung von Qualität und Zufriedenheit. Methodenvergleich und Entwurf eines Schweizer Kundenbarometers.* Wiesbaden: Gabler.

Bütikofer, P. (1999) 'Balanced Scorecard als Instrument zur Steuerung eines IT-Unternehmens im Wandel. Ein Praxisbericht über die Einführung der Balanced Scorecard bei der Systor AG', *Die Unternehmung*, 53 (5), 321–32.

Cadotte, E.R., Woodruff, R.B., and Jenkins, R.L. (1987) 'Expectations and Norms in Models of Consumer Satisfaction', *Journal of Marketing Research*, 24 (3), 305–14.

Cahill, D.J. (1995) 'The Managerial Implications of the Learning Organization. A New Tool for Internal Marketing', *Journal of Services Marketing*, 9 (4), 43–51.

Chandler, M.J. (1982) 'Egozentrismus und antisoziales Verhalten. Erfassen und Fördern der Fähigkeiten zur sozialen Perspektivenübernahme' in Geulen, D. (ed.) *Perspektivenübernahme und soziales Handeln. Texte zur sozialkognitiven Entwicklung (Perspective taking and social actions).* Frankfurt: Suhrkamp, 471–84.

Cherington, P.T. (1920) *The Elements of Marketing.* New York: Macmillan.

Choffray J.-M. and Lilien G.L. (1980) 'Industrial Market Segmentation by the Structure of the Purchasing Process', *Industrial Marketing Management*, 9, 331–42.

Chojnacki, K. (2000) 'Relationship Marketing at Volkswagen' in Hennig-Thurau, T. and Hansen, U. (eds.), *Relationship Marketing.* Heidelberg: Springer, 49–58.

Clark, M. (2000) 'Customer Service, People and Processes' in Cranfield School of Management (eds.), *Marketing Management. A Relationship Marketing Perspective.* New York, 210–27.

Coase, R.H. (1937) 'The Nature of the Firm', *Economica*, 4 (4), 386–405.

Cook, K.S. and Emerson, R. (1984) 'Exchange Networks and the Analysis of Complex Organisations', *Research in the Sociology of Organisations*, 3, Greenwich, 1–30.

Cornelsen, J. (1998) 'Kundenbewertung mit Referenzwerten. Theorie und Ergebnisse des Kooperationsprojektes "Kundenwert" in Zusammenarbeit mit der GfK AG', Working Paper No. 64, Betriebswirtschaftliches Institut, University of Erlangen-Nürnberg, Nürnberg, Germany.

Cox, W. (1967) 'PLC's as Marketing Models', *Journal of Business*, 40 (4), 375–84.

Cravens, D.W. and Piercy, N.F. (1994) 'Relationship Marketing and Collaborative Networks in Service Organizations', *International Journal of Service Industry Management*, 5 (5), 39–53.

Crosby, L.A. and Stephens, N. (1987) 'Effects of Relationship Marketing on Satisfaction, Retention, and Price in the Life Insurance', *Journal of Marketing Research*, 24 (4), 404–11.

Crosby, L.A., Evans, K.R., and Cowles, D. (1990) 'Relationship Quality in Services Selling. An Interpersonal Influence Perspective', *Journal of Marketing*, 54 (3), 68–81.

Cunningham, S.M. (1967) 'The major dimensions of perceived risk' in Cox, D.F. (ed.), *Risk Taking and Information Handling on Consumer Behavior.* Boston, MA: Harvard University, Graduate School of Business Administration, 82–108.

Czepiel, J.A. (1990) 'Service Encounters and Service Relationships. Implications for Research', *Journal of Business Research*, 23 (1), 13–21.

D'Aveni, R.A. (1994) *Hypercompetition: Managing the Dynamics of Strategic Maneuvering.* New York: Free Press.

Danaher, P.J. and Rust, R.T. (1996) 'Indirect Financial Benefits from Service Quality', *Quality Management Journal*, 3 (2), 63–75.

Darby, M.R. and Karni, E. (1973) 'Free Competition and the Optimal Amount of Fraud', *The Journal of Law and Economics*, 16 (1), 67–88.

Davis, M.H. (1983) 'Measuring Individual Differences in Empathy. Evidence for a Multidimensional Approach', *Journal of Personality and Social Psychology*, 44 (1), 113–126.

Day, G.S. (1981) 'The Product Life Cycle: Analysis and Application Issues', *Journal of Marketing*, 45, Fall, 60–7.

Deshpandé, R., Farley, J.U. and Webster, F.E. (1993) 'Corporate Culture, Customer Orientation, and Innovativeness in Japanese Firms. A Quadrad Analysis', *Journal of Marketing*, 57 (1), 23–7.

Deutsch, M. (1958) 'Trust and Suspicion', *The Journal of Conflict Resolution*, 2 (4), 265–79.

Dick, A.S. and Basu, K. (1994) 'Customer Loyalty. Towards an Integrated Conceptual Framework', *Journal of the Academy of Marketing Science*, 22 (2), 99–113.

Dickson, P.R. and Ginter, J.L. (1987) 'Market Segmentation, Product Differentiation and Marketing Strategy', *Journal of Marketing*, 51, April, 1–10.

Donabedian, A. (1980) *The Definition of Quality and Approaches to this Assessment. Explorations in Quality, Assessment and Monitoring*, I. Ann Arbor: Health Administration Press.

Doney, P.M. and Cannon, J.P. (1997) 'An Examination of the Nature of Trust in Buyer-Seller Relationships', *Journal of Marketing*, 62 (2), 1–13.

Dubinsky, A.J. and Ingram, T.N. (1984) 'A Portfolio Approach to Account Profitability', *Industrial Marketing Management*, 13 (1), 33–41.

Dukcevich, D. (2001) 'The Michael Jordan Portfolio', *Forbes.com*, September 28, 2001. (www.forbes.com/2001/09/28/0928jordan.html, accessed on May 28, 2002.)

Dwyer, F.R. (1989) 'Customer lifetime valuation to support marketing decision making', *Journal of Direct Marketing*, 3 (4), 8–11.

Dwyer, F.R. (1997) 'Customer Lifetime Valuation to Support Marketing Decision Making', *Journal of Direct Marketing*, 11 (4), 6–13.

Dwyer, F.R., Schurr, P.H. and Oh, S. (1987) Developing Buyer-Seller Relationships, *Journal of Marketing*, 51 (2), 11–27.

Easton, G. (1987) 'Competition and Marketing Strategy', *European Journal of Marketing*, 21 (2), 31–49.

Egan, J. (2001) *Relationship Marketing. Exploring relational strategies in marketing*. Harlow: Financial Times Prentice Hall.

Eisenhardt, K.M. (1989) 'Agency- and Institutional Theory Explanations: The Case of Retail Sales Compensation', *Academy of Management Journal*, 31, 488–511.

Ekeh, P.P. (1974) *Social Exchange Theory. The Two Traditions*. London: Heinemann Educational.

El-Ansary, A. (1997) 'Relationship Marketing: A Marketing Channel Context', *Research in Marketing*, 13, 33–46.

Elliott, G. and Glynn, W. (2000) 'Segmenting Industrial Buyers by Loyalty and Value', paper presented at the IMP Conference 2000, http://www.bath.ac.uk/imp/pdf/iElliotGlynn.pdf, accessed on May 28, 2002.

Engel, J., Blackwell, R., and Miniard, P. (1993) *Consumer Behaviour*, (7th edn). Fort Worth: Dryden Press.

Ewing, P. and Luhndahl, L. (1996) 'The Balanced Scorecard at ABB Sweden – the EVITA Project', *EFI Research Paper Nr. 6567*. Economic Research Institute, Stockholm School of Economics, Stockholm, Sweden.

Festinger, L. (1957) *A Theory of Cognitive Dissonance*. Stanford.

Fischer, T. and Tewes, M. (2001) 'Vertrauen und Commitment in der Dienstleistungsinteraktion', in Bruhn, M. and Stauss, B. (eds.) *Dienstleistungsmanagement. Jahrbuch 2001. Interaktionen im Dienstleistungsbereich*. Wiesbaden: Gabler, 299–318.

Ford, D. (1980) 'The Development of Buyer-Seller Relationships in Industrial Markets', *European Journal of Marketing*, 14, (5–6), 339–53.

Ford. I.D. (ed.) (1990) *Understanding Business Markets. Interaction, Relationships and Networks.* London: Academic Press.

Fornell, C. (1992) 'A National Customer Satisfaction Barometer. The Swedish Experience', *Journal of Marketing*, 56 (1), 6–21.

Fornell, C. and Wernerfelt, B. (1987) 'Defensive Marketing Strategy by Customer Complaint Management: A Theoretical Analysis', *Journal of Marketing Research*, 24, November, 337–46.

Fournier, S. (1998) 'Consumers and Their Brands. Developing Relationship Theory in Consumer Research', *Journal of Consumer Research*, 24 (3), 343–73.

Franzoi, S.L., Davis, M.H. and Young, R.D. (1985) The Effects of Private Self-Consciousness and Perspective Taking on Satisfaction in Close Relationships, *Journal of Personality and Social Psychology*, 48 (6), 1584–94.

Freiberg, K. and Freiberg, J. (1996) *NUTS! Southwest Airlines' Crazy Recipe for Business and Personal Strategies.* Austin: Bard Press.

Freter, H. (1983) *Marktsegmentierung.* Stuttgart: Kohlhammer.

Friedman, M.L. and Smith, L.J. (1993) 'Consumer Evaluation Processes in a Service Setting', *Journal of Services Marketing*, 7 (2), 47–61.

Gabbott, M. and Hogg, G. (1994) 'Consumer behaviour and services: a review', *Journal of Marketing Management*, 4 (10), 311–25.

Garbarino, E. and Johnson, M.S. (1999) 'The Different Roles of Satisfaction, Trust and Commitment in Customer Relationships', *Journal of Marketing*, 63 (2), 70–87.

Garman, E.T. and Forgue, R.E. (1994) *Personal Finance*, 4th edn. Boston: Houghton Mifflin Co.

Garvin, D.A. (1984) 'What does "Product Quality" really mean?', *Sloan Management Review*, 25 (1), 25–43.

Garvin, D.A. (1988) 'Die acht Dimensionen der Produktqualität', *Harvard Manager*, 10 (3), 66–74.

George, W.R. and Berry, L.L. (1981) 'Guidelines for the Advertising of Services', *Business Horizons*, 24, July–August, 52–6.

Georgi, D. (2000) *Entwicklung von Kundenbeziehungen.* Wiesbaden: Gabler.

Gibbons, R. (1998) 'Incentives in Organizations', *Journal of Economic Perspectives*, 12 (4), 115–32, http://papers.nber.org/papers/W6695.pdf, accessed on December 5, 2001.

Gilbert, X. and Strebel, P. (1987) 'Strategies to Outpace the Competition', *Journal of Business Strategy*, 8 (1), 28–37.

Goldberg, V.P. (1976) 'Regulation and Administered Contracts', *The Bell Journal of Economics and Management Science*, 7 (2), 426–48.

Goldstein, A.P. and Michaels, G.Y. (1985) *Empathy. Development, Training and Consequences.* Hillsdale, NJ: L. Erlbaum Associates.

Griffin, J. (1999) 'Customer Loyalty. Lost customers can be returned to your fold', *Small Business Insights*, February 19, 1999, http://austin.bcentral.com/austin/stories/1999/02/22/smallb3.html, accessed on January 22, 2002.

Grönroos, C. (1990) 'Relationship Approach to Marketing in Service Contexts. The Marketing and Organizational Behavior Interface', *Journal of Business Research*, 20 (1), 3–11.

Grönroos, C. (1994) 'From Marketing Mix to Relationship Marketing. Towards a Paradigm Shift in Marketing', *Management Decision*, 32 (2), 4–20.

Grönroos, C. (2000) *Service Management and Marketing. A Customer Relationship Management Approach*, (2nd edn). Chichester: John Wiley and Sons.

Gummesson, E. (1987) 'The New Marketing. Developing Long-Term Interactive Relationships', *Long Range Planning*, 20 (4), 10–20.

Gummesson, E. (1994) 'Making Relationship Marketing Operational', *International Journal of Service Industry Management*, 5 (5), 5–20.

Gummesson, E. (1996) 'Relationship Marketing and Imaginery Organizations A Synthesis' *European Journal of Marketing*, 30(2), 31–44.

Gummesson, F. (1999) *Total Relationship Marketing. Rethinking Marketing Management: From 4Ps to 30Rs*. Oxford: Butterworth-Heinemann.

Gup, B.E. and Agrrawal, P. (1996) 'The Product Life Cycle: A Paradigm for Understanding Financial Management', *Financial Practice & Education*, 6 (2), 41–48.

Gutman, J. (1982) 'A Means End Chain Model', *Journal of Marketing*, Spring, 60–72.

Håkansson, H. (ed.) (1982) *International Marketing and Purchasing of Industrial Goods: An Interaction Approach*. Chichester: Wiley.

Håkansson, H. and Snehota, I. (1993) 'The Content and Functions of Business Relationships', Paper of the 9th IMP Conference, Bath.

Håkansson, H. and Snehota, I. (eds.) (1995) *Developing Relationships in Business Networks*. London: Routledge.

Halinen, A. (1996) 'Service Quality in Professional Business Services. A Relationship Approach' in Swartz, T.A., Bowen, D.E and Brown, S.W. (eds.), *Advances in Services Marketing and Management*, 5. Greenwich: JAI, 315–41.

Hallowell, R. and Schlesinger, L.A. (2001) 'The Service Profit Chain. Intellectual Roots, Current Realities, and Future Prospects' in Swartz, T. and Iacobucci, D. (eds.) *Handbook of Services Marketing & Management*. Thousand Oaks, CA: Sage Publications, 203–21.

Hansotia, B.J. and Wang, P. (1997) 'Analytical Challenges in Customer Acquisition', *Journal of Direct Marketing*, 11 (2), 7–19.

Harris, L.C. and Piercy, N.F. (1999) 'Management behavior and barriers to market orientation in retailing companies', *The Journal of Services Marketing*, 13 (2), 113–25.

Hart, C. (1993) *Extraordinary Guarantees*. New York: Amacoms.

Hart, C., Heskett, J., and Sasser, W. (1990) 'The Profitable Art of Service Recovery', *Harvard Business Review*, 68 (4), 148–56.

Haywood, K.M. (1989) 'Managing Word of Mouth Communications', *Journal of Services Marketing*, 3 (2), 55–67.

Hefferan, C. (1982) 'Determinants and patterns of family saving', *Home Economic Research Journal*, 11 (1), 47–55.

Henn, H. (1995) 'Gestaltung des Wandels von der Funktions- zur Kompetenzhierarchie', *Zeitschrift für Organisation*, 64 (5), 304–9.

Hennig-Thurau, T. and Hansen, U. (eds.) (2000) *Relationship Marketing*. Heidelberg: Springer.

Hennig-Thurau, T. and Klee, A. (1997) 'The Impact of Customer Satisfaction and Relationship Quality on Customer Retention. A Critical Assessment and Model Development', *Psychology & Marketing*, 14 (8), 737–64.

Heskett, J.L., Sasser, W.E. and Schlesinger, L.A. (1997) *The Service Profit Chain*. New York: Free Press.

Hoekstra, J.C. and Huizingh, E.K.R.E. (1999) 'The Lifetime Value Concept in Customer-Based Marketing', *Journal of Market Focused Management*, 3 (3–4), 257–74.

Hogarth, J.M. (1991) 'Asset management and retired households: Savers, dissavers, and alternators', *Financial Counseling and Planning*, (2), 97–121.

Homans, G.C. (1961) *Social Behavior. Its Elementary Forms.* New York: Harcourt, Brace and World.

Homburg, Ch. (1998a) *Kundennähe von Industriegüterunternehmen,* 2nd edn, Wiesbaden: Gabler.

Homburg, Ch. (1998b) 'On Closeness to the Customer in Industrial Markets', *Journal of Business-to-Business Marketing,* 4 (4), 35–72.

Homburg, Ch. and Stock, R. (2000) *Der kundenorientierte Mitarbeiter.* Wiesbaden: Gabler.

Houston, F.S. and Gassenheimer, J.B. (1987) 'Marketing and Exchange', *Journal of Marketing,* 51 (4), 3–18.

Jackson, B.B. (1985) 'Build Customer Relationships that Last', *Harvard Business Review,* 63 (6), 120–8.

IMP Group (1982) *International Marketing and Purchasing of Industrial Goods* Håkansson, H. (ed.). Chichester: Wiley.

Jacoby, J. and Chestnut, R.W. (1978) *Brand Loyalty. Measurement and Management.* New York: Wiley.

Jensen, M.C. and Meckling, W. (1976) 'The theory of the firm: managerial behavior, agency costs, and capital structure', *Journal of Financial Economics,* 3, 305–60.

Johanson, J. and Mattson, L.-G. (1987) 'Interorganizational Relations. A Network Approach Compared to Transaction-Cost Approach', *International Studies of Management and Organization,* 17 (1), 34–48.

Johnston, W.J. and Lewin, J.E. (1996) 'Organizational Buying Behavior. Toward an Integrative Framework', *Journal of Business Research,* 35 (1), 1–15.

Jones, T.O. and Sasser, W.E. Jr. (1995) 'Why Satisfied Customers Defect', *Harvard Business Review,* 73 (12), 88–99.

Jones, M.A. and Suh, J. (2000) 'Transaction-specific satisfaction and overall satisfaction: an empirical analysis', *Journal of Services Marketing,* 14 (2), 147–159.

Jüttner, U. and Wehrli, H.P. (1994) 'Relationship Marketing from a Value System Perspective', *International Journal of Service Industry Management,* 5 (5), 54–73.

Kaas, K.P. (1995) 'Einführung. Marketing und Neue Institutionenökonomik' in Kaas, K.P. (ed.): 'Kontrakte, Geschäftsbeziehungen, Netzwerke – Marketing und Neue Institutionenökonomik', *Schmalenbachs Zeitschrift für betriebswirtschaftliche Forschung,* 47, extra edition No. 35/95, 1–17.

Kaas, K.P. (2000) 'Alternative Konzepte der Theorieverankerung' in Backhaus, K. (ed.) *Deutschsprachige Marketingforschung. Bestandsaufnahme und Perspektiven (German-speaking Marketing Research. Survey and Perspectives).* Stuttgart: Schäffer-Poeschel, 55–78.

Kano, N. (1984) 'Attractive Quality and Must-be Quality', *The Journal of the Japanese Society for Quality Control,* 2, 39–48.

Kaplan, L.B., Szybillo, G.J., and Tocoby, J. (1974) 'Components of perceived risk in product purchase: a cross validation', *Journal of Applied Psychology,* 59 (3), 287–91.

Kaplan, R.S. and Norton, D.P. (1992) 'The Balanced Scorecard – Measures That Drive Performance', *Harvard Business Review,* 70, January–February, 71–79.

Kaplan, R.S. and Norton, D.P. (1993) 'Putting the Balanced Scorecard to Work', *Harvard Business Review,* 71, September-October, 134–47.

Kaplan, R.S. and Norton, D.P. (1996a) 'Using the Balanced Scorecard as a Strategic Management System', *Harvard Business Review,* 74, January-February, 75–85.

Kaplan, R.S. and Norton, D.P. (1996b) *The Balanced Scorecard: Translating Strategy into Action.* Boston, MA: Harvard Business School.

KDnuggets (2002) www.kdnuggets.com/solutions/crm.html#W, accessed on May 3, 2002.

Keane, T.J. and Wang, P. (1995) 'Applications for the Lifetime Value Model in Modern Newspaper Publishing', *Journal of Direct Marketing*, 9 (2), 59–66.

Keaveney, S.M. (1995) 'Customer Switching Behavior in Service Industries. An Exploratory Study', *Journal of Marketing*, 59 (2), 71–82.

Keith, R.J. (1960) 'The Marketing Revolution', *Journal of Marketing*, January, 35–8.

Kelley, H.H. and Thibaut, J.W. (1978) *Interpersonal Relations. A Theory of Interdependance.* New York: Wiley.

Kennickell, A. and Shack-Marquez, J. (1992) 'Changes in family finance from 1983 to 1989: Evidence from the Survey of Consumer Finances', *Federal Reserve Bulletin*, January, 1–18.

Kinsey, J.D. (2000) 'The big shift from a food supply to a food demand chain', *Minnesota Agricultural Economist*, Fall 1999, No. 698, www.extension.iastate.edu/agdm/articles/others/KinApr00.htm, accessed on May 22, 2002.

Kirmani, A. and Rao, A.R. (2000) 'No Pain, No Gain: A Critical Review of the Literature on Signaling Unobservable Product Quality', *Journal of Marketing*, 64 (2), 66–79.

Klee, A. (2000) *Strategisches Beziehungsmanagement: ein integrativer Ansatz zur strategischen Planung und Implementierung des Beziehungsmanagement.* Aachen: Shaker.

Kleine, M. (2001) 'Amüsement abseits der breiten Massen', *Horizont*, 48, November, p. 31.

Kotler, P. (1972) 'A Generic Concept of Marketing', *Journal of Marketing*, 36, April, 46–54.

Kotler, P. (1989) 'From mass marketing to mass customisation', *Planning Review*, 18 (5), 10–13, 47.

Kotler, P. (1991) 'Philip Kotler Explores the New Marketing Paradigm', *Marketing Science Insitute Review*, Spring.

Kotler, P. (2000) *Marketing Management. The Millennium Edition.* New Jersey: Prentice Hall.

Kuhn, T.S. (1962) *The Structure of Scientific Revolutions.* Chicago, IL: University of Chicago Press.

Kumar, N., Scheer, L.K., and Steenkamp, J.-B. (1995) 'The Effects of Supplier Fairness on Vulnerable Resellers', *Journal of Marketing Research*, 32 (1), 54–65.

Laakmann, K. (1995) *Value-added Services als Profilierungsinstrument im Wettbewerb. Analyse, Generierung und Bewertung.* Frankfurt: Lang.

Lévi-Strauss, C. (1969) *The Elementary Structures of Kinship.* Boston: Beacon Press.

Levitt. T. (1965) 'Exploit the PLC', *Harvard Business Review*, 43, November–December, 81–94.

Levitt, T. (1983) 'After the Sale is Over', *Harvard Business Review*, 61, September–October, 87–93.

Liljander, V. (1994) 'Modeling Perceived Quality Using Different Comparison Standards', *Journal of Consumer Satisfaction, Dissatisfaction and Complaining Behavior*, 7, 126–142.

Liljander, V. and Strandvik, T. (1993) 'Different Comparison Standards as Determinants of Service Quality', *Journal of Consumer Satisfaction, Dissatisfaction and Complaining Behavior*, 6, 118–132.

Liljander, V. and Strandvik, T. (1995) 'The Nature of Customer Relationships in Services', in Swartz, T.A., Bowen, D.E. and Brown, S.W. (eds.), *Advances in Services Marketing and Management*, Vol. 4. Greenwich: JAI Press 141–167.

Lindqvist, L.J. (1987) 'Quality and Service Value in the Service Consumption', in Suprenant, C. (ed.), *Add Value to your Service*, Proceedings Series. Chicago: AMA, 17–20.

Lindskold, S. (1978) 'Trust Development, the GRIT Proposal and the Effects of Conciliatory Acts on Conflict and Cooperation', *Psychological Bulletin*, 85 (4), 772–93.

Lindsay, G. (2002) 'The Buzz: Etailers Go Offline for Holiday Promotions', http://www.sharpermedia.com/buzzarchive/buzz11_29_2001.htm, accessed on January 22, 2002.

Liu, H. (1995) 'Market orientation and firm size: an empirical examination of UK firms', *European Journal of Marketing*, 29 (1), 57–71.

Long, E.C.J. and Andrews, D.W. (1990) 'Perspective Taking as a Predictor of Marital Adjustment', *Journal of Personality and Social Psychology*, 59 (1), 126–131.

Loose, A. and Sydow, J. (1994) 'Vertrauen und Ökonomie in Netzwerkbeziehungen. Strukturationstheoretische Betrachtungen' in Sydow, J. and Windeler, A. (eds.) *Management interorganisationaler Beziehungen. Vertrauen, Kontrolle und Informationstechnik*. Opladen: Westdt. Verlag, 160–193.

Lovelock, C. (2001) *Services Marketing. People, Technology, Strategy*, (4th edn). Upper Saddle River, New Jersey: Prentice Hall.

Lutz, R. and Reilly, P.J. (1973) 'An Exploration of the Effects of Perceived Social and Performance Risk on Consumer Information Acquisition', in Ward, S. and Wright, P. (eds.), *Advances in Consumer Research*. Urbana: Association for Consumer Research, 393–405.

Mallak, L. (2001) 'Understanding and changing your organization's culture', *Industrial Management*, March–April, 18–24.

McCarthy, M. (2001) 'Marketers jump with Jordan's return', *USA TODAY*, http://www.usatoday.com/money/advertising/2001-09-26-jordan.htm, accessed on December 3, 2001.

McKenna, R. (1991) *Relationship Marketing. Successful Strategies for the Age of the Customer*. New York: Addison-Wesley.

Meffert, H. (2000) *Marketing. Grundlagen marktorientierter Unternehmensführung – Konzepte, Instrumente, Praxisbeispiele*, (9th edn). Wiesbaden: Gabler.

Meffert, H. and Bruhn, M. (2000) *Dienstleistungsmarketing (Services Marketing)*, (3rd edn). Wiesbaden: Gabler.

Miller, D. and Friesen, D.H. (1982) 'Innovation in Conservative and Entrepreneurial Firms. Two Models of Strategic Momentum', *Strategic Management Journal*, 3 (1), 1–25.

Miller, J.A. (1977) 'Exploring Satisfaction, Modifying Models, Eliciting Expectations, Posing Problems, and Making Meaningful Measurement', in Hunt, H.K. (ed.), *Conceptualizations and Measurement of Consumer Satisfaction and Dissatisfaction*, Cambridge, MA: Marketing Science Institute, 72–91.

Mintzberg, H. (1988) 'Generic Strategies. Toward a Comprehensive Framework', *Advances in Strategic Management*, Vol. 5, Greenwich.

Möller, K. (1992) 'Research Traditions in Marketing. Theoretical Notes', in Blomqvist, H. C., Grönroos, C. and Lindqvist, L.J. (eds) *Economics and Marketing: Essays in Honour of Goesta Mickwitz*, Economy and Society, (3), Helsinki: Swedish School of Economics, 197–218.

Monroe, K.B. (1991) *Pricing. Making Profitable Decisions*, (2nd edn). New York: McGraw-Hill.

Moorman, C., Zaltman, G., and Deshpandé, R. (1992) 'Relationships between Providers and Users of Market Research. The Dynamics of Trust within and between Organizations', *Journal of Marketing Research*, 29 (3), 314–29.

Moorthy, S. and Srinivasan, K. (1995) 'Signaling Quality with a Money-Back Guarantee: The Role of Transaction Costs', *Marketing Science*, 14 (4), 442–6.

Morgan, R.M. and Hunt, S.D. (1994) 'The Commitment-Trust Theory of Relationship Marketing', *Journal of Marketing*, 58 (3), 20–38.

Mudie, P. and Cottam, A. (1993) *The Management and Marketing of Services*. Oxford: Butterworth-Heinemann.

Mueller, D.C. (1972) 'A Life Cycle Theory of the Firm', *Journal of Industrial Economics*, 20 (3), 199–219.

Mueller-Heumann, G. (1992) 'Market and technology shifts in the 1990s: market fragmentation and mass customization', *Journal of Marketing Management*, 8 (4), 303–14.

Mulhern, F.J. (1999) 'Customer Profitability Analysis. Measurement, Concentration and Research Directions', *Journal of Interactive Marketing*, 13 (1), 25–40.

Murgulez, L., Dukeov, I., Eklöf, J. and Selivanova, I. (2000) 'Russian Customer Satisfaction Index 1999–2000: Main Results and Research Observations', in: Dermanov, V.K. (ed.) *Business Excellence. Russian and International State-of-the-Art Experience*, Stockholm School of Economics in St. Petersburg, Appendix, 223–9.

Murmann, B. (1999) *Qualität mehrstufiger Dienstleistungsinteraktionen. Besonderheiten bei Dienstleistungsunternehmen mit direktem und indirektem Kundenkontakt.* Wiesbaden: Gabler.

Murray, J.A. (1984) 'A Concept of Entrepreneurial Strategy', *Strategic Management Journal*, 5, 1–13.

Murray, K.B. (1991) 'A Test of Services Marketing Theory. Consumer Information Acquisition Activities', *Journal of Marketing*, 55 (1), 10–25.

Nevin, J.R. (1995) 'Relationship Marketing and Distribution Channels: Exploring Fundamental Issues', *Journal of the Academy Sciences*, Fall, 327–34.

Ngobo, P.V. (1997) 'The Standards Issue. An Accessibility-Diagnosticity Perspective', *Journal of Consumer Satisfaction, Dissatisfaction and Complaining Behavior,* 10, 61–79.

National Institute of Standards and Technology (NIST) (2002) Criteria for Performance Excellence, www.quality.nist.gov/PDF_files/2002_Business_Criteria.pdf, accessed on May 22, 2002.

Oldano, T.I. (1987) 'Relationship Segmentation. Enhancing the Service Provider/Client Connection', in Surprenant, C. (ed.), *Add Value to your Service. The Key to Success, Proceedings Series.* Chicago: AMA, 143–6.

Oliver, R.L. (1980) 'A Cognitive Model of the Antecedents and Consequences of Satisfaction Decisions', *Journal of Marketing Research*, 17 (4), 460–9.

Oliver, R.L. (1996) *Satisfaction. A behavioral perspective on the consumer.* New York: McGraw-Hill.

Olson, J.C. and Dover, P.A. (1979) 'Disconfirmation of Consumer Expectations Through Product Trial', *Journal of Applied Psychology*, 64 (2), 41–50.

O'Malley, L. and Tynan, C. (1997) 'A Reappraisal of the Relationship Marketing Constructs of Commitment and Trust', in: AMA (ed.), *New and Evolving Paradigms. The Emerging Future of Marketing* Dublin: AMA, 486–503.

Ostrom, A.L. and Hart, C. (2000) 'Service Guarantees. Research and Practice', in Swartz, T. and Iacobucci, D. (eds.) *Handbook of Services Marketing & Management.* Thousand Oaks, CA: Sage Publications, 299–313.

Palmer, A. (1994) *Principles of services marketing.* London: McGraw-Hill.

Palmer, A. (1996) 'Relationship marketing: a universal paradigm or management fad,' *The Learning Organization*, 3 (3), 19–26.

Palmer, A. and Cole, C. (1995) *Services Marketing, Principles and Practice.* New Jersey: Prentice Hall.

Palmer, R. (2000) 'Marketing Diagnostic Tools', in Cranfield School of Management (eds.), *Marketing Management. A Relationship Marketing Perspective.* New York: St. Martin's Press, 31–43.

Parasuraman, A., Berry, L.L. and Zeithaml, V.A. (1991), 'Refinement and Reassessment of the SERVQUAL Scale', *Journal of Retailing*, 67 (4), 420–50.

Parasuraman, A., Zeithaml, V.A. and Berry, L.L. (1985) 'A Conceptual Model of Service Quality and Its Implications for Future Research', *Journal of Marketing*, 49 (1), 41–50.

Parasuraman, A., Zeithaml, V.A. and Berry, L.L. (1986) SERVQUAL.'A Multiple-Item Scale for Measuring Consumer Perceptions of Service Quality', Marketing Science Institute, Report 86–108. Cambridge, MA.

Parasuraman, A., Zeithaml, V.A. and Berry, L.L. (1988) SERVQUAL. 'A Multiple-Item Scale for Measuring Consumer Perceptions of Service Quality', *Journal of Retailing*, 64 (1), 12–40.

Parasuraman, A., Zeithaml, V.A. and Berry, L.L. (1994) 'Alternative Scales for Measuring Service Quality: A Comparative Assessment Based on Psychometric and Diagnostic Criteria', *Journal of Retailing*, 70 (3), 201–230.

Pardo, C. (1997) 'Key account management in the business-to-business field: the Key Account's point of view', *Journal of Personal Selling and Sales Management*, 17(4), 17–26.

Parvatiyar, A. and Sheth, S.N. (2000) 'The Domain and Conceptual Foundations of Relationship Marketing', in Sheth, J.N. and Parvatiyar, A. (eds.), *Handbook of Relationship Marketing*. Thousand Oaks, CA: Sage Publications.

Payne, A. (ed.) (1995) *Advances in Relationship Marketing*. London: Kogan Page.

Payne, A. (2000a) 'Relationship Marketing: Managing Multiple Markets', in Cranfield School of Management (eds.) *Marketing Management. A Relationship Marketing Perspective*. New York: St. Martin's Press, 16–30.

Payne, A. (2000b) 'Customer Retention' in Cranfield School of Management (ed.), *Marketing Management. A Relationship Marketing Perspective*. New York: St. Martin's Press, 110–22.

Payne, A. and Frow, P. (1997) 'Relationship Marketing. Key Issues for the Utilities Sector', *Journal of Marketing Management*, 13 (5), 463–77.

Payne, A., Clarke, M., Coaton, A. and Hickmann, M. (1996) 'Creating success through relationship marketing at British Airways', in Peck, H., Payne, A., Christopher, M. and Clark, M. (eds.) (1999) *Relationship Marketing. Strategy and Implementation*. Oxford: Butterworth-Heinemann, 454–500.

Pearce, A.M. (1996) 'Efficient Consumer Response: Managing the Supply Chain for "Ultimate" Consumer Satisfaction', *Supply Chain Management*, 1 (2), 11–14.

Peck, H. (1995) 'Relationship Marketing: Lessons from Laura Ashley', in: Peck, H., Payne, A., Christopher, M., and Clark, M. (eds.) (1999) *Relationship Marketing. Strategy and Implementation*, Oxford: Butterworth-Heinemann, 432–53.

Peck, H., Payne, A., Christopher, M. and Clark, M. (eds.) (1999) *Relationship Marketing. Strategy and Implementation*. Oxford: Butterworth-Heinemann.

Peltier, J.W., Schibrowsky, J.A. and Davis, J. (1998) 'Using Attitudinal and Descriptive Database Information to Understand Interactive Buyer-Seller Relationships', *Journal of Interactive Marketing*, 12 (3), 32–45.

Perrey, J. (1998) 'Nutzenorientierte Marktsegmentierung im Verkehrsdienstleistungsbereich. Dargestellt am Beispiel der Deutschen Bahn AG', *Working Paper No. 124*. Organization for Marketing and Business Administration e.V. at the University of Münster: Münster.

Picot, A. (1982) 'Transaktionskostenansatz in der Organisationstheorie. Stand der Diskussion und Aussagewert (Transaction Cost Approach in Organization Theory)', *Die Betriebswirtschaft*, 42 (2), 267–84.

Picot, A. and Dietl, H. (1990) 'Transaktionskostentheorie (Transaction Cost Theory)', *Wirtschaftswissenschaftliches Studium*, 19 (4), 178–184.

Piller, F.T. (2000) 'Mass Customization Based E-business Strategies', www.mass-customization.de/engl_ebiz.htm, accessed on January 21, 2002.

Pine, B.J. (1993) *Mass Customization*. Boston: Harvard Business School Press.

Plinke, W. (1996) 'Kundenorientierung als Voraussetzung der Customer Integration', in Kleinaltenkamp, M., Fließ, S. and Jacob, F. (eds.), *Customer Integration. Von der Kundenorientierung zur Kundenintegration*. Wiesbaden: Gabler, 41–56.

Plummer, J.T. (1974) 'The Concept and Application of Lifestyle Segmentation', *Journal of Marketing*, 38 (1), 33–37.

Porter, M.E. and Fuller, M.B. (1989) 'Koalitionen und globale Strategien', in: Porter, M.E. (ed.), *Globaler Wettbewerb (Global Competition)*. Wiesbaden: Gabler, 363–399.

Quinn, R. and Rohrbaugh, J. (1983) 'A Spatial Model of Effectiveness Criteria. Towards a Competing Values Approach to Organizational Analysis', *Management Science*, 29 (3), 363–377.

Rao, A. and Bergen, M. (1992) 'Price Premium as a Consequence of Buyers' Lack of Information', *Journal of Consumer Research*, 19, December, 412–423.

Ravald, A. and Grönroos, C. (1996) 'The value concept and relationship marketing', *European Journal of Marketing*, 30 (2), 19–30.

Reichheld, F.F. (1993) 'Treue Kunden müssen auch rentabel sein', *Harvard Business Manager*, 14 (3), 106–14, first published as 'Loyalty-Based Management', *Harvard Business Review*, March–April 1993, 64–73.

Reichheld, F.F. (1994) 'Loyalty and the renaissance of marketing', *Marketing Management*, 2 (4), 10–21.

Reichheld, F.F. (1996) *The Loyalty Effect. The Hidden Force Behind Growth, Profits, and Lasting Value*. Boston: Harvard Business School Press.

Reichheld, F.F. and Sasser, W. (1990) 'Zero Defections. Quality Comes to Services', *Harvard Business Review*, 68 (5), 105–11.

Reinartz, W.J. and Kumar, V. (2000) 'On the Profitability of Long-Life Customers in a Noncontractual Setting: An Empirical Investigation and Implications for Marketing', *Journal of Marketing*, 64 (4), 17–35.

Reinecke, S., Sipötz, E. and Wiemann, E.-M. (eds.) (1998) *Total Customer Care*. Kundenorientierung auf dem Prüfstand. St. Gallen/Wien.

Reiß, M. (1995) 'Implementierungsarbeit im Spannungsfeld zwischen Effektivität und Effizienz', *Zeitschrift für Organisation*, 64 (5), 278–89.

Reynolds, Th. and Gutman, J. (1988) 'Laddering Theory, Method, Analysis, and Interpretation', *Journal of Advertising Research*, February–March, 11–31.

Richins, M.L. (1983) 'Negative Word-of-Mouth by Dissatisfied Consumers. A Pilot Study', *Journal of Marketing*, 47 (4), 68–78.

Roos, I. (1999) 'Switching Processes in Customer Relationships', *Journal of Service Research*, 2 (1), 68–85.

Roos, I. and Strandvik, T. (1997) 'Diagnosing the Termination of Customer Relationship', Proceedings of the "New and Evolving Paradigms: The Emerging Future of Marketing", Conference from June 12–15, 1997. Dublin: AMA, 617–31.

Rotter, J.B. (1967) 'A New Scale for the Measurement of Interpersonal Trust', *Journal of Personality*, 35 (4), 651–65.

Ruekert, R.W. (1992) 'Developing a market orientation: an organizational strategy perspective', *International Journal of Research in Marketing*, 9 (3), 225–45.

Rugg, G. and McGeorge, P. (1995). 'Laddering', *Expert Systems*, 12 (4), 339–46.

Rust, R.T, Zeithaml, V.A., and Lemon, K.N. (2000) *Driving Customer Equity: How Customer Lifetime Value is Reshaping Corporate Strategy*. New York: Free Press.

Rust, R.T. and Oliver, R.L. (1994) 'Service Quality. Insights and Managerial Implications from the Frontier', in: Rust, R.T. and Oliver, R.L. (eds.) *Service Quality. New Directions in Theory and Practice*. Thousand Oaks, CA: Sage Publications, 1–20.

Rust, R.T., Zahorik, A.J., and Keiningham, T.L. (1994) *Return on Quality. Measuring the Financial Impact of Your Company's Quest for Quality*. Chicago: Probus Publishing.

Ryals, L. (2000a) 'Planning for Relationship Marketing', in Cranfield School of Management (eds.), *Marketing Management. A Relationship Marketing Perspective*, New York, 231–48.

Ryals, L. (2000b) 'Organizing for Relationship Marketing', in Cranfield School of Management (eds.), *Marketing Management. A Relationship Marketing Perspective. New York*, 249–63.

Saaty T.L. (1980) *Analytic Hierarchy Process*. New York: McGraw-Hill.

Sahlins, M. (1972) *Stone Age Economics*. Chicago: Aldine-Atherton.

Salmon, K. (1993) *Efficient Consumer Response: Enhancing Consumer Value in the Grocery Industry*. Washington: Research Dept., Food Marketing Institute.

Sasser, W.E. Jr., Hart, C.W. and Heskett, J.L. (1991) *The Service Management Course. Cases and Readings*. New York: The Free Press.

Schauermann, J. (1990) 'A New Basis for Segmenting the Corporate Banking Market', in Teare, R., Moutinho, L. and Morgan, N. (eds.), *Managing and Marketing Services in the 1990's*. London: Cassell, 169–83.

Scheuing, E.E. and Johnson, E.M. (1989) 'A Proposed Model for New Service Development', *Journal of Services Marketing*, 3 (2), 25–34.

Schlesinger, L.A. and Heskett, J.L. (1992) 'Dem Kunden dienen. Das müssen viele Dienstleister erst noch lernen', *Harvard Manager*, 14 (1), 106–16.

Shani, D. and Chalasani, S. (1992) 'Exploiting Niches Using Relationship Marketing', *Journal of Consumer Marketing*, 9 (3), 33–42.

Shapiro, C. and Varian, H.R. (1999) *Information Rules. A Strategic Guide to the Network Economy*. Boston, MA: Harvard Business School Press.

Shaw, A. (1912) 'Some Problems in Market Distribution', *Quarterly Journal of Economics*, 26, August, 706–65.

Sheth, J.N. (1996) *Development, Management and Governance of Relationship*. Berlin: Humboldt-Universität zu Berlin, Germany.

Sheth, J.N. and Parvatiyar, A. (1995) 'Relationship Marketing in Consumer Markets. Antecedents and Consequences', *Journal of the Academy of Marketing Science*, 23 (4), 255–271.

Sheth, J.N., Gardner, D.M., and Garrett, D.E. (1988) *Marketing theory: Evolution and Evaluation*. New York: Wiley.

Shostack, G.L. (1984) 'Designing Services That Deliver', *Harvard Business Review*, 62 (1), 133–9.

Shostack, G.L. (1985) 'Planning the Service Encounter', in Czepiel, J.A., Solomon, M.R. and Surprenant, C.F. (eds.), *The Service Encounter*. Lexington: Lexington Books, 243–53.

Smith, J.B. (1998) 'Buyer-Seller Relationships. Similarity, Relationship Management and Quality', *Psychology & Marketing*, 15 (1), 3–21.

Spence, M. (1976) 'Information Aspects of Market Structure', *Quarterly Journal of Economics*, 90, 591–7.

Spence, M.A. (1973) 'Job Market Signaling', *Quarterly Journal of Economics*, 87 (3), 355–74.

Spence, M.A. (1974) *Market Signaling, Informational Transfer in Hiring and Related Sourcing Processes*. Cambridge: Harvard University Press.

Spremann, K. (1987) 'Agent and Principal', in Bamberg, G. and Spreman, K. (eds.) *Agency Theory, Information, and Incentives*. Berlin: Springer, 3–37.

Spremann, K. (1990) 'Asymmetrische Information', *Zeitschrift für Betriebswirtschaft*, 60, 5–6, 561–86.

St-Amour, D. (2001) 'Successful Organizational Change – Effective Management of people and cultural issues', *Canadian Manager/Manager Canadien*, Summer 2001, 20–22.

Stauss, B. (1997) 'Regaining Service Customers – Costs and Benefits of Regain Management', Discussion Contributions of the Department of Business Administration at the Catholic University of Eichstaett No. 66, Ingolstadt, Germany.

Stauss, B. (2000) 'Perspektivenwandel. Vom Produkt Lebenszyklus zum Kundenbeziehungs-Lebenszyklus', *Thexis*, 17 (2), 15–18.

Stauss, B. and Friege, Ch. (1999) 'Regaining Service Customers. Cost and Benefits of Regain Management', *Journal of Service Research*, 1 (4), 347–61.

Stauss, B. and Neuhaus, P. (1995) 'Das Qualitative Zufriedenheitsmodell', Discussion Contributions of the Department of Business Administration at the Catholic University of Eichstaett No. 66, Ingolstadt, Germany.

Stauss, B. and Seidel, W. (1998) *Beschwerdemanagement. Fehler vermeiden, Leistung verbessern, Kunden binden (Complaint Management)*, (2nd edn). Munich: Carl Hanser.

Stauss, B., Chojnacki, K., Decker, A. and Hoffmann, F. (2001) 'Retention effects of a customer club', *International Journal of Service Industry Management*, 12 (1), 7–19.

Steins, G. (2000) 'Motivation in Person Perception: Role of the Other's Perspective', *The Journal of Social Psychology*, 140 (6), 692–709.

Stephens, N. (2000) 'Complaining', in Swartz, T. and Iacobucci, D. (eds.) *Handbook of Services Marketing & Management*. Thousand Oaks, CA: Sage Publications, 287–98.

Stewart, K. (1998) 'The customer exit process – a review and research agenda', *Journal of Marketing Management*, 14 (4), 235–50.

Storbacka, K. (1997) 'Segmentation Based on Customer Profitability. Retrospective Analysis of Retail Bank Customer Bases', *Journal of Marketing Management*, 13 (5), 479–92.

Storbacka, K., Strandvik, T. and Grönroos, C. (1994) 'Managing Customer Relationships for Profit. The Dynamics of Relationship Quality', *International Journal of Service Industry Management*, 5 (5), 21–38.

Strandvik, T. and Törnroos, J.-A. (1997) 'Discovering Relationscapes. Extending the Horizon of Relationship Strategies in Marketing', in AMA (ed.), *New and Evolving Paradigms. The Emerging Future of Marketing*. Dublin: AMA, 381–93.

Swartz, T.A. Bowen, D.E., and Brown, S. W. (eds.) (1992) *Advances in Services Marketing and Management*, Vol. 1, Greenwich: JAI Press.

Sydow, J. (1992) 'On the Management of Strategic Networks', in Ernste, H. and Meier, V. (eds.), *Regional Development and Contemporary Industrial Response*. London: Belhaven, 115–31.

Tax, S.S., Brown, S.W. and Chandrashekaran, M. (1998), 'Customer Evaluations of Service Complaint Experiences: Implications for Relationship Marketing', *Journal of Marketing*, 60, April, 60–76.

Teas, R.K. (1993) 'Consumer Expectations and the Measurement of Perceived Service Quality', *Journal of Professional Services Marketing*, 8 (2), 33–53.

Tesar, G., Moini, H. and Boter, H. (2000) 'Marketing Orientation and International Industrial Network Involvement: An Exploratory Perspective', Working Paper, Proceedings of the 16th Annual IMP Conference, September 7–9, 2000, University of Bath, School of Management, Bath, UK (http://www.bath.ac.uk/management/imp/pdf/50_ TesarMoiniBoter.pdf, accessed on December 3, 2001).

Thanner, J.F. (1999) 'Organizational Buying Theories: A Bridge to Relationships Theory', *Industrial Marketing Management*, 28, 245–55.

Thibaut, J.W. and Kelley, H.H. (1959) *The Social Psychology of Groups*. New York: Wiley.

Tse, D.K. and Wilton, P.C. (1988) 'Models of Consumer Satisfaction Formation. An Extension', *Journal of Marketing Research*, 25 (2), 204–12.

Urban, G.L. and v. Hippel, H. (1988) 'Lead User Analyses for the Development of New Industrial Products', *Management Science*, 34 (5), 569–82.

v. Hippel, E.A. (1986) 'Lead Users. A Source of Novel Product Concepts', *Management Science*, 32 (7), 791–805.

van Raaij, W.F. (1991) 'The Formation and Use of Expectations in Consumer Decision Making', in Robertson, T.S. and Kassarjian, H.H. (eds.) *Handbook of Consumer Behavior*. Englewood Cliffs: Prentice Hall, 401–18.

van Waterschoot, W. and van den Bulte, C. (1992) 'The 4P Classification of the Marketing Mix Revisited', *Journal of Marketing*, 56, October, 83–93.

Walter, A. (1999) 'Relationship Promotors: Driving Forces for Successful Customer Relationships', *Industrial Marketing Management*, 28 (5), 537–551.

Wang, P. and Splegel, T. (1994) 'Database Marketing and its Measurements of Success: Designing a Managerial Instrument to Calculate the Value of a Repeat Customer Base', *Journal of Direct Marketing*, 8 (2), 73–81.

Webster C. (1990) 'Industrial Buyer's Level of Involvement with Services', in Lichtenthal J.D., Spekman R.E. and Wilson D.T. (eds.), *Marketing Theory and Application*, AMA Proceedings Winter. Chicago, IL: AMA, 69–74.

Weiber, R. (1993) 'Was ist Marketing? Ein informationsökonomischer Erklärungsansatz', Working Paper No. 1, ed. Rolf Weiber, University of Trier, Trier, Germany.

Weiber, R. and Adler, J. (1995) 'Informationsökonomisch begründete Typologisierung von Kaufprozessen', *Zeitschrift für betriebswirtschaftliche Forschung*, 47 (1), 43–65.

Wilkie, W. (1994) *Consumer Behavior*, (3rd edn). New York: Wiley.

Williamson, O.E. (1975) *Markets and Hierarchies. Analysis and Antitrust Implications*. New York/London: Free Press.

Williamson, O.E. (1991) 'Comparative Economic Organizations. The Analysis of Discrete Structural Alternatives', *Administrative Science Quarterly*, 36 (2), 269–96.

Woodruff, R.B. and Gardial, S.F. (1996) *Know Your Customer: New Approaches to Understanding Customer Value and Satisfaction*. Blackwell Business: Cambridge, MA.

Xiao, J.J. (1996) *Effects of Family Income and Life Cycle Stages on Financial Asset Ownership*, Finanical Counseling and Planning, 7, 21–30.

Yi, Y. (1991) 'A critical review of customer satisfaction', in Zeithaml, V.A. (ed.) *Review of Marketing 1989*. Chicago, IL: AMA, 68–123.

Yip, G.S. (1982) *Barriers to Entry: a corporate-strategy perspective*. Lexington, MA: Lexington Books.

Zeithaml, V.A. (1981) 'How Consumer Evaluation Processes Differ between Goods and Services', in Donnelly, J.H. and George, W.R. (eds.), *Marketing of Services*. Chicago, IL: AMA, 186–190.

Zeithaml, V.A. (1988) 'Consumer Perceptions of Price, Quality and Value. A Means-End Model and Synthesis of Evidence', *Journal of Marketing*, 52 (2), 2–22.

Zeithaml, V.A. (1991) 'How Consumer Evaluation Processes Differ between Goods and Services', in Lovelock, C.H. (ed.), *Services Marketing*, (2nd edn). Englewood Cliffs: Prentice Hall, 39–47.

Zeithaml, V.A., Berry, L.L. and Parasuraman, A. (1993) 'The Nature and Determinants of Customer Expectations of Service', *Journal of the Academy of Marketing Science*, 21 (1), 1–12.

Zeithaml, V.A., Berry, L.L. and Parasuraman, A. (1996) 'The Behavioral Consequences of Service Quality', *Journal of Marketing*, 60 (2), 31–46.

Zeithaml, V.A. and Bitner, M.J. (2000) *Services Marketing. Integrating Customer Focus Across the Firm* (2nd edn). Boston: McGraw-Hill.

Zeithaml, V.A., Parasuraman, A. and Berry, L.L. (1990) *Delivering Quality Service*. New York: Free Press.

Zeithaml, V.A , Parasuraman, A. and Berry, L.L. (1992) *Qualitätsservice*. New York/Frankfurt am Main, Campus Verlag.

Zeyer, U. (1995) 'Zeitaspekte der Implementierung aktueller Managementkonzepte', *Zeitschrift für Organisation*, 64 (5), 283–9.

Zoller, M.A. (1998) 'Customer Focus – Total Customer Care bei ABB Schweiz', in Reinecke, S., Sipötz, E. and Wiemann, E.-M. (eds.), *Total Customer Care. Kundenorientierung auf dem Prüfstand*. St. Gallen/Wien: THEXIS, 26–53.

Subject Index

Company Name Index